Frederick Douglass and the Philosophy of Religion

Frederick Douglass and the Philosophy of Religion

An Interpretation of Narrative, Art, and the Political

Timothy J. Golden

LEXINGTON BOOKS
Lanham • Boulder • New York • London

Published by Lexington Books
An imprint of The Rowman & Littlefield Publishing Group, Inc.
4501 Forbes Boulevard, Suite 200, Lanham, Maryland 20706
www.rowman.com

86-90 Paul Street, London EC2A 4NE, United Kingdom

Copyright © 2022 by The Rowman & Littlefield Publishing Group, Inc.

All rights reserved. No part of this book may be reproduced in any form or by any electronic or mechanical means, including information storage and retrieval systems, without written permission from the publisher, except by a reviewer who may quote passages in a review.

British Library Cataloguing in Publication Information Available

Library of Congress Cataloging-in-Publication Data

Names: Golden, Timothy Joseph, author.
Title: Frederick Douglass and the philosophy of religion : an interpretation of narrative, art, and the political / Timothy J. Golden.
Description: Lanham : Lexington Books, [2022] | Includes bibliographical references and index. | Summary: "Timothy J. Golden presents an existential, phenomenological, and political interpretation of Douglass's use of narrative. Reading Douglass with Kierkegaard, Kafka, Kant, and Levinas, Golden argues that analytic theism is an inauthentic preoccupation with knowledge at the expense of a concrete moral sensibility that Douglass's narrative provides"— Provided by publisher.
Identifiers: LCCN 2021043314 (print) | LCCN 2021043315 (ebook) | ISBN 9780739191675 (cloth) | ISBN 9780739191682 (epub) | ISBN 9781666907018 (paperback)
Subjects: LCSH: Philosophical theology. | Douglass, Frederick, 1818–1895—Philosophy. | Knowledge, Theory of. | God—Proof, Ontological.
Classification: LCC BT40 .G59 2022 (print) | LCC BT40 (ebook) | DDC 230.01—dc23/eng/20211008
LC record available at https://lccn.loc.gov/2021043314
LC ebook record available at https://lccn.loc.gov/2021043315

For C. James Trotman

Contents

Preface and Acknowledgments	ix
Introduction: The Dawn: A New Day for a New Song	1
Chapter One: The Word Made Flesh: Narrative and the Jurisdiction of History	17
Chapter Two: The Truth in Fiction: Narrative, Art, and Subjectivity	51
Chapter Three: Overcoming Theodicy: Narrative, Poetry, and the Phenomenology of Suffering	97
Chapter Four: A Demand for Universality: Narrative, Art, and the Politics of Moral Suasion	131
Chapter Five: An Ethical Metaphysics of the Flesh: Narrative, Theology, and Justice	187
Epilogue: Toward a Philosophical Theology of History: Narrative and Resurrection	225
Bibliography	235
Index	243
About the Author	257

Preface and Acknowledgments

"Some of the Epicurean and Stoic philosophers also were conversing with him. Some said, 'What does this babbler want to say?' Others said, 'He seems to be advocating foreign deities,' because he preached Jesus and the resurrection. They took hold of him, and brought him to the Areopagus, saying, 'May we know what this new teaching is, which is spoken by you? For you bring certain strange things to our ears. We want to know therefore what these things mean.' Now all the Athenians and the strangers living there spent their time in nothing else, but either to tell or to hear some new thing."

—*Holy Bible*[1]

Paul's encounter with the Stoics and the Epicureans in the book of Acts is a microcosm of the tension—indeed, the antagonism—between philosophy and Christianity. Augustine's and Aquinas's incorporations of Plato and Aristotle into Christianity notwithstanding, there remains a fundamental shortcoming of the ontotheological: it causes the moral problem of what Martin Heidegger referred to as the "god of philosophy," an idol made into an *imago hominis*, which is a philosophical reversal of the Judeo-Christian notion of human beings who are made *imago Dei*. Philosophy demands rational, explanatory consistency according to the dictates of the *logos*, whereas Christian theology embodies the *logos* in the story, the Gospel (the good news), of Jesus Christ, a colonized Hebrew carpenter turned itinerant preacher from Nazareth. Christian theology thus turns away from the *logos* of Greek philosophy and toward the *mythos* akin to the poetic, aesthetic tradition of Homer and Hesiod. It is this difference between *logos* and *mythos*, between the morally anemic philosophical demand for rational explanation, on one hand, and the theologically motivated, socially and politically potent power of poetic testimony, on the other, that forms the framework for this book. This is not to say that demands for epistemic verification and metaphysical certainty do not have their place—indeed, they do, especially in the realm of the social and the political as related to public policy discourse.[2] Their usefulness, however, is restricted to what Immanuel Kant would call "the land of truth," that sphere of human activity in which empirical cognition is what counts as knowledge. But as it relates to a theoretical consideration of God, which is the subject of this book—and a matter far beyond the reach of empirical verification—I submit that epistemic and metaphysical demands for rational explanation do much more harm than good, as they are conducive to a preoccupation with reason that demands a theological withdrawal from (rather than a robust engagement with) moral, social, and political life. And it is in this book that I attempt to show how such harm assumes the form of analytic theism's relentless pursuit of rational explanation at the expense of a theologically motivated, robust, moral, social, and political engagement that one finds in Frederick Douglass's use of narrative. In the former, a sort of abstract Christian philosophical theology emerges from the work of Alvin Plantinga, Nicholas Wolterstorff, and William Alston; in the latter, a very different sort of Christian philosophical theology emerges from Douglass. My aim here is to argue that, as it relates to Christian theology, the existential, phenomenological, aesthetic, social, and political interpretation of Douglass's use of narrative that I develop throughout these pages has much greater theological and moral force than the reformed epistemology of analytic theism, which, I believe, has rational explanation as its principal motivation, thus doing Christianity more harm than good.

This book is an extension of several of my published essays in academic journals, edited books, and another monograph. To situate this book in this broader context, I will briefly discuss some of this research. Broadly understood, my research develops a moral critique of epistemology, particularly epistemology's use in the context of Christian-based, religious beliefs. This research began in 2012, when I published two essays that were moral critiques of epistemology that are especially concerned with the problem of morality and Christianity. The first of these essays presented a reading of James Baldwin's short story "Sonny's Blues."[3] There, I developed the concept of "epistemic addiction," which is central to my research agenda overall and to this book. The addiction motif is prominent in "Sonny's Blues," and

I was interested in problematizing the all-too-easy practice of condemning Sonny for his heroin addiction while absolving his brother, the narrator of the story, of any wrongdoing whatsoever. My claim in this essay was that the narrator had an addiction that was, in many ways, just as bad as (if not worse than) Sonny's: his "epistemic addiction" caused him to overlook Sonny as he was and instead transform Sonny into who he wanted him to be, into what the narrator "knew" to be "right." So I argued that the real problem in "Sonny's Blues" was not Sonny's heroin addiction, but rather his brother's failure to allow Sonny to present himself *kath-auto*. I reimagined the Christian religious doctrine of the fall of humanity as a preoccupation with gaining knowledge at the expense of moral concerns, which is also the subject of this book. This essay aimed to show how—especially under the guise of paternalistic care—one can engage in forms of epistemic domination in ways that occlude one's moral responsibility to accept people as they are rather than as we would like them to be. And I attempted to make my case for this proposition reading "Sonny's Blues" with Emmanuel Levinas, Søren Kierkegaard, and Friedrich Nietzsche (Levinas and Kierkegaard also figure prominently in this book).

Reading Baldwin's "Sonny's Blues" with Levinas, I pointed out that there is something mystical about Sonny that remains beyond the epistemic grasp of his brother. Sonny was a literary depiction of *L'Autre*, from *Totality and Infinity*; he represents infinity making a heteronomous moral demand on his brother, the narrator of the story, who attempts to fix Sonny's identity within a scheme of epistemic and metaphysical intelligibility. But Sonny's brother, despite his best attempts, fails to grasp and comprehend Sonny, and he ultimately occupies the position of subjectivity from Levinas's *Otherwise than Being*: he is a subjectivity in crisis, experiencing the insomnia and restlessness that comes from a radical confrontation with his infinite moral obligation to help his brother, but not by demanding that his brother change in order to be worthy of his help. Instead, the narrator must learn to accept Sonny as he is. This is the best help that he can offer to Sonny.

When reading Baldwin's "Sonny's Blues" with Kierkegaard, I argued that the narrator and Sonny correspond to Constantin Constantius and the young man in love, respectively, from Kierkegaard's novella *Repetition*. Both the narrator and Constantin Constantius are addicted to knowledge: the narrator believes that he "knows" what is best for Sonny, and Constantin is unable to understand the young man's existential dilemma because of his preoccupation with detached observation. Baldwin also uses flashback to juxtapose the aesthetic movement of recollection with the ethical movement of repetition, for although the narrator fondly remembers his childhood, he does so at the expense of his future-oriented, ethical obligation to his brother Sonny that demands an inward, passionate repetition to love Sonny anew each day stronger than the day before.

Finally, in reading Baldwin's "Sonny's Blues" with Nietzsche, two insights speak to an end of epistemic addiction in the face of moral responsibility. First, there is a critique of Christianity when the narrator realizes, after the death of his daughter, that he must help Sonny. The narrator's daughter's name, "Grace," is significant, for grace is the central tenet of Christian soteriology. So I argued that Grace's death represents the death of God in a Nietzschean sense. Christianity can no longer be used to conceal the narrator's lack of responsibility to help Sonny. The death of God thus makes way for a post-metaphysical world where the mendacity of bourgeoisie Christian culture yields to an acceptance of moral responsibility. And it is in this context that the narrator writes his brother, Sonny, acknowledging his moral obligation to care for him. Second, Sonny's occupation as a jazz musician, when juxtaposed with his brother's life as a high school algebra teacher, frames the narrative of the story in terms that resonate strongly with Nietzsche's *The Birth of Tragedy*: the symmetry of algebraic formulae and the stability of a bourgeoisie life puts the narrator in the position of an Appollonian influence in the story, and the improvisational nature of jazz music, combined with Sonny's heroin addiction, gives Sonny a Dionysian persona. Once the narrator learns to accept Sonny, a drink of scotch and milk at the end of the story portrays an enduring image of familial bonding: the wholesome, nourishing milk of the narrator's Appollonian nature is combined with Sonny's intoxicating, improvisational, and thoroughly Dionysian life, represented in the scotch. Reading Baldwin's short story with Levinas, Kierkegaard, and Nietzsche is thus an attempt to reestablish the importance of balancing epistemic and moral interests when epistemic interests have gone too far.

Another published essay in 2012 also dealt with a critique of epistemic interests based on moral concerns.[4] There, I built upon the work of Frank M. Kirkland and Bill E. Lawson regarding Douglass's conception of the self, pointing out that the preoccupation with metaphysical and epistemological justifications for religious beliefs led to a neglect of pressing moral concerns, and Kant and Douglass offer solutions to this neglect of praxis that are rooted in an interrogation of rationality's extensions beyond the bounds of experience that serves as a check on reason in the interest of morality. I argued in part that Douglass's critical engagement with slaveholding Christianity has Kantian overtones, for Douglass pointed out that in contrast to the metaphysical sophistication of Dr. Godwin's Cartesian-styled argument for baptizing slaves was a woeful lack of practical morality. Douglass would rather have an infinite moral obligation that is "immortal" in a practical sense and not real in an ontological sense. Again, I concluded that morality is more important than ontology and epistemology. I continue this engagement with Kirkland and Lawson in chapter 4 of this book, where I read Kant's *Critique of Judgment* with Douglass to show a general resonance between their respective anthropologies, epistemologies, ethics, and aesthetics that I argue shows itself in Douglass's politics of moral suasion as an abolition strategy.

I continued to address the problem of morality and religious beliefs—those of a Christian sort—in the context of epistemology in another essay that was published in 2013.[5] In this essay, I provide a more explicit engagement with Christian theology, arguing that Black philosophy and Black theology are correctives to the moral problem of abstraction in analytic theism, which inverts the soteriological paradigm from the Word of God being made flesh to the flesh of God being made a word. Drawing from the liberation theology of David Walker, I argued that in contrast to the hyper-abstractions of analytic theism (which transform God's flesh into a word), Walker, in his *Appeal to the Colored Citizens of the World, but in Particular, and Very Expressly to those of the United States of America*, through his trenchant, Christian-based, critique of slaveholding Christianity and his radical identification of God with the moral cause of abolition and the plight of enslaved Africans, makes the word flesh. I also point to the aesthetic sensibilities of Douglass, who, in his 1845 narrative, predates Nietzsche's insights about music in *The Birth of Tragedy* when he points out that slave songs did more to express the real plight of slaves than "volumes of philosophy" could ever do. Douglass's insight about music points in the direction of this book: like music, I argue that Douglass's use of narrative is an aesthetic methodology that opens a space for religious experience that is, morally speaking, I think, far superior to the explanatory doctrines of analytic theism.

My criticisms of metaphysical and epistemological conceptions of religion continue in my book *Reason's Dilemma: Subjectivity, Transcendence, and the Problem of Ontotheology*.[6] This book is a critique of ontotheology as a form of epistemic and metaphysical desire for totality that I argue is run amok. I contend that ontotheology not only has a religious and theological manifestation that Kant and Kierkegaard critique but also has a social and political dimension, as seen in Christianity's support of American chattel slavery and its enduring legacy of racial violence and oppression. Reading Black philosophy (Lewis R. Gordon, George Yancy, and Bill E. Lawson) with Miranda Fricker, I argue for a phenomenological suspension of ontotheology's idolatrous construction of an epistemic framework of oppression in the name of God. Douglass emerges in the midst of this oppression as one who abides in the system of American chattel slavery and who displays remarkable affinities with Kant and Kierkegaard as they relate to subjectivity, demanding a theology of *praxis* over *doxa*. As I have discussed above, I continue my engagement of Douglass with Kant in this book, and I likewise continue my engagement of Douglass with Kierkegaard that I first articulated in a 2016 essay, a book chapter on the affinities between the two on morality, art, and the self.[7]

In this essay, I built upon the work of Lewis Gordon and George Yancy, whose pioneering work in Black existentialism and phenomenology inspired my reflections on Douglass and Kierkegaard and my attempt to develop an interpretation of Douglass's deep existentialist affinities—affinities that Gordon and Yancy had already developed throughout their work on Douglass and existentialism—with Christianity. The book concludes with urging an emptying of the white self of epistemic and metaphysical desire—a *kenosis*—in favor of what Levinas calls an "atheism" in an ethical sense, in which the moral responsibilities of the interhuman order take priority over metaphysical and epistemological demands for philosophical explanation. I urge a theology of ethical metaphysics rather than a theology of epistemic and metaphysical certainty, as in analytic theism. I develop this argument here at much greater length.

A point needs to be made about ontotheology and its connection to analytic theism: the two work together to produce a state of affairs that I want to interrogate in this book. Evidence of this is found in Marylin McCord Adams's essay "What's Wrong with the Ontotheological Error?"[8] There, she argues, contrary to critics of ontotheology such as Merold Westphal, that ontotheology is not morally problematic; rather, when it is rightly conceived, it reflects a certain awe and reverence for God and may even be considered as a form of prayer of thanksgiving to God for the perpetual revelation of Himself to human beings. Without fully addressing the substance of this argument here, I point out this connection to show the continuity in my prior research and this book: my moral objections to epistemology are also moral objections to ontotheology, which is ultimately an epistemologically and metaphysically driven attempt to construct, articulate, and maintain a theology of God. And such a theology of God is precisely what is at work in the project of analytic theism, as exemplified by Adams in her defense of ontotheology.

Finally, the prelude on Kant's racism in chapter 4 draws from a previous essay of mine on the importance of my own "historically effected consciousness" in the hermeneutic endeavor.[9] As I wrote in this previous essay, drawing from the work of Hans Georg Gadamer, no textual interpretation occurs that is independent of the interpreter. Text and self, separated by Enlightenment thinking, are actually united in the hermeneutic process in a way that results in a merging of horizons, which is what happens here with my interpretation of Douglass: my racial and religious background affects my interpretation of philosophical texts.

This book is the product of the collegiality and indulgence of many colleagues, as well as the love and support of my family and many friends. I have endured great personal hardships over the past several years, and without the overwhelming personal and professional support that I have received, this book would not have been possible. Thanking people by name is a risky proposition, for human frailty may lead to omissions perceived as neglect. So I ask those who are unnamed to forgive me in advance. My failure to mention you by name results not from a mean-spirited heart, but rather from a forgetful head. Thank you for understanding.

With this disclaimer aside, I want to first thank my editor, Jana Hodges-Kluck, for her extraordinary patience with me throughout the completion of this book. Jana, without your limitless patience and understanding, this project would not have been possible. Thank you. I also want to thank my colleagues in the Department of History and Philosophy at Walla Walla University, Gregory Dodds, Terrie Aamodt, Hilary Dickerson, Monique Roddy, and Linda Emmerson (my fellow philosopher), for their support of my research generally and for their encouragement in the completion of this project in particular. An advantage of being a philosopher in a department of mostly historians is that I now read philosophy with a greater historical sensibility, which helped inspire my approach to this book. Thanks to all of you for being such wonderful colleagues and good friends. I am also grateful for the aid of my research assistant, Carmen Lopez. Thank you, Carmen, for your discerning eye and your superb work ethic, which made the task of completing this book much more efficient than it would have been without your help.

I also want to thank George Yancy for his continuing support of this project and for his groundbreaking work on Douglass. George, our many conversations reinvigorated me and provided a renewed determination to finish this work—a work that some of your philosophical reflections on Douglass helped to inspire. Your intellect, mentoring, and friendship have nurtured my scholarly development and, I am certain, will continue to do so. Thank you, George. I also want to thank Jim Trotman, to whom this book is dedicated. Jim, your enduring interest in and affection for Douglass is, in part, responsible for this book. I cannot thank you enough for being such a fine person and friend to me through the years. I have learned much from you and benefited so much from your example that, at times, I find myself unworthy of the blessing of our friendship. Thank you for being such a fine mentor, colleague, and, above all, good friend to me.

Finally, I am deeply grateful for the love and support of my family and friends. To my sisters, Joyce, Debbie, and Rita Golden, and my brothers, James Jr. and Dennis Golden, although we are physically far apart, each of you are close to my heart. I am at my best when I incorporate the finest virtues of each of you into my daily life. James B. Golden Sr. and Margaret Catherine Golden, our parents, put me in the best position possible in the family because, as the youngest sibling, I benefited from being able to observe and learn so much from the fine examples of decency and integrity that each of you has shown me throughout my life. It is your love, kindness, and support that has given me the strength to be a philosopher—an occupation that imposes great demands on the intellect and is simply not possible without the emotional security and stability that the quality of our familial relationship provides. My identity is anchored in the joy that comes from knowing that I am part of such a loving and supportive family. All of you, and our beloved, late brother, Marshall Golden, whose passion and pathos is a source of daily inspiration to me, are responsible for my success. I salute each of you, and I love each of you beyond measure. Thank you for your love and support.

As for my friends, Keith Davidson, Jason Hall, Adia Taliaferro, Tameka Lafayette, Donald Cantrell, Dwayne Wyre, Aaron and Nicky Scott, Charles and Michelle Cammack, Maurits and Katherine Hughes, Larry and Ina Farrell, Steven L. Garner, James and Jacqueline Winston, and Dwayne and Marissa Leslie, without each of you, I would be far worse off than I am. Your support during the most difficult times of my life in recent years has meant the world to me. Without your enduring care and concern for me, I would be in no condition—intellectual, spiritual, psychological, or otherwise—to complete a scholarly, philosophical work of this nature. Each of you have my deep gratitude and endless love. Thank you.

NOTES

1. Acts 17: 18–21 (World English Version).

2. Consider Tommy J. Curry, whose pioneering philosophical work relies heavily on the empirical data and methodologies of social science research and has given rise to the emerging philosophical subfield of Black male studies. See especially *The Man-Not: Race, Class, Genre, and the Dilemmas of Black Manhood* (Philadelphia, PA: Temple University Press, 2017) and "Decolonizing the Intersection: Black Male Studies as a Critique of Intersectionality's Indebtedness to Subculture of Violence Theory," in *Critical Psychology Praxis: Psychosocial Non-Alignment to Modernity/Coloniality*, ed. Robert Beshara (New York: Routledge, 2021).

3. Timothy Joseph Golden, "Epistemic Addiction: Reading 'Sonny's Blues' with Levinas, Kierkegaard, and Nietzsche," *Journal of Speculative Philosophy* 26, no. 3 (2012): 554–71.

4. Timothy Joseph Golden, "From Epistemology to Ethics: Theoretical and Practical Reason in Kant and Douglass," *Journal of Religious Ethics* 40, no. 4 (2012): 603–28.

5. Tim Golden, "From *Logos* to *Sarx*: Black Philosophy and the Philosophy of Religion," *Black Scholar* 43, no. 4 (Winter 2013): 94–100.

6. Under contract (Palgrave MacMillan, forthcoming 2022).

7. Timothy Golden, "Morality, Art, and the Self: Existentialism in Frederick Douglass and Søren Kierkegaard," in *Existentialist Thought in African American Literature before 1940*, ed. Melvin G. Hill (Lanham, MD: Lexington Books, 2016), 1–20.

8. Marilyn McCord Adams, "What's Wrong with the Ontotheological Error?" *Journal of Analytic Theology* 2 (May 2014).

9. See Timothy J. Golden, "German Chocolate: Why Philosophy Is So Personal," in *Philosophy and the Mixed Race Experience* (Lanham, MD: Lexington Books, 2016), 231–66.

Introduction
The Dawn: A New Day for a New Song

"He said, 'Please show me your glory.' . . . He [God] said, 'You cannot see my face, for man may not see me and live.'"

—*Holy Bible*[1]

Alvin Plantinga makes a significant admission in his essay, *God, Freedom, and Evil*. After articulating the difference between a "Free Will Theodicy" and a "Free Will Defense," he points out that neither of these will "enable someone to find peace with himself and with God in the face of the evil the world contains."[2] This admission follows a long and logically rigorous exposition of numerically ordered propositions that consists of sets and subsets in which Plantinga attempts to defeat John L. Mackie's claims that religious beliefs are "positively irrational" and "that the several parts of the theological doctrine are inconsistent with one another" because of the problem of evil. After making this admission about the inability of either a Free Will Theodicy or a Free Will Defense to bring human beings peace in a time of need, Plantinga writes, "But then, of course, neither is intended for that purpose."[3] This statement of Plantinga's raises a question: *what is* the purpose of these philosophical and theological doctrines if they fail to bring peace amidst an existential storm? The context of Plantinga's essay gives us a clue. Recall that Plantinga is responding to Mackie's claim that the problem of evil makes theism irrational and inconsistent. Presumably, then, the intended purpose for a Free Will Theodicy and a Free Will Defense is a rational, intellectual interest that a theist has in defending the logical consistency of a belief in God in the face of the problem of evil. The interests of reason are paramount in this effort. Reason must vindicate its interest in a rationally and logically consistent account of God through an extensive engagement with those who say that such an account of God is impossible. The intellect thus becomes the site of extensive discussion and debate over the rational and logical status of God. Such debates, are, at bottom, despite the reformed epistemology of analytic theism's resistance to the Enlightenment, ultimately Enlightenment-inspired debates that make human rationality the ultimate arbiter of theological matters. Accordingly, reason becomes what Immanuel Kant called a sort of "tribunal" in which God is accused of injustice. Human beings both hale God into court and then rush to God's defense. Reason thus both accuses and represents the divine defendant.[4] Metaphysics and epistemology are the order of the day in this tribunal of reason, where debates between Plantinga and Mackie are akin to Homer and Hesiod attempting to provide rigorous, philosophical defenses of the gods because of an accusation of logical incoherence from Aristotle. Surely, Homer and Hesiod were not interested in engaging in such a debate. And that is because Homer and Hesiod understood what Plantinga did not: supernatural beliefs are not intended to be intellectually sound and logically defended. Are such beliefs cultural and social narratives? Yes. Are they reflections of humanity's flaws? Indeed. Can we derive inspiration from them to help us amidst life's most tragic and sad difficulties? We can. But what we *cannot do* without changing the fundamental character of religion is make religious beliefs—whether they be Greek or Christian—"rational" in the sense that they can be defended against all accusations of irrationality. For in doing so, we cheapen the legitimate cultural, social, and existential purposes that religion has. Indeed, rigorous rational debate over God goes too far whenever belief is rationally justified at the expense of the very God that it attempts to defend. Martin Heidegger emphasizes this problem when he writes:

> The deity enters into philosophy through the perdurance of which we think at first as the approach to the active nature of the difference between Being and beings. The difference constitutes the ground plan in the structure of the essence of metaphysics. The perdurance results in and gives being as the generative ground. This ground itself needs to be properly accounted for by that for which it accounts, that is, by the causation through the supremely original matter—and that is the cause as *causa sui*. This is the right name for the god of philosophy. Man can neither pray nor sacrifice to this god. Before the *causa sui*, man can neither fall to his knees in awe, nor can he play music and dance before this god.[5]

In this passage, Heidegger develops what he calls the "ontotheological" dimension of metaphysics, which is the attempt to ground reason in an ultimate theological grounding that reason terms "god." We see this at work in Aristotle, who, with no tolerance for infinite regress, truncates the infinite in the interest of rational explanation and metaphysical closure. In this way, Aristotle's god is the ground of philosophy, or what Heidegger would call an "ontotheological" ground that justifies the entire enterprise of Western philosophy, which has the *logos* as its *telos*. But for Heidegger, this is merely the "god of philosophy"; a metaphysical and epistemological starting point for human reason. This "god" is a means to the end of rationality and is not an end in itself. Unlike the God of the Judeo-Christian tradition, whose existence is a matter of religious assumption rather than rational justification, Aristotle's "god" is, in Heidegger's terms, unworthy of adoration or praise, for one can "neither pray nor sacrifice to this god" or "play music and dance before this god."

In this juxtaposition of Aristotle's "god" and the God of the Judeo-Christian tradition, one can hear Tertullian's poignant question echo through the ages: "What hath Athens to do with Jerusalem?" The difference between Greek philosophy and the Judeo-Christian theological tradition could not be clearer: the former has an abiding and paramount interest in reason, while the latter is a matter of religious faith. Thus understood, it seems that Christian absorptions of Greek philosophy, the great traditions of Augustine and Aquinas notwithstanding, would concern Christians enough to avoid such ontotheological commitments in the interest of avoiding the idol that is the "god of philosophy." And yet Christian theology too often not only welcomes reason but does so at the expense of moral responsibility, which takes a back seat to reason's demands for metaphysical and epistemic justification.

Despite its best attempts at a reformed epistemology, analytic theism sacrifices God for the sake of metaphysical and epistemological clarity far too often, and the aim of this book is to not only critique analytic theism on this basis but also offer an alternative to its metaphysical and its epistemological preoccupations. I offer this alternative in the form of an existential, phenomenological, and aesthetic reading of Frederick Douglass, who was thoroughly engaged with religion and religious questions—in their Christian form—throughout his public life.

Phenomenology emerges from a crisis of a certain forgetfulness of subjectivity. As it relates to analytic theism, this crisis assumes the form of an illicit relationship between Christian theology and Enlightenment reason, despite Christian philosophy's objections to the Enlightenment. Even as Edmund Husserl called for a suspension of the natural attitude because a forgetfulness of human subjectivity resulted in a scientific conception of the world that had little regard for the human contributions to science, there is a need for a suspension of the abstract and hyper-theorized accounts of God such as those that we see in much of analytic theism. Husserl understood that although

Enlightenment science had produced a vision of the world in which we were mathematically and scientifically assured of objective truth, we were missing the humanity, the richness, and the diversity of the *lebenswelt*, which was inaccessible because of our preoccupation with Enlightenment science.

I argue something similar: Christianity, for all of its complaints about science, has (unwittingly, perhaps) adopted an Enlightenment, scientific conception of truth, applying it to religious beliefs. This is seen in the reformed epistemology of analytic theism's "parity argument," which, relying on the epistemology of Scottish Enlightenment philosopher Thomas Reid, argues that religious beliefs are on par with perceptual beliefs. Contemporary Christian philosophers such as James K. A. Smith have referred to this as a sort of "theological positivism," and it is the deeply modern application of an Enlightenment-based theory of meaning and coherence (correspondence?) theory of truth to religious concerns.[6] On this theological account of truth, religion becomes subject to scientific methodologies and debates over historical matters such as whether there actually was a flood that covered the Earth, and the creation versus evolution debate. But what is the real upshot of these arguments for the religious believer? There is no real point of having a scientifically based Christian apologetics, especially when, as Kierkegaard's pseudonym, Johannes Climacus, reminds us, Christianity is an "existence-communication" that is thoroughly "unscientific."[7] Moreover, importing a coherence theory of meaning into Christian theology does not somehow make Christianity more credible. Instead, it raises more questions than it answers; questions such as, what are we to make of the virgin birth, and the resurrection of Jesus? These questions leave Christianity in a place where it must cherry-pick its beliefs that it wants to scientifically prove, and this ultimately makes Christianity look much less credible, not more. And even if one accepts Plantinga, William Alston, and Nicholas Wolterstorff's reformed epistemology and its rejection of classical foundationalism's demand for evidence and empirical verification, one is still left with a preoccupation with rationality without any real attentiveness to the urgency of moral life. Indeed, it seems as if, foundationalist or not, Christianity is more interested in proving itself to be a rational worldview in the marketplace of ideas than it is interested in its adherents living the principles of its teachings. This perhaps helps to explain why the history of Christianity is fraught with hegemony in the West, whether it be in the form of the Inquisitions of the medieval period or the Christian-based justifications of chattel slavery, Jim Crow, lynching, and their enduring legacies of racial violence and racial injustice throughout American history. In the interest of a more robust and authentic morality, this book argues that the theoretical explanation and justification of analytic theism must yield to the existentially and phenomenologically driven, aesthetically oriented testimony that one finds in the narrative methodology of Frederick Douglass.

BLACK INVISIBILITY IN CONTEMPORARY THEOLOGY

Why this book? After all, there is nothing new about criticizing ontotheology and analytic theism. Much has been written in postmodern theology about this problem of ontotheology. But as much as I agree with many of these critiques, even some of the critics have fallen into a recurring problem in the extant literature on ontotheology, which is a neglect of Black philosophical and theological thought as it relates to Christianity's self-critique coming from Black theological voices who condemn Christianity's complicity in racial oppression in the modern West. This problem is discernible in the work of radical orthodoxy, which draws heavily from John Milbank's work. Milbank's work, in turn, which purports to be Christian theology, contains little to no discussion of Black philosophy or Black theology. For example, the closest that Milbank comes to addressing social issues is his critique of liberation theology in his *Theology and Social Theory*. But even there, his criticism takes Latin American liberation theology to be the only sort of liberation theology that exists. There is no mention of James H. Cone's Black liberation theology, nor is there any reference to nineteenth-century Black abolitionist Christian thought, which never encountered Marxist social theory—the secularity of Marxist social theory is a consistent target of Milbank's—and was thoroughly engaged with the Christian Gospel. This blindness toward Black theology persists in several of the seminal Milbank-inspired texts in the radical orthodoxy book series.

For example, Daniel Bell writes an entire book purporting to be about liberation theology and without even so much as an acknowledgment that there are other forms of liberation theology, Bell proceeds in his book as though Latin American liberation theology is the only sort of liberation theology that there is.[8] James K. A. Smith makes a similar omission. In his book, *Introducing Radical Orthodoxy: Mapping a Post-Secular Theology*—John Milbank wrote the foreword—Smith continues to treat liberation theology monolithically. Every reference in the book is a reference to Latin American liberation theology, and no mention is made of nineteenth-century Black abolitionist thought as the thoroughly Christian response to the moral abomination of American chattel slavery that it was in the work of Maria Stewart, David Walker, Frederick Douglass, and Henry Highland Garnet, or twentieth-century Black theology in the work of William R. Jones, Anthony B. Pinn, Delores S. Williams, or James H. Cone.

So serious is the omission that even some of the critics of radical orthodoxy neglect to mention its failure to engage Milbank's vision in light of Black philosophy's and Black theology's critiques of Christianity's complicity in the project of white racial empire.[9] The essays in *The Poverty of Radical Orthodoxy*, ironically written as a liberationist critique of radical orthodoxy, still do not explicitly engage Black theology or Black philosophy as a means to critique radical orthodoxy. To this volume's credit, several of these essays come close to addressing, and in some ways, do address problems of race and racism.[10] But none of the essays provide any explicit discussion of Black theology's extensive structural critique of societal institutions—like the church—that help maintain the abject material, social, and economic conditions of anti-Black racism. So although this latter critique of radical orthodoxy comes close to addressing the cultural and religious hegemony of white Christianity, there is nothing in this volume on radical orthodoxy's failure to meaningfully engage Black philosophy and Black theology. My critique here is at the meta level: this volume, which purports to critique radical orthodoxy, presents a critique that must itself be critiqued by pointing out its failure to see Black philosophy and Black theology. Indeed, the continuing omission of Black philosophy and Black theology from mainstream academic discussions of broader philosophical and theological discourse is itself a by-product of racial oppression in the postmodern West.

So, neither contemporary theology nor its critics, who claim liberation theology as the reading site of their critique of radical orthodoxy, engage the moral and political problems with which Black theology and Black philosophy are engaged. This results in an invisibility of Black philosophy and Black theology. Despite their motivations to disable and destabilize modernity's and Christianity's respective roles in establishing and maintaining white supremacy, Black philosophy and Black theology are not only made necessary by the ontotheological narrative of Scholasticism and its progeny of analytic theism but also excluded from postmodern critiques of Scholasticism and modern theology, which purport to manumit religion from the clutches of hegemonic metaphysically and epistemologically driven religious systems. What is more remarkable here is that considering Christianity's support for American chattel slavery, Jim Crow, lynching, and their attendant legacies in, for example, police brutality and voter suppression efforts, perhaps no group of people in the history of the modern West is more motivated to question—and actually questions—modernity's presuppositions more than Black people, and yet Black people are routinely overlooked in broader philosophical and theological conversations. This is a serious problem in the philosophy of religion.

This problem of invisibility in contemporary theology is, I believe, similar to a problem of invisibility that Charles W. Mills confronted and grappled with in political philosophy and a problem that James H. Cone dealt with in Christian theology. In *The Racial Contract*, Mills argued that ideal theorizing in political philosophy was morally deficient because the abstractions of thought experiments like the "state of nature" and the Rawlsian "original position" failed to account for racial oppression. Such thought experiments, according to Mills, subject historical realities to the whimsical fancies of the white philosophical imagination, contributing to the erasure of centuries of racial oppression and violence, resulting in an abiding reality of injustice that persists to this day. And in *The Cross and the Lynching Tree*, Cone argues that Reinhold Niebuhr failed to recognize the moral abomination of lynching by connecting it to the Cross, despite being considered to be one of the great moral theologians of the twentieth century. I discuss Mills and Cone in greater detail in chapter 1. An important point here, however, is that Niebuhr is to Christian theology for Cone what Rawls is to political philosophy for Mills: a representation of white theorizing that neglects the pressing social, political, and moral concerns of Black people. As I will argue in chapter 1, drawing from Mills and Cone in more detail, another layer to the devastating results of abstraction becomes real in this book project. It is here where it is argued that the reformed epistemology of analytic theism is as culpable of the sort of neglect in the philosophy of religion as Rawls is neglectful in political philosophy and as Niebuhr is neglectful in Christian theology. My interpretation of Douglass in this book aims to critically discuss this state of affairs.

ONTOTHEOLOGY, PHENOMENOLOGY, AND THE PROBLEM OF ANTERIORITY

Recent scholarship has called certain responses to ontotheology into question. Tyler Tritten writes that "I intend to reject both that the overcoming of ontotheology must consist in the silencing of an ontology of God, or theology, and in the death of religion."[11] Tritten wants to "find a way to speak of God that is both philosophically, i.e., ontologically, and religiously adequate, yet without relapsing into the tradition of ontotheology." Having stated his aims, Tritten states his thesis as follows:

> My hypothesis is that a contingently existing God is able to be both religiously adequate as well as the "paradigmatic" existent, which is a different concept than that of a first cause or self-caused being. The attempt is to engage in a "speculative" theology that could find itself in line with contemporary (and currently quite fashionable) appeals for a speculative realism.[12]

Through his appeal to speculative realism, Tritten hopes to find a third way of speaking about God as post-ontotheological and post-phenomenological. As Tritten points out, he wants to break "from the ubiquity of the philosophy of religion as a phenomenology of religious experience in the post-Kantian tradition in favor of a speculative and ontological account of God" while adhering "to the contemporary conviction that ontotheology is a dead project."[13] Tritten thus does not want to challenge Heidegger's assertions about ontotheology—he indeed affirms them—but rather wants to offer an alternative to phenomenology as a response to ontotheology's problems. Tritten continues on to a discussion of Friedrich Schelling's late lectures on mythology and revelation, which he believes avoids the problems of the ontotheologically driven principle of sufficient reason. Specifically, he points to Schelling's discussion of Moses's encounter with God in the Old Testament book of Exodus to show that what he calls God's "contingency" is rooted in a facticity-based necessity rather than an ontological necessity, juxtaposing it to both the necessity of ontotheology and the subjectivity of phenomenology. In the end, Tritten seeks a third way of "contingency," which, for him, will enable one to speak about God in ontological terms without resorting to ontotheology, and without resorting to what he believes is contemporary phenomenology's neglect of the being of God.

Tritten criticizes phenomenology because it does not "actually offer an ontology of God, but only a phenomenology of religious experience."[14] It is on this basis that Tritten finds phenomenology unacceptable as an alternative to ontotheology. I differ with Tritten's account of phenomenology on this point. With Jean-Luc Marion, Emmanuel Levinas, and Heidegger, I agree that phenomenological approaches to theism refocus our attention on the interhuman moral order, while eschewing a theology of idolatry. So unlike Tritten, who seeks a way of understanding God beyond ontotheology and phenomenology, I seek a way beyond ontotheology from within the phenomenological. But I am less interested in criticizing Tritten's understanding of phenomenology than I am interested in how I think Schelling's work on revelation opens the way for an aesthetic phenomenology of narrative that never sees God's "face," but rather only sees what God has left behind; that is, I am interested in how one only sees God's "backside." I want to use Schelling's account of revelation as discussed in his commentary on Moses's encounter with God to show how the difference between seeing God's "face" and God's "backside" is the difference between a religion of metaphysical and epistemological explanation as represented by the ontotheological work of analytic theism and a religion of testimonial narrative and art in the work of Frederick Douglass. This difference is grounded in what I shall call the problem of anteriority.

THE PROBLEM OF ANTERIORITY

Anteriority, as I conceive of it here, is an ontotheological problem. When Moses demands to see God, he demands a frontal view; a facial view; a view of God's anterior. Moses wants to "see God coming," to render God metaphysically explainable and epistemologically justifiable. Moses wants to be able to grasp and comprehend God in an ontotheological sense. This is the way of analytic theism; it aims at understanding God's being through the use of philosophical argumentation. But God declares that Moses is unable to do this, as He tells Moses that "no man" can "see" him and "live."[15] This is to say that living, or life—with all of its existential perplexities and difficulties—ceases if one "sees God coming," or if one grasps, comprehends, and understands God. Part of what makes life—especially our moral lives—rich and vibrant is a lack of epistemic certainty with respect to God. Our epistemic failure is conducive to an honest and mature mysticism, in which I must allow my uncertainty take root and trust God that all will be well. Kant points this out in the *Critique of Practical Reason*, when he argues that human beings have been "wisely adapted" to their "moral vocation" because of our epistemic limitations with respect to God.[16] He argues that if we knew God with certainty, we would be like puppets, moving without there being any real "life in the figures."[17] And so life in this existential and moral sense would cease if we knew God—and, I would argue, even when we seek to know God as analytic theism does—with epistemic and metaphysical certainty. I return to Kant's argument on this point later in greater detail, but I touch on the argument here to show that the problem of anteriority is that problem arising from a pursuit of theoretical knowledge about God at the expense of one's existential and moral life.

By contrast, seeing God's "backside" implies that we can see what God has left behind. The problem of anteriority gives way to the power of narrative testimony. As a sort of art form, "testifying," as it is often called in many Christian denominations, is less interested in explaining how God did something according to the *logos* than it is interested in rejoicing about what one believes God has already done in the *mythos*. Here, *mythos* is not used pejoratively, but rather refers to an aesthetic use that is a sort of poetry; it does not explain what God has done. Instead, it is a living, vibrant, creative expression of a first-person experience accompanied by a gratitude for what God has done despite the epistemic and metaphysical failures of rational explanation. This book aims to develop an aesthetic-phenomenological interpretation of Douglass that demonstrates the value of a Black theological and philosophical voice in the midst of oppression, not through a moribund anteriority, but rather through a life-giving view of God's backside, a testimony of what God has left behind. So it is that Douglass would say on December 28, 1862, as the signing of the Emancipation Proclamation drew near, "Today is not a day for prose. It is a day for song, a new song."[18] This "new song," or perhaps a new version of some old songs, begins in this book with my aesthetic-phenomenological interpretation of Douglass. It is a song of existential and phenomenological life that challenges theodicy, elevates the philosophical canon, reinvigorates poetic expression with moral feeling, uplifts community, and resists epistemic oppression.

CHAPTER SUMMARIES

The first chapter, titled "The Word Made Flesh: Narrative and the Jurisdiction of History," adumbrates the overall argument of the book by doing three things. First, it articulates the framework for my interpretation of Douglass, which is the Christian theological framework of the Incarnation of Jesus Christ as the *logos* made flesh. I choose Christian theology to interpret Douglass because Douglass lived with Christianity throughout his life as a slave and critically engaged Christianity as a public intellectual after his escape from slavery.

Second, this chapter explains that even as Douglass's voice both spoke from within Christianity and critiqued it, here, I use the framework of the Incarnation to discuss two distinct philosophical and theological approaches to Christianity, and to argue that one of them is preferable to the other. These two philosophical and theological approaches to Christianity are (1) the reformed epistemology of analytic theism, and (2) an existential, phenomenological, aesthetic, social, and political interpretation of Douglass. The thesis of this book is that the reformed epistemology of analytic theism, because of its preoccupation with philosophical abstraction, is morally, creatively, and politically deficient as compared with my interpretation of Douglass. I argue that these deficiencies of analytic theism in the philosophy of religion result from a form of white philosophical and theological reflection similar to what happens in Christian theology and in political philosophy. Again, James H. Cone has articulated this problem of abstraction in Christian theology, and Charles W. Mills has addressed the problem of abstraction in political philosophy. Abstraction is problematic, I argue, because rather than following the Christian paradigm of the *logos* made flesh, the flesh is made into an abstract *logos*. Philosophical and theological abstraction thus turn Christianity, for which *logos* is merely a beginning (John 1:1), into philosophy, for which *logos* is an end in itself. What makes abstraction so problematic is that it disregards what I call the jurisdiction of history, meaning that rather than human beings respecting the authority of history, the authority of history submits to human beings.

And third, drawing from an example in my own experience, I discuss the importance of reading Douglass as I do, with white thinkers, arguing that reading Douglass with Søren Kierkegaard, Franz Kafka, Edmund Husserl, Emmanuel Levinas, and Immanuel Kant shows how my interpretation of Douglass that unfolds in the subsequent chapters addresses existential subjectivity and art (chapter 2), a phenomenology of suffering (chapter 3), political engagement (chapter 4), and an ethical metaphysics of alterity (chapter 5) in ways that demonstrate how both Douglass's philosophical and theological rigor and his lived experience are improvements on the work of his white dialogue partners. I begin with an existential interpretation of Douglass in chapter 2, reading him with Kierkegaard and Kafka on the importance of subjectivity, art, and communication.

Chapter 2, titled "The Truth in Fiction: Narrative, Art, and Subjectivity," interprets Douglass with Kierkegaard and Kafka. I want to develop an existentialist interpretation of Douglass in this chapter through his use of narrative that demonstrates its attentiveness to subjectivity and creativity—two emphases that are missing from analytic theism's reformed epistemology, thus enabling Douglass to make the word flesh. As for Douglass and Kierkegaard, both thinkers were critical of objectivity in Christian thought, an objectivity that led entire communities of Christians to have strong epistemic commitments, on one hand, while lacking any real moral commitments, on the other hand. For Kierkegaard, one such community was the Danish State Church, and for Douglass, this sort of community was the community of slave-holding Christians that he writes about in his *Narrative*. Existential subjectivity and its attendant moral responsibility played little to no role in either of these communities, and both Douglass and Kierkegaard resorted to literary communication strategies to effect change in these communities. Douglass did so through his use of narrative and Kierkegaard did so through his use of pseudonyms. It is against this backdrop that I read Douglass's critique of slave-holding Christianity in his *Narrative* with Kierkegaard's (Johannes Climacus's) Incarnational theology from *Philosophical Fragments* and his account of Christianity as an "existence-communication" from *Concluding Unscientific Postscript to Philosophical Fragments*. What I argue is that Climacus's contrast of Platonic recollection with Incarnational Christian theology in *Philosophical Fragments* is an analogue to the difference between analytic theism's reformed epistemology and Douglass's much more robust notion of existential subjectivity. For Climacus, the emphasis in Christianity is on a radical change in the subject, as opposed to a mere recollection of truth that can be attained based upon what one already knows. And this is exactly what Douglass wanted to see among slave-holding Christians: a genuine conversion and repentance from the ways of slave-holding Christianity.

My existentialist interpretation of Douglass with Kafka unfolds in close proximity to both the absurdities of the world in which Douglass lived and the absurdities of the world that Kafka created for his protagonist, Josef K., in his novel, *The Trial*. To establish the absurdities of Douglass's world, I draw from the work of American legal historian Ariela J. Gross, whose book *Double Character: Slavery and Mastery in the Antebellum Southern Courtroom* is, in her words, an exploration of "the paradoxes that arose from slaves' double identity as human subjects and the objects of property relations *at one and the same time*." Taking this existential absurdity as my point of departure, I then present a discussion that compares the absurdities of Douglass's reality as both person and property with certain parts of *The Trial*, trying to show how the novel's emphasis on the importance of subjectivity, existential freedom, indirect communication, and responsibility in the face of the absurd is a message that Douglass was able to appropriate in a way that Josef K., quite tragically, was not.

Chapter 3, titled "Overcoming Theodicy: Narrative, Poetry, and the Phenomenology of Suffering," tries to show the moral inadequacy of what many consider analytic theism and its reformed epistemology. I try to show this moral inadequacy in the way that the philosophy of religion treats the problem of evil. Here, I read Douglass with an interpretation of Levinas's account of suffering from his essay "Useless Suffering" to show how suffering ought not to be thematized into a polarity between good and evil, as is done in the philosophy of religion with the issue of theodicy. Contrary to analytic theism, both Douglass's and Levinas's phenomenological accounts of suffering suspend all theoretical judgments about suffering and evil and present them as a "datum" of consciousness, according to Levinas, and as experienced, giving priority to the first-person experience of suffering through narrative, according to Douglass. When reading Levinas, I deal with the subtleties of his critique of Edmund Husserl's phenomenological reduction, for, on one hand, Levinas is critical of Husserl's methodology because of the primacy of subjectivity. But, as Levinas is careful to admit, he is doing phenomenology nonetheless. I thus conclude that what Levinas presents to us in "Useless Suffering" is a phenomenological analysis of the Other's experience of suffering. In "Useless Suffering," then, rather than suffering being part of a naïve, thematized polarity between "good and evil" that one might be inclined to observe in the "natural attitude," Levinas suspends the natural attitude for the sake of the Other, giving us a pre-theoretical account of suffering as the Other experiences it. Levinas's insights, phenomenological though they may be, find their fullest expression in the existential embodiment of Douglass, whose phenomenological "datum" of suffering is prominently displayed throughout his narratives. On one level, then, although Levinas wrests the phenomenological reality of suffering from the clutches of violent conceptual polarities that maintain the usefulness of evil and ignore the Other's suffering, Douglass takes Levinas to the deeper level of existential embodiment, exposing us to the datum of his consciousness throughout his narratives, thus making the Word flesh.

As chapter 1 has argued, reading Black philosophy and Black theology with white philosophers not only shows the defects in white philosophical and theological reflection but also provides new insights to old philosophical and theological musings. With this in mind, my aim in chapter 4, titled "A Demand for Universality: Narrative, Art, and the Politics of Moral Suasion," is to show how Douglass's use of narrative functions as an art form allowing him to speak not only morally but also poetically and politically in the face of suffering. As it relates to the poetic, this chapter attempts to show a connection between Kant and Douglass with respect to the faculty of judgment and its mediation between the understanding and reason in Kant's *Critique of Judgment*. In support of this connection, I read Kant's *Critique of Judgment* with his essay "On the Miscarriage of All Philosophical Trials in Theodicy." Kant's aesthetic theory and its connection of the mental power of feeling to judgment creates a space for Douglass to express himself through narrative with aesthetic feeling according to the power of judgment, when both empirical cognition and practical reason demand his stoic silence, as it did for Job in Kant's essay on theodicy. In this chapter, I discuss the moral reasons that Kant provides for rational psychology in the paralogisms of the *Critique of Pure Reason*, and the way that Douglass's narrative brings us closer to those moral reasons. And I provide an analysis of Douglass's literary technique as a type of poetic expression that is neither propositional knowledge—as it would be if it were operating according to what Kant would call the "understanding"—nor moral silence—as it would be if it were operating in contrast to the self-righteousness of Job's three friends. Douglass's narrative methodology is instead an artistic one that reveals his *Geist* (spirit) or feeling, allowing him a mode of expression that lies between the rigorous certainty of predication in the attainment of knowledge, on one hand, and the uncertainty of epistemic failure combined with stoic moral duty, on the other hand. Chapter 4 also points to what I believe are some deep anthropological connections between Kant and Douglass as it relates to Douglass's use of moral suasion. I attempt to develop an interpretation of Douglass's *Narrative* as a work of art that induces reflective judgment that is disinterested in its quality, universal in its quantity, purposive in its relation, and necessary in its modality, assuming that others in the *sensus communis* will be compelled to judge it beautifully. Understanding the problems that Kant has on issues of race and racism in his critical philosophy, the chapter has a brief prelude to my interpretation of Kant and Douglass on Kant and the problem of race.

The fifth and final chapter interprets Douglass's fight with Covey as an encounter of totality with infinity. Infinity, a concept that may be theorized *ad nauseam* in the philosophy of religion, is, for Levinas, not a concept, but rather the Other. Using theological language, Levinas invests the Other with infinity by regarding the Other as "the Most High," whereas the philosophy of religion keeps infinity in the realm of the conceptual. "Totality," however, a concept that Levinas believes has serious political implications, is that tendency to render all of being intelligible to the ego. Being epistemologically driven, totality presumes to even be able to reduce infinity to the conditions of finitude. As it relates to the traditional conception of God, the philosophy of religion's epistemological/ontotheological impulse de-values infinity by making God conform to the conditions of finitude. Levinas argues that the self does the same thing to the Other: it forces the Other to conform to the horizons of itself, disregarding its alterity and its transcendence. For Levinas, then, totality and infinity are at odds with each other. Carrying the social and the political implications of totality to their conclusion, I argue that when Covey assaults Douglass, he is acting within an oppressive epistemological framework in which Douglass is already "known" as a slave. Within this epistemological framework, Douglass, on Levinas's account, becomes the mere *noema* of a *noesis*, preserving only the minimal amount of transcendence that is necessary to preserve Douglass as an "object" "to" and "for" Covey. Thus transformed into an intentional object, Covey can render Douglass intelligible to himself, making Douglass play a role in which he no longer recognizes himself: that of a slave. And in contrast, when Douglass resists Covey, Covey's subjectivity is, as Levinas argues in *Otherwise than Being*, "thrown back onto itself" in a sort of "anarchic passivity." Anarchic in that Covey is no longer a self-regulating subject operating according to the laws of his own instrumental rationality, and passive in the sense that now instead of acting on Douglass, he himself is acted upon by the infinity of Douglass as the Other. Douglass's narrative methodology, when read with Levinas in this way, thus makes the Word flesh: it transforms the overly theoretical reflections of "infinity" as a concept into the existentially/phenomenologically lived experience of Douglass.

NOTES

1. *Holy Bible*, World English Version, Exodus 33:18, 20.
2. Alvin Plantinga, *God, Freedom, and Evil* (New York: Harper and Row, 2002), 29.
3. Ibid.

4. Kant describes theodicy as a "juridical process . . . instituted before the tribunal of reason." In this process, "The author of theodicy . . . consents to represent the accused side as advocate through the formal refutation of all the plaintiff's complaints; he is not therefore allowed to dismiss" the complaints "in the course of the process of law through a decree of incompetency in the tribunal of human reason . . . he must rather attend to the objections, and make comprehensible how they in no way derogate from the concept of the highest wisdom by clarifying and removing them." See Immanuel Kant, "On the Miscarriage of All Philosophical Trials in Theodicy," in *Religion and Rational Theology*, trans. George di Giovanni (Cambridge: Cambridge University Press, 1996), 24–25. I must say that, considering the seemingly endless proliferation of abstractions in analytic theism, if reason were an honest judge, it would dismiss the accusations against God from before its tribunal for a lack of both subject matter and personal jurisdiction. For what authority has human reason over either the attributes of God or God Himself? My answer is none.

5. Martin Heidegger, "The Onto-Theo-Logical Constitution of Metaphysics," in *Identity and Difference*, trans. Joan Stambaugh (Chicago: University of Chicago Press, 2002), 71–72.

6. "Theological positivism" is the term that Smith gives to the kataphatic project of predication in theology. See James K. A. Smith, *Speech and Theology: Language and the Logic of Incarnation* (London: Routledge, 2002), 154, and *Introducing Radical Orthodoxy: Mapping a Post-Secular Theology* (Grand Rapids, MI: Baker Academic Publishing, 2004), 63–64. See also James K. A. Smith and Shane R. Cudney, "Postmodern Freedom and the Growth of Fundamentalism: Was the Grand Inquisitor Right?" *Studies in Religion/Religieuses* 25 (1996): 35–49.

7. See generally Søren Kierkegaard, *Concluding Unscientific Postscript to Philosophical Fragments*, trans. Howard V. and Edna H. Hong (Princeton, NJ: Princeton University Press, 1992).

8. See Daniel M. Bell Jr., *Liberation Theology After the End of History: The Refusal to Cease Suffering* (London: Routledge, 2001).

9. *The Poverty of Radical Orthodoxy*, ed. Lisa Isherwood and Marko Zlomislic (Eugene, OR: Wipf and Stock, 2012).

10. Ibid. There are two essays in this volume that I am referencing here: (1) "Radical Orthodoxy and the Closed Western Theological Mind: The Poverty of Radical Orthodoxy in Intercultural and Interreligious Perspective," by Paul Hedges at pp. 119–43, and (2) "Communities of Faith, Desire, and Resistance: A Response to Radical Orthodoxy's Ecclesia," by Christopher Newell at pp. 196–212. Regrettably, these essays are not the best efforts at meaningfully addressing problems of race and racism, particularly from the sorts of trenchant institutional and structural critique of the material conditions of racism that are characteristic of liberationist theological discourse. Here I am thinking of James H. Cone's works, such as *A Black Theology of Liberation* and *God of the Oppressed*.

11. Tyler Tritten, "The Contingency of God," *Heythrop Journal* 59, Issue 3 (2018): 448–55.

12. Ibid., 448.

13. Ibid.

14. Ibid., 449.
15. *Holy Bible*, King James Version, Exodus 33:20.
16. Immanuel Kant, "Critique of Practical Reason," *Practical Philosophy*, trans. and ed. Mary J. Gregor (Cambridge: Cambridge University Press, 1996), 257.
17. Ibid., 258.
18. Frederick Douglass, "The Day of Jubilee Comes," speech delivered on December 28, 1862, in *The Frederick Douglass Papers*, vol. 3, ed. John W. Blassingame (New Haven, CT: Yale University Press, 1985), 543.

Chapter One

The Word Made Flesh

Narrative and the Jurisdiction of History

"In the beginning was the Word, and the Word was with God, and the Word was God. . . . And the Word was made flesh, and dwelt among us, (and we beheld his glory, the glory as of the only begotten of the Father), full of grace and truth."

—*Holy Bible*[1]

WORD AND FLESH

This chapter outlines my existential, phenomenological, and aesthetic interpretation of Frederick Douglass, which unfolds in the remaining chapters of this book. Each of the three modes that I use to interpret Douglass—existentialism, phenomenology, philosophical aesthetics, and social theory—overlap extensively with Christian theology and also with politics. And this makes sense when interpreting Douglass, since Christianity and politics are two subjects that concerned him throughout his life as a public intellectual after his escape from slavery, and which thus form the basis for so much of his philosophical and theological reflection. Douglass was astute enough and pragmatic enough to understand that if he was to adequately champion the cause of abolition and the plight of the freed slave, it was essential, considering the legal, social, and political culture of his day, for him to understand the basics of Christianity and thus to be able to communicate in Christian terms. And Douglass did just that. So whether he accepted any of the doctrines of Christianity is irrelevant for my purposes. I am thus not making any strong claims about Douglass being an evangelical Christian, nor am I attempting to make any strong claims that Douglass was an Enlightenment deist or skeptic. Others have taken on that debate, and that is simply not my interest here.[2] Instead, I am interested in developing a philosophical and theological interpretation of Douglass from within the Christian Incarnational theological tradition, as Douglass spoke both from within that tradition and against it. Indeed, it is the narrative of Incarnational theology, whether one accepts it or not, that provides compelling explanatory force as it relates to interpreting Douglass's criticisms of Christianity. So rather than argue that Douglass either was or was not a Christian, I am interested in his broader orientation to Christianity as an escaped slave turned public intellectual, especially the implications of his orientation to Christianity when studied with certain philosophical traditions, such as existentialism and phenomenology, and philosophical subfields such as aesthetics and social theory. My existential and phenomenological interpretations of Douglass are both meta-philosophical and theological. That is, I am interested in philosophical questions about the task of philosophy itself as it relates to Christian theology. In my aesthetic interpretation of Douglass, I try to show how the political, the theological, and the aesthetic merge in the interest of justice. And in social theory, I try to show how epistemic and ontological forms of domination pervaded Douglass's life and how Douglass resisted them. I conclude that existentialism, phenomenology, aesthetics, and social thought work together to form an interpretation of Douglass that is not only consistent with his own philosophical and theological views on Christianity but also a corrective to the problem of philosophical and theological abstraction that is so prevalent in analytic theism, its reformed epistemology notwithstanding.

The remainder of this chapter will proceed as follows. In the next section, I discuss the broad framework for my interpretation of Douglass. This discussion is an exposition of the Christian account of the Incarnation of Jesus Christ. It is here that I juxtapose word and flesh, concepts and moral action, philosophical musings and political engagement, and abstraction and embodiment, laying the foundation for my comparison of analytic theism and its reformed epistemology with Douglass's use of narrative. It is this comparison which forms the thesis of the book, which, again, is that my existential, phenomenological, and aesthetic interpretation of Douglass is morally preferable to the reformed epistemology of analytic theism because, when viewed within an Incarnational theological framework, analytic theism's neglect of artistic creativity and subjectivity, its theorization of suffering, its lack of a prophetic political engagement, its emphasis on a rationally driven epistemology, and its overuse of abstraction ultimately makes the flesh a word, while Douglass's narrative methodology makes the word flesh. I believe that my interpretation of Douglass reveals a richness of subjective moral and religious life that is more interested in justice than it is interested in any metaphysical or epistemic (i.e., rational) justification of Christian beliefs.

Following the discussion of the Incarnation, I explore the two philosophical approaches to Christianity from which my thesis emerges: the reformed epistemology of analytic theism, on one hand, and Douglass's existential, phenomenological, aesthetic, social, political, and moral use of narrative, on the other hand. There are two analogues to the difference of my interpretation of Douglass as compared with analytic theism that provide my argument with explanatory force. The first is from political philosophy, and the other from Christian theology. In political philosophy, Charles W. Mills critiques the abstractions of classical contractarian and Rawlsian political theory as compared with what he calls "non-ideal" political theory.[3] And in Christian theology, James H. Cone critiques the abstractions of academic theology as compared with the concrete existential point of departure of Black theology and with the activism of Black writers, poets, and artists.[4] Both Cone and Mills see a similar problem with white philosophical and theological thought, which is the problem of abstraction. And I argue that a similar problem of abstraction in white philosophical and theological reflection exists in the philosophy of religion, specifically in the analytic theism of Nicholas Wolterstorff, William P. Alston, and Alvin Plantinga. So whether it is Christian theology (Niebuhr's failure to adequately engage Black suffering despite his work in moral theology), political philosophy (Rawls's failure to adequately engage chattel slavery despite his concern for justice), or the philosophy of religion (reformed epistemology's failure to have a prophetic voice despite its adherence to Christian beliefs), all use abstraction in a way that renders moral problems in general and Black life in particular, invisible, as Ralph Ellison would put it. My interpretation of Douglass along existential, phenomenological, and aesthetic lines aims to address this problem by arguing, as do Cone and Mills, that abstraction is best countered with embodiment, or, to put it in Incarnational theological terms, that the word is best when it is made flesh. I conclude this section of the chapter with a discussion of a concept underlying the juxtaposition of word and flesh that I shall call "the jurisdiction of history."

The next section argues that because of the difference between abstraction and embodiment, it is important—as Cone does with Karl Barth, Paul Tillich, Karl Marx, and Feuerbach—to read the Black philosophical and theological traditions with the thinking of canonical philosophical and theological figures. This is not done to legitimize Black philosophy and theology, claiming that Douglass is somehow not really a philosopher unless one interprets him with white philosophical and theological figures. No. To the contrary, I defend the view that one should read Black philosophical and theological figures such as Douglass with canonical philosophical and theological figures to *interrogate the canonical figures*, for, as Cone points out in *The Cross and the Lynching Tree*, with respect to Niebuhr, there is much left to be desired of his moral theology as compared with James Baldwin, Countee Cullen, and W. E. B. Du Bois. But one cannot see just how far Niebuhr falls short *until one reads him with* Baldwin, Cullen, and Du Bois. Similarly, I submit that reading Douglass with Husserl, Levinas, Kafka, Kierkegaard, and Kant is important because Douglass's reading site of Christianity, his hermeneutical horizon, is a site of racialized, dehumanized embodiment, rather than a site of academic philosophical, literary, and theological white privilege as with Kierkegaard, Kafka, Husserl, Kant, and Levinas. Reading Douglass with these white philosophical figures breathes life into their theoretical insights, making their theoretical word embodied flesh. And reading Douglass with analytic theism's reformed epistemology (Plantinga, Wolterstorff, and Alston) does the same thing for me that reading Black theology with Niebuhr did for Cone: it demonstrates the inadequacy of the abstractions of white philosophical thinking to address moral problems at the level of praxis. To help make my case, I recount a personal moment when my reading of Douglass with a white philosopher—Kant—was called into question. I then conclude the chapter.

THE BIG PICTURE: INCARNATIONAL THEOLOGY

The central feature of Christianity is God's intervention in history. God does not function in the Judeo-Christian tradition as an abstract, conceptual entity apart from human life. The biblical tradition illustrates this basic idea. Whether it was God's intervention in ancient Egypt to save the Hebrew slaves from Pharaoh's army at the shores of the Red Sea, or God's intervention in the fiery furnace or in the den of hungry lions, the Judeo-Christian tradition depicts a God who is intensely interested in human history. Perhaps this is why God—who, on the Judeo-Christian account is atemporal and without a past—becomes a historical being in the person of Jesus Christ in order to rescue humanity from what Christians believe is its wretched condition. The Christian Gospel, or "good news" is the story of a God who loves his creation so much that He becomes one of them in order to save them from their doom. This soteriological paradigm is recited in the Gospel according to John: "In the beginning was the Word, and the Word was with God and the Word was God. . . . And the Word was made flesh, and dwelt among us, (and we beheld his glory, the glory as of the only begotten of the Father,) full of grace and truth."[5] The use of the Greek word *logos* (λόγος) in John 1:1 is significant, for it implies a word, speech, or language; it implies rational explanation—perhaps an explanation of how the universe is structured, ordered, or how *logos* is a sort of organizing principle that somehow holds the universe together. And then in the fourteenth verse, we are told that this reason, this explanation, this ordering, this structuring, becomes flesh. The Greek word for flesh in John 1:14 is *sarx* (σάρξ), which means embodiment, flesh, bone, and blood, and it represents that part of human nature that is prone to moral wrongdoing. Regardless of whether one accepts Incarnational theology as a matter of historical or epistemic truth, what is, I think, undeniable is that this theology is compelling, for even taken as a myth, it describes a radical commitment to a symbiotic relationship between transcendence and immanence; between abstraction and materiality; between word and flesh. The significance of the Incarnation to the Christian story thus cannot be overstated, for if the salvation of humanity was merely a good idea, then the *logos* of John 1:1 remains rational and conceptual; God remains at the level of an idea without ever making any genuine moral commitment to His creation. It is only after the Word has become flesh—after the Word has become historical—that people are delivered. If salvation was merely the Word of John 1:1, then no one would actually be saved. The organizing principle, apart from fleshly embodiment, is a mere abstract notion incapable of salvation or deliverance.

To further appreciate the nature of the Incarnation, consider its comparison to the nature of Western philosophy. Thales of Miletus is generally thought to be the first of the ancient Greek philosophers. His basic claim was that "All is water." The significance of this claim is not in what Thales accomplished, for he never succeeded in proving that all things were water, but rather it is in what he attempted: he articulated a rational, naturalistic account of reality, in stark contrast to the mythical account of the Homeric tradition. It is this subtle but profound movement away from tradition of *mythos* that is the origin of Western philosophy. To be sure, Thales did not make a clean break from ancient Greek religion, as his fragments indicate that he still believed in the gods. But what he did do was attempt an explanation of all that is in rational and naturalistic terms rather than mythical and supernatural terms. And it is this attempt that defines the nature of Western philosophy: an attempt to explain all of reality in rational terms, or according to the *logos*. The contrast with the Incarnation is stark on this point, for in Christian theology, the *logos* is merely the beginning, according to John 1:1. The *logos*, or notions of word, reason, and language, is the starting point, but, again, rational explanations of salvation are inadequate to effect deliverance; only the Word as it is made flesh can accomplish this task. In contrast, *logos* is not a beginning for Greek philosophy—or Western philosophy, for that matter. Philosophy *begins and ends* with the *logos*, with rational argument, with metaphysical explanation, and with epistemic justification. *Logos* is thus a rational "Alpha and Omega"—a term that God gives to Himself in the Judeo-Christian tradition—of sorts. The entire goal of philosophy is to provide a rational account of being, or of what is. Hence metaphysics and epistemology lie at the very foundation of Western philosophy. Whereas on the Christian theological view, the Word (*logos*) is a mere beginning that is made flesh and delivers people, on the philosophical view, *logos* is both a beginning and an end in itself that provides ontological and epistemic assurance. The contrast here is striking.

Considering the significance of the Word of God being made flesh—that is, considering its centrality to the Christian Incarnational narrative—Christianity, it seems, ought to eschew abstraction, for to abstract from the person and work of Jesus Christ is to reverse the Incarnational paradigm from a life-giving, soul-delivering Word made flesh into a moribund flesh made into a word. Abstraction brings to mind the image of birds scavenging a carcass: they pick at its flesh and fly away, taking it to a place far from the carcass to consume it. Eventually, all that will be left is a skeleton, a structure, a form of what the animal used to be. Its flesh, its embodiment—indeed, its life—is gone from it. In this way, abstraction picks from the flesh of the historical Jesus until all that is left is a formal structure of rational, ontological, and epistemic justification. Like the birds scavenging the carcass, abstraction brings with it a desire for consumption until only an empty skeleton and framework remains. This imagery emphasizes two serious problems with abstraction. First, the resulting religion is empty, formal, and without any real moral engagement. Here, we are reminded of Levinas's admonition about theology:

> It is our relations with men . . . that give to theological concepts the sole signification they admit of. . . . Metaphysics is enacted in ethical relations. Without the signification they draw from ethics theological concepts remain empty and formal frameworks. The role Kant attributed to sensible experience in the domain of the understanding belongs in metaphysics to interhuman relations.[6]

Philosophical and theological concepts are useless apart from the human relationships in which they are to be applied. The principle of the Golden Rule, for example, means little except that there is some human relationship in which I can actually treat someone as I want to be treated. Kant put it this way in his metaphysics and epistemology: "concepts without intuitions are empty." As Levinas points out, for Kant, sensible experience provides intuitions which are then subject to the formal, empty framework of the categories of pure reason. For Kant, without any sensory experience, we would have no knowledge at all. Similarly, in Christian theology, when we have a philosophically sophisticated, abstract, formal religion without any concrete ethical relationships, we have no morality. The second problem with abstraction that the imagery of the scavenging birds brings to mind is the problem of consumption. Consumption here can be interpreted as a metaphor for ontological and epistemic desire. This is the "desire to know" of Aristotle's *Metaphysics*,[7] and in this context, it is a metaphor for abstraction's incessant epistemic and ontological explanations in the interest of subjecting God to human standards of rationality. The consumption metaphor can be explained with reference to the Judeo-Christian tradition. In John's gospel, Jesus feeds five thousand people with five loaves of bread and two fish.[8] Twelve baskets of bread were left over after the meal. The fish, as created beings according to the Christian theological narrative, represent finitude. There was no fish left over. Jesus, as God Himself in human flesh, identifies himself as the "bread of life."[9] Finitude was consumed, but divinity was not. There was a remainder, a residue, a portion that, despite the hunger of five thousand people, was left over because it could not be consumed. So it is that no matter how hard one tries to epistemically and ontologically abstract from Jesus—that is, no matter how "hungry" our rational desire may be—there will always be something "left over" that our rationality cannot consume. So not only does abstraction leave Christian theology empty, but even rationality's most fervent attempts at comprehending God will be futile, as something will always escape its grasp; something will always be, like the twelve baskets of bread, "left over."

This is what makes abstraction problematic for a religion whose God becomes historical, a God who not only intervenes in human affairs from a distance but also subjected Himself to the vagaries of human existence, not the least of which is embodiment and death, in order to save humanity. In becoming human, so goes the Christian narrative, God subjected himself to a human nature that is prone to wrongdoing—this is a meaning of the Greek word for flesh (*sarx*) in John 1:14. On the traditional Christian accounts of God in philosophical theology, God is an atemporal being with no past, present, or future. Indeed, in the Hebrew tradition, God's name is "I AM," indicating a present state of being not subject to the flow and flux of time. So it is that Jeremiah will say that in God there is "no variableness, neither shadow of turning,"[10] indicating a sense of consistency and stability, in contrast to the world that He entered and the body that He inhabited that was the God-man, Jesus Christ. As Kierkegaard's pseudonym, Johannes Climacus points out, the Incarnation is the great paradox that leaves human rationality utterly befuddled; it is the paradox that becomes the "passion" of rational thought that defies explanation.[11] Indeed, according to Johannes Climacus, one cannot accept this as truth without also having the condition for receiving the truth, which is faith.[12] And faith is necessary precisely because the Word of God became flesh and yet remained God—again, something that philosophical reasoning cannot explain. So the broad contrast that is the backdrop for this book is a contrast between two very different approaches to Christian thought that represent, on one hand, the use of philosophical abstraction that makes the flesh an abstract word and, on the other hand, an attentiveness to embodiment and a respect for what I shall call the "jurisdiction of history" that makes the word flesh. Each of these approaches is discussed in the next section.

ABSTRACTION AND THE JURISDICTION OF HISTORY

Since Christian theology depends upon the Word being made flesh, it stands to reason that philosophical thinking about God—thinking with the *logos* as its alpha and omega—apart from human beings as an abstract concept would be inconsistent with the nature of the Christian Gospel. And yet that is what happens so often in a certain mode of Christian theological and philosophical reflection. As I pointed out in the introduction, so much of Christian philosophical theology in both its modern (Leibniz) and its postmodern[13] (the reformed epistemology of analytic theism) iterations is more interested in rational, epistemic justification than it is in any sort of existential, embodied, historical particularity of Jesus Christ. Broadly understood, the philosophical theology of Wolterstorff, Alston, and Plantinga are representative of this sort of abstraction. The emphasis of their project in what they call "reformed epistemology," I think, rightly critiques modernity's emphasis on epistemic foundationalism and evidentialism as the sole arbiter of truth. But its objective is still to render a belief in God *rational*. And so long as rationality—*logos*—is the goal, then this sort of philosophical theology, despite its attempt to affirm Christian beliefs as properly basic, works against the biblical Incarnational paradigm of *logos* being a beginning (John 1:1), rather than being an end in itself, as it is for the reformed epistemology of analytic theism. Considering this, it is not surprising that Alston points out with reference to his own work in religious epistemology that "This is basically a work in epistemology, the epistemology of religious perceptual beliefs."[14] And his recognition of the abstraction inherent in his project of epistemic justification is also quite telling: "The reader is warned, however, that fairly heavy doses of abstract epistemological discussion can be expected."[15] This is what I am referring to as the flesh is being made word instead of the Word being made flesh: an overemphasis on abstraction in the interest of rationality rather than an emphasis on concrete moral, social, political, and aesthetic life in the interest of justice. And this is, I believe, the fundamental problem with the reformed epistemology of analytic theism. Again, this level of abstraction is unavoidable, precisely because reason is still the determining factor in the task of reformed epistemology. Some explanation of the project of reformed epistemology and its deep connections to rational justification—the *logos*—will be useful here.

Reformed epistemology is analytic theism's robust and rigorous challenge against two modern philosophical notions: classical epistemic foundationalism and evidentialism. The former being the claim that it is only rational to hold beliefs that are properly grounded in other beliefs, or that are otherwise immediate to us, thereby satisfying the criterion of incorrigibility.[16] And the latter is the claim that it is only rational to hold beliefs for which there is sufficient credible evidence to support them.[17] Wolterstorff has argued that although Descartes was certainly a classical foundationalist, he adhered to foundationalism only with respect to science, and that it was John Locke who expanded foundationalism, applying it to theological concerns.[18] The one modern philosopher upon whom much of reformed epistemology is based is Thomas Reid, as according to Wolterstorff, he represents an exception to the Enlightenment tradition of demanding justification and evidence for beliefs. Wolterstorff writes:

> It has to be said that the main representatives of the epistemological tradition . . . all take the existence of belief forming "mechanisms" in human beings, they devote scant attention to this phenomenon as such. A characteristic result of this oversight is that the rules they give for "the direction of the mind" prove limited and myopic in application. To these generalizations, Thomas Reid . . . is the great exception. It was Reid's great genius to perceive that if we want to understand knowledge and rationality, we cannot only talk about the abstract relations holding among propositions, along the way making unreflective assumptions about the "mechanisms" which form our beliefs. We must look head-on at the psychological "mechanisms" involved in belief formation. Articulate epistemology requires articulate psychology.[19]

According to Wolterstorff, then, Foundationalism has paid insufficient attention to the mechanisms at work in the formation of our beliefs. Reid, however, is attentive to such mechanisms, and this attentiveness leads him to conclude that there is no difference between the beliefs that we trust because of external verification and sense perception on one hand and the beliefs that we hold based on introspection and intuition on the other hand. We see this reliance on Reid not only in Wolterstorff but also in Alston, who elucidates on Reid's contribution to reformed epistemology as follows:

> Reid's point is that the only (external) basis we have for trusting rational intuition and introspection is that they are firmly established doxastic practices, so firmly established that we "cannot help it"; and we have exactly the same basis for trusting sense perception, memory, nondeductive reasoning, and other sources of belief for which Descartes and Hume were demanding an external validation. They all "came out of the same shop," and therefore if one of them is suspect so are all the others.[20]

The philosophical aim of Alston's reformed epistemology is, then, to show that the foundationalist and evidentialist objections to theism do not hold because established doxastic practices provide the same justification for external beliefs such as "The glass of water is on the table," as they do for an intuitive or introspective belief that "God exists," or that "God is love," or that "God has forgiven me." So we are entitled to trust theistic beliefs as properly "basic" and without epistemic foundation, because, as Reid points out, we have innate belief-forming habits and self-governed mechanisms that each realize "a function that yields beliefs with a certain kind of content from inputs of a certain type."[21] And since, as Reid puts it, our rational intuition and our sense perception all come from "the same shop," one is not entitled to a privileged epistemic status over the other. So the reformed epistemologist of analytic theism concludes that religious beliefs are epistemically on par with perceptual beliefs: the former being based on religious experience and the latter being based on perceptual experience. This is what Alston has called "the parity argument."[22] The aim here is to establish religious beliefs, or what Alston calls "M-beliefs" (manifestation beliefs, such as the belief that God is doing this or that thing at a given time vis-à-vis a human subject "strengthening," "comforting," etc.) as beliefs that are epistemically justified—and thus rational—as a set of beliefs that are not based upon any other beliefs at all.[23] Such beliefs, again, are considered "properly basic" in the reformed epistemology of analytic theism.

Alvin Plantinga presents a similar argument in which he rejects the foundationalist notion of proper basicality. Plantinga first describes the classical criterion of verificationist epistemology that says that a belief is properly basic if and only if the belief is either incorrigible or self-evident to the believer. Plantinga describes this criterion of proper basicality as follows: "(8) For any proposition A and person S, A is properly basic for S if and only if A is incorrigible for S or self-evident to S."[24] Plantinga goes on to critique the basis for accepting this claim as a criterion of proper basicality, arguing that there is nothing properly basic about this criterion at all unless the epistemic foundationalist violates his own criterion of proper basicality, essentially making the foundationalist position incoherent. Plantinga writes:

> Of course a philosopher might find (8) so appealing that he simply takes it to be true, neither offering argument for it, nor accepting it on the basis of other things he believes. If he does so, however, his noetic structure will be self-referentially incoherent. (8) itself is neither self-evident nor incorrigible; hence in accepting (8) as basic, the classical foundationalist violates the condition of proper basicality he himself lays down in accepting it. On the other hand, perhaps the philosopher has some argument for it from premises that are self-evident; it is exceeding[ly] hard to see, however, what such arguments might be like. And

until he has produced such arguments, what shall the rest of us do—we who do not find (8) at all obvious or compelling? How could he use (8) to show us that belief in God, for example, is not properly basic? Why should we believe (8), or pay it any attention?[25]

Plantinga goes on to argue that rather than use a foundationalist criterion for proper basicality of a belief in God that is deductive or self-evident in nature, an inductive, experiential-based criterion must be used. Examples of beliefs and conditions for those beliefs together form what Plantinga calls a "noetic structure."[26] And it is within this noetic structure that Plantinga argues that "We must assemble examples of beliefs and conditions such that the former are obviously properly basic in the latter, and examples of beliefs and conditions such that the former are obviously not properly basic in the latter.... Accordingly," claims Plantinga, "criteria for proper basicality must be reached from below rather than above; they should not be presented as obiter dicta, but argued to and tested by a relevant set of examples."[27] And it is these examples which must come from within Christianity, not from without it. On this view of proper basicality, the Christian can suppose that a belief in God is properly basic as grounded in the Christian tradition of believing that God has given us an innate rational capacity to discern his work in the world around us, whereas a belief in the Great Pumpkin is not grounded in such a belief. The Christian, then, may be able to properly dismiss a belief in the Great Pumpkin as a thoroughly irrational belief, while accepting a belief in God as a rational basic belief.

There is, then, in the reformed epistemology of analytic theism, an attempt to attain rational justification of certain religious beliefs as properly basic. It is present in Wolterstorff, Alston, and Plantinga. All three attempt to put religious beliefs on par with perceptual beliefs, and all three do so with a strong interest in defeating the claim that religious beliefs are irrational. But why must rationality be the standard-bearer? Is there not something problematic for religious belief if its ultimate justification is that of rationality? Here, one hears an echo of Levinas when he writes,

> The philosophical discourse of the West claims the amplitude of an all-encompassing structure or of an ultimate comprehension. It compels every other discourse to justify itself before philosophy. Rational theology accepts this vassalage. If, for the benefit of religion, it reserves a domain for the authority of philosophy, one will know that this domain will have been recognized to be philosophically unverifiable.[28]

Levinas's point about rational theology being in "vassalage" or in a subordinate position to philosophy is compelling. For at bottom, reformed epistemology, despite its objections to natural theology and epistemic foundationalism, ultimately pays homage to reason in furtherance of a deeply philosophical agenda that is entirely committed to the *logos*. And it is this pursuit of epistemic parity and rational consistency which comes at the expense of subjectivity, morality, creative expression, and political engagement, each of which the Christian Gospel demands. Although there are some moral and political concerns for the reformed epistemology of analytic theism, they are, I think, far too peripheral to the overall project, and too narrowly restricted to evangelical Christian belief to be considered as meaningful, except in some very dubious ways.[29]

To summarize, the reformed epistemology of analytic theism has as its aim to place religious beliefs on par with perceptual beliefs in order to show that religious beliefs are rational. With rationality firmly ensconced as the goal, the reformed epistemologist engages in a high level of abstraction and generality. It is precisely reformed epistemology's pursuit of rational justification—the *logos*—that inverts the Incarnational theological paradigm from the Word made flesh into the flesh made into an abstract word, converting Christian theology into a species of Greek philosophy. Insufficient attention is paid to both existential subjectivity and prophetic moral concerns, concerns that, as I shall discuss throughout the book, are paramount in my existential, phenomenological, and aesthetic interpretation of Douglass.

The problem of abstraction in the reformed epistemology of analytic theism is not unique to the philosophy of religion. Political philosophy and Christian theology also grapple with the problem of abstraction, and political philosopher Charles W. Mills and Christian theologian James H. Cone discuss the problem of abstraction at length, locating its origin, discussing its effects, and proposing alternatives to this mode of philosophical and theological thinking. After discussing Mills and Cone, I try to think through the problem of abstraction as a neglect of what I shall call the "jurisdiction of history," a phenomenon in which oppression and injustice arise through an inversion of what I submit ought to be the relationship between historical authority and human authority. I first discuss Mills and Cone.

Mills confronts the problem of abstraction in political philosophy. His critique of political philosophy (specifically, contractarianism) is that it is too "ideal" in nature—that Thomas Hobbes, John Locke, and John Rawls, for example, in beginning with abstract thought experiments about the conditions under which societies are formed and political obligations are first imposed (Hobbes's and Locke's "state of nature" and Rawls's "original position"), are overlooking the historical conditions under which modern social and political arrangements were actually made. Such historical conditions include a plethora of unjust, oppressive imperial and colonial projects that are grounded in white supremacy. In contrast to the hypothetical thought experiments of political philosophy, Mills finds, in Jean-Jacques Rousseau, a non-ideal political theory, which, rather than overlooking the role of injustice in the formation of the social contract, actually accounts for it. For Mills, Rousseau's account of the state of nature, unlike those of Locke and Rawls, for example, does not describe the formation of a just society based on rational principles of natural freedom and equality. Instead, Mills argues that according to Rousseau, "technological development in the state of nature brings into existence a nascent society of growing divisions in wealth between rich and poor, which are then consolidated and made permanent by a deceitful 'social contract.'"[30] On Rousseau's account, inequality is grafted into the very foundation of the modern social and political structure. And this is the basis for Mills's appropriation of Rousseau in his notion of the racial contract. Mills wants to eliminate the abstractions of political theory in favor of a non-ideal political theory that will no longer overlook the litany of social and political oppression in the modern West, but rather will account for it. These two contrasting social and political frameworks—the ideal and the non-ideal—are the framework for Mills's notion of the racial contract. Mills describes the differences between the two as follows:

> Whereas the ideal contract explains how a just society would be formed, ruled by a moral government, and regulated by a defensible moral code, this nonideal/naturalized contract explains how an unjust, exploitative society, ruled by an oppressive government and regulated by an immoral code, comes into existence. If the ideal contract is to be endorsed and emulated, this nonideal/naturalized contract is to be demystified and condemned.[31]

To bridge this gap between the philosophical abstractions of political theory and the historical realities of political life, Mills proposes what he calls "The Racial Contract," which is

> a set of formal or informal agreements or meta-agreements (higher-level contracts about contracts, which set the limits of the contracts' validity) between the members of one subset of humans, henceforth designated . . . as "white," and coextensive . . . with the class of full persons, to categorize the remaining subset of humans as "nonwhite" and of a different and inferior moral status, subpersons, so that they have a subordinate civil standing in the white or white-ruled polities the whites either already inhabit or establish or in transactions as aliens with these polities, and the moral and juridical rules normally regulating the behavior of whites in their dealings with one another either do not apply at all in dealings with nonwhites or apply only in a qualified form . . . but in any case the general purpose of the contract is always the differential privileging of the whites as a group with respect to the nonwhites as a group, the exploitation of their bodies, land, and resources, and the denial of equal socioeconomic opportunities to them. All whites are beneficiaries of the Contract, though some

whites are not signatories to it . . . it is a contract between those categorized as white *over* the nonwhites, who are thus the objects rather than the subjects of the agreement."[32]

Mills also explains how the Racial Contract is intended to work:

> The "Racial Contract," then, is intended as a conceptual bridge between two areas now largely segregated from each other: on the one hand, the world of mainstream (i.e., white) ethics and political philosophy, preoccupied with discussions of justice and rights in the abstract, on the other hand, the world of Native Americans, African American, and Third and Fourth World political thought, historically focused on issues of conquest, imperialism, colonialism, white settlement, land rights, race and racism, slavery, Jim crow, reparations, apartheid, cultural authenticity, national identity, *indigenismo*, Afrocentrism, etc.[33]

The point of Mills's Racial Contract is to, as he put it, "bridge" a gap—indeed, a chasm—between the ideal political thought of white political and ethical thought and the non-ideal, historical reality of oppression and injustice, with which Black social and political thought has always been concerned. What makes ideal political theory—particularly that of Rawls—so problematic for Mills is its conception of an ideally just society, which is "a society without any previous history of injustice," as opposed to an "ideally just" society as one that has "an unjust history that has now been *completely corrected for*." Without any historical attentiveness whatsoever, except for what Mills calls the "ritualistic genuflection" at the name of Martin Luther King Jr., Rawls's ideal political theory misses an entire tradition of Black social and political thought that grapples extensively with the very moral, social, and political problems that Rawlsian political theory overlooks[34]—precisely the same thing that I am arguing happens here in the philosophy of religion, specifically in the reformed epistemology of analytic theism.

Even as Mills grapples with the problem of abstraction in political philosophy and proposes the Racial Contract as a corrective to the problem, James H. Cone deals with the problem of abstraction in Christian theology and proposes a Black theology of liberation as a remedial measure. According to J. Kameron Carter, "Cone is acutely sensitive to the problem of abstraction in theology. He understands it to be the perennial problem of white theology and Euro-American racism as a whole. Indeed, as he sees it, a commitment to thinking and acting abstractly is central to why neither white theology nor the white church authentically expresses the Christian faith."[35] Indeed, Cone's critique of abstraction is extensive and is seen throughout his oeuvre.[36] In some of his earliest work, Cone points out that "The prophets of Israel are prophets of social justice, reminding the people that Yahweh is the author of justice. It is important to note in this connection that the righteousness of

God is not an abstract quality in the being of God, as with Greek philosophy. It is rather God's active involvement in history, making right what human beings have made wrong."[37] Like Mills, who argues that there is something problematic about white theorizing in moral and political philosophy, Cone points out that white theology "tends to make the Jesus-event an abstract, unembodied idea."[38]

Abstraction thus does in Christian theology what it does in political philosophy: it almost immediately erases moral responsibility by creating fictive and hypothetical worlds. These worlds are akin to the "state of nature" in what Mills calls "ideal" political theory. Nothing exists in these worlds but an ontotheological god made in the *imago hominis* of white rationality. This is an idol of the white theological and philosophical imagination that, through the various white imperial projects of Western civilization, not only makes a world of Christian-based white supremacy but also, through the endless proliferation of thought experiments of its progeny of the reformed epistemology of analytic theism, maintains this Christian-based, white supremacist world.[39] What is especially problematic in the theological context is that white theology purports to transcend the jurisdiction of history, to be beyond history's reach. Rather than human reason submitting to the authority of history, history submits to the authority of white rationality. This is problematic for Christian theology precisely because as Black theology has pointed out, the Judeo-Christian narrative portrays a God who is intimately involved in history, repeatedly intervening on behalf of the oppressed, who are his chosen people in the Old Testament, and the victims of a corrupt theo-political regime in the New Testament. And yet, despite the historicity of the Judeo-Christian God, the reformed epistemology of analytic theism, through abstraction, presents us with a god that has no resemblance at all to the God that parted the Red Sea for the Hebrews, delivering them from Egypt; it produces instead an ersatz god that, through its theodicies and its free will defenses, will justify the slavery that put the Hebrews in bondage in the first place. At the core of this problem in the reformed epistemology of analytic theism is that rationality is what drives its entire project; that is, it has epistemic and ontological preoccupations to explain God in rational terms. Here, the reformed epistemologists take on what is essentially an Aristotelian project, in which their aim is to, using the *logos*, provide a rational account of God. In doing so, they neglect an entire history of Christianity's complicity in a vast array of moral evils throughout Western civilization, not the least of which was its support for American chattel slavery. So, as I have argued earlier, because rationality is the driving concern behind the reformed epistemology of analytic theism, problems of concrete existence fall by the wayside.[40] In this regard, it is no accident that Aristotle's *Metaphysics* informs his *Politics*. Consider that the *Metaphysics* gives us a god that is not the God of the Bible, but rather an explanatory metaphysical first principal, a god made in the image of Aristotle, a Greek philosopher. This god justifies a certain teleological ordering of nature, in which all things have a variety of natural dispositions and potentialities, including human beings. So for Aristotle, there are certain people who "From the hour of their birth" are "marked out for subjection."[41] This is, of course, the same line of reasoning that justified American chattel slavery—a different type of slavery than that which Aristotle references, to be sure, but the claim was that Africans were slaves by nature, a claim that Christianity, through theological arguments such as the Hamitic curse, supported. An attentiveness to Douglass is important here, as John Stauffer argues that in Douglass's speech "Pictures and Progress," he refers to human beings as the only "picture-making" beings in the natural world, paraphrasing the opening of Aristotle's *Poetics*. Stauffer argues that this is an attempt to humanize Black people by Douglass reading Aristotle's *Poetics* against his *Politics*.[42] Aristotle's notion of natural slavery became a theoretical, philosophical, and theological foundation of American chattel slavery. The moral omissions of reformed epistemology can perhaps be understood as a way of avoiding a reckoning with a past that white theology needs to ignore to maintain its rational, Aristotelian, pursuit of an ontotheological "god," or what Martin Heidegger calls the "god of philosophy."

Abstraction in philosophical theology causes a neglect of historical wrongs done in the very name of the religion that the reformed epistemology of analytical theism purports to be defending. And these omissions—the various colonial and imperial projects carried on in the name of Christianity that justified white supremacy—are significant and legion. Cone points to a huge omission in his book *The Cross and the Lynching Tree* when he highlights Reinhold Niebuhr's failure to see the connection between Jesus's death on the cross and the lynching of African Americans as a significant problem, especially considering Niebuhr's other work on race in his moral theology. Of this failure, Cone writes:

> Few theologians of the twentieth century focused as much attention on the cross, one of the central themes of his work. And yet even he failed to connect the cross and its most vivid reenactment in his time. To reflect on this failure is to address a defect in the conscience of white Christians and to suggest why African Americans have needed to trust and cultivate their own theological imagination.[43]

Cone elsewhere addresses this "defect in the conscience of white Christians" by asking the rhetorical question, "What difference does it make if one should 'prove' a philosophical point, if that point has nothing to do with spreading freedom throughout the land?"[44]

So, similar to Mills and Cone, I argue that "ideal" theorizing in analytic theism is morally deficient in that it overlooks Christianity's complicity in the ongoing suffering resulting from racial oppression. And more important, it overlooks Black philosophy's and Black theology's responses to this suffering. Through my emphasis on Douglass and his narrative methodology, this book is an attempt to bring a much needed focus on social and political engagement into contemporary philosophical and theological discussion from my own Black philosophical and theological voice, a voice that is attempting to cultivate what Cone calls the "African American theological imagination." In both political philosophy and Christian theology, abstraction results in the neglect of historical atrocities as well as their legacies. And it is this ongoing neglect that, for Mills and Cone, demands a more concrete point of departure for political and theological reflection. Here, I am attempting a more concrete point of departure in the philosophy of religion because of the problem of abstraction, specifically the abstractions of analytic theism's reformed epistemology. And to discuss the need for this more concrete point of departure in the philosophy of religion, I now turn to a fundamental concept at work in my interpretation of Douglass. I call this concept "the jurisdiction of history."

As a legal concept, the term "jurisdiction" refers to the authority of a court that translates into the adjudicative power of the state over property, subject matter, or a person. To say that a court has jurisdiction over something, someone, or some subject matter is to say that not only is the case justiciable in that court as a legal forum, but the litigants, once in that court, also cannot avoid the court's authority; there is no escaping the court's power of adjudication and enforcement of its judgments. So to be subject to a court's jurisdiction is significant, for it means that one must both answer to and account for one's conduct giving rise to the cause that joins the litigants in court. The coercive power of the state makes one who is subject to the jurisdiction of its courts legally accountable for one's action or inaction. And the penalties for one who ignores the jurisdiction of the court—that is, the penalties for disregarding the court's authority—can be significant, ranging from a judgment against one's property (sometimes called a "default" judgment in a civil action to recover money damages) to a judgment against one's liberty, as in criminal cases, in which a criminal defendant fails to take a criminal case seriously and, because of that failure, suffers the penalty of incarceration. Whether ignoring the jurisdiction of the court affects one's property or liberty, such consequences are significant, for once the judgment is rendered in a civil case, or a guilty verdict is reached in a criminal case, the court now has the power of enforcing that judgment and, by judicial order, may either seize one's property or send one to the penitentiary. In short, there are very real consequences for ignoring jurisdiction in this legal sense of that term.

Here, I use the term "jurisdiction" not in its legal sense but in a philosophical sense. I am analogizing the legal consequence of disregarding jurisdiction to the social, political, and theological consequences of disregarding the jurisdiction of history. What I want to emphasize with this juridical metaphor is the inescapable authority of history over human affairs; that even as a court of competent jurisdiction holds its litigants accountable for their action or inaction, their crimes of commission and omission, history has that same hold on humanity because all human beings, as temporal beings, have a past, a history. No one just appears without any past whatsoever. And as it is with individual persons, so it is with families, communities, governments, nations, and religions. So it is that the reach of history's jurisdiction, its authority, its power over persons, groups, religions, and nations is all-encompassing; it is universal. In the temporal order of things, the jurisdiction of history is plenary. This is not to say that there is any sort of determinism with respect to one's past or one's history, for people remain free to part with their past, or to do things inconsistent with their past behavior. But it is to say that anything that occurs whatsoever, occurs in history, in time, and it becomes a part of our past and, ultimately a part of our identity—political, religious, or otherwise. So ignoring the history of a person, nation, religion, family, or community has social and political consequences that are just as devastating as the legal consequences of ignoring jurisdiction. But instead of losing property or liberty (that is, liberty in the literal, physical sense of being incarcerated), one is stripped of one's identity, which can result in a tremendous loss of liberty in the social and political sense. So when Rawls employs theoretical abstraction to articulate his notion of the original position, history submits to abstract, philosophical reflection, rather than abstract, philosophical reflection submitting to history. And with history thus subordinated to reason, as Mills points out, philosophical abstraction succeeds in producing an ideal just society at the expense of an actual, unjust society. Justice is achieved in the abstract, but it can never be concretely realized because rationality's abstractions have effectively eliminated history from having any consideration whatsoever. Exalting reason over history is thus a zero-sum game: reason's handmaiden of abstraction wins, and actual justice loses. So history, whose jurisdiction is plenary, when ignored, leads to a loss of social and political freedom, often resulting in social and political death, which I will discuss below in greater detail. Since the consequences of ignoring history are so devastating, this raises a question: Why ignore the jurisdiction of history?

We often ignore the jurisdiction of history because of an evasion of responsibility. That is, there is some interest—usually a corrupt one—in ignoring historical moments that make us uncomfortable. Here, I am not referring to mere unpleasant memories, but rather to historical atrocities of such magnitude that they demand not only our recollection but also our remedial action. And since we prefer not to be morally responsible, we either, through a process of abstraction—as in political philosophy, theology, and the philosophy of religion—ignore the historical events and context altogether or revise history to suit our moral complacency, interpreting historical events and contexts as compatible with our evasion of responsibility. Such events and contexts, stripped of their historical, social, political, and cultural moorings, are the result of the jurisdiction of history's neglect, and the consequences are significant. For example, in some interpretations of Jesus in the Judeo-Christian tradition, the Christian life is a life of personal piety, and in some extreme cases, a neurotic and narcissistic obsession with one's personal "salvation" from sin that takes precedence over the moral obligation to care for the widow, the orphan, and the stranger.[45] Little, if any, consideration is given to the actual historical circumstances of Jesus's life—that he was, for example, a colonized Jew, from a first-century ghetto (Nazareth), who was born in to poverty and whose life was subject to the corruption of a nefarious band of theo-political elites who, in the name of God, used the power of the state to execute him despite his innocence. To interpret Jesus in this way is to understand Christianity's complicity in contemporary socioeconomic, religious, and racial oppression. Indeed, an attentiveness to the jurisdiction of history, as found, for example, in the work of Cone and Ched Meyers,[46] holds Christian theology accountable for its maintenance of the status quo in the face of injustice. Such interpretations that respect the jurisdiction of history have a way of helping us see the complicity of Christianity in the spread of colonialism and imperialism; something that many Christians would, because of a lack of moral accountability, prefer to avoid.

So it is important to allow history to assert its authority—its jurisdiction—over reason rather than allowing reason to assert its authority over history. The former respects the nature of temporality, whereas the latter is a corruption of temporality.[47] On this latter view, history is changed, manipulated, or, worse, ignored (as in Rawlsian political theory, white theology, and the reformed epistemology of analytic theism). The human jurisdiction (authority) over history lies at the very foundation of oppression, and it includes the outright neglect of history, which, in turn, produces a status quo that both ignores and perpetuates injustice, which is the end of oppression; to ignore history is to ignore the identity of persons—it is to disembody them, to make them into beings who have no sense of who they are. And it is here where we see the most devastating consequence of ignoring the jurisdiction of history: the invisibility of an Ellisonian sort, where people who are, to use Ellison's words, "flesh and bone, fiber and liquid," are treated as though they don't exist or as if they never existed at all.[48] So it is that many oppressed people die twice: their physical death is a belated pronouncement of a social and political death that long since sealed their fate as second-class citizens, a tragic consequence of human beings disregarding the jurisdiction of history. Christian theology is often the culprit here, and its most devastating weapon is theoretical abstraction, which results in an inversion of the soteriological paradigm: instead of the Word of God being made flesh, God's colonized, ghettoized flesh is transformed into the abstract word of immoral theological reflection, resulting in an idol of the corrupt theological imagination that is a far cry from Jesus of Nazareth.

Considering God's involvement in history in the person of Jesus Christ, the human attempt to avoid it becomes significant in this way: it becomes an attempt to undo that which God Himself has already done. And this is precisely the role of abstraction in analytic theism: it attempts to disincarnate the historical, Hebrew flesh of Jesus into the "word" of Christian beliefs. Epistemic justification is thus an assertion of rationality's authority over history, and as such, it ignores the jurisdiction of history. The effects of this disregard of the jurisdiction of history are twofold: the oppressed have ceased to be oppressed, and the oppressors have ceased to be oppressors. The fictive world created is one in which everyone is somehow magically "equal" despite the historical realities to the contrary. As Charles Mills points out, this methodology of abstraction creates a false world in which injustice has never occurred instead of a world in which one has already accounted for corrected injustices. For Mills, this problem exists because of

> Rawls's methodological decision to focus in *A Theory of Justice* on "ideal theory"—the reconstruction of what a perfectly just society would look like. If this might have seemed reasonable enough when first propounded—after all, what's wrong with striving for the asymptotic realization of perfect justice?—it is, I propose, because of a crucial ambiguity: "ideally just" as meaning a society without any previous history of injustice and "ideally just" as meaning a society with an unjust history that has now been completely corrected for. Rawls means the former, not the latter.[49]

Rawls advocates for a "color-blind" political philosophy in which there is only an ideally just world without an actual world in which there was injustice. And it is the failure to account for the actual world of injustice that leads to a maintenance of the political status quo, meaning that the historical denial of social and political freedom not only will not be addressed but also will be maintained. This denial of social and political liberty is seen in the claims of those who advocate for an abstract—and thus color-blind—theology in which one's principal concern is personal piety. This, in turn, results in a neglect of public policies that exploit the vulnerabilities of the widow, the orphan, and the stranger, for to engage in abstraction is to ignore the jurisdiction of history over both Black and white, especially in America, where the history is fraught with oppression and injustice; it is not only to ignore the identity of Black people as oppressed people but also to ignore the identity of white people as both oppressors and privileged. We are then left with abstract "persons," who can only agree on principles of justice in the abstract, apart from human history. Such principles, derived from reason's authority over history place racial, ethnic, and gender identities behind a "veil of ignorance" and with them, the sordid histories of each that produced the thoroughly unjust world that is being ignored. Douglass, of course, never ignored that history. Indeed, Douglass not only did not ignore history but also lived it and sought to change it in ways that the reformed epistemology of analytic theism, because of its exaltation of reason over the jurisdiction of history, does not—and, indeed, cannot—do.

There are at least two approaches to Christian theology that emerge within the broader Christian Incarnational theological framework as I have described it thus far. These are the reformed epistemology of analytic theism and my existential, phenomenological, aesthetic interpretation of Douglass. Just as Mills and Cone do in political philosophy and Christian theology, I do with the philosophy of religion: I critique its use of abstract philosophical and theological thought as an exaltation of reason over history, which is the hallmark of oppression. To address history, which is what I aim to do throughout my various arguments in this book, is to provide for a meaningful engagement with injustice rather than using abstraction to ignore and thus perpetuate it.

READING DOUGLASS WITH THE CANON

The interpretation of Douglass that I develop throughout this book is one in which Douglass is read with a variety of dialogue partners, all of whom are white philosophers, and at least one—Kant—who held openly racist views. Considering the criticisms of white philosophy and white philosophical thinking that I have offered throughout this chapter, one may ask, "Why use such thinkers to interpret Douglass?" There are at least three good reasons, I think, to interpret Douglass by reading him with the white thinkers I have chosen. First, as I have spoken of "white philosophy" or "white philosophical thinking" throughout the chapter thus far, I have done so with regard to the problem of abstraction and its pernicious effects on a sort of Christian philosophizing as viewed against the backdrop of Incarnational theology, and the white thinkers that I use for my interpretation of Douglass are not interested in the abstractions of conceptual analysis, which are my real target here. It is not my claim that any white philosopher is somehow always already deficient in their understanding of subjectivity, morality, art, and politics. Instead, I am claiming that the problem of abstraction is present when certain white thinkers philosophically reflect on a set of theoretical, theological problems. Furthermore, I use the terms "white philosophy," or "white philosophers," to refer not so much to the persons doing the conceptual analysis—although in this case, all happen to be white—but rather to the very task of conceptual analysis itself and its attendant abstraction. I refer to it as "white" in contrast to what it both ignores and enables, which are the moral problems that plague Christianity as related to its complicity in the racism and white supremacy of the modern West. In contrast to this methodology of abstraction, all of the thinkers with whom I interpret Douglass eschew this sort of abstraction and conceptual analysis at some level. Kierkegaard and Kafka are part of the existentialist philosophical tradition, which, while not monolithic, is generally deeply concerned about the moral problems that confront human subjectivity. Husserl and Levinas, both part of the phenomenological tradition, have profoundly moral overtones to their work, with Husserl's entire phenomenological methodology devoted to reconnecting subjectivity to the world that it inhabits. Levinas interrogates the entire Western philosophical tradition for its pursuit of epistemic and ontological accounts of the world, favoring an approach where first principles are ethical rather than metaphysical. And Kant's transcendental idealism admits to reason's epistemic failure in the case of rational theology, advocating a practical moral basis for theology rather than an objective, epistemic basis for theology—a task which the reformed epistemologists of analytic theism seem determined to complete. Kant, because of his racist views and his role in the construction of the modern philosophical account of race, has other serious problems that I address in chapter 4, but even those problems, as serious as they are, do not preclude a dialogue partnership with Douglass. In fact, I will argue in chapter 4 that Kant's problems demand such a partnership with Douglass instead. So first, I interpret Douglass with philosophers whose reflections resonate with those of Douglass on the philosophical issues of subjectivity, morality, art, and politics.

Second, there is a sense in which reading Douglass with the thinkers that I have chosen, far from being an attempt to legitimize Douglass by reading him with white "canonical" philosophers, is actually not about legitimizing Douglass at all, but rather about interrogating the canon. As white philosophers, Kierkegaard, Kafka, Kant, Husserl, and Levinas, despite their resonance with Douglass, write from a position of privilege from within academic and literary circles, while Douglass, as an escaped slave, plainly does not. Writing from the perspective of an escaped slave, Douglass has seen issues of moral theory, subjectivity, and artistic expression at the concrete level of praxis. So interpreting Douglass with this unique array of white philosophers interrogates their existentialist, phenomenological, and aesthetic theories and puts them to the test. Douglass, a Black philosopher with his own unique voice, does not need legitimacy by associating him with white thinkers. But there does need to be an interrogation of the thinkers that I have assembled here as Douglass's dialogue partners insofar as all of their work is done from a position of privilege. The question needs to be raised: Does the theoretical reflection of white philosophers sustain its insights at the level of praxis? I think so, and my arguments in support of this conclusion are presented throughout this book.

Third, as an interpreter myself (that is, as one who is reading philosophy from a certain hermeneutic standpoint), my interpretation of Douglass in this book is, in part, a reflection of my own identity as a mixed-race person. I have written of this at length elsewhere,[50] and here I will argue—as I do in chapter 4 with respect to Kant—that my philosophical interpretations reflect in some way personal identity. My father was African American with a Jewish lineage, and my mother was German. I identify myself as an African American, and this book is an interpretation of an African American philosopher (Douglass), in conjunction with German and Jewish thinkers (Kafka, Kant, Husserl, and Levinas). Moreover, my religious identity is also part of this interpretation of Douglass, as I am a member of a Christian Protestant denomination, and Kierkegaard—a Lutheran—is an important part of my work in this book. As Gadamer points out, it would be a "prejudice against prejudice" to pretend that I can approach this subject completely free from any hermeneutic background whatsoever as "the history of effect" is always at work in philosophical hermeneutics. Akin to the jurisdiction of history as I discussed that concept earlier in this chapter to address the problem of philosophical abstraction, the "historically effected consciousness" (*wirkungsgeschichtliches Bewußtsein*) prevents what Gadamer calls the "deformation of knowledge" by allowing for a fusion of horizons—namely, mine and those of the authors of the philosophical text. What emerges is a fresh, new, interpretation that demands something more of us than either I as an interpreter or any of the other philosophical figures in this book could demand standing alone. In this way knowledge is advanced rather than made static through biases against recognizing the role of the interpreter in the hermeneutic endeavor.

So, I read Douglass because the existential and phenomenological issues that he faces are issues that are connected to the broader philosophical traditions of existentialism and phenomenology. All of the thinkers with whom I interpret Douglass are facing profound existential and phenomenological issues related to subjectivity, morality, creativity, and responsibility, as is Douglass, and these thinkers are important because of their philosophical resonance with Douglass. Also, the philosophical canon must be interrogated for the extent to which it either may or may not be consistent with Black philosophical insights from Douglass, who, as an escaped slave, not only contemplates at the level of *theoria* but also engages at the level of praxis.

And, finally, I am perhaps bound to interpret Douglass in this way because of my mixed-race background. While I could interpret Douglass independent of my hermeneutical horizon, to do so would perhaps prevent me from breaking some new ground or providing some interpretive insight that advances the cause of philosophical knowledge. I thus am avoiding the "prejudice against prejudice." To close this chapter, I now turn to a story of an objection that I have received for my reading of Douglass with Kant. I share this personal story because, like Douglass's narrative methodology, it will, I believe, help us to see ourselves and perhaps lead to some positive change for how we do interpretive work in academic philosophy. This is my story.

When I was a graduate student in philosophy, I attended a philosophy conference with a member of my dissertation committee to present a portion of a chapter of my dissertation. The aims of the conference were to both develop my scholarship and prepare me for the rigors of the job market by pairing me with a veteran faculty member. I was ABD ("all but dissertation") at the time, so this conference was perfect timing for me, as I was just a few months away from beginning my job search. To put the conference in its proper context, I will provide a brief summary of the chapter of my dissertation pertinent to this discussion. My dissertation was a critique of a concept that Martin Heidegger referred to as "ontotheology." As I briefly discussed in the introduction, ontotheology is a philosophical understanding of God, where God is viewed as the ground of all that is (being). As its name implies, on the ontotheological conception of God, reason requires that being ("onto," from the Greek word *ontos*, which means being) must have a ground outside of it; and that ground is God (theology). For Heidegger, this is the only way that the deity "enters into" philosophy; human rationality and its need for completeness demand it. Otherwise, being is an infinite regress of causes, and being itself has no absolute ground. On the ontotheological account, then, rationality renders infinity intelligible. The resulting "god" of ontotheology is, I argued, as compared with the God of the Judeo-Christian tradition, an ersatz one—a mere product of rationality that is only as strong as the human desire that created it. In my dissertation, I argued that ontotheology is rooted in the human impulse toward epistemology. In short, all human beings, as Aristotle claims in the first sentence of his *Metaphysics*, "desire to know." Using Heidegger's insights about ontotheology as my point of departure, I argued that the human "desire to know" demands totality and completeness at every philosophical turn, God included; that this human "desire to know," to use Aristotle's phraseology, creates a "god" that, as the product of a rational, human interest in totality and completeness, is purely philosophical; that this "god," unlike the God of the Judeo-Christian tradition, who creates human beings to serve Him and His interests, is created by human beings to serve the interests of human beings; that when human interests are corrupt—as they often are—the "god" of ontotheology is there to serve corrupt human interests; that such a corruption of interests occurred in chattel slavery both in America and throughout the Western world in the seventeenth, eighteenth, and nineteenth centuries; that the "god" of ontotheology found its way into a perverted form of Christianity in order to provide a philosophical and theological grounding for chattel slavery and all of its moral, social, and political abominations; and that Frederick Douglass, in his critical engagement with slaveholding Christianity, articulated a brand of selfhood that had features akin to the self in Kant and Kierkegaard that can overcome the dangers of ontotheology. A chapter of my dissertation was devoted to the similarities in subjectivity between Douglass, Kant, and Kierkegaard. At the conference, I presented that portion of the chapter about Douglass and Kant.

Consistent with the protocols of academic philosophy, I had to read my essay after which there would be commentary from a philosophy professor, and after I responded to the faculty member's commentary, the floor would be open for questions. Although I was a graduate student and thus concerned about what the faculty commentator thought of the quality of my work, I was not afraid of criticism or engaging in an argument where I had to defend my position. After all, at that time I practiced law as a criminal defense lawyer in Philadelphia, Pennsylvania, for twelve years, with much more on the line than a mere theoretical "position." With all due respect to the rigors of philosophical critique, fighting for people's lives and liberty—defending the constitutional rights of criminal defendants before judges and juries with so much at stake—was a task far more daunting to me than responding to a critique from a philosophy professor.

So after I read my essay, the professor's commentary began. Initially favorable, it characterized my essay as "informed" and "interesting." But not too long into the commentary, the tone of the professor's remarks changed dramatically. The professor was highly critical of my approach to doing African American philosophy. He critiqued my reading of Douglass with a white European philosopher—especially one with Kant's racist baggage. He thus went on at length about how ill conceived it was for me to associate Douglass with Kant and about how the essay was an attempt—a rather poor one, in his view—to vindicate a Black philosopher by associating him with a white "canonical" and "philosophical" figure. After suggesting that Douglass could never possibly have anything in common with a racist like Kant, he continued on for several pages of his commentary to "educate" me about the horrors of slavery and how Kant remained silent on slavery's moral abomination, his great moral theory notwithstanding. He concluded his remarks by indicating both that I ought to abandon my "Kantian" approach to Douglass altogether and that my faculty mentor—himself an accomplished scholar who at the time held the rank of distinguished professor of philosophy, and who has read Kant and Douglass together (in fact, in my essay, I was attempting to expand upon his work on Douglass and Kant)—was as misguided as I was. So, in the end, neither I nor my dissertation committee member and faculty mentor—both African Americans, I might add—were reading Douglass the "right" way—which presumably was the way that the white commentator wanted us to read Douglass!

Then the floor opened up for questions and answers, and things worsened. I recognized a prominent African American philosopher who was in attendance so that he could make his comment and/or ask his question. In dramatic and comical fashion, depicting the body language of a street fight, this philosopher began to remove his jacket, draping it over the rear of the chair in which he was sitting, rolled up the sleeves on his dress shirt, cleared his throat, and, with frustration, sarcasm, and hostility in his voice, began to ask me questions like "Are you crazy?" "Do you think that we're stupid?" "You can't possibly read Douglass and Kant together and expect to be taken seriously, can you?" (I paraphrase but still come close to the hostile tone of the questions.)

At this point, I realized that this professor's gestures were supposed to intimidate me. But they did not. Rather than behave like an intimidated graduate student, I switched into full philosopher and lawyer mode, vigorously defending every assertion in my essay and demanding specificity from my two critics. I responded by telling my critics that I was not crazy at all, I did not think that they were stupid, and I fully expected to be taken seriously when reading Douglass with Kant, offering detailed reasons for my methodology in doing African American philosophy as I was doing it. The exchange was lively and lasted for more than an hour. In the end, I walked away from the conference feeling rather good about my essay, especially since my faculty mentor told me that nothing that was said in criticism of my work would cause me to have to radically revise it. In contrast, my faculty mentor thought that the essay, with some minor revisions unrelated to those raised in the criticisms of my work at the conference, would eventually make its way into a quality academic journal. And he turned out to be right; that essay is now a journal publication.

So I left the conference and returned to campus feeling good about my essay and feeling equally good about how I was able to handle the confrontation that it engendered. But I was left asking some lingering questions: What if my critics were right? What if I *was* simply trying to legitimize Douglass by associating him with white philosophers? What would affirmative answers to such questions imply for African American philosophy? Would it mean that Black philosophers such as Douglass could never be read with white "canonical" philosophical figures? If so, would African American philosophy have to be a self-contained unit—likely to be transformed into a philosophical "ghetto"—where Black philosophers could only be read with one another?

I thus found myself grappling with questions similar to those that Lewis Gordon posed to those skeptical of a call for papers on Black existential philosophy. Summarizing the claims of some of his detractors in his essay "Douglass as an Existentialist," Gordon writes that his critics wrote things like "There is no black existential philosophy . . . since existentialism is a European phenomenon addressing European experience. Looking for thought from Søren Kierkegaard to Simone de Beauvoir, and one would find more bourgeois *Angst* than material conditions of black misery."[51] "In my replies to the skeptics," writes Gordon, "I asked them if slaves did not wonder about freedom; suffer anguish; notice paradoxes of responsibility; have concerns of agency, tremors of broken sociality, or a burning desire for liberation."[52]

Gordon's "skeptics" about Black existential philosophy, as he calls them, were, in a sense, doing something similar to the critics of my essay at the conference: calling into question the propriety of reading Black philosophers with white European philosophers. Gordon's response to the skeptics was a powerful one: "The body of literature that constitutes European existentialism is but one continent's response to a set of problems that date from the moment human beings faced problems of anguish and despair. Conflicts over responsibility and anxiety, over life-affirmation and suicidal nihilism preceded Kierkegaardian formulations of fear and trembling and raised questions beyond Eurocentric attachment to a narrow body of literature."[53] Gordon thus argued—correctly, in my view—that existentialism transcends Eurocentrism, extending to the entirety of humanity. Now, to be sure, there are different existential concerns depending upon one's social, cultural, political, and economic circumstances, but such concerns are transculturally present nonetheless, making existentialism not simply a "white," "European" philosophical subfield, but rather a philosophical subfield that can be—and, thanks to scholars like Gordon and George Yancy, *is*—used to address questions of profound Black existential and phenomenological import.

I began to raise some of these lingering questions to the member of my dissertation committee who accompanied me to the conference. Having written extensively on Douglass himself, this faculty member kept pressing me on using Douglass with a figure like Kant, but for another reason: Douglass was a slave, considered to be property, but Kant was not. As a white European philosopher, Kant's humanity was presupposed. Douglass, however, could not even own the texts that he wrote, because—at least in the southern, slaveholding United States—he was property himself, and property cannot own property. As I thought carefully about his question, I began to formulate an answer to it, as well as to the questions of my critics. And the answer was that Kant, as a white European philosopher, has the luxury of having his humanity presupposed, whereas Douglass had to prove that he was human. And Kant's whiteness had another advantage: it enabled him to *theorize* about morality, whereas Douglass had to *live* it. Kant could write at length about dignity, respect for persons, autonomy, and the categorical imperative, but Douglass had no such luxury. As a slave, Douglass had to deal with matters at the hard level of phenomenological and existential experience. And although Douglass gives us theoretical moral insights, he does not give them to us from the ethereal mist of a Kantian Mount Olympus, where theoretical musings take the form of canonical writings as a bequest to future philosophical generations. No. Douglass gives us moral insights from an existential level of moral praxis. As I thought more about this contrast between Kant and Douglass in terms of their respective designations as human and property, I reversed the question of my critics from the conference: What if, instead of Kant legitimizing Douglass, Douglass's life and moral insights somehow interrogates the Kantian moral and theological corpus? What if it is not Douglass who needs the legitimizing at all? What if Kant's moral theory needs to be tested at the level of praxis to determine its fitness for the Western philosophical canon? Affirmative answers to these questions were, I thought, certain. It is the affirmative answers to these questions that, at least in part, prompted this book.

REFLECTION AND ANTICIPATION

Christianity deeply influenced the social and political world in which Douglass lived. So it was inevitable that, in his abolition work—a work that was thoroughly socially and politically engaged—Christianity would be a profound influence on him as well. With Christianity's influence on Douglass in mind, in this chapter I have sketched the broad parameters of this book within a Christian Incarnational theological framework to draw a contrast between the Word of God made flesh (John 1:14) and the flesh of God made into an abstract word of conceptual analysis and epistemic certainty. Within this framework are two distinct philosophical approaches to Christianity: the reformed epistemology of analytic theism and my existential, phenomenological, and aesthetic interpretation of Douglass. Besetting the former is the problem of philosophical abstraction, which turns God's flesh into a word, and augmenting the latter is a reading of Douglass with Kierkegaard, Kafka, Husserl, Levinas, and Kant that makes the word flesh. Abstraction is problematic because it inverts the relationship between history and reason, allowing for reason to assert its authority over history rather than allowing history to have its proper jurisdiction over reason.

It is important to read Douglass with the canon because of a deep philosophical resonance between Douglass and the thinkers I use to interpret him in this book—thinkers whose concerns are not abstract and theoretical, but rather concrete and practical. The canon must also be interrogated at the level of praxis, which Douglass provides through his autobiographical narrative. And because I recognize that my "historically effected consciousness" is always at work, I, as a mixed-race person, read Douglass with thinkers that reflect my own racial and religious identity in a way that aims to advance philosophical dialogue about important matters of subjectivity, morality, social political theory, and art rather than leaving these issues unaddressed. I now begin my interpretation of Douglass in the next chapter with his two existentialist dialogue partners, Kierkegaard and Kafka.

NOTES

1. John 1:1 and John 1:14.
2. For a discussion of this debate, see Scott C. Williamson, *The Narrative Life: The Moral and Religious Thought of Frederick Douglass* (Macon, GA: Mercer University Press, 2002).
3. See Charles W. Mills, *The Racial Contract* (Ithaca, NY: Cornell University Press, 1997).
4. See James H. Cone, *A Black Theology of Liberation* (Maryknoll, NY: Orbis Books, 1970), *God of the Oppressed* (Maryknoll, NY: Orbis Books, 1997), and *The Cross and the Lynching Tree* (Maryknoll, NY: Orbis Books, 2011).
5. *Holy Bible*, King James Version, John 1:1 and John 1:14.
6. Emmanuel Levinas, *Totality and Infinity: An Essay on Exteriority*, trans. Alphonso Lingis (Pittsburgh, PA: Duquesne University Press, 1969), 79.
7. Aristotle, *Metaphysics*, 980a.
8. *Holy Bible*, John 6:9–13.
9. *Holy Bible*, John 6:48.
10. *Holy Bible*, James 1:17.
11. Søren Kierkegaard, *Philosophical Fragments*, ed. and trans. Howard V. and Edna H. Hong (Princeton, NJ: Princeton University Press, 1985), 37.
12. Ibid., 59.
13. Here, I use the word "postmodern" in its broadest sense to mean a calling into question of the epistemic and metaphysical approaches developed in modern philosophy, especially epistemic foundationalism. For example, Plantinga, Wolterstorff, and Alston, drawing from Thomas Reid, call into question the epistemic foundations of modernity to develop the view that there are such things as basic beliefs that can be rationally justified without regard to any sort of epistemic verification. It is in this sense that the reformed epistemology of these thinkers is "postmodern."
14. See William P. Alston, *Perceiving God: The Epistemology of Religious Experience* (Ithaca, NY: Cornell University Press, 1991), 1.
15. Ibid., 2. Alston sounds much like John Rawls, who, in the preface to *A Theory of Justice* points out that what he is trying to do is to "generalize and carry to a higher order of abstraction the traditional theory of the social contract as represented by

Locke, Rousseau, and Kant." See John Rawls, *A Theory of Justice* (Cambridge, MA: Harvard University Press, 1971), viii. For both Alston in the philosophy of religion and Rawls in political philosophy, abstraction is the principal methodology.

16. See Nicholas Wolterstorff, "Introduction," in *Faith and Rationality: Reason and Belief in God*, eds. Alvin Plantinga and Nicholas Wolterstorff (Notre Dame, IN: Notre Dame University Press, 1983), 3.

17. Wolterstorff, "Can a Belief in God be Rational?" in *Faith and Rationality: Reason and Belief in God*, eds. Alvin Plantinga and Nicholas Wolterstorff (Notre Dame, IN: Notre Dame University Press, 1983), 136.

18. Wolterstorff, "Introduction," 6.

19. Wolterstorff, "Can a Belief in God Be Rational?" 149.

20. See Alston, *Perceiving God*, 151. Alston differentiates his notion of "doxastic practices" from Ludwig Wittgenstein's notion of a "language game." He points out that he does not

> accept for a moment Wittgenstein's verificationist restrictions on what assertions, questions, and doubts are intelligible . . . I will simply testify that I can understand perfectly well the propositions that sense perception is (is not) reliable, that physical objects do (do not) exist, and that the earth has (has not) been in existence for more than a year, whether or not I or anyone else has any idea of how to determine whether one of these propositions is true. This confidence reflects a realistic concept of truth, on which a proposition's being true is not a matter of anyone's actual or possible epistemic position vis-à-vis the proposition. Hence I cannot accept Wittgenstein's solution to skepticism about perception, and his answer to the question of the reliability of basic doxastic practices, the solution that seeks to dissolve the problem by undercutting the supposition that it can be meaningfully posed. With this realist orientation I am ineluctably faced with the question of whether a given practice is a reliable source of true beliefs, and hence with the question of whether it is rational or justified to suppose this. Moreover, since from this perspective it is not the case that each practice creates its own reality, but rather seeks to tell it like it is with respect to the one reality (or some segment thereof), there is a live possibility that the outputs of one practice contradict those of another. We will exploit this possibility in taking interpractice inconsistencies as a reason for disqualification. (*Perceiving God*, 155)

Alston differentiates himself from Wittgenstein on the basis that Wittgenstein's notion of a "language game" makes some concessions to verificationism that he is unwilling to make—namely, that Wittgenstein concedes that an ontological realism of certain beliefs is untenable, and instead relocates those beliefs in the sphere of human subjectivity rather than in the realm of objective knowledge. Instead, Alston commits himself to a "realist orientation to doxastic practices, as he wants to "tell it like it is" rather than how people may interpret it based on linguistic or cultural conventions, in the same way that people purport to do with sense perception.

21. Ibid.

22. Ibid.

23. Ibid., 1.

24. Alvin Plantinga, "The Reformed Objection to Natural Theology," *Proceedings of the American Catholic Philosophical Association* 54 (1980), 59.

25. Ibid., 59–60.

26. Ibid., 54.

27. Ibid., 60.

28. Emmanuel Levinas, "God and Philosophy," in *Basic Philosophical Writings*, eds. Adriaan T. Peperzak, Simon Critchley, and Robert Bernasconi (Bloomington: Indiana University Press, 1996), 129–30.

29. See Plantinga's essay "A Defense of Religious Exclusivism," in *Philosophy of Religion: An Anthology*, eds. Michael Rea and Louis Pojman (Stamford, CT: Cengage Learning, 2015), 645–59, and George Marsden's essay, "The Collapse of American Evangelical Academia," in *Faith and Rationality: Reason and Belief in God*, eds. Alvin Plantinga and Nicholas Wolterstorff (Notre Dame, IN: Notre Dame University Press, 1983), 219–64.

30. Charles W. Mills, *The Racial Contract* (Ithaca, NY: Cornell University Press, 1997), 5.

31. Ibid.

32. Ibid., 11.

33. Ibid., 4.

34. Charles W. Mills, "Rawls on Race/Race in Rawls," *Southern Journal of Philosophy* 47, no. S1 (2009), 177.

35. J. Kameron Carter, *Race: A Theological Account* (Oxford: Oxford University Press, 2008), 160.

36. See especially James H. Cone, *A Black Theology of Liberation* and *God of the Oppressed*.

37. Cone, *A Black Theology of Liberation*, 2. In Greek philosophy, Plato considers the good *epekeina tes ousias*, or transcendent from this world. Cone is contrasting the concreteness and immanence of Black theological reflection with the Greek way of transcendence as something beyond this world. Kierkegaard also juxtaposes Scripture with Greek philosophy under the pseudonym, Johannes Climacus in *Philosophical Fragments*. In Kierkegaard's juxtaposition, however, immanence is considered the way of Greek Philosophy and transcendence is contrasted as the way of the Christian Gospel. I discuss this more extensively in chapter 2.

38. Ibid., 5.

39. I address the problem of the *imago hominis* of white theology in greater detail in my forthcoming monograph, *Reason's Dilemma: Subjectivity, Transcendence, and the Problem of Ontotheology* (Palgrave Macmillan, under contract).

40. See Frantz Fanon, *Black Skin, White Masks*, trans. Charles Lam Markmann (New York: Grove Press, 1967), where Fanon writes, "Ontology—once it is finally admitted as leaving existence by the wayside—does not permit us to understand the being of the black man" (110). Fanon's statement is apt here, as I am arguing that the ontological preoccupations of analytic theism's reformed epistemology do nothing to allow us to understand the moral problems surrounding Black life, because white philosophical abstraction in the interest of ontology and epistemology leaves Black existence "by the wayside," as Fanon put it.

41. Aristotle, *Politics*, 1254a 21–23.

42. John Stauffer, "Frederick Douglass and the Aesthetics of Freedom," *Raritan* 25, no. 1 (2005), 116.

43. Cone, *The Cross and the Lynching Tree*, 32. Cone's objections to Niebuhr are based upon more than his failure to see the connection between the cross and the lynching tree. See especially *God of the Oppressed*, where Cone takes Niebuhr to task for claims that African Americans are "culturally backward" and "We must not consider the Founding Fathers immoral just because they were slaveholders." In light of the statement about America's founders, Cone rhetorically asks, "What else can this ethical judgment mean than that Niebuhr derived his ethics from white culture and not biblical revelation?" (184).

44. Cone, *God of the Oppressed*.

45. In the Judeo-Christian tradition, these are broad references to certain groups of people who represent the weakest and most vulnerable persons in society. One sees these references in both the Old and the New Testaments (Deut. 27:19, Exodus, 22:21–24, Isaiah 1:17, and James 1:27). One also sees such references in philosophical texts, such as Levinas's *Totality and Infinity* (78).

46. Ched Myers, *Binding the Strong Man: A Political Reading of Mark's Story of Jesus* (Maryknoll, NY: Orbis Books, 2008).

47. One must distinguish between an assertion of human authority over history for the sake of aesthetic and political purposes that seeks justice, and an assertion of human authority over history for the sake of maintaining oppression. On the former assertion of human authority over history, creative license is afforded to those such as Derrick Bell, who retell historical narratives in such a way as to create a counter-narrative of resistance to a dominant narrative that has either ignored oppression or discussed it in a misleading fashion. Here, I am thinking of Derrick Bell's "The Chronicle of the Constitutional Contradiction" from his book *And We Are Not Saved: The Elusive Quest for Racial Justice*. There, Bell reconstructs the debates at the 1787 Constitutional Convention in Philadelphia by inserting a Black heroine (Geneva Crenshaw) who is teleported into the past and pleads with the American framers of the Constitution not to proceed without first ending slavery. Although Bell is certainly asserting his creative authority over history, he is doing so in the interest of resisting a dominant narrative that either pays little to no attention to historical instances of oppression—and thus perpetuates oppression by neglect—or, in a much more sinister fashion, asserts its authority over history in the form of distortions that are employed to cast aspersions against one side or another in some historical conflict. W. E. B. Du Bois confronts such distortions in the final chapter of *Black Reconstruction in America*, where he demonstrates how Reconstruction was distorted "because the nation was ashamed." See W. E. B. Du Bois, *Black Reconstruction in America* (New York: Oxford University Press, 2007), 582.

48. One finds a direct reference to the problem of invisibility in James Cone's *God of the Oppressed*, where he points out that "Any time God is not derived from the biblical theme of the oppressed, it is to be expected that Christian ethics will be at best indifferent toward the oppressed struggle of freedom. . . . Here racism appears in the form of *invisibility*. White theologians and ethicists simply ignore black people by suggesting that the problem of racism and oppression is only one social expression of a larger ethical concern." See Cone, *God of the Oppressed*, 184 (emphasis in original).

49. Mills, "Rawls on Race/Race in Rawls," 162.

50. See Timothy J. Golden, "German Chocolate: Why Philosophy Is So Personal," in *Philosophy and the Mixed Race Experience*, ed. Tina Fernandes Botts (Lanham, MD: Lexington Books, 2016), 231–66.

51. Lewis R. Gordon, *Existentia Africana: Understanding Africana Existential Thought* (New York: Routledge, 2000), 6.

52. Ibid., 7.

53. Ibid.

Chapter Two

The Truth in Fiction
Narrative, Art, and Subjectivity

"He taught them many things in parables."

—*Holy Bible*[1]

THE MISCHIEF OF EMPTINESS

The central feature of analytic theism's reformed epistemology is rational justification; that is, it is committed to refuting the claim that a belief in God is irrational.[2] In its quest to prove the rationality of a belief in God, reformed epistemology, through logical abstraction, departs from the subjectivity of Jesus's human flesh and moves toward a sort of objectivity that will, in its view, provide the *logos* for theistic belief. A result of this abstraction is a neglect of existential subjectivity, which, I believe, for the Christian, is far more important than rationally justified theistic beliefs. Douglass understood this well, for he dwelt in a community of slaveholding Christians who were certain about their "Christian" beliefs, but who were living in flagrant contradiction of those beliefs. This is because of their commitment to objective doctrine at the expense of subjective moral and religious practice. To put this problem in the Incarnational language of the previous chapter, slaveholding Christians embraced the abstract word of their religion without any attentiveness to either the concrete flesh of Jesus or the concrete flesh of their own behavior. So it is that Douglass addresses religious hypocrisy in a way that speaks from within the Christian tradition and is aimed at not only exposing slaveholding Christianity for its profound moral and theological shortcomings but also effecting a genuine change in the hearts and minds of white slaveholding Christians through the method of storytelling. Faced with the difficulties of minds that were theologically, sociologically, and politically "made up" in favor of chattel slavery, Douglass—and other slaves—used narrative as an art form to penetrate the layers of determination that so many white Christians had for preserving the "peculiar institution." And I will argue in this chapter that within Douglass's *Narrative*, he shows how the power of storytelling affected him, making himself an example for others to follow. Douglass thus emphasized the importance of the moral consistency of belief and action, and he used a creative means to get slaveholding Christians to see themselves and change their behavior. Analytic theism is not primarily interested in either of these endeavors. Again, because analytic theism wants to rationally justify a belief in God, its principal interest is to employ logical abstraction to show the formal structure of theistic belief without regard for the concerns of subjective Christian life. What makes this so morally and theologically hazardous for Christianity is that the abstract, formal structures of analytic theism are devoid of moral content—the word does not become flesh. Instead, the word remains just that—a rational explanation at the level of formal, logical abstraction. This raises a question, which is that apart from the concrete moral realities of human life, of what real value are abstract, formal, theological structures such as those of analytic theism? I submit that their moral and social value is dubious at best, except as what Merold Westphal has called a "standing invitation to evil."[3] Westphal writes of the parable where Jesus speaks of the exorcised demon that returned to an empty house, only to re-inhabit it with demons who were worse than himself.[4] Westphal points out that "Religion that is not bound to the scene of the ethical relation consists of 'empty and formal frameworks' . . . However rich it may be in images, narrative, concepts, theories, practices, and institutions, it is utterly devoid of anything that would prevent it from being the home, the shelter, the base, the legitimizer of the various evils that deface the Other."[5] On this account, analytic theism becomes an empty, logical framework that is inclined toward a sort of evil that can be rationally justified. This is a severe consequence of analytic theism's neglect of the jurisdiction of history; a breeding ground for mischief in the name of Christianity. Such mischief can be found, for example, in the rational justification of evil as found in either free will theodicy or a free will defense. Indeed, as I will argue in the next chapter, a major flaw of the reformed epistemology of analytic theism that necessitates a phenomenology of Black suffering is that in its attempt to render a belief in God rational, its theodicy and its free will defense both result in evil being a rational and epistemically justified constituent of Christian philosophical thought. It is in this sense that Westphal's point rings true: the abstraction of analytic theism, insofar as it provides an empty theoretical framework, becomes the habitation for a rational justification for evil at the expense of moral action against it. Consider that through abstraction, there is an expulsion of historical evils done in the name of Christianity. This can be likened to the exorcised demon in Jesus's parable. And because what analytic theism gives us is a formal structure, it is empty. This emptiness then creates a space for new occupants in the Christian philosophical framework: theodicy and the free will defense. And both of these ultimately justify evil for the sake of explaining a rational belief in God. This is, in Jesus's parabolic language, "more wicked" than before, because not only are the historical moral evils of Christianity absent from this new brand of Christian philosophy, but there are now new occupants—theodicy and the free will defense—that justify such evils in the first place. Indeed, as Plantinga himself acknowledges, neither theodicy nor the free will defense does the religious believer much good on a concrete, subjective, existential level.[6] So the conclusion of Jesus's parable seems to be applicable here: this latter condition of Christian thought is worse than the first.

In the interest of combating the mischief-making of empty, formal, abstract, Christian theological frameworks, this chapter offers an interpretation of Douglass with Søren Kierkegaard and Franz Kafka. Through an emphasis on existential subjectivity and its artistic, creative dimension, I argue that Douglass succeeds in making the word flesh, and in doing so, provides a philosophical and theological approach to Christianity that pursues justice rather than sacrificing justice for the sake of rational justification, as in the case of analytic theism. There are three remaining sections to this chapter. The next section is a discussion of Douglass and Kierkegaard. I do three things in this section of the chapter. First, I frame my discussion of Douglass and Kierkegaard in the context of Incarnational theology. I do this by first situating Kierkegaard within the broader Danish debate over the implications of Georg Wilhelm Friedrich Hegel's speculative logic for Incarnational theology, which helps us understand precisely what is at stake for Kierkegaard in that debate as he articulates it in his pseudonymous work, *Philosophical Fragments*. Second, I draw from Kierkegaard's *Concluding Unscientific Postscript* and Douglass's *Narrative* to argue that both Kierkegaard and Douglass lived in what they thought were corrupt Christian communities that had a profound shortage of religious integrity. And third, I argue that both Douglass and Kierkegaard approached their respective communities through artistic, creative means: Douglass through narrative, and Kierkegaard through pseudonyms.

Following Douglass and Kierkegaard, I discuss the affinities between Douglass's *Narrative* and Kafka's novel, *The Trial*. Since a major theme of *The Trial* is the absurd, I begin this section of the chapter with a discussion of two examples of the absurdities, paradoxes, and contradictions that American law and legal systems facilitate in contemporary Black American life. I argue that these absurdities originate in the law of chattel slavery in antebellum

America—when Douglass is writing his *Narrative*—and that the legal system foisted these absurdities upon slaves. Against this historical backdrop, I present a discussion of various aspects of *The Trial* with parts of Douglass's *Narrative* to show how Douglass navigates these absurdities in a way that is far more constructive than how Josef K., the protagonist of *The Trial*, navigates the absurdities that confront him. This comparison between Douglass and Josef K. demonstrates the importance of existential subjectivity and creating meaning in the face of the absurd. I conclude the chapter after this discussion of Douglass and Kafka by pointing toward my phenomenological interpretation of Douglass with Husserl and Levinas in the next chapter.

DOUGLASS AND KIERKEGAARD

Chapter 1 frames the thesis of the book in the context of the Christian theology of the Incarnation. I use Incarnational theology here, on a much smaller scale, to frame my discussion of Douglass and Kierkegaard. My aim in doing so is to lay the foundation for the problem of moral complacency that both Douglass and Kierkegaard believed plagued their respective Christian communities. I begin with Kierkegaard.

Situating Kierkegaard

Much of Kierkegaard's writing—what he called his pseudonymous authorship—was directed at removing what he thought were serious delusions among Christians in the broader Christian culture. He wrote extensively about the problem of deception and how it affected Christians in the Danish State Church, whose theology he believed had contributed to a cultural and social decadence, where people understood their Christianity to consist in familial connections and the outward participation in liturgical practices. This "objective" approach to Christianity resulted from Kierkegaard's interpretation of Hegelian theology, which certain influential thinkers in the Danish theological intelligentsia embraced.[7]

A central feature of Hegel's philosophical and theological thought was his rejection of Aristotelian logic. The logical structure of thought, he argued, alienated consciousness from fully understanding reality. And so rather than accept the three laws of thought derived from Aristotle, Hegel saw himself as making an advance upon logic by arguing that the principle of noncontradiction, the principle of the excluded middle, and the principle of identity were not the bedrock principles that they had been assumed to be. Some explanation of Hegel's logic will be helpful here, as it will provide background for his Danish reception, which includes, of course, Kierkegaard's critique of Hegel.

Hegel criticizes Aristotle's logic in part because he views it as being fundamentally at odds with the purpose of philosophy, which is to comprehend God as the ultimate source of all truth. The opening paragraph of Hegel's *Science of Logic* makes this point:

> Philosophy misses an advantage enjoyed by the other sciences. It cannot like them rest the existence of its objects on the natural admissions of consciousness, nor can it assume that its method of cognition either for starting or for continuing, is one already accepted. The objects of philosophy, it is true, are upon the whole the same as those of religion. In both the object is Truth, in that supreme sense in which God and God only is the Truth. Both in like manner go on to treat of the finite worlds of Nature and the human Mind, with their relation to each other and to their truth in God. Some acquaintance with its objects, therefore, philosophy may and even must presume, that and a certain interest in them to boot, were it for no other reason than this: that in point of time the mind makes general images of objects long before it makes notions of them, and that it is only through these mental images, and by recourse to them, that the thinking mind rises to know and comprehend thinkingly.[8]

For Hegel, philosophy cannot, like the natural sciences, base its conclusions solely on empirical observation and experimentation. Philosophy has a calling to go beyond finite cognition, as its object is the same as that of religion, which is God. So if philosophy has stopped at the finitude of empirical observation (that is, the way that things appear to the senses as they do in the natural sciences), then philosophy is not fulfilling its purpose of pursuing the truth in the sense that God is the truth. Anything that would cause philosophy to cease in this manner must be reevaluated for short-circuiting philosophy from its ultimate purpose of seeking all truth about God. It is in this context, then, that one ought to view Hegel's critique of Aristotelian logic.

There are three basic logical principles that emerge from Aristotle. These principles are the principle of identity, the principle of noncontradiction, and the principle of the excluded middle. Hegel rejects Aristotle's logical method as vapid and static in its failure to allow for a more dynamic, truth-revealing understanding of logic such as that of his speculative logical method. Hegel begins with his criticism of the principle of identity. The principle of identity, or $p = p$, was a mere tautology. To say that anything is identical to itself is to say nothing that enlarges my knowledge about the world. In its place, Hegel argued for a conception of identity that actually *contains* difference. To do this, he argued that the logical structure of predication connects identity with difference, rather than merely asserting a one-sided relationship of one thing to itself. For example, if one said, "The table is the table," this is the principle of identity. For Hegel, it is the copula—"is"—that suggests that something new and interesting will be said after it, but nothing is said. Hegel expresses his criticism this way: "The propositional form itself contradicts it: for a proposition always promises a distinction between subject and predicate; while the present one does not fulfill what its form requires."[9] Consider, however, the statement "The table is blue." Now, there is a relationship between table and blue, but it is not a relationship of identity. Instead, it is a relationship of difference, as the table is not the same thing as the abstract blueness that is attributed to it, and blueness is not the same thing as the table. The two are mutually exclusive and are thus different. So according to Hegel's speculative logical method, since one already knows that a table is a table (identity), and now one knows that the table is blue (difference), identity and difference are held together; they imply one another in a dialectical relationship that is dynamic, rather than in a static, one-sided relation. Jon Stewart describes Hegel's speculative criticism of Aristotle's principle of identity as follows:

> As a corrective [to Aristotle's logical notion of identity], Hegel proposes the speculative concept of identity that contains an element of difference within itself. In this way, one avoids the abstract tautology of classical logic; moreover, this new concept of identity is not a non-starter like the previous one, but instead leads to further conceptual development. Thus identity implies difference, which is the next category in the sequence.[10]

So for Hegel, the Aristotelian concept of logical identity is fundamentally static and banal; it does nothing to advance the cause of philosophy, which is to know truth as completely as possible. Hegel believes, however, that his speculative logic provides a dynamism that allows for the discovery of more knowledge.

Hegel also critiques the law of noncontradiction. His critique is somewhat nuanced here, as he argues that there are three distinct notions of the concept of difference. The first two (absolute difference and diversity) show noncontradiction's failure by the standards of Hegel's speculative thought, whereas the final concept of difference is Hegel's speculative, dynamic understanding of difference that he calls "opposition or contrariety." As for the classical notion of absolute difference, consider that in classical Aristotelian logic, this is the principle that two contradictory statements cannot both be true in the same sense and at the same time. For example, the statements "I am in the kitchen" and "I am not in the kitchen" cannot both be true, assuming that "I," "am," "in the," and "kitchen" are used in precisely the same senses in both statements and that both statements refer to the same exact time. If every sense of each statement is exactly the same and refers to exactly the same time, then one of these two statements must be false. There are no exceptions. Hegel argues that according to the classical logical notion of absolute difference, the negation of me being in the kitchen is simply an abstract, indeterminate negation; in other words, there is no knowledge advanced as to my whereabouts except to indicate—in a most uninteresting way, Hegel would add—where I am not. And it is this indeterminacy that leads Hegel to conclude that much like the principle of identity, classical logic has failed to provide anything interesting or dynamic that would advance the cause of philosophical knowledge. The same holds true for the notion of diversity. With this concept of difference, one may negate any subject with any other subject at all. For example one may negate the concept of "chair" with "sky" or with "tiger," or "lion." Although our negations are now determinate objects, there is still an abiding sense of indeterminacy because we could negate any object with any other object whatsoever. We still have not acquired the requisite determinacy that would indicate an advancement of philosophical knowledge. Moreover, the principle of diversity leaves us with a random comparison of terms that are wholly unrelated to one another—hardly the way to advance the cause of philosophy, on Hegel's view. Hegel then introduces his concept of opposition, which he argues is an improvement on the classical notions of absolute difference and diversity. With opposition we have a determinate other, as in the case of positive and negative, or north and south. If I negate north with south, then I am introducing a new determinate concept. But unlike diversity, the determinacy is not random and unrelated. Instead, south is inextricably connected to north as a geographical direction. So north is not simply negated by any random other, but rather by its own other. Hegel writes, "Essential difference is therefore Opposition; according to which the different is not confronted by any other but by its other. That is, either of these two . . . is stamped with a characteristic of its own only in its relation to the other: the one is only reflected into itself as it is reflected into the other. And so with the other. Either in this way is the other's own other."[11]

The principle of the excluded middle is that every statement is either true or false. Symbolically, this may be represented as p v ~p. On the Aristotelian account, there is no such thing as "p" being neither true nor false. Hegel disagrees. For Hegel, the very form of the statement p v ~p, indicates a "p" that is neither true nor false. Although it appears that there are only two terms, +p and –p, there is actually a third term that is neither true nor false. Hegel gives the following example: "If +W mean 6 miles to the West, and –W mean 6 miles to the East, and if the + and – cancel each other, the 6 miles of way or space remain what they were with and without the contrast."[12] There are, then, 6 miles that are neither West nor East, making it the common middle term. Again, Hegel employs his speculative method to show that Aristotelian logic is inconsistent with the task of philosophy as he understands it. For Hegel, philosophy is not one-sided and finite, but rather dynamic and progressive. And it is classical logic that impedes the philosophical task because it takes the most trivial and insipid logical analysis to be the very foundation of truth itself, leaving philosophy unable to do its work, unlike speculative logic, which moves philosophy forward toward its end of understanding all truth.

Hegel's critique of classical logic had profound implications for Christian theology, especially his critique of the principle of the excluded middle, and it provoked intense debate in Denmark that sided either with or against Hegel.[13] On one side of this debate was Bishop Jakob Peter Mynster, who disagreed with Hegel's speculative logical method, and on the other side was academic theologian Hans Lassen Martensen, who was a proponent of Hegel's insights on classical logic. The Danish reception of Hegel's speculative logic was more about Christian theology than it was about Hegel's logic. Hegel's significance for these Danish thinkers became about the extent to which one could apply Hegel's logic to Incarnational theology. Some proponents of Hegel's speculative logical method argued that if the principle of the excluded middle holds true, Jesus could not be the God-man—that Jesus cannot be the mediator between divinity and humanity. On this view, divinity and humanity are viewed each as a part of the logical relation of the statement +A or –A, taking +A to be divinity and –A to be humanity. There is no middle term that mediates between the two, so Christian theology, which claims there is a third term that is neither fully human nor fully divine, fails on this account. Martensen makes this point as follows:

> It is difficult to see how this law can be applied to theology, the task of which has always been to grasp the identity of what is contradictory for the understanding. This law and the law of contradiction seem to say only that contradictions, as long as they remain what they are, namely contradictions, and as long as they are maintained in their abstraction or untruth, necessarily exclude one another. Since the law contains only the empty proposition that contradictions are contradictions and that, as long as they remain contradictions, they exclude the third, then judgments regarding the possible sublation of contradictions would appear to fall completely outside its jurisdiction. That this law cannot be a final court of appeals for theology appears obvious in practice when we see how Christianity continually sublates it. This must make us suspicious about its application where what is at issue is the truth of spirit. The central point of Christianity—the doctrine of Incarnation, the doctrine of the God-man—shows precisely that Christian metaphysics cannot remain in an either/or, but that it must find its truth in the third that this law excludes.[14]

From this passage, one can see how the debate became a theological debate in Denmark. Christianity's principal claim, that Jesus is the God-man, the mediator between God and humanity is, for defenders of Hegel's logic, dependent upon Hegel's speculative method. It also seems here that Martensen and Hegel share similar views about the task of theology and philosophy, for Martensen identifies the theological task as one "which has always been to grasp the identity of what is contradictory for the understanding." Given their similar stances on theology and philosophy, one also sees how Martensen would agree with Hegel.

On the other side of this debate was Bishop Jakob Peter Mynster, who opposed Hegel's speculative method as it relates to Christianity. In an essay titled "Rationalism and Supernaturalism," Mynster is responding to the claim of a young theology student and enthusiastic supporter of Hegel's speculative method who boldly asserted that "In theology both rationalism and supernaturalism are antiquated standpoints, which belong to an age which has disappeared."[15] This view is based on the notion that Hegel's logic has rendered the polarities of reason and revelation obsolete, mediating them into his speculative method. In support of his view that rationalism and supernaturalism are still theologically relevant, Mynster argues that "When we say 'the revelation which Christianity rests upon either is supernatural or is not supernatural,' it presumably is immediately clear that all mediation is impossible here and that all such attempts towards it can only lead to a halfway point, to a teetering and oscillation back and for the between rationalist supernaturalism and supernaturalist rationalism."[16] For Mynster, rationalism and supernaturalism are not antiquated concepts in theology, because theological thinking, unlike Hegel's logic is an "activity of the soul."[17]

It is in this broader context that Kierkegaard enters the debate on the side of Mynster. Toward the end of Mynster's essay on rationalism and supernaturalism, he invokes the Latin phrase *Aut/aut*, translated as "Either/Or," which would be the title of Kierkegaard's 1843 text published under the pseudonyms "A" and "B" (Judge William) and edited by the pseudonym "Victor Eremita." With this title, Kierkegaard establishes his firm commitment to Aristotelian logic and his stance against the logic of Hegel's speculative method, particularly its Christian theological reception in Denmark. For Kierkegaard, when Martensen argues that Hegel's speculative method makes the Incarnation comprehensible, Martensen lays the theoretical foundation for the negation of existential subjectivity. The mystery of God has ceased, and God is now understood as a Hegelian mediation of divinity and humanity. Interestingly, Hegel critiques Aristotle's logic because, for him, it is too abstract, meaning that in the case of the principle of identity, we only get an abstract indeterminacy, as we do with the principle of noncontradiction. And with the principle of the excluded middle, abstract thinking prevents us from seeing the third term that is neither true nor false. For Hegel, the notion of abstraction is any sort of thinking that does not advance the cause of philosophical knowledge. But Kierkegaard's view of abstraction is different. Kierkegaard views Hegel's speculative method as abstract thinking because of its elimination of concrete human dilemmas that people face with regularity—the life choices that people have to make, choices such as whether to marry, have children, and so forth. Douglass would also, I believe, view Hegel's speculative method as a manner of thinking that is entirely too abstract because of the concrete dilemmas that Douglass had to face; dilemmas about his freedom, his bondage, and his resistance. I submit that for both Kierkegaard and Douglass, Hegel's speculative method is too abstract because it badly oversimplifies divine as well as human existence. And it is precisely this theoretical oversimplification that has devastating sociological and practical consequences on Danish life, specifically on the culture of the Danish State Church, as well as on Douglass, for if slaveholding people could call themselves "Christian," then they are only Christians abstractly, not concretely. For Douglass, surely Christianity demands more of us than the mediation of the God-man in the person of Jesus Christ. Christianity demands moral consistency, decisions with real-world, practical consequences, and placing one's life on the line rather than simply making an abstract argument. So Kierkegaard and Douglass, I believe, want to reclaim the conceptual and practical difficulties of Christian theology and the Christian life in order to remove the social and cultural malaise of Christendom by affirming the primacy of existential subjectivity and the qualitative difference between Christianity and the abstractions of Greek philosophy and Hegelian philosophy. And this is, in part, what I argue here about the abstractions of the reformed epistemology of analytic theism. I begin with Kierkegaard, who devotes much effort to this task in his two pseudonymous works, *Philosophical Fragments* and *Concluding Unscientific Postscript to the Philosophical Fragments*.

Kierkegaard, Douglass, and the Need for Conversion

Kierkegaard begins his argument in *Philosophical Fragments* with the learner's paradox. A puzzle taken from Plato's dialogue *Meno*, the paradox is presented as follows. It begins with the question "Can the truth be learned?" If one already knows the truth, then the truth cannot be learned, for one cannot learn what one already knows. And if one does not know the truth, then how will one recognize the truth when one finds it? Climacus calls this question of how the truth can be learned, given this disjunction and its ensuing paradox, a Socratic question, which, he believes, the Platonic doctrine of recollection resolves. In Plato's *Meno*, Socrates is able to get a slave boy to articulate the steps of a mathematical proof simply by asking him the right questions. So on the Platonic account of truth, the moment of learning is anticlimactic; it is incidental, for the truth was already contained within the slave boy and all he did was simply recall it. Plato uses this example to support his psychological doctrine of the soul's communion with the Forms prior to birth. Socrates, through asking questions, gets the slave boy to recollect the knowledge that is already within him because of his prior kinship with the Forms, and the learner's paradox is resolved through the Platonic doctrine of recollection.

In stark contrast to this Platonic way of recollection, Climacus introduces another way of learning the truth. On this new account of learning the truth, one does not learn the truth through recollection of that which is immanent to one's soul. Instead, the truth is transcendent and comes to the individual from without, causing a genuine change in the person. So complex is this truth that it does not come by itself; if it did come alone, it would not be effective. When the truth comes, it also comes with the condition necessary for receiving it, which Climacus calls "faith." On this view of transcendent truth, the learner's paradox is not resolved at all. Indeed, it is deepened. Not only is the truth not already present within the individual, but now there are other phenomena that make the paradox more complex. Who or what is this entity that externally brings the truth to the individual? And what are we to make of this notion of "faith" as a condition for receiving the truth? The answers to these questions for Climacus, are, first, the one that externally brings the truth is God in the person of Jesus Christ, and second, that the Incarnation of God in Jesus is itself paradoxical, and cannot be resolved through the use of any Greek philosophical concepts such as recollection. This, then, is a paradox on top of a paradox that demands faith as a condition for believing it. Upon receiving both the truth and the faith necessary to accept it, the individual is changed in a way that the slave boy from Plato's *Meno* was not. The individual has experienced a conversion: there was a way of life prior to receiving the truth (Climacus calls this life "sin"), and there is a way of life after receiving the truth, which is a life of faith; a life of believing in that which cannot be explained; a life of epistemic humility that emphasizes the radical change that comes with one's newfound truth, rather than the incidental moment of recollection that arrives merely Socratically; this life after conversion is a life that pursues an authentic existential subjectivity that will, in turn, demand self-reflection and self-concern.

In juxtaposing these two ways of coming to know the truth, Climacus is contrasting the difference between a philosophical approach and a religious approach to Christian theology. He wants to show that the philosophical approach—the approach of Danish theologians originating with Hegel's speculative method—has cheapened the Christian experience to the point of not requiring faith at all. For Climacus, because Hegelian theology claims to have understood the Incarnation through Hegel's rejection of Aristotelian logic and his account of mediation, faith is unimportant because one already "knows" the truth of Christianity. And on the philosophical approach to Christianity, not only is faith unnecessary, but the entirety of Christian religious experience is lacking in any real significance because all one needs to do is recollect the truth, so there is no moment of conversion. On the philosophical approach to Christianity, then, the existing individual's subjectivity, personhood, and destiny remain unaffected. Indeed, in the absence of faith and of a genuine conversion, people will assume themselves to be Christians because they have accepted a badly oversimplified Hegelian-influenced brand of Christianity to be the truth, not realizing that the reduction of Christianity's paradoxical transcendence to an epistemic immanence, which ultimately leads them to assume a state or condition of *being* a Christian has actually deprived them of the experience of what it means to *become* a Christian. These categories of being and becoming are important in understanding the problem of *Philosophical Fragments*, because they represent the contrast of the philosophical approach to Christianity, where one is a Christian and simply makes rational justifications for it (the way of analytic theism), and an Incarnational account of Christianity, where the word being made flesh is an event of great significance that demands a conversion, an actual change of the person. This is the concern for existential subjectivity that is lacking in the reformed epistemology of analytic theism, and that is present in both Douglass and Kierkegaard.

Against the backdrop of the philosophical way of truth and the Incarnational way of truth, it is important to analyze the culture of the Christian communities in which both Douglass and Kierkegaard lived. Reflecting on the cultural realities of Douglass and Kierkegaard in the context of Incarnational theology emphasizes the need for conversion, which, for both of them, was severely lacking in their respective communities.

Kierkegaard describes the culture of his Christian community as an age in which the philosophical and theological certainty of Hegelian mediation has supplanted the conceptual and practical difficulties of Christian life. Christians in "Christendom," the broader culture of Christianity, thus resting on their Hegelian philosophical understanding of Christianity make the mistake of assuming that they are Christian solely in virtue of objective factors such as one's assent to and understanding of doctrinal beliefs. Christendom has transformed Christianity into philosophy. Through his pseudonym, Johannes Climacus, he points to an example of this sort of deception, drawing a comparison between Hegelian theology and the pre-Socratic, Eleatic arguments about motion:

> Christianity pertains to existence, to existing, but existence and existing are the very opposite of speculation. The Eleatic doctrine, for example, is not related to existing but to speculation; therefore it must be assigned its place within speculation. Precisely because Christianity is not a doctrine, it holds true, as developed previously, that there is an enormous difference between knowing what

Christianity is and being a Christian. With regard to a doctrine, this distinction is unthinkable, because the doctrine is not related to existing. I cannot help it that our age has reversed the relation and changed Christianity into a philosophical theory that is to be comprehended and being a Christian into something negligible. Furthermore, to say that Christianity is empty of content because it is not a doctrine is only chicanery. When a believer exists in faith, his existence has enormous content, but not in the sense of a yield in paragraphs.[18]

Climacus's point here is emphatically stated: Christianity is intended to be lived and experienced rather than agreed to and understood. But his "age," as he puts it, has "changed Christianity into a philosophical theory that is to be comprehended and being a Christian into something negligible." Christianity is a religion of existence. Now the contrast between Hegel and Kierkegaard is clearer: Kierkegaard's concern with dynamism and progress is related to an existing person who must live with faith and make hard choices in comparison to the abstractions of Hegel's speculative logical method which simply does not take the concreteness of existential life into account. And it is this failure to account for the difficult choices of Christian life that make for a community of persons that are nominal Christians, but who lack any concern whatsoever for how they are living. Indeed, to question whether one is even living as a Christian is considered to be problematic. Climacus explains:

Yet one thing is assumed: Christianity as given. It is assumed that we are all Christians. Alas, alas, alas, speculative thought is much too courteous. Yes, how strange the course of the world is! At one time it was perilous to profess being a Christian; now it is precarious to doubt that one is. . . . No, if someone were to say, plainly and simply, that he was concerned about himself, that it was not quite right for him to call himself a Christian, he would not be persecuted or executed, but people would give him an angry look and say, "It is really boring of this fellow to make so much ado about nothing; why can't he be like the rest of us, who are all Christians . . ." If he were married, his wife would tell him, "Hubby, darling, where did you ever pick up such a notion? How can you not be a Christian? You are Danish, aren't you? Doesn't the geography book say that the predominant religion in Denmark is Lutheran-Christian? You aren't a Jew, are you, or a Mohammedan? What else would you be, then? It is a thousand years since paganism was superseded; so I know you aren't a pagan. Don't you tend to your work in the office as a good civil servant; aren't you a good subject in a Christian nation, in a Lutheran-Christian state? So of course you are a Christian."

Lo, we have become so objective that even the wife of a civil servant argues from the whole, from the state, from the idea of the society, from geographic scientificity to the single individual. It follows so automatically that the single individual is Christian, has faith, etc. that it is flippant to make so much ado about it, or certainly capricious.[19]

Climacus has just described the phenomenon that makes Kierkegaard's Christendom so problematic: geography, science, occupation, familial connections, and church membership are the objective determinants for being a Christian. The subjective life is utterly unaccounted for on this view. So what we end up with for Kierkegaard is a community of persons who believe that they are Christians, but who have had no real conversion experience. There is a fundamental lack of what Climacus calls "appropriation" and "inwardness." There has been no application of the beliefs to the life of the existing individual. There is only an assent to an objective set of beliefs. These persons need only "recollect," in the Platonic sense, their church membership, geography, and so on, and they can immediately "know" that they are Christians. Later in the *Concluding Unscientific Postscript*, Climacus connects the problem of Christian culture to the conversion issue that he raised in *Philosophical Fragments*, where he explains why he took paganism (Greek philosophical thought) as his point of departure in that text: "speculative thought makes paganism the outcome of Christianity, and to be Christian as a matter of course by being baptized changes Christendom into a baptized paganism."[20] A "baptized paganism" will yield a community of baptized pagans, a designation that Douglass no doubt would use to describe the hypocritical "Christian" community in which he lived as a slave.

That Douglass believed that the community in which he spent a portion of his life as a slave was in need of religious conversion is difficult to doubt. In chapter nine of his *Narrative*, Douglass describes the condition of his master, Captain Auld, both before and after his experience with Christianity and, in doing so, provides some compelling insights into the character of the community of Christians in which Douglass lived:

> In August, 1832, my master attended a Methodist camp-meeting held in the Bayside, Talbot county, and there experienced religion. I indulged a faint hope that his conversion would lead him to emancipate his slaves, and that, if he did not do this, it would at any rate, make him more kind and humane. I was disappointed in both these respects. It neither made him to be human to his slaves, nor to emancipate them. If it had any effect on his character, it made him more cruel and hateful in all his ways; for I believe him to have been a much worse man after his conversion than before. Prior to his conversion, he relied upon his own depravity to shield and sustain him in his savage barbarity; but after his conversion, he found religious sanction and support for his slave-holding cruelty. He made the greatest pretensions to piety. His house was the house of prayer. He prayed morning, noon and night. He very soon distinguished himself among his brethren, and was soon made a class-leader and exhorter. His activity in revivals was great, and he proved himself an instrument in the hands of the church in converting many souls.[21]

The lack of authentic existential subjectivity and self-reflection is significant in this passage. What first stands out is that the "conversion" to Christianity does not improve Captain Auld, but rather makes him worse off than he was before the religious experience. Here again, we see the insight from Merold Westphal earlier in the chapter about the danger of empty and formal religious frameworks: they become the habitation of evils worse than those that were there before. As if the emptiness of slaveholding is not bad enough, what we now have is, in the words of Douglass, "religious sanction" for the "slave-holding cruelty" of Captain Auld. Thus Jesus, the central religious figure of Captain Auld's newfound religion, would say that "the last state" of Captain Auld was "worse than the first." The sort of Christianity that Captain Auld has experienced is one where he participates in rituals and ceremonies without any real inwardness or appropriation of the Christian message. Indeed, Douglass's conjecture that Captain Auld would be improved after his religious experience is based on the notion that Christianity improves people rather than worsens them. To put Captain Auld's religion in Incarnational theological language, there was no word that was ever made flesh. An empty and formal theological framework of doctrinal beliefs was more than enough to effectively eliminate the possibility of any authentic existential subjectivity. Instead, Auld's religion was one that rendered impossible a genuine, inward, moral conversion, in favor of a descent to an even deeper level of moral corruption. It stands to reason that since this happened to Captain Auld, it perhaps happened to other members of Auld's "Christian" community. Later in the *Narrative*, Douglass tells us that indeed the more Christian such persons profess to be, the worse their behavior toward the slaves.

At the end of chapter nine of Douglass's *Narrative*, Douglass tells us that Mr. Covey, whom he would be with as a slave for one year, was "a professor of religion—a pious soul—a member and a class-leader in the Methodist church. All of this added weight to his reputation as a 'nigger-breaker.'"[22] Douglass was being sent to Covey because, according to his previous master, his "city life" "had a very pernicious effect" upon him.[23] So he was sent to Covey to be purged of his difficult ways. Significantly, among Covey's qualifications for being a good "nigger-breaker" was that he was also a good Christian. After being with Covey for a year, and describing some of his worst and most formative experiences as a slave and as a human being in chapter ten of his *Narrative*, Douglass describes what it was like for him after leaving Covey, a good, Christian "nigger-breaker," whom he had been with for one year, to work as a slave for Mr. Freeland. Douglass's description of Freeland as compared with Covey is significant:

> I soon found Mr. Freeland a very different man from Mr. Covey. Though not rich, he was what would be called an educated southern gentleman. Mr. Covey,

as I have shown, was a well-trained negro-breaker and slave-driver. The former (slaveholder though he was) seemed to possess some regard for honor, some reverence for justice, and some respect for humanity. The latter seemed totally insensible to all such sentiments. Mr. Freeland had many of the faults peculiar to slave-holders, such as being very passionate and fretful; but I must do him the justice to say, that he was exceedingly free from those degrading vices to which Mr. Covey was constantly addicted. The one was open and frank, and we always knew where to find him. The other was a most artful deceiver, and could be understood only by such as were skillful enough to detect his cunningly-devised frauds. Another advantage I gained in my new master was, he made no pretensions to, or profession of, religion; and this, in my opinion, was truly a great advantage. I assert most unhesitatingly, that the religion of the south is a mere covering for the most horrid crimes,—a justifier of the most appalling barbarity,—a sanctifier of the most hateful frauds,—and a dark shelter under which the darkest, foulest, grossest, and most infernal deeds of slaveholders find the strongest protection. Were I to be again reduced to the chains of slavery, next to that enslavement, I should regard being the slave of a religious master the greatest calamity that could befall me. For of all slaveholders with whom I have ever met, religious slaveholders are the worst. I have ever found them the meanest and basest, the most cruel and cowardly of all others. It was my unhappy lot not only to belong to a religious slaveholder but to live in a community of such religionists.[24]

Covey not only professed Christianity but also was pious, which qualified him to be a "nigger-breaker." Freeland made no religious profession at all and yet still managed to have "some regard for honor, some reverence for justice, and some respect for humanity." Covey was a Christian and "a most artful deceiver" who perpetrated "cunningly-devised frauds," while Freeland, who was not religious, "was exceedingly free from those degrading vices to which Mr. Covey was constantly addicted." Covey was a Christian who was an "artful deceiver," and Freeland was "open and frank." The contrast here could not be clearer. Douglass then assigns blame to "the religion of the south" to account for this difference in disposition between Covey and Freeland. There was something about slaveholding Christianity that Douglass thought was more corrupting than the absence of any religion at all, and I believe that something is the assent to abstract beliefs without any genuine moral and religious conversion. The Platonic doctrine of recollection merely allows for Covey to be reminded—perhaps by his church attendance, or by his recitation of Bible verses—that he is a Christian. It is often said of Christian hypocrites that they are in the church but that the church is not in them. Considering the Platonic notion of recollection from Climacus's *Philosophical Fragments*, one may say that the church was in Covey, but that something corrupt—the slaveholding religion of the American antebellum south—put it there. Covey did not experience his Christianity from the God outside of him, so as to cause a genuine moral conversion within, resulting in a life of moral integrity and faith. Instead, Covey experienced his religion from the corruption inside of him, so as to cause a disturbing hypocrisy without, resulting in a religious life where he had fellowship with other such persons as what Climacus would call "baptized pagans."

That such other persons existed is plain enough from Douglass's claim that he lived in a community of religionists like Covey. Two that are named in chapter ten of Douglass's *Narrative* are Reverend Daniel Weeden and Reverend Rigby Hopkins. Both men "were members and ministers in the Reformed Methodist Church."[25] And both men were slaveholders. Of Weeden, Douglass says that his maxim was "Behave well or behave ill, it is the duty of a master occasionally to whip a slave, to remind him of his master's authority."[26] And to this maxim he held true, for, according to Douglass, Weeden "owned, among others, a woman slave, whose name I have forgotten. This woman's back, for weeks, was kept literally raw, made so by the lash of this merciless, religious wretch."[27] So it is that Douglass writes of Weeden, "Such was his theory, and such his practice."[28] Hopkins, we are told, was "even worse than Mr. Weeden." His greatest "virtue" as a slaveholder was to whip his slaves in advance of any offense deserving it. This was intended to keep the slaves in check. Douglass experienced the height of this community's religious corruption when he organized a Sabbath school that was devoted to teaching his fellow slaves how to read. Just as this literacy initiative was gaining momentum, several of the religious leaders of the community "rushed in upon" Douglass's small group that was learning to read "with sticks and stones" and "broke up" the class, "all calling themselves Christians! Humble followers of the Lord Jesus Christ!"[29] Both Douglass and Kierkegaard, then, were confronted with a similar problem: they faced communities of people whose religion remained abstract and was thus too far removed from human experience to make any appreciable difference in their moral and religious lives. Instead of an authentic existential subjectivity, their selves have fallen by an epistemological wayside of sorts, for while they make commitments to religious beliefs, they make no commitment whatsoever to authentic, subjective moral and religious practice. Their Incarnational paradigm is short-circuited by a social and cultural Platonic "recollection" where all that matters are the reminders that come from the epistemic and ontological markers of their "Christianity," rather than the radical change of inwardness that comes from the God-man, who not only delivers the truth but also delivers the faith necessary to believe and, more important, to live it.

Kierkegaard, Douglass, and Communication

Having seen the deeply troubling circumstances of Kierkegaard's and Douglass's corrupt religious communities, their task of moral reform is no small matter. Both thinkers are confronting people who genuinely believe that their Christianity is morally legitimate, and who are thoroughly deceived, greatly overestimating the quality of their religious lives. How do they address this problem? How do you tell people who believe that they are right that they are wrong? In both cases, philosophical debate seems to be incapable of dealing with the problem, for the debate rages on in Kierkegaard's Denmark, while the Hegelian theologians have not changed their mind. And for Douglass, the abolition movements were an abiding presence in public life and debate, while slavery in the antebellum American south was thriving. Intellectual debates and discussions seem to only aggravate rather than mitigate the conditions that both Douglass and Kierkegaard want to eliminate, driving people deeper into their respective opinions and positions, and making them more committed to their causes. In light of these difficulties with theoretical, intellectual discussion as a means for social change, Douglass and Kierkegaard turn away from the objective and toward the subjective. From the discussion thus far in this chapter, we have seen that both thinkers are deeply committed to an authentic existential subjectivity; both are interested in the word being made flesh, and this, combined with the difficulties of objective, theoretical, and intellectual discussion and debate when confronting these social and cultural problems, brings Douglass and Kierkegaard to a deeper understanding of the self, and both decide that the best way to reach the self is not directly through objective theory, but rather subjectively through creative, artistic interventions. For Kierkegaard, this is done through the use of pseudonyms, and for Douglass, this is done through his use of narrative.

Kierkegaard on Indirect Communication

Indirect communication is a major aspect of Kierkegaard's corpus. Kierkegaard is known for transmitting many of his ideas through pseudonyms who he inserts between himself and his audience. Kierkegaard uses pseudonyms because he is attempting to influence the social and cultural life of the Danish State Church.[30] This communication strategy is an important part of Kierkegaard's overall view of subjectivity. The relationship between existential subjectivity and communication is important because indirect communication is intended to effect change within the individual in a way that direct communication cannot. Some discussion of these terms is useful here.

A direct communication is a communication of objective knowledge. So, for example, if I said, "George Washington was the first president of the

United States," that is a historical fact. According to Kierkegaard, this is a statement that I can make directly without being expected to do anything because of that statement. All that I can do with this statement is hear it, verify it, and perhaps recall it as a matter of objective knowledge. But again, this sort of objective, historical knowledge does not demand anything of me. And because it does not demand anything of me, my capacity to receive this sort of historical truth is presumed to be in good working order if something is communicated to a person directly. So with a direct communication, as long as my perceptual faculties—sight, hearing, cognition, etc.—are in good working order, the transmission of knowledge is a straightforward task. Direct communications are intended for people who are not already deceived about something. If someone is deceived, however, an indirect communication is appropriate because it removes the deception. Kierkegaard explains the differences between direct and indirect communication and one's ability to receive such communications as follows: "But direct communication presupposes that the recipient's ability to receive is entirely in order, but here that is simply not the case—indeed, here a delusion is an obstacle. That means a corrosive must first be used, but this corrosive is the negative, but the negative in connection with communicating is precisely to deceive."[31] By way of further explanation, Kierkegaard writes:

> No, an illusion can never be removed directly, and basically only indirectly. If it is an illusion that all are Christians, and if something is to be done, it must be done indirectly, not by someone who loudly declares himself to be an extraordinary Christian, but by someone who, better informed, even declares himself not to be a Christian. That is one who is under an illusion must be approached from behind. . . . By a direct attack he only strengthens a person in the illusion and also infuriates him. Generally speaking, there is nothing that requires as gentle a treatment as the removal of an illusion. If one in any way causes the one ensnared to be antagonized, then all is lost. And this one does by a direct attack.[32]

Kierkegaard believes that Christendom is laboring under the delusion that they are Christians. Since this is the deception, if Kierkegaard's attempt at removing this deception is going to be successful, then he must communicate indirectly with Christendom. The average person in Christendom is deceived into thinking that he or she is a Christian, when he or she is not a Christian. The pseudonyms, then, are intended to communicate the message of Christianity indirectly so that people will see themselves and change, rather than seeing Kierkegaard and being driven deeper into their deception about their status as Christians.

The delusion in Christendom stems from the mistaken belief that Christianity is objective; that Christianity is a mere collection of doctrinal beliefs, and that on assenting to such beliefs, one is a Christian. Christianity has simply become an exercise in Hegelian logic. As I have pointed out earlier in this chapter, Martensen refers to the "Christian metaphysics" as that which makes the Hegelian move of mediation.[33] Martensen also refers to the "metaphysics" of the Jewish religion, which, for him, fails to make such a move.[34] Again, Kierkegaard's objection here is that in reducing Christianity to a theological exercise in Hegelian logic, one has eclipsed the conceptual and practical difficulties of being Christian, and Christianity has become a matter of Platonic recollection. This is why the point of departure in *Philosophical Fragments* was taken from Greek paganism: to show that the Christian life is one in which paradoxical theological beliefs remain paradoxical. Aristotelian logic rather than Hegelian logic applies, and for Johannes Climacus, the pseudonymous author of *Philosophical Fragments*, the principle of the excluded middle remains a bedrock of human thought that frustrates epistemic and metaphysical pursuits of Christian doctrines such as the Incarnation. God and humanity are not reconciled in any third term, but rather remain fundamentally different from one another while being one and the same. This is the paradox that demands a measure of faith to believe it. Christianity is then not a mere matter of intellectual assent due to Hegelian mediation, but rather a conceptually difficult thing to understand (and even more difficult to live). This is why Kierkegaard wants to show that from the standpoint of existential subjectivity, one is likewise often presented with difficult choices and paradoxical situations that are not easily resolved and that are endured under great trial and difficulty. Kierkegaard is trying to reclaim these conceptual and practical difficulties through the use of his pseudonyms, which he hopes will enable people to see themselves and make the double reflection—hearing the communication, and then applying it to themselves—that will change their behavior from complacency because of an assent to the doctrine of Hegelian theology and toward an inwardness and a subjective passion because of a genuine faith in Christianity. Unlike the transcendence of Incarnational theology, which brings the truth to the learner and results in a genuine change in the person, Christendom is holding fast to the immanence of Platonic recollection as represented in Hegelian mediation and is thus a mere "baptized paganism."

What Kierkegaard wants Christendom to do is understand that Christianity is fundamentally "unscientific," as in the title of his *Concluding Unscientific Postscript to Philosophical Fragments*. In science, one must remove oneself from any of the scientific laboratory work so as to not skew the results of the testing on one's hypothesis. But Christianity demands the opposite of science, which is that instead of removing oneself, one should completely immerse oneself in Christianity to achieve the best results. Indeed, notions of "inwardness" and passion are so important for Kierkegaard precisely because they represent the sort of total commitment that Kierkegaard believes Christianity demands of an authentic Christian, and that they are also the missing ingredients that fall by the wayside because Hegelian theology has, without any subjective existential accounts of faith, suffering, and evil, effectively made Christianity into a matter of Hegelian mediation. This is why Climacus refers to Christianity repeatedly in the postscript as an "existence-communication." This passage is instructive:

> The introducing that I take upon myself consists, by repelling, in making it difficult to become a Christian and understands Christianity not as a doctrine but as an existence-contradiction and existence-communication. Therefore, it introduces psychologically, not world-historically, by evoking an awareness of how much must be lived and how difficult it is to become really aware of the difficulty of the decision. . . . When culture and the like have managed to make it so very easy to be a Christian, it is certainly in order that a single individual, according to his poor abilities, seeks to make it difficult, provided, however, that he does not make it more difficult than it is.—But the more culture and knowledge, the more difficult to become a Christian.[35]

Christianity, or what it means to become a Christian, cannot be communicated directly because direct communication is for the "what" of objective knowledge, but Christianity is for the "how" of subjective appropriation. From this passage what we see is that for Climacus, contemporary Christian culture has made it "easy" to be a Christian because of doctrinal assent. This is why Climacus points out "the more culture and knowledge, the more difficult to become a Christian." It is through the use of pseudonyms that Kierkegaard works against the Christian culture of his day to problematize Christianity—a religion that once required one to risk so much, but in Kierkegaard's Denmark, he saw as requiring little more than a few lessons in Hegelian logic. This was the world of "baptized paganism" that Kierkegaard attempted to change. Douglass faced a similarly corrupt Christian community and employed a similar strategy that I will now discuss.

Douglass's Use of Narrative and the Problem of Anteriority

The delusions of slaveholding Christians regarding their religious life, despite intense public debate over abolition and the myriad abolitionist arguments of moral suasion, remained deeply entrenched in their hearts and minds. This is not to say that direct communications that pointed to statistics and other facts and figures could not shed light on the desperate plight of the American slave, but rather that such efforts, standing alone, would be insufficient to change the culture. And the same goes for legal reform. Though there were great strides toward political freedom for former slaves, neither the Emancipation Proclamation nor Reconstruction-motivated federal civil rights legislation would be sufficient, in themselves, to change the social and cultural realities for enslaved Africans or for newly freed slaves. The former, while necessary, resulted in a mere absence of restraint without any support from a federal government that sanctioned and facilitated the slave trade for 244 years, leaving the illiterate former slave to a life of vagrancy, and the latter was subject to restrictive Supreme Court interpretations that effectively nullified the legislation for nearly one hundred years. It is in this context that Douglass turns to his use of narrative as a form of artistic storytelling that will draw in the hearts and minds of his white, Christian, slaveholding audience in a way that the best of his philosophical argumentation—and Douglass was a fine philosophical thinker—could not. To develop my interpretation of Douglass's use of narrative, I return to a concept that I mentioned in the introduction that I have called "the problem of anteriority."

The problem of anteriority is based on the biblical account of Moses's request to see God.[36] God tells Moses in response that no one can see him and live. I have argued in the introduction that Moses's demand is a philosophical plea for epistemic and ontological clarity. That is, Moses wants to know precisely who God is. Moses wants to be able to provide an ontological account of God so that when others ask about Him, Moses will be able to, through resort to the *logos*, provide a rational account of God's being. It is in this way that Moses wants God to conform to the conditions of human intelligibility; to fit within human epistemic and ontological restraints. In response to Moses, God reminds him that He will decide the conditions under which to reveal Himself, and then hides Moses in the cleft of a rock, telling Moses that He will allow all of his goodness to pass by him, but His face, His front, shall not be seen. Instead of seeing God's face, God allows Moses to see His backside.

I call this the problem of anteriority because of the demarcation between God's front and His back that He introduces when he forbids Moses from seeing his front. What does this sort of prohibition mean? Why would God prevent a frontal, or an anterior view? An insight from this biblical story is that even if God did allow Moses to see His anterior, Moses would have been unable to comprehend it. And even if Moses could comprehend God, what sort of life would result from that encounter but a life of Platonic recollection in which Moses would be able to recall God as an object of human knowledge? To put the problem of anteriority in Climacus's Incarnational language from *Philosophical Fragments*, God would be immanent to Moses rather than transcendent from him. God would be, contrary to the Cartesian argument for His existence from the third meditation, contained within human consciousness; God would simply be another idea of equal to or lesser value than Moses. And as I have discussed throughout this chapter, one can see precisely the sort of life that ensues from such epistemic immanence and recollection: a life where there is no real moral conversion because the transcendence of God is disregarded. Indeed, not only is there not a moral conversion born of authentic existential subjectivity, but there is also an ersatz version of the Christian Gospel in its place. So when God says that no one can see Him and live, I submit that means that the life resulting from ontological and epistemic certainty, the life that results from the attempt of the reformed epistemology of analytic theism to prove that a belief in God is rational, is no life at all. In contrast, it is a death—a death of one's spirit; a death of one's imagination; a death of one's creativity; a death of oneself. The need for spirit, imagination, creativity, and one's own subjectivity becomes irrelevant, because, in seeing God's front—or at least in convincing ourselves that we have seen God's front—we already have all of the answers. Indeed, to see God from the front is not really to see God at all, but rather to see a mirror image of one's rational self staring back at you. This religion (if one can even call it that) is essentially an ontotheological mode of self-projection. Xenophanes and Feuerbach condemn and diagnose this sort of philosophical theology.[37] Anteriority, then, is a problem precisely because one purports to "know" God at the expense of oneself.

But the view of God's backside is different. In contrast to what is seen from the front in a religion of epistemic and ontological certainty, what is seen from the back is what was never known in advance, but rather can only be related *after experience*. So whereas God's front provides a religion of epistemic and ontological rational explanation, the sight of God's backside provides a poetic religion of testimony. One cannot see God's front, but one can always see and discuss what God has left behind. And this is how Douglass uses his *Narrative*. As he recounts his various harrowing experiences, from his escape to freedom to his fight with Covey, one realizes that in Douglass, there is a qualitatively different power in his story than there is in intellectual debate and argument. Again, this is not to say that Douglass did not engage in argument, nor is it to say that philosophical arguments are not present in his *Narrative*. Indeed, they are. But my point here is that all of those arguments are not presented on their own; they are part of a much larger overall story of, for example, his journey to literacy, without which the skill of his philosophical argumentation would not be possible. Moreover, it is, I think, far more compelling to find oneself cheering for Douglass to learn to read as he describes the discontent that whites experienced when they heard the term "abolition," before he knew what it meant, than it is to listen to philosophical argumentation apart from the backstory of how Douglass not only learned to read but also developed his rhetorical and analytical skill. Douglass himself makes this point:

> Dry logic and illaborate arguments—though perfect in all their appointments and though knitted together as a coat of mail, lays down the Law to Empty benches. But he who speaks to the feelings, who enters the soul's deepest meditations, holding the mirror up to nature, revealing the profoundest mysteries of the human heart to the eye and ear by action and by utterance, will never want for an audience.[38]

No amount of philosophical argumentation, standing alone, can penetrate the heart and mind like the feeling that one experiences as one reads, for example, of Douglass's determination to transform himself from slave to man in his fight with Covey.[39] Douglass understood this well, which is why his *Narrative* is not the "dry logic" of epistemic and ontological rationality, but is instead the window through which we are permitted a glimpse into Douglass's soul and its "deepest meditation" that reveals "the profoundest mysteries of the human heart to the eye and ear by action and utterance." William Lloyd Garrison, Douglass's white ally in the abolition struggle, remarks, "This narrative contains many affecting incidents, many passages of great eloquence and power. . . . Who can read [it], and be insensible to its pathos and sublimity."[40] The power of pathos in Douglass's story is undeniable. And so much of that power resides in what he relates to us about what he experienced as opposed to what he knows. Again, this is the difference between Douglass seeing God's face and Douglass seeing what God has left behind. By Douglass telling us what he saw when he beheld God's "backside," Douglass is able to tap into what Kierkegaard would call his reader's "existential pathos," "inwardness," his "passion," not for the sake of entertainment, but for the sake of self-reflection and moral reform. So it is much more fruitful for Douglass to testify about what he experienced than it is to only argue about what he knows. Testimony, then, in this sense, does not supplant philosophical argumentation, but rather augments it, doing what philosophical argumentation alone cannot do. The other side of this dynamic is the commitment to anteriority, to the Mosaic philosophical desire for the *logos*. This is by and large the way of the reformed epistemology of analytic theism: sophisticated, extensive, abstract, and formal philosophical argumentation about what we have convinced ourselves that we know about God at the expense of existential subjectivity. Reformed epistemology stimulates the intellect, and it may even reassure some Christians that their belief in God is rational. But if one can rationally justify a belief in God, is God still God, or is it the god of ontotheological explanation? When rationality is the driving force for theistic belief, we create what Martin Heidegger termed "the god of philosophy." This god is the product of reason. Rationality—that is, the Mosaic desire for God's front, for God's anterior—drives us to invert the biblical model of creation, for instead of God making human beings in His image, we create God in our image, in an image of human rationality. The problem of anteriority, described in Kantian terms, is a problem of the faculty of reason, which, by its own nature, makes demands that also by its own nature, it cannot fulfill. So the problem of anteriority is an enduring problem. We will always want to see God's front. But we will also always see what God has left behind. It is up to us to tell the story. God's front represents reason and intellect, and God's back represents the creativity of storytelling and the power of testimony. Douglass understood this, and, through the power of his *Narrative*, told us about what God had left behind in his life.

Another virtue of seeing God's backside—storytelling and the artistic use of narrative—is that, unlike philosophical explanation and argumentation, it creates a world in which people are able to see themselves. So in addition to the accessibility to hearts and minds through moral feeling, narrative enables us to create a world apart from ourselves, as Douglass does through his use of autobiographical narrative. It is the creation of this world that allows us enough distance to be able to see ourselves. We see an example of this in Douglass's reaction to a fictional dialogue that he read between a master and a slave. The slave had escaped and been captured three times. After being captured for the third time, the master argued the entire cause for slavery, but the slave intelligently and persuasively refuted every point the master made, resulting in the master voluntarily manumitting the slave. Douglass writes of his takeaway from this dialogue, "The moral which I gained from the dialogue was the power of truth over the conscience of even a slaveholder."[41] Douglass's point here is significant, for the dialogue was fictional, but what he learned from the dialogue was the power of truth. So there is, it seems, a profoundly moral side to narrative in that one can glean the truth from fiction. This truth is not, however, the truth of epistemic and ontological argumentation, but rather the truth of existential subjectivity in the sense that Kierkegaard claims that "truth is subjectivity." On the former account of truth, the principal interest is the truth of propositions, or the truth of beliefs as properly basic based on human cognitive dispositions, as in the case of reformed epistemology.[42] On the latter account, the truth is not argued or learned, instead, it is appropriated, resulting in an actual change in one's life. This is what Climacus means in the *Concluding Unscientific Postscript* when he claims that "truth is subjectivity." Climacus writes:

> The inquiring, speculating, knowing subject accordingly asks about the truth but not about the subjective truth, the truth of appropriation. Accordingly the inquiring subject is indeed interested but is not infinitely, personally, impassionedly

interested in his relation to this truth concerning his own eternal happiness. Far be it from the objective subject to be so immodest, so vain.[43]

Douglass was not an inquiring, speculating subject in the philosophical sense. Although he was reading the *Columbian Orator* out of an intellectual curiosity, he walked away from this dialogue "infinitely, personally, impassionedly interested in his relation" to the truth that slavery was morally wrong. Interestingly, Douglass, as he writes his *Narrative* in 1845, is, I submit, able to see himself in the dialogue as the escaped slave who uses the power of argument to gain his freedom. Indeed, as he writes his *Narrative*, he sees himself both in the present and in his future life as a public intellectual. Here also we see philosophical argumentation presented in the context of artistic creativity, which in a sense, makes the dialogue in the *Columbian Orator* a sort of Platonic dialogue, for Plato presents his philosophical ideas in dialogue form, and even argued, in the "Myth of the Metals" from book three of his *Republic* that fictional dialogue was essential for social and cultural renewal. So the authors of the *Columbian Orator* and Douglass are in good philosophical company.[44]

In sum, I have attempted an existential interpretation of Douglass by reading him with Kierkegaard. Viewing both thinkers from within the Incarnational theological paradigm, they each address the problem of abstraction, which results in a perverse inversion of the Incarnation in which rather than the word being made flesh, the flesh is made into a word. Abstraction thus results in corrupt communities of Christians who have never experienced a genuine conversion and yet still see themselves as Christians. To address this deluded community, in an attempt to access the inner lives of their corrupt cultures, both Kierkegaard and Douglass employ similar creative strategies. Kierkegaard communicates indirectly through pseudonyms, and Douglass does so through the use of narrative. Both of these strategies address existential subjectivity and morality in a way that is, I have argued, far superior to that of the reformed epistemology of analytic theism. To complete my existential interpretation of Douglass in this chapter, I now turn to my reading of Douglass with Kafka.

DOUGLASS, KAFKA, AND THE ABSURD

Among the prominent themes of existentialism is the notion of the absurd. In the twentieth century, the absurd is taken up in existentialist literature, especially the literary works of Kafka. In this section of the chapter, I interpret Douglass by reading his *Narrative* with Kafka's novel, *The Trial*. I choose *The Trial* as an interpretive partner for Douglass for two reasons. First, because of its setting against the backdrop of law and legal systems, the novel emphasizes the significance of the oppressive effects of law not only in the fictional life of its protagonist, Josef K., but also in the actual life of Douglass as a slave and the actual lives of contemporary African Americans. Second, I am interested in the affinities between the reality of Douglass's life as a slave and the fictional world of Josef K. Kafka's novel teaches us, through its stories within the story, something about how we ought to face the absurd when it confronts us. Navigating the absurd is not easy. But Douglass somehow managed to do so in a way that Josef K. could not, and we learn this through Kafka's compelling presentation of story from within the broader story of the novel, as compared with Douglass's presentation of his *Narrative*.

What is so striking about *The Trial* is how the legal authority penetrates the lives of people at the level of the quotidian. Apartments are transformed into courtrooms, and the jurisdiction of the court is so far reaching that one cannot go anywhere without its presence being known, and without its influence being felt. It is for this reason that before I begin my interpretation of Douglass's *Narrative* with *The Trial*, I want to discuss two contemporary instances in the lives of ordinary people doing ordinary things, who, like Josef K., find themselves facing the ubiquitous presence of the legal system in ways that, I will argue, can only be described as absurd. These two contemporary instances of the absurd have a very disturbing connection to the life of Douglass, in that they are representative of the legacy of chattel slavery through which Douglass lived. In both of these instances, a Black person, through some ordinary, mundane activity, sees his subjectivity emerge in paradoxical and absurd circumstances. As Saidiya Hartman points out, it is these ordinary, everyday encounters which are actually far more terrifying than bloody spectacles. To put Hartman's point in contemporary terms, the instances of the absurd that I will describe are, I believe, much more frightening than the spectacle of watching Philando Castille's death or Eric Garner's death on social media videos. Hartman notes that this is why she focuses not on the terror inflicted upon Douglass's Aunt Hester, but rather upon those more routine instances that, on the surface, appear to be harmless:

> I have chosen not to reproduce Douglass's account of the beating of Aunt Hester . . . rather than try to convey the routinized violence of slavery and its aftermath through invocations of the shocking and the terrible, I have chosen to look elsewhere and consider those scenes in which terror can hardly be discerned—slaves dancing in the quarters, the outrageous darky antics of the minstrel stage, the constitution of humanity in slave law, and the fashioning of the self-possessed individual. By defamiliarizing the familiar, I hope to illuminate the terror of the mundane and the quotidian rather than exploit the shocking

spectacle. What concerns me here is the diffusion of terror and the violence perpetrated under the rubric of pleasure, paternalism, and property.[45]

Hartman is interested in how Black subjectivity is formed within the crucible of fear and social control at the level of the mundane. The examples that I provide attempt to show how Hartman's analysis of nineteenth-century slave life is pertinent today, in the twenty-first century. I do this by showing with these contemporary examples what George Yancy has so aptly termed the "confiscation" of the Black body by the white gaze: a radical, incessant, and often tragic set of ontological and epistemic claims that the white gaze imposes on the Black body, always already understanding it as marked with suspicion and criminality that demands immediate attention from law enforcement. Thus, reading Yancy with Hartman, in these examples, I will show how anti-Black racism functions at the level of the mundane to instill fear and maintain social control over Black bodies, not unlike the Black subjectivities of nineteenth-century America that Hartman terms "scenes of subjection." But more than that, both of these contemporary examples are encounters with the absurd and the paradoxical that are fundamentally no different from those that confronted Douglass when he was simultaneously considered both person and property.

After discussing these contemporary examples of the absurd in Black life, I then draw from the work of legal historian Ariela J. Gross, who points to the many paradoxes, contradictions, and absurdities that were foisted upon slaves in the legal system of the American antebellum south. This discussion, in conjunction with the two contemporary examples of the absurd as it relates to the emergence of Black subjectivity, sets the stage for my analysis of Douglass's *Narrative* and Kafka's *The Trial*, through which one can see that the absurdities of the world that Douglass inhabited, though separated by more than a century from my contemporary examples, are, in many ways, still the same today. The upshot of my Douglass-Kafka interpretation is to show the need for a creative, courageous confrontation with the absurd in such a way that one can find, in the words of Paul Tillich, "the courage to be," something that the reformed epistemology of analytic theism ignores altogether.

Contemporary Examples of the Absurd in Black Life

Byron Ragland

Byron Ragland is a nine-year veteran of the U.S. Air Force. After his military service, he returned to life as a civilian and was employed as a court-appointed supervisor of noncustodial parents during visitation hours by the court system in King County, Washington, and was enrolled as a psychology student at the

University of Washington, Tacoma. In his capacity as the supervisor, he was legally required to be present, on the premises, during noncustodial, parental visitations. In November 2018, while supervising a visit of a noncustodial parent at Menchie's yogurt shop in Seattle, the owner called the police after his employees reported Ragland as looking suspicious because he had not bought anything and was looking at his cell phone and would periodically look up at them. According to the shop's owner, Ramon Cruz, who owns several businesses in the area, there were some recent robberies that occurred at some of his other business locations, and so this, in conjunction with the call from his two teenage employees at the shop, made him nervous. So he called the police to report a man who was sitting in his shop without buying anything, and that, in light of the recent robberies of his other businesses, he was concerned. The police told him that they would investigate. When the police arrived, they told Ragland that he had to "move along," despite his explanation that his job—a job with the same legal system that employs the police, no less—required him to be there. The law first told Ragland to be at the yogurt shop, and then the law told him that he had to leave the yogurt shop.

Here, we are reminded of the maddening, absurd, and oppressive relationship between African Americans and the American legal system: the legal system that demanded Ragland's presence in the yogurt shop for court-appointed supervision is the same legal system that demanded Ragland's absence from the yogurt shop because the employees were "uncomfortable." It seems, then, that the white gaze of two teenage employees at a local yogurt shop is sufficient to nullify the demands of the legal system that requires Ragland to be in the yogurt shop for his court-appointed job. Not only is this maddeningly absurd, but it is also an act of violence, for, as Levinas points out, "violence does not consist so much in injuring and annihilating persons as in interrupting their continuity, making them play roles in which they no longer recognize themselves, making them betray not only commitments but their own substance, making them carry out actions that will destroy every possibility for action."[46] Ragland's identity was confiscated, distorted and returned to him in such a way that he could not recognize himself. This is precisely what Yancy terms the "confiscation" and the "return" of the Black body. And this is a hallmark of a sort of racial violence that African Americans have historically endured—not physical violence, but violence nonetheless. Ragland's situation is representative of the myriad ways that African Americans are thus always already subjected to the absurd from a legal system that is supposed to have rationality as its cornerstone. When the legal system simultaneously demands his presence in and his absence from the yogurt shop, Ragland's existential situation is Kafkaesque, to say the least.

Wesley Michel

A viral video on social media and news websites shows Christopher Cukor, a white man in San Francisco, calling the police to report Wesley Michel, a Black man, outside of an apartment building who refused to identify himself. Michel is a thirty-five-year-old software engineer who was waiting outside of the San Francisco apartment building for a friend—a rather routine, ordinary activity. Cukor called the police because he saw Michel closely trailing someone who lived in the building to gain access to the building. Cukor demanded to know the name of Michel's friend, to which Michel replied, "I don't have to tell you shit." Cukor is seen on the video calling the police, over the protest of his small child (approximately five to six years old). Michel's friend eventually emerged from the apartment building, the police arrived, and, after a brief investigation, they sent everyone on their way. Cukor has since apologized, citing both recent crime in the area and the shooting death of his father as his reason for calling the police. Several lessons can be learned from this video.

First, the video indicates a certain temporality to the absurd. In this ordinary circumstance, the child's pleading with his father not to call the police represents a temporal struggle between the hopes of the future (the child) and the racism of the present and the past (Cukor). This is pertinent because white people are often the first to demand that African Americans stop talking about America's racist past without doing anything to secure a future free of racism. "How can we move forward," many whites argue, "if we keep living in the past?" Interestingly, the child in this video represents a future America pleading with its racist past and present—a racist past and present that his father represents—to stop its racist practice of using 911 as customer service for non-emergencies. But even as the future demands that the present and the past let go, both maintain their grip, destroying our future. So when white people demand that African Americans "let go of the past," what they really mean is "Stop complaining about the past while we continue to treat you the same way in the present." Out of this mundane situation emerges a Black subjectivity that is discouraged in light of the failure of its hopes for a bright future in the midst of such a dismal and racist past and present. Black people cannot let go of the past when the past is always already the present, and also face a future that, while beckoning for an end to such quotidian racist microaggressions—even as Cukor's small child beckons for his father not to call 911—remains unheard. The Black subject, then, is formed in a temporal context in which the absurdity of the social control of white domination is not only past and present but also, almost predictably, in the future.

Second, the incident occurs in San Francisco, a supposed bastion of progressive thought, what some might call a "safe space." James Baldwin once pointed out that there is no difference between the north and the south. The only difference, according to Baldwin, is "in the way that they castrate you." Anti-Black racism and whiteness are nationwide phenomena that aren't restricted to Mississippi and Alabama. Indeed, so-called "progressive" political locations are sometimes an even greater danger to Black people than conservative political spaces, especially when one considers how racism and whiteness are masked by and function within other progressive communities, such as the LGBTQ community.[47] In this way, the Black subject is not only temporally situated within the absurd but also spatially situated. There are no spaces that are "safe" from the absurdity of white dominance, not even in spaces in which one would be inclined to feel safe for other political reasons, such as being in San Francisco, a place considered a bastion of "progressive" thinking.

Finally, Cukor, toward the end of the video, decides to deflect attention away from his racism by pointing out Michel's use of profanity. This is the father straining at the gnat of the Black man's foul language—foul language that is used out of frustration in response to a racist act—while swallowing the camel of his own racism. Suddenly, the resistance to racism in the form of a stressful use of profanity and in the face of the absurd, in the mind of Cukor, outweighs his racist act of calling the police on an innocent Black man who was waiting for his friend. Here, Michel realizes that the slightest act of resistance to oppression will be met with a false moral condemnation—false because in criticizing the manner of resistance, it has no critique of the racist action that made the protest necessary.

With these two examples, I have tried to show how the Black self is both temporally and spatially situated within the absurd and dangerous world of white social control. Temporally, Black subjectivity is forged in the context of a future relentlessly, furiously, and unsuccessfully trying to overcome its past. Spatially, it is situated in the midst of a pervasively racist social and cultural context, all while being blamed for its mode of resistance and without any critique of the oppression that made its resistance necessary in the first place.

The Double Character of Slavery

Byron Ragland and Wesley Michel represent contemporary examples of how whites use American law and the American legal system as an instrument of social control and white domination. When whites deploy these sorts of legal strategies against Black people in ordinary, everyday situations, Black subjectivity is transformed from a United States Air Force veteran doing his job (Ragland) and a software engineer waiting for his friend (Michel) into people who are "suspicious" and "up to no good." Again, this is what Yancy has so aptly referred to as the confiscation and the return of the Black body.

What makes Ragland and Michel important examples for my purposes in this section of the chapter is the role that law plays in the re-formation of Black subjectivity. When Ragland and Michel are seen as objects of suspicion and criminality by the white gaze, they are thrust into a paradoxical, absurd, dual identity of criminal object and law-abiding subject. Indeed, the very phraseology of "criminal object" is absurd because criminality presupposes a voluntary *actus reus* and a culpable *mens rea*, both of which are attributes of subjects only. The white gaze forces a social identity upon Ragland and Michel such that it is held in tension with who they actually know themselves to be. So Ragland and Michel now have a double character: they are simultaneously both object and subject, law abiding and criminal. Here, I do not mean that they are object and subject in the sense that Jean-Paul Sartre argues in *Being and Nothingness*, as in when one peeks through a keyhole and then realizes that another is looking at him. This is a sort of soft objectification of one's personhood that finds no social or political reinforcement. In contrast, when Ragland and Michel are objectified as "criminal," "suspicious," or "up to no good," one may say that their objectification is a hard sort of objectification because unlike Sartre's examples, their objectification by the white gaze occurs in a historical context of an American legal system that reinforces, and indeed legalizes their objectification. This is because the racial-legal dynamic and its resulting existential absurdity that Ragland and Michel confront in the twenty-first century is nothing new, for long before Ragland and Michel, there were millions of Black slaves who were subject to an entire *corpus juris* that was responsible for their dehumanization, forcing Black slaves into the absurd position of being both person and property. The incidents involving Ragland and Michel and their attendant existential absurdities occur in this troubling historical context.

Legal historian Ariela Gross chronicles "the paradoxes that arose from slaves' double identity as human subjects and the objects of property relations *at one and the same time*."[48] For Gross, the law had a "double character" that manifested itself during the civil trials over white property rights in their slaves. Gross points out:

> Trials also illuminate the double character of white Southerners' racial ideology. At the day-to-day working level, slave masters had no choice but to deal with slaves as people in some respects; to acknowledge that they had preferences, volition, personality, relationships, families—whether or not their masters chose to override all of these by force. Thus in witnesses' testimony as in private slave lists, descriptions of slaves went far beyond the simple "Sambo" and "Nat Turner" stereotypes; while they may not have recognized the full range of human personality, they did include comments on slaves' intelligence, playfulness, and pride. On the other hand, the second quarter of the nineteenth century

saw the development of a highly articulated, stylized racial ideology used in the defense of slavery as a positive good. As legal historians have shown, appellate opinions were part of this highly articulate, outward-looking proslavery defense; judges knew that abolitionists in the North scoured the published reports to find damning evidence of the inhumanity of slavery. It was quite possible for these two discourses of racial ideology to coexist: a white slaveholder could believe on one level that all black people were children; at the same time in his daily life he could expect his slave blacksmith to complete very skilled work, and he could get angry when the work was not completed. [49]

Gross makes a significant contrast in this passage between the realities of whites in their everyday interactions with slaves as people and the development of a *corpus juris* in defense of the white paternalism that saw slaves as property. And it is this double character of the law which translates into an absurd social reality for the slave: on one hand, the slave is treated as a person, and on the other hand, the slave is treated as property. To put this in legal terms, whereas civil trials showed the slaves to be persons, appellate review of those trials and the well-established body of appellate law guaranteed the slaves status as property, despite some arguments to the contrary. Gross points out a tension in the law because despite the best efforts of appellate judges to eliminate any consideration of the slaves as moral agents, the slaves' moral agency nevertheless found its way into the trial process. She writes of the slave legal doctrine known as the "sound price rule." The essence of this rule was "a sound price for a sound commodity," and the legal issue arising from this rule was whether, in ordinary slave sales, the "sound price rule" extended to moral as well as physical characteristics of a slave. Judge Abraham Nott of South Carolina held that it did not. Part of his reasoning, according to Gross, reflected "a deeper uneasiness about the wisdom of opening up slave character as a subject of inquiry at the very moment slaves were to be treated as objects of ownership and transfer."[50] Gross goes on to argue that the very nature of the trial process as it relates to the legal rights of white slave owners to testify as witnesses about their interactions with their slaves on some contested factual issues created a tension in the slave system. Despite white attempts to diminish the slaves' moral agency during the civil slave trial, the tension was inevitable. Gross writes:

> Moral agency meant more than simply that slaves had human qualities. What was threatening to the legal system's effort to treat slaves as chattel was evidence that slaves behaved as morally reasoning, self-governing agents. Yet the logic of the legal system itself guaranteed that litigants in civil disputes would open the door to such evidence, and that it would take work to rationalize this evidence away—to explain it in other terms . . . it was in the legal arena that white men were forced to confront the contradictions such agency raised. . . . Slaves acting

as moral agents in disputes between white men were slaves acting out of their place. When they did so, they raised the stakes in courtroom conflicts over commerce, and legal actors worked hard to put them back in their place.[51]

The slave is thus, before the law, both subject and object. The appellate courts, in the interest of maintaining the slave economy, saw slaves as property, and the trial courts inevitably undid this characterization of slaves through the testimony of white slaveholders about their everyday interactions with their slaves. Thus it is that the law was a catalyst for the absurd, casting the slave in daily life as a person and but theorizing the slave as property in the abstract reflection of appellate review. Relating this to Ragland and Michel, in their daily lives, they consider themselves to be people. But the moment they face the American legal system, indeed the moment they realize that a white person may invoke the power of the legal system against them, they, like the slave, despite their own self-understanding, become objects not only of the white gaze that calls the police but also of a legal system that has historically done them harm. This is the world of the absurd that Ragland, Michel, and Black bodies in general all inhabit. And it was also the world of Douglass.

Douglass's *Narrative* and Kafka's *The Trial*

Douglass inhabits a world in which the law operates to both create and maintain the absurd. Ragland and Michel have inherited this world; a world in which law enforcement are the representatives of the absurd. The etymology of the word "enforcement" is significant here. Enforcement is taken from Old French and it implies "strengthening," "fortification," "rape," "compulsion," and "coercion." So to say that laws are enforced in the context of American chattel slavery and its legacy is to say that there is something nonconsensual about the role that Black bodies such as Ragland's and Michel's play in their interactions with whites and with the police. Ragland and Michel are "raped" insofar as the law is "enforced" upon them. And they are raped because they are "forced" into an existential moment of absurdity in which their identity is called into question, and they must hold—or at least entertain—conflicting and paradoxical beliefs about themselves: one belief based on who they know themselves to be, and the other based upon the historically, socially, and culturally oppressive force of the white gaze. Indeed, as it applies to Black racial embodiment and its relationship to American law and the American legal system, one can credibly argue that Kafka's novel *The Trial* is one that almost any African American could have written. For Black bodies on the receiving end of law enforcement—again, the word "enforcement" is so terribly important here—the absurd has never been their fiction; rather, it has always been their reality, including, of course, Douglass and the millions of slaves who lived with him who suffered the absurdities of chattel slavery. In this last section of the chapter, what I want to do is point out the affinities between Douglass's *Narrative* and *The Trial* to emphasize the importance of existential subjectivity and moral courage in the face of the absurd. As with Kierkegaard, many of Kafka's most important messages to his reader are communicated indirectly; first through the overall story of the novel, and second through a story within a story at the end of the novel with the parable of the law. If Kant was right, the predictability of objective knowledge has its limitations; it can only take us so far. After all, this is why Kant calls mathematics and the natural sciences the "land of truth." Kant points out that if human beings really do understand their place in the world, we will realize that there comes a time when we must set aside our theoretical ambitions and turn to subjective life, which includes the benefit of rational autonomy and the burden of moral responsibility. And this is the great lesson for the reformed epistemology of analytic theism: the end of objectivity is the beginning of responsibility. This is, I believe, the message to be gleaned from my interpretation of Douglass *Narrative* and Kafka's *The Trial*.

The Trial opens, as does Douglass's *Narrative*, with references to birthdays. Kafka tells us that "Someone must have slandered Josef K., for one morning, without having done anything wrong, he was arrested."[52] We are later told that K. thought to himself that maybe the entire incident of his arrest was staged because it was his birthday: "of course he could treat the whole thing as a joke, a crude joke his colleagues at the bank were playing on him for some unknown reason, perhaps because today was his thirtieth birthday."[53] Douglass indicates in the opening pages of his *Narrative* that, as a slave, he did not know his birthday: "I have no authentic record of my age, never having seen any authentic record containing it. By far the larger part of the slaves know as little of their ages as horses know of theirs . . . I do not remember to have ever met a slave who could tell of his birthday."[54] Birthdays are identity indicators. They are, among other things, a way that we distinguish ourselves from one another. Birthdays also represent the beginning of our lives. Each year marks the anniversary of when our life's journey began. These notions of identity and beginning are significant for both K. and Douglass. K., we are told, is an employee at the bank. He seems to be the sort of person who lives a life of regularity and predictability. In fact, from the opening pages of the novel, K.'s shock and his reaction to the officers who came to arrest him suggest that he was caught completely off-guard. Prior to his thirtieth birthday, then, one may say that K. has a certain identity as a productive, predictable creature of habit—a bit boring in his lifestyle, but nonetheless a vivid portrait of bourgeoisie respectability. But on his thirtieth birthday, K. was "born again"; that is, his identity changes into a new life that demands a level of courage from him that he has perhaps never had to use before, insofar as before his thirtieth birthday, the meaning of his life was secure. But on his thirtieth birthday, everything changed. And for the next year of his life, he will be called upon to live very differently than he ever has. Douglass never knew his birthday, so insofar as birthdays represent one's identity, Douglass, unlike K., does not know who he is. The only identity Douglass knows is that he is a slave. His particularities are subsumed within the framework of slavery. K.'s life became absurd. Douglass's life was absurd from the very beginning. K. had to learn to handle the absurdity of existence. Douglass knew how to handle absurdity, but had to learn to navigate freedom. The birthday motif in both works sets the tone for existential subjectivity and its attendant demand for responsibility in the face of freedom.

Both Kafka and Douglass live in worlds surrounded by people who are living in what Sartre would call "bad-faith." The prospect of their freedom, their "forlornness," to borrow a Heidegerrean term, leads them to engage in projects of self-reification, literally manufacturing essences to precede their existences so as to eliminate the need for authentic existential subjectivity and moral responsibility. We see this in *The Trial* with Kafka's account of the floggers, who are the two men who came to his residence to arrest him at the beginning of the story. K. is at work at the bank and he encounters the two men in an old junk room. These two men are being flogged because K. complained about them. K., feeling sorry for the men, attempts to bribe the flogger to stop the beating. The following dialogue ensues between K. and the flogger, with K. speaking first:

> "Is there any possibility of sparing these two a flogging?" . . . "No," said the flogger, and shook his head with a smile. "Strip," he ordered the guards. And to K. he said: "you mustn't believe everything they say. They're already a bit weak in the head because they're so afraid of the flogging" . . . "I'll reward you well if you'll let them go," said K., taking out his wallet without looking at the flogger again, such matters being best conducted by both parties with lowered eyes . . . "I'd pay you extra, to strengthen you in your good work." "I believed what you say," said the flogger, "but I can't be bribed. I've been hired to flog, and flog I will."[55]

Compare the flogger with Douglass's account of Mr. Gore, an overseer on Colonel Lloyd's plantation, where he was a slave:

> Mr. Gore was a grave man, and, though a young man, he indulged in no jokes, said no funny words, seldom smiled. His words were in perfect keeping with his looks, and his looks were in perfect keeping with his words. Overseers will sometimes indulge in a witty word, even with the slaves; not so with Mr. Gore. He spoke but to command, and commanded but to be obeyed; he dealt sparingly with his words, and bountifully with his whip, never using the former where the

latter would answer as well. When he whipped, he seemed to do so from a sense of duty, and feared no consequences. He did nothing reluctantly, no matter how disagreeable; always at his post, never inconsistent. He never promised but to fulfill. He was, in a word, a man of the most inflexible firmness and stone-like coolness.[56]

In both of these situations, there is a socially constructed essence that precedes the existence of these two men. In K.'s encounter with the flogger, we see that the flogger is so committed to his job that he seems to have no agency. He cannot even be persuaded to take a bribe. His role as a flogger has transformed him into what Sartre would call an automaton. In robotic fashion, all that he is able to do is flog. And the same is true of Mr. Gore, who is likewise driven by a strong sense of duty to ensure that his job as an overseer is properly done. Both of these people have allowed themselves to be grafted into oppressive social and political systems to the point where their existential subjectivity is lost. Both the flogger and Mr. Gore have lost themselves. This says something about the effects of oppressive regimes upon those who partake in them. Douglass often spoke of how American chattel slavery dehumanized not only Black slaves but also white slave masters and overseers. Kafka gives us a similar warning with the flogger, who seems to prefigure the excuses of the Nazis who manned the German death camps during the Holocaust. Their steady refrain was often "I was just doing my duty," as though they were not responsible for their murderous actions. Indeed, part of what makes the absurd so problematic is that people perform intentional actions in the name of their employment and then refuse to accept responsibility for those actions. The absurd can thus result in complete abandonment of authentic existential subjectivity, and with it, an abandonment of moral responsibility. K. inhabits this danger in a world of fiction, while Douglass inhabited this danger in reality.

Douglass's and Kafka's works also tell us something important about the relationship between existential subjectivity and the creative insights that allow the self to remain free despite oppressive circumstances. Here, I am interested in the existential contrast between the outer life of scientific natural laws, which describe the external world, and the inner life of poetic, literary, lyrical, and musical expression that reveal the internal word of existential subjectivity. Art takes center stage here in both Kafka and Douglass. Recall that with his arrest on his thirtieth birthday, K. has been "born again." He has assumed a new identity. The predictability and regularity of his objectively lived bourgeoisie existence has died, and he must begin his life all over again in a subjective rather than an objective mode. He must learn to live subjectively and come to understand that his life cannot be explained theoretically, but instead must be lived practically—that he is better off living his life without regard for its absurd circumstances rather than desperately trying to figure out each and every detail of his situation, and must turn inward toward himself and find the courage to be free despite his oppression. But K. never learns this lesson. Instead, he hires a lawyer, Huld, to represent him in his case before the court. Huld is a character in the story who represents the essence of rationality because he does what lawyers do: they make arguments. But they can only make arguments after the basic requirements of notice and an opportunity to be heard are afforded to their clients. Here, we can see that hiring a lawyer is a nonstarter for K. because there cannot be any notice of the charges, as no one has ever told him the charges lodged against him. And though his lawyer will have ample time to talk in court, what will he discuss? What arguments will he make? How will he ever know what precedents to discuss in his written arguments to the court without knowing the charges against his client? Huld cannot do anything to help K. because as a character representative of rationality, his skills are useless in the face of the absurd. Moreover, we are told that Huld has a heart problem. This is significant. As a character who represents rationality, Huld's problem is internal; it is in his heart. Huld is lacking in the passion and inwardness that he needs to be able to turn from objectivity and deal with the absurd through an authentic existential subjectivity. We can see this heart problem at work in his representation of Block, the merchant, who once had a thriving business, but now, because he has spent so much money on Huld's representation of him, he finds himself destitute and hopeless. This is because Huld never made the move away from objective rationality and toward subjective inwardness, and it has severely affected his client.

In contrast to Huld, K. comes across a painter named Titorelli, who paints portraits of the judges on the court. The painter, Titorelli, seemingly allows an essence to determine his existence—he is a third/fourth-generation painter. But this is disrupted because he paints the judges as he sees them, not as anyone tells him. This speaks to a space of existential freedom based upon his phenomenological standpoint. From his vantage point, he cannot help but paint the judges as *he sees them*, and not as anyone else sees them. Titorelli has thus found a way to exercise his freedom in the midst of the absurd because of art. However, not only does Titorelli find a place for existential freedom, but he also is able to give K. some insight into the possible outcomes of his case, which is something that Huld, despite all of his work on the case as K.'s lawyer, could never do. This tells us something about the role of art in oppressive social and political regimes: through creativity, one can gain insight into the absurdities of life and can use that insight to thrive despite the oppressive circumstances. This is precisely what the slaves were able to do, according to Douglass. In the *Narrative*, Douglass describes the slave songs:

I have sometimes thought that the mere hearing of those songs would do more to impress some minds with the horrible character of slavery, than the reading of whole volumes of philosophy on the subject could do. . . . To those songs I trace my first glimmering conception of the dehumanizing character of slavery. I can never get rid of that conception. Those songs still follow me, to deepen my hatred of slavery, and quicken my sympathies for my brethren in bonds. If any one wishes to be impressed with the soul-killing effects of slavery, let him go to Colonel Lloyd's plantation, and, on allowance-day, place himself in the deep pine woods, and there let him in silence, analyze the sounds that shall pass through the chambers of his soul,—and if he is not thus impressed, it will only be because there is no flesh in his obdurate heart.[57]

Douglass's first statement here is a compelling one, for he juxtaposes the art of musical expression with philosophical knowledge. The slave song gave him an insight into the wretchedness of slavery that no rational discourse could do. Somehow, the slaves, like Titorelli, the painter, found a way, through the power of artistic expression, to create meaning in their lives despite their oppressive circumstances. If, like K., the slaves had tried to make sense of the absurdities that confronted them in daily life, they, also like K., would have continued to frustrate themselves. But despite their bondage, they found freedom through an inward turn to existential subjectivity, understanding that art reaches a place where the chains of captivity cannot bind them: their spirit. In fact, there is a biblical notion of spirit that one may employ here to show the need for internal artistic expression. In Scripture, before God created the heavens and the earth, the spirit moved.[58] The word for spirit here is the Hebrew word, רוּחַ, transliterated as *ruwach*, which means "breath," and in one of its meanings, also means courage. It takes courage to be creative in the face of the absurd, particularly when, as I have pointed out earlier in this chapter, the problem of anteriority prevents any coherent epistemological or metaphysical explanation for one's plight. In the face of an absurd world, art becomes the site of free expression and of the solace of the soul. Both Titorelli, through painting, and the slaves, through music and song, illustrate this important principle.

Communication plays a significant role in the life of Douglass and K. For Kierkegaard, indirect communication is how one accomplishes subjective appropriation and double reflection. For K., however, the attempt at indirect communication was unable to reach him. But for Douglass, the indirect communication was successful. Near the end of K.'s year-long journey through his arrest and his court case, he encounters a priest who tells him a parable. Now famously known as the parable of the law, the story is about a man who came from the country and sought admission to the law. But there was a doorkeeper who told the man that he could not grant him admission to the law, but even if he did, the man from the country would encounter many other doorkeepers who were more intimidating than him. The doorkeeper tells the man from the country that he cannot grant him admittance to the law right now, but that later "it's possible" he'll be allowed to enter. So the man from the country spends his entire life waiting to be admitted to the law, and when he is old and his senses are failing him, the doorkeeper tells the man from the country that "No one else could gain admittance here, because this entrance was meant solely for you. I'm going to go and shut it now."[59] K.'s initial reaction to the parable is to tell the priest that the doorkeeper deceived the man. But the priest explains to K. that the doorkeeper has not deceived the man at all. The doorkeeper says, "The story contains two important statements by the doorkeeper concerning admittance to the Law. . . . The one passage says: 'that he can't grant him admittance now'; and the other: 'this entrance was meant solely for you' . . . the first statement even implies the second."[60] One can interpret the parable to mean that the doorkeeper did nothing other than say to the man from the country that he could not grant him admittance to the law because it was the man's responsibility to simply walk through the door himself. This is precisely the reason for the second statement that the entrance was meant solely for the man from the country. If the entrance was meant solely for him, then he was the only one who could go through the door on his own, without permission from anyone else, including the doorkeeper. The priest is trying to show K. himself and how he is approaching his trial. Rather than passively wait for things to happen to him, K. has to accept some responsibility and make things happen. That is, K. can best deal with his trial without losing himself in it, something that is happening because he is not approaching the trial subjectively, but rather objectively. It is the lack of authentic existential subjectivity in the face of the absurd that has K., as it has the man from the country, paralyzed, and losing his entire life waiting for others to do for him what only he can do for himself.

In contrast to the man from the country, Douglass confronts an indirect communication and sees himself, applies it to himself, and proceeds to make the most of his life as a free person after his escape from slavery. This indirect communication is the fictional dialogue between the master and the slave in the *Columbian Orator*, as discussed earlier in the chapter. Douglass ends up doing the very thing that the slave did in the dialogue; he finds himself standing before slavery's supporters for the rest of his life making arguments against slavery and in favor of newly freed slaves. Unlike K., Douglass made what Kierkegaard would call the move of "subjective appropriation": he actually applied the communication to himself such that it created a change in him. Rather than waste away waiting to gain "admittance" to the law, Douglass accepted full responsibility for his life, doing for himself, rather than waiting for others to do for him. Douglass went on to become one of the most world-renowned abolitionists, ambassador to Haiti, and an advisor to President Abraham Lincoln. In contrast, K. had relinquished his existential subjectivity—himself—to such a degree that he walks so closely with his captors as to assume the place of "lifeless matter."[61] Thus it is that K. dies, not like a human being, but instead "Like a dog."[62]

Douglass's *Narrative* and Kafka's *The Trial* both illustrate how literary strategies are intended to reawaken existential subjectivity in the face of the absurd. They accomplish this by emphasizing the importance of identity, creativity, and responsibility, which are enduring themes in the existentialist philosophical and literary tradition.

TOWARD A PHENOMENOLOGY OF BLACK SUFFERING

The framework of Incarnational theology was applied in this chapter on a much smaller scale than the overall project of the book in an attempt to emphasize the corruption in the communities of Kierkegaard and Douglass. And it is through this application that we saw that contrary to the Incarnational way of transcendence, which causes a genuine conversion in the individual, there is a Greek philosophical way of immanence in which religious experience is reduced to the incidental moment of recollection. The latter was the way of the Danish State Church and the slaveholding Christians of Saint Michael's, who both desperately needed a genuine conversion. Both Kierkegaard and Douglass employ creative strategies to reach such deluded people, Kierkegaard through pseudonyms and Douglass through his use of narrative. Douglass's life also bears the strong imprint of the absurd at the level of the quotidian. American law and its legal systems are the catalyst for this absurdity, as they allow for the absurd and paradoxical formulations of Black subjectivity from contemporary situations all the way back to Douglass. Despite these absurdities, Douglass manages his situation a bit better than Josef K., who finds himself unable to make the move of existential subjectivity in the face of the absurd. Douglass becomes a normative philosophical figure, showing us how one ought to courageously and creatively face the absurd.

For all that this chapter says about Douglass as an existentialist in a Kierkegaardian vein, there is also much to be said about the phenomenological dimensions of Douglass's work. These dimensions have far-reaching implications for philosophical and theological reflection, as phenomenology introduces us to a methodology designed for a different access into subjectivity than existentialism, demanding an attentiveness to the pre-theoretical aspects of subjective life. How this methodology can be used to interpret

Douglass is what I discuss in the following chapter, where I introduce Husserl and Levinas as Douglass's dialogue partners in phenomenology. This dialogue is needed, in part at least, because I believe the phenomenological method helps to alleviate the disturbing philosophical, theological, and moral implications of Black suffering.[63] Let us now turn to this dialogue.

NOTES

1. *Holy Bible*, Mark 4:2 (World English Version).
2. Here, I am referring to Alvin Plantinga's rejoinder to John Mackie's essay "Evil and Omnipotence," in Plantinga's *God, Freedom, and Evil* (Harper & Row, 1974).
3. Merold Westphal, "Teleological Suspensions," in *Levinas and Kierkegaard in Dialogue* (Indianapolis: Indiana University Press, 2008), 50.
4. Ibid., 50–51.
5. Ibid.
6. See Alvin Plantinga, *God, Freedom, and Evil*.
7. An excellent discussion of the debate over Hegelian theology and its role in Christian theology in Kierkegaard's Denmark, along with the principal texts of that debate, is found in *Mynster's "Rationalism, Supernaturalism" and the Debate about Mediation*, ed. and trans. Jon Stewart (Copenhagen: Museum Tusculanum, 2009).
8. Georg Wilhelm Friedrich Hegel, "The Science of Logic," in *Hegel's Logic*, trans. William Wallace (London: Oxford University Press, 1975), 3.
9. Ibid., 167.
10. Jon Stewart, "The Debate Surrounding Hegel's Criticism of the Laws of Classical Logic in Golden Age Denmark," in *Mynster's "Rationalism, Supernaturalism" and the Debate about Mediation*, 11.
11. Hegel, "The Science of Logic," 172.
12. Ibid.
13. See *Mynster's "Rationalism, Supernaturalism" and the Debate about Mediation*.
14. Ibid., 130.
15. Ibid., 95.
16. Ibid., 110.
17. Ibid., 109.
18. Søren Kierkegaard, *Concluding Unscientific Postscript to Philosophical Fragments*, trans. and ed. Howard V. and Edna H. Hong (Princeton, NJ: Princeton University Press, 1992), 380.
19. Ibid., 50–51.
20. Ibid., 368.
21. Frederick Douglass, *Narrative of the life of Frederick Douglass, an American slave*, with preface by William Lloyd Garrison (Boston: Anti-Slavery Office, 1849), 53–54. Retrieved from https://www.loc.gov/item/82225385/.
22. Ibid., 57.
23. Ibid., 56.

24. Douglass, *Narrative*, 77–78.
25. Ibid., 78.
26. Ibid.
27. Ibid.
28. Ibid.
29. Ibid., 81.
30. That Kierkegaard is attempting to achieve social and cultural renewal finds support in the *Concluding Unscientific Postscript*, where Climacus writes of another pseudonymous work, *Fear and Trembling*, that

> To call this book "*eine erhabnene Lüge* [a noble lie]" . . . is in my opinion significant, inasmuch as the expression itself contains a contradiction. The contrast of form is altogether necessary for every production in these spheres. In the form of direct communication, in the form of bellowing, fear and trembling are insignificant, because the direct communication expressly indicates that the direction is outward, toward screaming, not inward into the abyss of inwardness, where fear and trembling first become terrible, with when expressed can be only in a deceptive form. Of course, I cannot know with certainty Johannes de Silentio's actual situation, since I do not know him personally, and even if I did, I am not exactly inclined to think that he would want to make a fool of himself by giving a direct communication. (Kierkegaard, *Concluding Unscientific Postscript*, 262)

Climacus is making the point here that even as Plato used the phraseology of "noble lie" to refer to the Myth of the Metals in his *Republic* to encourage cultural renewal and solidarity, he is doing something similar with *Fear and Trembling*, which is the story of Abraham's near sacrifice of his son, Isaac (Gen. 22: 1–14). I discuss the Myth of the Metals from Plato's *Republic* in more detail in note 44 below, as it relates to Plato and Douglass. The point here is that, for Kierkegaard, none of his pseudonymous works are intended to be taken directly or, one might say, literally. Instead, pseudonymity, as a method of indirect communication, is more about the creation of another person in another world to help disabuse people of false ideas than it is about the communication of divine commands or imperatives. So in this passage, Climacus is making the point that *Fear and Trembling* is to be understood more as a metaphor for the difficulties attending a life of faith than it is about a direct communication about child sacrifice. See Ronald M. Green, "Enough Is Enough! 'Fear and Trembling' Is Not about Ethics," *Journal of Religious Ethics* 21, no. 2 (1993): 191–209.

31. Søren Kierkegaard, *The Point of View for My Work as an Author*, trans. Howard V. and Edna H. Hong (Princeton, NJ: Princeton University Press, 1998), 54.
32. Ibid., 43.
33. Hans Lassen Martensen, "Rationalism, Supernaturalism, and the *principium exclusi medii*," in *Mynster's "Rationalism, Supernaturalism" and the Debate about Mediation*, ed. and trans. Jon Stewart (Copenhagen: Museum Tusculanum, 2009), 130.
34. Ibid.
35. Kierkegaard, *Postscript*, 383.
36. *Holy Bible*, Exodus 33:12–23.

37. For an excellent discussion of Xenophanes, see Sarah Broadie, "Rational Theology," in *The Cambridge Companion to Early Greek Philosophy*, ed. A. A. Long (New York: Cambridge University Press, 1999), 205–24. The discussion on Xenophanes's critique of anthropomorphic theology can be found at 208–12. For Feuerbach, see *The Essence of Christianity*, trans. George Eliot (Amherst, NY: Prometheus Books, 1989).

38. Frederick Douglass, "Pictures and Progress," speech delivered on December 3, 1861, *The Frederick Douglass Papers*, vol. 3, ed. John W. Blassingame (New Haven, CT: Yale University Press, 1985), 462.

39. Douglass was careful to point out that philosophical discussions of slavery paled in comparison to artistic creativity. He wrote in his *Narrative* that the music of slave songs could do more to portray the plight of slaves than "volumes of philosophy" could ever do. See Douglass's *Narrative*, 14.

40. William Lloyd Garrison, *Narrative*, ix.

41. Douglass, *Narrative*, 40.

42. I am referring to the notion of basic beliefs in reformed epistemology that is based upon the work of Thomas Reid. See especially William P. Alston's discussion of "The Autonomy of Doxastic Practices" in *Perceiving God: The Epistemology of Religious Experience* (Ithaca, NY: Cornell University Press, 1991), 149–53.

43. Kierkegaard, *Concluding Unscientific Postscript*, 21.

44. Although Plato doesn't want the poets in the *Kallipolis* because of the mimetic and violent nature of their poetry, in book three of the *Republic*, he advocates a poetic form of expression through storytelling in the myth of the metals to build solidarity in the *Kallipolis*. See *Republic* (414b7–415d-4). Moreover, the presentation of Plato's work is not straightforward philosophical argument as one finds in, say, Aristotle. In contrast, Plato gives his reader an admixture of poetic dialogue and philosophical argumentation. Plato thus attempted to engender national solidarity and political obligation. Douglass did something similar throughout his corpus to both abolish slavery and help shape the future of a world without it: he employed a rich combination of substantive, rigorous, philosophical argumentation (his use of moral suasion) and creative, methodological, artistic presentation (his use of first-person narrative and story). Douglass recognized that, on one hand, logic helps us clarify our theoretical position, but, on the other hand, it is art in general and the art of storytelling in particular that can change our behavior. That this was Douglass's approach is important in a country like America, which has always had difficulty getting her conduct toward its citizens to correspond to the level of her rhetoric, and thus has needed her conduct to change; especially her conduct toward African Americans. Indeed Cone points out that poetry and other art forms like narrative and music remind us, in a way that theoretical reflection alone cannot, of America's profound political and moral failures when it comes to African Americans. If we can, as Plato did, conceive of theoretical reflection as "knowledge" and poetry as "inspiration," and if poetic inspiration can be such a sobering reminder of moral and political obligation, then perhaps one can read the following statement from Plato's *Ion* as complementing rather than castigating the poets: "For a poet is an airy thing, winged and holy, and he is not able to make poetry until he becomes inspired and goes out of his mind and his intellect is no longer in

him. As long as a human being has his intellect in his possession he will always lack the power to make poetry or sing prophecy" (534b4-c1). Thus it may be a *virtue* that a poet is out of his "mind" when inspired; for to be out of one's mind is to be free from the temptations of abstraction, generality, and hyper-theorization long enough to recognize one's moral and political obligations. And perhaps Douglass, in using his narrative methodology, was "out of his mind" not in the sense that he was insane, but rather in the sense of understanding that there are times when changing the world can only occur if either a new world is created (the notion of "poetic justice" in fiction) or people are allowed access into a world that is otherwise strange to them (Douglass's use of narrative).

45. Saidiya Hartman, *Scenes of Subjection: Terror, Slavery, and Self-Making in Nineteenth Century America* (London: Oxford University Press, 1997), 4.

46. Emmanuel Levinas, *Totality and Infinity: An Essay on Exteriority*, trans. Alfonso Lingis (Pittsburgh, PA: Duquesne University Press, 1969), 21.

47. See Rae Rosenberg, "The Whiteness of Gay Urban Belonging: Criminalizing LGBT Youth of Color in Queer Spaces of Care," *Urban Geography* 38, no. 1 (2016): 137–48, and Jane Ward, "White Normativity: The Cultural Dimensions of Whiteness in a Racially Diverse LGBT Organization," *Sociological Perspectives* 51, no. 3 (2008): 563–86.

48. Ariela J. Gross, *Double Character: Slavery and Mastery in the Antebellum Southern Courtroom* (Athens: University of Georgia Press, 2006), 3.

49. Ibid., 5.

50. Ibid., 72.

51. Ibid., 73.

52. Franz Kafka, *The Trial*, trans. Breon Mitchell (New York: Shocken Books, 1998), 3.

53. Ibid., 6.

54. Douglass, *Narrative*, 1.

55. Kafka, *The Trial*, 82–83.

56. Douglass, *Narrative*, 22.

57. Ibid., 14.

58. *Holy Bible*, Gen. 1:2.

59. Kafka, *The Trial*, 217.

60. Ibid., 217–18.

61. Ibid., 226.

62. Ibid., 231.

63. Scholars have provided extensive critiques of accounts of Black suffering in Black theology and its connection to theodicy and free will defenses. See Anthony Pinn, *Why Lord? Suffering and Evil in Black Theology* (New York: Continuum, 1995) and *Is God a White Racist? A Preamble to Black Theology* (Boston, MA: Beacon Press, 1998).

Chapter Three

Overcoming Theodicy

Narrative, Poetry, and the Phenomenology of Suffering

"Can you fathom the mystery of God? Or can you probe the limits of the Almighty? They are high as heaven. What can you do? They are deeper than Sheol. What can you know? Its measure is longer than the earth, and broader than the sea."

—*Holy Bible*[1]

"The King will answer them, 'Most certainly I tell you, inasmuch as you did it to one of the least of these my brothers, you did it to me.'"

—*Holy Bible*[2]

"If a man says, 'I love God,' and hates his brother, he is a liar; for he who doesn't love his brother whom he has seen, how can he love God whom he has not seen?"

—*Holy Bible*[3]

DOUGLASS AND LEVINAS

Frederick Douglass and Emmanuel Levinas have plenty of differences. Douglass was an African American; Levinas was a European Jew. Douglass, born a slave, had no formal philosophical education or training, as it was illegal for slaves to read, let alone pursue graduate level education, whereas Levinas not only studied philosophy but also wrote a dissertation on the theory of intuition in Edmund Husserl's phenomenology. Douglass, through much of his life, was, legally speaking, considered ordinary chattel, no different from a table or a chair, and according to American chattel slavery's jurisprudence, Douglass was unable to even legally own a copy of his autobiographical narrative. This was because, legally speaking, property could not own property. Indeed, to say that Douglass owned a copy of his narrative was as ridiculous as saying that the sofa owns the clock. Douglass also had to indicate that his autobiographical narrative was "written by himself" because of the widespread belief that white abolitionists wrote slave narratives as part of anti-slavery propaganda machine, because slaves were not only illiterate—again, it was illegal for a slave to read—but also considered intellectually inferior and thus incapable of producing any written document whatsoever. Levinas, however, while having the claims of his philosophical texts exegeted, elaborated upon, scrutinized, interrogated, and critiqued as an ordinary part of scholarly discourse, has never had the authorship of his texts called into question.

But despite these vast cultural, religious, and sociological differences, Douglass and Levinas have some philosophical and theological things in common. They both lived with oppression: Douglass lived in the oppressive regime of American chattel slavery, and the Germans captured Levinas, forcing him to live as a prisoner of war during World War II, while many of his family members were killed in concentration camps as part of the Jewish Holocaust. Both lived through these atrocities sequentially in two different centuries and on different continents—Douglass in nineteenth-century America, and Levinas in twentieth-century Europe. The worst atrocities of the nineteenth century are arguably chattel slavery, its Christian justification, and its legacy of Jim Crow and lynching that Christianity likewise justified. And among the worst atrocities of the twentieth century was the Jewish Holocaust of World War II. Throughout their lives, both thinkers sought ethical solutions to the problems that they faced, and these solutions assumed philosophical and theological proportions throughout their respective oeuvres. Douglass's work was philosophical and theological because he was involved in an ongoing critical engagement with slaveholding Christianity, Jim Crow, and lynching,[4] and Levinas interrogated the entirety of Western philosophy for its emphasis on the autonomy and freedom of the self at the expense of a genuine care and concern for the Other. Their moral struggles within the systems of oppression that they resisted led both philosophers to a more human-centered understanding of God, arguing for a grounding of religious life in the terrestrial rather than the celestial sphere. Both are interested in what Levinas calls "the interhuman order," rather than the abstract realm of metaphysical speculation about God and epistemic justification of beliefs in God, as with the reformed epistemology of analytic theism. Indeed, the interhuman order is not only a concrete reality in the here and now as opposed to an eschatological beyond; it is, as I will discuss later in the chapter, prior to all positive law, hypothetical states of nature, and legal and political arrangements between people termed "citizens," for prior to the citizen is the face of infinity in the Other who beckons me not to do it any harm.

My aim in this chapter is to interpret Douglass and Levinas together, considering their moral struggles within their respective crises of oppression to show how they both question the legitimacy of philosophical and theological abstraction—specifically, theodicy. I am interested in their critiques of theodicy in light of the extensive amount of evil and suffering in their respective worlds, evil that is overlooked in analytic theism, except as a resource for a vast proliferation of hypotheticals, thought experiments, and abstractions that ignore pressing moral, social, existential, and political concerns. I interpret Douglass and Levinas with Husserl in this chapter to show how a crisis demands a radical return to human responsibility. I argue that Douglass's narrative methodology prefigures Husserl's phenomenological reduction during the nineteenth-century crisis of American chattel slavery. Husserl was, of course, responding to what he termed the "crisis of the European sciences" in the twentieth century, and Levinas works in the shadow of the crisis of the European sciences during the crisis of the Jewish Holocaust in the twentieth century. Specifically, I argue that Douglass and Levinas, on either chronological side of Husserl, produce phenomenological insights that move from the transcendence of God as a mere object of ontotheological speculation to the immanence of God in the face of the Other that calls us to infinite moral responsibility within the interhuman order through a suspension of what I shall call the "theological attitude." I conclude that both Douglass and Levinas are doing phenomenology, for, as Levinas points out, adherence to the rigorous phenomenological method is not required for one to do phenomenology. All that is required is a "proceeding back from the thought" (of God) to the "fullness of the thought" (of God).[5] For both Douglass and Levinas, I argue that the "fullness of the thought" of God is a phenomenological-aesthetic depiction of human suffering in the form of poetry that demonstrates the uselessness of suffering and demands a moral attentiveness to the Other in the interhuman order.

My interpretation of Douglass and Levinas develops in four phases. First, in the next section of this chapter, I situate both Douglass's and Levinas's work within the ethical realm of concrete moral life here on Earth, as opposed to the abstract speculation of a metaphysically and epistemologically driven attempt to develop and maintain a theology of God. Such abstract speculation, which is the task of the ontotheologically based reformed epistemology of analytic theism, results in a philosophical god that is an explanatory first principle rather than an existentially authentic religious deity. This god is the god before whom, as Heidegger declared, no one can sing or dance, but who provided—and continues to provide—explanatory force for myriad evils based upon the principle of sufficient reason.⁶ Both Douglass and Levinas eschew this god of abstract theorizations in favor of a more concrete and authentic understanding of moral and religious life. I conclude in this section that Douglass's suspension of the theological attitude prefigures what Husserl will call a suspension of the "transcendence of God,"⁷ and that Levinas's "atheism" does the same, causing Levinas to admit that "in spite of everything, what I do is phenomenology."⁸

In phase two of my interpretation of Douglass and Levinas, I argue that Douglass's narrative methodology is consistent with his humanistic conception of religion in that it effects a prefigured phenomenological "suspension" of metaphysical speculation and epistemic justification in favor of exposing a life-world in which Douglass experiences suffering. And not only does Douglass experience suffering, but, through his turn to the poetic and away from the propositional function of language, predication (Levinas's notion of "the said") gives way to aesthetic, poetic, creativity (Levinas's notion of "the saying") that demands our moral attention. Douglass functions here within the theological, providing a poetic depiction of suffering that is consistent with the Judeo-Christian tradition. Using two previously discussed examples of poetry from his autobiographical narrative, I attempt to show in the next phase of my argument that by drawing attention away from himself to the death of his grandmother and to the plight of slaves in bondage, Douglass effects a "holy aesthetic," moving from the ontologically fixed meaning of the said to the ethical import of the saying. Within this realm of the saying, Douglass establishes a "poetic said" that "communicates the profundity of the saying through writing."⁹ Douglass, though pointing out the problem of evil in these poetic examples, does not attempt to resolve it through philosophical speculation. Instead, Douglass articulates the problem of evil, and then leaves the problem where he finds it, disrupting the ontologized, fixed nature of the said of analytic theism, with a poetic demonstration of the saying, in writing, thus creating a phenomenological, "poetic said." Douglass's phenomenological aesthetics is thus a demonstration of Levinas's understanding of poetry as distinguished from other, mimetic art forms.

Douglass's aporetic treatment of the problem of evil in favor of a first-person account of his suffering that is poetic rather than propositional has some affinities with Levinas as it relates to the issue of theodicy and to Levinas's project of ethics as first philosophy. In his essay, "Useless Suffering," Levinas points to the need to see suffering not as part of a thematized, metaphysical, and epistemological dialectic, but rather as a "useless" "datum of consciousness." Suspending the theoretical understanding of suffering and evil, Levinas, like Douglass, leaves the problem of evil where he finds it, and is instead interested in the "unassumability" of suffering that makes it "useless." And despite Levinas's criticisms of art, his embrace of poetic discourse as a sort of "holy aesthetic"[10] means that Douglass's poetic reflections on suffering, which occur in the aporetic space created by his refusal to engage what I have called the "problem of anteriority" in the introduction, represent precisely such a holy aesthetic: they call us toward a demand for moral treatment of the Other.

SETTING THE STAGE FOR PHENOMENOLOGY: MORAL RESPONSIBILITY IN DOUGLASS AND LEVINAS

Douglass's conception of religion was humanistic in nature. His critical view of Christian arguments in favor of chattel slavery led him to suspect that an over-reliance on God and on divine providence was not the most constructive way to achieve either abolition or long-term liberation for slaves. There is a debate in the extant literature on Douglass as to whether he was religious at all, or whether his assessment of Christianity was that of an enlightenment deist, who saw religion as an immoral form of superstition.[11] I am not interested in entering this debate here. Instead, I want to show that, with respect to Douglass's relationship to Christianity, there is ample evidence to suggest that Douglass rejected metaphysical and epistemological subtleties because of their philosophical and theological use from within Christianity to justify chattel slavery. Instead, Douglass—and Levinas, who writes after him in the twentieth century—wanted a radical acceptance of human responsibility both for the existence of injustice and for continued resistance to it. Slaves and other people of good will could not wait for the supernatural to accomplish what the natural was able to accomplish. Moral responsibility for humans and by humans was Douglass's message. Humans brought slavery into existence, and it would take humans to abolish it. Douglass argued that "The great difficulty about our Christianity is, we have got certain notions that turn off our attention from humanity all together."[12] Earlier in that same speech, Douglass argues that ignoring the human dimension of religion is the main reason for slavery:

> I believe the grand reason why we have Slavery in this land at the present moment is that we are too religious as a nation, in other words, that we have substituted religion for humanity—we have substituted a form of Godliness,[13] an outside show for the real thing itself. We have houses built for the worship of God, which are regarded as too sacred to plead the cause of the down-trodden millions in them. They will tell you in these churches that they are willing to receive you to talk to them about the sins of the Scribes and Pharisees, or on the subject of the heathenism of the South Sea Islands, or on any of the subjects

connected with missions, the Tract Society, the Bible Society, and other societies connected with the Church, but the very moment you ask them to open their mouths for the liberation of Southern slaves, they tell you, that is a subject with which they have nothing to do, and which they do not wish to have introduced into the Church; it is foreign to the object for which churches in the country were formed, and houses built.[14]

Douglass's critique of institutionalized Christianity is strong here. When he points to the "form" of Godliness, he is arguing that a formal, abstract understanding of religion has eclipsed the human dimension of religion, where one does justice to one's neighbor. Matters of personal piety, condemnation of "heathens" from foreign lands,[15] and the distribution of Bible literature—all "forms" of religiosity—take precedence over rendering aid to slaves who are held in bondage. On slavery, which was, for Douglass, the most important issue, the Church remained silent, and it was this silence that spoke loudest and most directly to the reality of slavery as an ongoing problem. For Douglass, the moral responsibility to address slavery could not be greater, and the same can be said for the moral failing of the church to address this most important issue. Again, Douglass believed that since human beings created slavery, it was up to human beings—not God—to abolish it. In some ways, as Lewis Gordon and George Yancy have pointed out, Douglass prefigures twentieth-century Sartrean and Fanonian existentialism on this point.[16] Indeed, Douglass not only understood, as did Jean-Paul Sartre and Simone de Beauvoir, that his politically and socially constructed essence of "slave" did not determine his existence[17] but also understood, as did Frantz Fanon, the dangers of metaphysical speculation when compared with the more urgent matters of Black existence. Douglass would certainly agree with Fanon that "ontology leaves existence by the wayside."[18] Indeed, one can argue that Douglass wants to reverse this problem so that existence leaves ontology by the wayside.

There are other instances of Douglass's criticisms of an overemphasis on religion. For example, there is Douglass's criticism of Reverend Godwin's argument for Negro baptism. I have written more extensively about this argument elsewhere,[19] but I recount the argument and Douglass's response to it here because I think that it exemplifies that sort of philosophical reasoning that led Douglass to move away from theoretical approaches to Christianity and more toward humanistic approaches. In other words, arguments like the one for Negro baptism are Douglass's motivation for a narrative approach that "suspends" theoretical discussions of God and enables a "proceeding back from what is thought"—God—"toward the fullness of the thought itself"[20]—a creative, poetic, and deeply moral fullness that enables the Other to make demands upon the self from within the utterly asymmetrical and non-reciprocal interhuman order rather than in an eschatological beyond.

According to Douglass, there was a controversy in the late eighteenth-century American slaveholding Christianity over whether it was permissible to baptize a slave. Douglass points out that the controversy was significant because it addressed whether and to what extent a slave could be considered human. If the slave had a soul that could be baptized, then the slave was a human and a moral being. And if the slave was a human and a moral being, then there was a clear basis for the slaveholding Christian church to perhaps admit that they were wrong in their participation and justification of chattel slavery and the slave trade. So there was much at stake as it related to the argument for Negro baptism. Douglass says that the real issue was not baptism, but rather "what might follow such baptism. The sprinkling him with water was a very simple thing and easily gotten along with, but the slaveholders of that day saw in the innovation something more dangerous than cold water."[21] What they saw about baptizing slaves was the much more serious problem that would arise, when, upon baptism, slaves were made to be members of the church of Christ, heirs to the legacy of Christ, and humans that were now part of the body of Christ—the same body of Christ of which whites claimed to be a part. Beyond that, baptizing the slave would "take him out of the category of heathenism and make it inconsistent to hold him a slave, for the Bible made only the heathen a proper subject for slavery."[22] For Douglass, then, baptism of the slave seemed to go hand-in-hand with abolition. Douglass reasons that because of this connection, "Christian slaveholders of that day viewed these consequences with immeasurable horror. It was something more terrible and dangerous than the Civil Rights Bill and the Fourteenth and Fifteenth Amendments to our Constitution."[23] So it was that because of such devastating consequences for slaveholding Christianity, "It was a difficult thing, therefore, at that day to get the Negro into water."[24]

None of this deterred Dr. Godwin, who, according to Douglass, was both "a celebrated divine of his time"[25] and "a skilled dialectician."[26] Godwin could "not only divide the word with skill, but he could divide the Negro into two parts. He argued that the Negro had a soul as well as a body, and insisted that while his body rightfully belonged to his master on earth, his soul belonged to his master in heaven."[27] Douglass continues by saying that "By this convenient arrangement, somewhat metaphysical, to be sure, but entirely evangelical and logical, the problem of Negro baptism was solved."[28] Douglass then, somewhat disappointed, critiques the argument:

> But with the Negro in this case, as I have said, the argument was not entirely satisfactory. The operation was much like that by which the white man got the turkey and the Indian got the crow. When the Negro looked for his body, that

belonged to his earthly master; when he looked around for his soul, that had been appropriated by his heavenly Master; and when he looked around for something that really belonged to himself, he found nothing but his shadow, and that vanished into thin air, when he might most want it.[29]

Significantly, before Douglass critiques the argument, he refers to it as being "somewhat metaphysical, to be sure."[30] And one can see why. After all, Godwin's resort to a Cartesian psychological dualism rent the slave into a body and a soul and, all at once, justified both their baptism into the faith and their continued enslavement. Douglass complains that this argument was "metaphysical" in nature and thus was of no benefit at all to slaves, despite acknowledging that they had souls. Douglass thus had good reason to believe that metaphysical reasoning about souls, bodies, and God was more likely to be responsible for maintaining rather than abolishing slavery. One sees this in Douglass's critique of philosophical and theological abstraction when he argues that "when a child first comes into the world, it don't cry for metaphysics or theology, but for a little milk."[31]

We also see Douglass's humanistic approach to Christianity at work in his defense of William Lloyd Garrison. Douglass speaks of how when he was a member of the Methodist Episcopal Church, he heard criticism of Garrison for being an infidel.[32] Looking for a substantiation of such a charge, Douglass said that he "wanted to hear what his infidelity consisted in."[33] So he carefully listened to Garrison. Douglass says "the moment I heard him pour out his soul in behalf of the downtrodden bondsman and utter his voice against the oppressor as if his own wife and children were in chains, I wanted to know nothing further of his religious views."[34] This was enough for Douglass, as he was convinced after hearing Garrison's support for the slave and disdain for the slave holder that Garrison was not an infidel, but rather a true Christian. Douglass continues on to say that once he heard Garrison condemn slavery,

> I felt that in his heart was the love of Christ, and that was the Christianity for me. I did not want to know anything of his *abstract faith*, for I felt very much as I suppose John the Baptist felt when he received the tidings from Christ, saying: "Go tell John that the deaf hear, the blind see, the poor have the Gospel preached unto them." Those works testified as to what manner of man he was, as to whence he came, and what his objects were. When we see men binding up the wounds of those who fall among thieves, administering to the necessities of the down-trodden, and breaking off the chains of the bondsmen, it is evidence enough that their works are of God, and, *whatever may be their abstract notions*, Christ himself lives within them; for this was his spirit. He went about doing good to the souls and bodies of men. Whenever the cry of sorrow saluted his hear there he was to soothe and console the afflicted heart. Among the cries of joy and triumph that surrounded him as he marched amid the multitudes, he

heard the single voice of the blind man, and when the multitude bid him hold his peace, Christ rebuked them and turning to the poor man, said: "What will thou have me do unto thee?" I believe if he had been on his way to create a world, he would have stopped to attend to the wants of that poor blind man. "I will have mercy and not sacrifice" is the great doctrine which distinguishes the Christian religion from the Jewish ceremonial ritual and the current religion of our times. The Christian religion is one of mercy, lifting up the bowed down and disconsolate. O for revival of this religion![35]

This passage is significant for three reasons. First, it demonstrates Douglass's rejection of abstract theological doctrine in favor of human action. Douglass uses the word "abstract" twice in this passage, with reference to one's theological beliefs in contrast to one's actions. The first time that Douglass uses the word "abstract," he is referencing his disregard of Garrison's "abstract faith" because of Garrison's actions. And the second time that Douglass uses the word "abstract," he expresses an indifference toward "abstract notions" of belief in favor of a greater attentiveness to the works of human beings who render help to other human beings in need. Second, Douglass's biblical references are significant in this passage as they point to instances in the life of Jesus that exalt ethical and compassionate human conduct. Douglass's interpretation of Jesus's message to John the Baptist and Jesus's encounter with blind Bartimaeus point to a liberationist Christology that eschews abstract theological doctrine to emphasize moral action to help the oppressed. Reginald F. Davis discusses this at length in his book, *Frederick Douglass: A Precursor to Liberation Theology*, as does Waldo E. Martin Jr. in his book, *The Mind of Frederick Douglass*. Finally, this passage is significant because of its reference to the parable of the Good Samaritan when Douglass mentions "binding up the wounds of those who fall among thieves." Recall that in the parable of the Good Samaritan, Jesus is addressing a question that comes to him from one learned in the Mosaic Law who asks what he can do to inherit eternal life. Jesus responds to him by referring him to the book of the law where he then reads the two great commandments to love God and love his neighbor. He then asks Jesus, "Who is my neighbor?" The lawyer asked this question trying "to justify himself." It seems, then, that the lawyer was hoping that Jesus would provide an abstract, conceptual definition in the form of something like "Your neighbor is one who lives no farther than one hundred paces from your front door." Had Jesus provided such an abstract, conceptual definition, the lawyer could have justified a narrow moral obligation to those who were within the parameters of the law. But Jesus does not provide such a definition. Instead, his response to the lawyer is "A man was on his way from Jerusalem to Jericho. . . ." Thus it is that Jesus begins to tell a story to his lawyer-interlocutor. Jesus does something here that I think Douglass would be glad that he did: he suspends abstract, conceptual, and generalized legal definitions in favor of a creative story that not only does not justify the lawyer in his moral complacency but also heightens the lawyer's moral obligation to an astonishing degree, as, by the end of the parable, the lawyer realizes that the "neighbor" is not a mere legal concept to be narrowed for the sake of a legalistic self-justification, but rather a moral imperative to help anyone who is in need. So when Douglass references the parable of the Good Samaritan, he references—knowingly or not—an ethical impulse in the Judeo-Christian tradition that not only eschews abstraction but also does so in the interest of creative, narrative storytelling. Douglass does the same thing in avoiding theological and philosophical abstractions in favor of a narrative methodology that, as I will argue in the next section of this chapter, shows itself as poetry.

Having survived the Jewish Holocaust, Levinas reflects on politics, war, justice, and ethics in his *magnum opus*, *Totality and Infinity*. In this text, Levinas interrogates Western philosophy because of what he believes is a sort of violence associated with philosophy itself. Philosophy has what Levinas believes is a totalizing tendency. By "totalizing," Levinas means that philosophy, because its first principles are metaphysical and epistemological, has as its chief interest the *logos*, or providing a comprehensive account of being that can be rationally justified. One can see this at work in the first sentence of Aristotle's *Metaphysics*: "All human beings by nature desire knowledge."[36] The term for desire in Greek is *oregontai*, and it implies a hand reaching out in the distance to grasp something and bring it closer for inspection. And it is this notion of grasping, of seizure, of control, that Levinas associates with the Western philosophical tradition. Levinas argues that we see the notion of totality at work as early as the Milesian school of pre-Socratic philosophy. He argues that Thales, with his claim that "All is water," exemplifies a metaphysical impulse to render *all things* knowable and comprehensible to the "I," or the philosophical self. In *Totality and Infinity*, Levinas problematizes the philosophical self with his notion of infinity, which he claims resists the impulse of totality. Levinas locates infinity in the face of the other person, whom he refers to as "the Other" (*l'Autre*). Being resistant to totality, infinity is divinity that is located, not in an unknowable beyond, but rather in the face of the other person. The self is inclined toward totality, but the Other, which is infinity personified, is resistant to the totality. The Aristotelian self-assured hand that reaches out to grasp an object and bring it closer for inspection is transformed, on Levinas's account, into the hand of a self that moral obligation overwhelms so much that it reaches out in a feeble attempt to render assistance to the infinite Other. So for Levinas, philosophical first principles ought to be ethical rather than metaphysical and epistemological. The first thing that we encounter should not be a world that we attempt to grasp and know, but rather the face of another person who demands our help. Levinas thus wants to replace metaphysics and epistemology with ethics as first principles, or it may be said that Levinas wants to develop an "ethical metaphysics."

So like Douglass, Levinas wants a radical sense of moral responsibility among human beings. Levinas is so committed to this project that he refers to himself as an atheist. But he does not mean that he is an atheist in the epistemological sense of the term, where one purports to "prove" that God does not exist. Instead, Levinas develops a conception of God that collapses into human beings so that God—the infinite—is in the face of the other person. Throughout Levinas's corpus, he invests the face of the Other with divine attributes. Levinas thus makes a phenomenological move in theology akin to what Husserl does with the European sciences: even as Husserl suspends the "natural attitude" to access the *lebenswelt* in the interest of a more responsible scientific culture, Levinas suspends what I will call the "theological attitude" to access the interhuman order, revealing a pre-theological *lebenswelt* in which there is a radical moral responsibility to and for the Other that the theological attitude ignores.

This is why Levinas writes that "To relate to the absolute as an atheist is to welcome the absolute purified of the violence of the sacred."[37] The "violence of the sacred" refers here to the theological attitude that posits God as existing in a sacred and holy space above and beyond human reach. Thus situated, the theological attitude, while it engenders much mystery and speculation, does so at the expense of ethics and moral action. Levinas writes that "The idea of infinity, the metaphysical relation, is the dawn of a humanity without myths.... Atheism conditions a veritable relationship with a true God καθ' αυτό."[38] In contrast to the theological attitude which conditions a relationship with God on rational, philosophical terms such that God is reduced to the rational conditions of human intelligibility, or what one might call the violence of the *logos*, an "atheist," as Levinas uses the term, refuses to accept the vassalage of philosophical theology that allows for the subordination of the moral to the rational and instead allows God to appear on His own terms. For Levinas, such an appearance will not be the appearance of Heidegger's "god of philosophy"; instead, it will be "a substance overflowing its own idea in me," overflowing what Descartes calls its "objective existence." When simply known and thematized, the substance no longer is "according to itself." God must be allowed to appear on God's own terms, not on the terms of human intelligibility. Levinas's reference to Descartes's third meditation is significant here. In the third meditation, Descartes argues for God's existence on the basis that of all his ideas, the idea of God as an infinite being is so overwhelming that he is unable to contain it. Descartes applies the principle of cause and effect to argue that the cause of any of his ideas must have at least as much reality as its effect. If the effect of the idea of God is that Descartes is overwhelmed by the idea of an infinite being, then the cause of that idea must be an infinite being. Descartes concludes that since he, a finite being, cannot be the cause of an idea of an infinite being, such an idea can only come from a being equally as infinite as the idea itself. And, for Descartes, that being is God. Levinas is not trying to prove God's existence. He is not falling into an ontotheological trap. As Levinas often does, he draws from examples in the history of philosophy that aid him in the illustrations of the deeply metaphorical and imagery-rich points that he is trying to make. So here, Levinas wants to demonstrate the overwhelming sense of moral obligation that emerges from the face of the Other when the Other gives itself on its own terms—terms that are incompatible with an ontotheological appearance of God according to the dictates of philosophical intelligibility.

Thus suspended, the "theological attitude" enables one to see that positing "the transcendent as stranger and poor one is to prohibit the metaphysical relation with God from being accomplished in the ignorance of men and things. The dimension of the divine opens forth from the human face." Removing the theoretical assumptions, metaphysical speculations, and epistemic justifications of the "theological attitude" enables one to see that divinity is not transcendent in a metaphysical beyond, but rather immanent, being present in the human face. That there must be such a removal of theory and rational, philosophical interests—a suspension of the "theological attitude"—is shown when Levinas continues on to claim that "A relation with the Transcendent free from all captivation by the Transcendent is a social relation. It is here that the Transcendent, infinitely other, solicits us and appeals to us." The first sentence here is important because the first time the word "Transcendent" is used, it is a reference to one's relationship with the face of the Other, which is always transcendent, or beyond the self's metaphysical and epistemic grasp or reach (i.e., the face of the infinite God). But the second time the word "Transcendent" is used, it refers to the transcendence of the God of the theological attitude that is theorized, ontologized, and epistemically justified in the philosophy of religion. Transcendence in this second sense, then, according to Levinas, "captivates" us to the point of preventing any meaningful realization of a social relation that is the actual site of the ethical. Levinas further emphasizes this point when he writes that "There can be no 'knowledge' of God separated from the relationship with men." Levinas is explicit about the nature of his work in *Totality and Infinity*: "The establishing of this primacy of the ethical, that is, of the relationship of man to man—signification, teaching, and justice—a primacy of an irreducible structure upon which all the other structures rest . . . is one of the objectives of the present work."[39]

Both Douglass and Levinas, then, call for a departure from a metaphysical and epistemic transcendence of God in favor of an ethical transcendence of

God that is situated in human relationships. It is this departure from metaphysics and epistemology and toward ethics that I am loosely referring to as the suspension of the "theological attitude." Akin to the "natural attitude" that Husserl argues must be suspended, the theological attitude is that body of naïve theoretical assumptions that we make about God as a transcendent being without accounting for the much deeper and richer connection that religious beliefs have to the existential immanence of human personhood. This is not to say that beliefs are altogether unimportant; rather, they are not as important as one's conduct toward one's fellow human beings—especially in the midst of the human crises that were American chattel slavery in the nineteenth century and the Jewish Holocaust of the twentieth century. When there is such a crisis, we must find a way to access the best of our humanity. For Husserl, this meant that the crisis of European sciences demanded a suspension of theoretical reflection for the sake of rehumanizing science. Husserl was concerned that theorizing would be an impediment to the task of phenomenology, especially theorizing about God. In §58 of *Ideas I*, Husserl writes that his concern is that the transcendence of God would hint "at various groups of such rational grounds for the existence of an extraworldly, 'divine' being [and] that this being would transcend not merely the world but apparently also 'absolute' consciousness." For Husserl, such a being would "thus be *an 'absolute' in a sense totally different from the absolute of consciousness*, just as, on the other side, it would be something *transcendent in a totally different sense* vis-à-vis the transcendent in the sense of the world."[40] And for Douglass and Levinas, both living through humanitarian crises in consecutive centuries, it became necessary to make a similar exclusion of God from the field of their philosophical and theological works, because their work needed to respond to the crisis with a radical sense of human responsibility.

This is consistent with Husserl's account of suspending God's transcendence in §58 of *Ideas I*. Indeed, Douglass prefigures the Husserlian suspension of God's transcendence and Levinas works in the shadow of it. As Levinas points out in *Of God Who Comes to Mind*, whether Husserl's rigorous phenomenological method is adhered to is not the sine qua non of phenomenology. The only thing that needs to happen is that we turn back from what is thought—an analysis of God and his attributes—toward the fullness of the thought itself—moral responsibility for the Other—to discover something new. I explore this idea in greater detail in the next section of the chapter.

DOUGLASS'S PHENOMENOLOGICAL "AESTH-ETHICS"

Silvia Benso develops the neologisim "Aesth-ethics" in her essay, "Aesth-ethics: Levinas, Plato, and Art."[41] In this essay, she discusses the relationship between art and the primacy of the ethical in Levinas by reading Levinas with Plato and vice versa. Benso concludes—as I do here—that Levinas, despite his reluctance to accept certain art forms as ethical, makes room in his ethics for the art form of poetry as an aesthetic expression consistent with his ethical metaphysics. Douglass, I argue, likewise approves of poetry for moral purposes. He is not interested in any philosophical resolution to the problem of anteriority, which I discussed in the introduction. Indeed, considering Douglass's humanism, it makes sense that Douglass is less interested in seeing God's anterior than he is interested in seeing God's backside, or what is left over after God has passed by. Again, the difference between seeing God's anterior and his posterior, or backside, is the difference between a religion of philosophical explanation and a religion of testimony. Theodicy is the way of the former, but poetic narrative is the way of the latter. When Douglass prefigures the phenomenological reduction by suspending the "theological attitude," he simultaneously brings propositional language to a close and opens the way to access a *lebenswelt* of creative, poetic, testimony that is less interested in explaining divinity in philosophical and theological terms than it is in pointing to humanity's suffering in poetic terms. Two examples from Douglass's narrative exemplify this dynamic between reason and language. In both of these examples, Douglass identifies the problem of evil, but then resists its temptation to rational indulgence. Before discussing these examples, however, some preliminary discussion of the problem of evil and theodicy is in order.

Theodicy arises because of the philosophical problem of evil, which claims that God's attributes cannot be reconciled with the existence of evil in the world. The problem may be set forth as follows:

1. God is omnibenevolent.
2. God is omniscient.
3. God is omnipotent.
4. Evil exists.

The theist faces the following conundrum: the existence of evil at (4)—this evil may be either moral evil, which originates in corrupt human behavior, or natural evil, in the form of natural disasters that bring widespread destruction and loss of life—compromises at least one of the attributes of God at

(1) through (3). If God is omnibenevolent at (1), then God cannot be both omniscient at (2) and omnipotent at (3), because a God who was all good and all knowledgeable would see evil coming and stop it. But God does not stop evil from happening, so either God is not omnipotent or, if God is omnipotent, then God is not all good, because if God was both all powerful and all good, God would use His omnipotence to stop evil. The point here is that (1) through (4) cannot all be the case. And since (4) is indubitable, (1) through (3) are all called into question.

Theism responds to this problem with theodicy. Derived from the Greek words for God (*Theos*), and justice (*dikē*), theodicy defends God's attributes at (1) through (3) against the charge of rational incoherence. Among some of the more notable debates involving theodicy is the debate between J. L. Mackie and Alvin Plantinga that I referenced in the introduction. Although the questions raised in debates such as this one strike at the core of theistic belief, the context in which such questions are raised affect both the manner and the extent of the engagement with such questions. So when Mackie and Plantinga address the issues that the problem of evil raises, the manner of the engagement is typical of professional philosophers and theologians: the debate occurs in a series of publications in scholarly essays. And since the scholarly forum is the locus of the debate, there will be an extensive proliferation of abstractions that will relentlessly address theoretical issues without ever addressing concrete moral and political concerns. The reformed epistemology of analytic theism, then, as practiced in professional philosophical and theological circles, becomes, perhaps unwittingly, a handmaiden to injustice because its abstractions force a retreat from the *sarx* (flesh) of concrete experience to the *logos* (word, reason, or language) of thought experiments. We thus see on this point the inherent secularity of theology,[42] for analytic theism is more interested in an ontotheological, Scholastic, and Aristotelian explanation, than it is interested in the existential, phenomenological, concrete life of testimony. Preoccupied with rational explanation, analytic theism finds itself facing the problem of anteriority as I have identified it in the introduction. Like Moses, analytic theists make a demand to "see God coming," to see God's face. This is the religion of explanation.

But theodicy is not strictly an academic, professional, endeavor. William R. Jones points this out when he observes, "Theodicy is also defined too narrowly if it is perceived as an abstract and theoretical enterprise executed only by professional philosophers and theologians."[43] One does not need to be a professional academic to recognize the problem of evil and grapple with the question of whether an omnibenevolent, omniscient, omnipresent God exists. Indeed, Douglass himself pondered these questions when he was a slave. Two instances from Douglass's 1845 narrative are instructive. First is Douglass's description of his grandmother's death; second is Douglass's fight with Covey. Both indicate that Douglass is less interested in theodicy than he is in pointing out the problem of evil, leaving it alone, and pointing toward poetic responses to it, and both are consistent with Douglass's social and political strategy of suspending the "theological attitude" in favor of a more humanistic—and here I argue phenomenological—understanding of religion.

In chapter eight of Douglass's first autobiographical narrative, Douglass paints a sad and tragic portrait of his grandmother's life. She is described as one who, throughout her life, was dutiful to her tasks as a slave despite the wretched conditions of slavery. Douglass writes that "she had peopled his plantation with slaves; she had become a great grandmother in his service. She had rocked him in infancy, attended him in childhood, served him through life, and at his death wiped from his icy brow the cold death-sweat, and closed his eyes forever."[44] Standing in stark contrast to her faithfulness was the pain of her life as a slave that separated her from her children, grandchildren, and great-grandchildren taken from her and "divided, like so many sheep, without being gratified with the small privilege of a single word, as to their or her own destiny."[45] And now that she was old, instead of reaping the joy, comfort, and security that she has sown into the lives of others, in her last years, she reaps a bitter harvest of loneliness and despair. Having been sold to a new master, who found that she "was of but little value, her frame already racked with the pain of old age, and complete helplessness fast stealing over her once active limbs," this new master "made her a little hut, put up a little much-chimney, and then made her welcome to the privilege of supporting herself there in perfect loneliness; thus virtually turning her out to die!"[46] After depicting the scene of how Douglass imagines her sad demise as contrasted with all of her efforts to improve the lives of others, Douglass says, "Will not a righteous God visit for these things?"[47] This depiction of the loneliness and desolation of his grandmother's life, when contrasted with the faithfulness of her life, raises the question of how an omnibenevolent, omniscient, and omnipotent God can allow such injustice to occur. Why is such suffering and evil permitted? God, as an omnipotent, omniscient, and omnibenevolent being, must take responsibility for this terrible injustice. This is the problem of evil. But unlike the analytic theist, Douglass makes no effort to resolve this question with a theodicy. Instead, after raising the problem of evil with his question "Will not a righteous God visit for these things?" Douglass moves to an entirely different subject.[48]

But it is what Douglass does before he articulates the problem of evil that is so significant. Trying to describe the pain of his grandmother's loss of her children, the loss of her grandchildren, and the loss of her great-grandchildren, who are gone from her forever, Douglass turns to the poetry of John Greenleaf Whitter, who penned this poem:

> Gone, gone, sold and gone
> To the rice swamp dank and lone,
> Where the slave-whip ceaseless swings,
> Where the noisome insect stings,
> Where the fever demon strews,
> Poison with the falling dews,
> Where the sickly sunbeams glare
> Through the hot and misty air:—
> Gone, gone, sold and gone
> To the rice swamp dank and lone,
> From Virginia hills and waters—
> Woe is me, my stolen daughters![49]

Douglass, at a complete loss for propositional speech to describe his grandmother's pain and plight, turns to poetry. The *logos* of the "theological attitude" is suspended here, leaving Douglass with poetry as his only recourse to draw attention to the suffering of his grandmother, and of so many other women slaves who endured the emotional trauma of losing generations of children to the cruelty of the slave auction block. Douglass empties himself here to get us to see the suffering of someone else. Drawing this sort of attention to the plight of another is far more important for Douglass in this situation because "solving" the problem of evil, rather than drawing attention to the suffering of another, by thematizing suffering as part of a rational, coherent, whole, justifies that suffering through rational explanation, and thus altogether ignores the plight of the suffering. Despite his grandmother's faithfulness, generations of Douglass's grandmother's children are, in the words of Whittier, "Gone, gone, sold and gone." This is a creative expression, a cultural achievement, of a life-world that is accessible through a suspension of the "theological attitude" during the humanitarian crisis of American chattel slavery. It is in this way that I believe Douglass prefigures Husserl's phenomenological reduction with an aesthetic-phenomenological call to moral responsibility to his grandmother, the Other, who is the "the stranger and poor one" of the prophetic, Judeo-Christian tradition.

Douglass turns to poetry again in his narrative when he reflects on his desire to be free. Enchanted and transfixed by the boats and ships in Chesapeake Bay, Douglass writes that the sight of the vessels "always affected me powerfully" as he "traced, with saddened heart and tearful eye, the countless number of sails moving off to the mighty ocean." He continues: "The sight of these affected me powerfully. My thoughts would compel utterance; and there, with no audience but the Almighty, I would pour out my soul's complaint, in my rude way, with an apostrophe to the moving multitude of ships." Douglass then moves to a poetic description of his desire to be free, speaking to the vessels in the Chesapeake Bay as though they are persons:

You are loosed from your moorings, and are free; I am fast in my chains, and am a slave! You move merrily before the gentle gale, and I sadly before the bloody whip! You are freedom's swift-winged angels, that fly round the world; I am confined in bands of iron! O that I were free! O, that I were on one of your gallant decks, and under your protecting wing! Alas! Betwixt me and you, the turbid waters roll. Go on, go on. O that I could also go! Could I but swim! If I could fly! O, why was I born a man, of whom to make a brute! The glad ship is gone: she hides in the dim distance. I am left in the hottest hell of unending slavery. O God, save me! God, deliver me! Let me be free! Is there any God? Why am I a slave?[50]

The last five sentences of this passage articulate the problem of evil as arising from the reality of suffering—three exclamatory sentences—as followed by rational questioning—two interrogatory sentences. Donald Gibson writes of these five sentences that they indicate that Douglass reasoned as follows: "If there were a God, then I would not be a slave; since I am a slave, the possibility exists (hence the question, not a positive assertion) that there is no God. Also implicit in his reasoning is the assumption that, if there were a God, he would 'save me,' 'deliver me,' 'let me be free.'"[51] Again, Douglass never intellectually attempts to resolve the problem of evil. Instead, this poetic moment results from a suspension of the "theological attitude" that enables Douglass to empty himself of his rational desire in a way that enables us to experience the plight of the slave in bondage. The poetic moment with the boats in the bay speaks to the plight of an enslaved body yearning to be free. Such a moment is not possible if Douglass develops a theodicy or a free will defense in an attempt to intellectually solve the problem of evil. In fact, any such attempt will not result in his freedom, but rather will seek to justify his bondage. Suspending the "theological attitude" is thus morally significant because it grants access to a new way of seeing the world that enables insight into the suffering of one who longs to be free.

Douglass's engagement with poetry extends beyond his narrative to his speeches and writings. For Douglass, poetry was a backbone of the abolitionist movement. In his 1855 speech that he titled "The Nature, Character, and History of the Anti-Slavery Movement," he points out that poetry is an indispensable component of the abolitionist's cause. Citing John Greenleaf Whittier, Henry Wadsworth Longfellow, James Russell Lowell, John Pierpont, and William Cullen Bryant, Douglass argues that their poetry is a source of political agitation and inspiration for the abolitionist movement.[52] Poetry thus has a political dimension for Douglass. And poetry has a political dimension for Levinas, which is connected to his notion of "the saying" and "the said." The latter refers to an ontologized, fixed meaning of language where the speech is part of a coherent whole, and the former disrupts the coherence of speech, often in the form of either a poetic or prophetic call for justice, as Douglass has demonstrated with his poetic turns away from rational theology and toward a phenomenological aesthetics in his narrative that I discussed in this section. For Levinas, coherent discourses—which, for Douglass may sound a lot like "servants obey your masters"—originate in a state-sponsored, oppressive attempt to maintain a totalized whole. Indeed, Levinas asks rhetorically in *Otherwise than Being* "Does not the coherent discourse, wholly absorbed in the said, owe its coherence to the State, which, violently excludes subversive discourse?"[53] Levinas's understanding of poetry and language, when read with Douglass's phenomenological and political uses of poetry indicate an even stronger connection between these two thinkers.

THE SAYING, THE SAID, POETRY, AND NARRATIVE

Art is a nuanced subject in Levinas studies.[54] In an essay titled "Reality and Its Shadow," Levinas expresses his disapproval of art because its mimetic nature moves us away from the reality of the Other's suffering.[55] Certain art forms such as plays or dramatic performances, for Levinas, lack a grounding in anything that is actually connected to the concrete realm of ethical life, a life that Levinas wants to emphasize.

But Levinas's relationship to written art such as poetry is different. Speech presupposes the presence of the Other, and thus language is integral to the ethical relation. There are, however, differences in the purposes and uses of language. These differences are seen in Levinas's distinction between "the saying" and "the said." "The said" is a manner of speaking with a fixed ontological meaning; a meaning that is part of a scheme of rational discourse and intelligibility. The said has a meaning that is thus situated within a network of propositions, perhaps even in logical or syllogistic form. The aim of the said is to convey meaning clearly and carefully so as to render absolutely certain the intentions of the speaker or the author. The principal concern with the said is self-driven; that is, it is the self that demands to be understood and comprehended. The self's comprehension or the comprehension of what is said occurs at the expense of the Other, who is absorbed into the totality of rational discourse, and whose alterity and transcendence is sacrificed for the sake of fixed logical and ontological meaning. The said represents the ultimate expression of immanence in language: it is the linguistic demand of the self without regard for the Other. The Other is sacrificed, as it were, on an altar of logical meaning and grasping in the interest of a totalized whole expressed in language. In *Otherwise than Being*, Levinas writes of the said that its origin in Western philosophy and politics is seen in that "the history of Western philosophy has not been the refutation of skepticism as much as the refutation of transcendence. The logos said has the last word dominating all meaning, the word of the end, the very possibility of the ultimate and the result. Nothing can interrupt it."[56] The logos is an all-consuming form of politically based speech, necessary to justify the state such that "Every contestation and interruption of this power of discourse is at once related and invested by discourse. It thus recommences as soon as one interrupts it. In the logos said, and written, it survives the death of the interlocutors that state it, and assures the continuity of culture."[57] Significantly, even God becomes, for Levinas, a term and a concept that is re-inscribed within an ontology of meaning, and is put "at the disposition of the philologists, instead of confounding philosophical language."[58] The said, then, according to Levinas, is a certain orientation to language that is preoccupied with the development and maintenance of a coherent whole for the sake of social, cultural, and political stability that appropriates theological notions as part of its fixed theory of meaning. The said then develops into a philosophically based narrative that sees itself as beyond reproach in virtue of its rationality, intelligibility, coherence, and seeming indestructability as its rational narrative is generationally transmitted.[59]

Consider the said in light of Douglass's and Levinas's world. Both lived in the midst of oppressive regimes with correspondingly oppressive narratives. For Douglass, it was the narrative of America's founding and racist notions of manifest destiny that simultaneously enslaved Africans and authorized the slaughter of innocent indigenous persons, and the hypocrisy of slaveholding Christianity, which justified all of the above. And for Levinas, the situation was very similar, as there was the propaganda machine of National Socialism, which spewed a message of hatred toward the Jews and promoted false notions of Christian, Aryan superiority. "The said" functions in both instances as a form of highly ontologized discourse that, through the power of the logos, fixes all meaning within a "rational" and "logical" scheme of intelligibility that reduces persons to concepts and consumes them within the vast field of ontological meaning, epistemic justification, and theological "reasoning." When Levinas speaks of "the said," he speaks of the way of anteriority, as I have begun to develop that concept in the introduction. The way of the said is the way of anteriority because it sees God coming from a frontal view as always already "understood," "grasped," and "comprehended." This is what Moses wanted to see. The said as anteriority is ontotheology; it is the said made theo-logos, or theo-logical, living up to its actual etymological root for "theo-logy," "theo-ry," "thought," and "thinking." Anteriority is a problem precisely because God's transcendence is reduced to the immanence of analytic theists who are engaged in scholarly debates. This is what Levinas means when he refers to a theology "that thematizes the transcending in the logos, assigns a term to the passing of transcendence, congeals it into a "world behind the scenes," and installs what it says in war and in matter."[60] The said is thus the ultimate expression of oppression's linguistic control and domination.

The saying, however, is different. It is, for Levinas, "Antecedent to the verbal signs it conjugates, to the linguistic systems and the semantic glimmerings, a foreword preceding languages, it is the proximity of one to the other, the commitment of an approach."[61] Although the saying is language, it is not of the sort of language as the said. The saying bears the indelible imprint of infinity insofar as it is a beckoning from the Other that disrupts the self's scheme of intelligibility and demands to be heard. "Saying is not a game," writes Levinas. Instead, it is the language of infinity in which moral responsibility is found prior to the autonomous, rational, agential behavior of the deontological, utilitarian, or virtue ethicist. The saying is "The original or pre-original saying, what is put for the in the foreword." It "weaves an intrigue of responsibility. It sets forth an order more grave than being and antecedent to being. By comparison being appears like a game. Being is a play or détente, without responsibility, where everything possible is permitted."[62] As Pamela Carralero has pointed out, the saying, in the form of "the spoken word can shatter the closed world of the ego, thus jump starting being's transcendence into holiness."[63] When spoken, the saying maintains its ethical priority. The written word, however, is prone to absorption into the fixed meaning of the logos. Carralero continues: "When written, however, thought communicated through the spoken word becomes disfigured into the documents of the ontological realm that connote a system of prescriptions in which words become fixed into legitimated truths," and thus "the written word is traditionally unable to establish an unending relation of proximity with the other."[64]

But when the written word is in book form, it retains the ethical import of the saying: "Books belong to a world they do not include, but recognize by being written and printed, and by being prefaced and getting themselves preceded with forewords. They are interrupted and call for other books and in the end are interpreted in a saying distinct from the said."[65] The internal structure of the book—its preface, its foreword, and its text—retain the fluidity of the saying and resist the ontology of the said because they allow for a continuous disruption of the text, enabling the text to admit of an infinite variety of interpretations. And it is precisely this infinite variety of interpretations that Levinas refers to as the "poetic said," which is what happens when "Language exceeds the limits of thought."[66] For Levinas, language implies "a meaning distinct from that which comes to signs from the simultaneity of systems or the logical definition of concepts. This possibility is laid bare in the poetic said, and the interpretation it calls for ad infinitum."[67]

On this account of the saying and the said, both Douglass's autobiographical narrative and the poetry that I discussed in the previous section of this chapter reveal a fresh meaning to Douglass's text. Douglass's narrative, being in book form, belongs to a world of ontologized meaning that fixes his identity as a slave, and yet the content of the book runs counter to the ontology of the said as represented in the literature of pro-slavery discourse, so Douglass's narrative excludes the world to which it belongs. Social, political, religious, and cultural commentary have been extensively made on Douglass's autobiographical narratives, and as such, there are myriad interpretations of Douglass's work—"the saying"—including this one, which disrupted and continues to disrupt the ontologized "said" of racial violence that occurs in all manner of anti-Black racist ideology that persists today. For example, this book aims to interpret Douglass so as to disrupt traditional standards for what counts as philosophy, considering Douglass's status as a former slave and his philosophical reflections on slavery, a topic that traditional philosophy has, until late in the twentieth century, generally ignored.

And Douglass's poetic turn, which comes on the heels of his aporetic treatment of the problem of evil, when read with Levinas's notion of the saying, exemplifies the importance of abandoning the said in favor of a poetic demand to recognize the suffering of the Other. It is with Douglass's poetry that our attention is drawn to the suffering of his grandmother and to the majority of Douglass's fellow slaves; a suffering that cannot be thematized into a dialectical "said" as part of a philosophical theology; a suffering that does not account for evil as some sort of inauthentic Augustinian privation that denies the reality of evil in favor of some sort of overarching, rational necessity of perfect being theology, but rather a suffering that has an ontological status as something that is quite real and, as Levinas argues, quite useless.

USELESS SUFFERING

Douglass's poetic depiction of his grandmother and his fellow slaves exposes a world of suffering that cannot be captured in the ontologized language of the said. Indeed, it is the said of analytic theism that demands a justification of evil and suffering as some sort of divine will, or as a rational, dialectical necessity for a thorough conceptual analysis of God's attribute of omnibenevolence in the context of theodicy. Suffering, then, on the account of analytic theism, has a certain usefulness that makes it not only rationally acceptable but also rationally necessary. This is where Levinas begins his critique of suffering in his essay "Useless Suffering": with a suspension of the theological attitude that first provides a phenomenology of suffering, second a critique of theodicy, then a declaration of radical human responsibility in the midst of unspeakable evil and horror, and, finally, an ethical discussion of the *lebenswelt* that is what Levinas calls the "interhuman order." Through an analysis of this important text, one sees the continuity between Levinas's and Douglass's criticisms of theodicy, Levinas's account of the saying and the said, and Douglass's use of poetry.

Levinas begins his essay "Useless Suffering" with a phenomenological account of suffering. The first subheading of the essay, "Phenomenology" is an indication that Levinas wants to provide a pre-theoretical account of suffering. He is interested in what suffering is as experienced prior to the thematization and systematization of rational theology. Although "Useless Suffering" does not explicitly and rigorously perform the phenomenological reduction, one can reasonably conclude that Levinas is not interested in the traditional account of suffering, as later in the essay, he engages in an extensive critique of theodicy. Again, it behooves us, I think, to heed Levinas's own admonition about his relationship to phenomenology, when he says that what he is doing is phenomenology, and that it is not necessary to employ "the rules required by Husserl; even if all of the Husserlian methodology is not respected."[68] For Levinas, the hallmark of phenomenological analysis is the "proceeding back from what is thought toward the fullness of the thought itself."[69] This leads to the discovery of "dimensions of meaning, each time new."[70] "Useless Suffering," then, read as a whole, is a phenomenological (i.e., pre-theoretical) account of suffering; an account of suffering that, though informal, bypasses theoretical accounts of suffering to show how suffering appears—indeed, this is the very meaning of phenomenology—to oneself.

Levinas refers to suffering as "a datum in consciousness, a certain "psychological content," similar to the lived experience of color, sound, contact, or any other sensation."[71] Phenomenologically speaking, one would speak of color, sound, contact, or other sensations as being the *noema* of a *noesis*, being understood as the content of consciousness that is cast in terms of one's directedness toward the object or one's intentionality toward the object. The color, sound, and so on is a consciousness of the color or the sound precisely because of its relationship to the ego's intentionality; its relevance for the intentions of the self. Suffering thus has a certain immanent characteristic. But unlike the color, sound, or other sensation, which the ego absorbs completely in the grasp of its intentionality, suffering is both immanent to consciousness and yet, as Levinas puts it, "an in-spite-of-consciousness, the unassumable. The unassumable and 'unassumability.'"[72] This "unassumability" is not, however, a mere excess that results from an excess of something. Instead, unassumability refers to "an excess, an unwelcome superfluity, that is inscribed in a sensorial content, penetrating as suffering, the dimensions of meaning that seem to open themselves to it, or become grafted onto it."[73] Likening suffering to a refractory resistance to Kant's transcendental cogito,[74] but expanding suffering to mean something much worse than that, Levinas points out that suffering is not merely resistant to rational cognition and thematization, but also that suffering operates not as a "grasp" but as a "revulsion." Suffering is not merely resistant to the rational thematization of the said; it cannot merely be defined in negative terms as that which consciousness cannot absorb. Instead suffering is, in this failure to absorb, an affirmative reality of nauseating odium, disgust, and loathing that is literally good for nothing; it is useless. Realizing this uselessness of suffering does, however, bring us closer to what Levinas calls the "interhuman order." He writes that as the twentieth century came to a close, there emerged a "just suffering in me for the unjustifiable suffering of the other" that "opens suffering to the ethical perspective of the inter-human. In this perspective there is a radical difference between the suffering in the Other, where it is unforgivable to me, solicits me and calls me, and suffering in me, my own experience of suffering, whose constitutional or congenital uselessness can take on a meaning, the only one of which suffering is capable, in becoming a suffering for the suffering (inexorable though it may be) of someone else."[75] Suffering's only "use," then, is to awaken, within the ego, the ultimate ethical principle of an attentiveness to the suffering of the Other. This ethical principle demands our moral attention and responsibility to such a high degree that, according to Levinas we cannot await deliverance "from an all-powerful God . . . without lowering ourselves." In this way, suffering brings us closer "to God in a more difficult, but also a more spiritual, way than does confidence in any kind of theodicy."[76] Phenomenologically understood, then, suffering is utterly useless for the Other, but useful for the self insofar as it awakens a moral obligation in the self to relieve the suffering of the Other; any resort to a God shrouded in mystery and religiosity is morally corrupt and humanly degrading. And this is precisely what Douglass hoped to do with his autobiographical writings: provide a pre-theorectical, first-person account of suffering that demands moral action.

But despite its uselessness, theodicy makes suffering useful. In the next section of "Useless Suffering," Levinas points out how suffering loses "its modality of uselessness in various ways." Likening suffering to the phenomenon of pain, Levinas points out that pain becomes useful as a symptom of a larger problem in that, if there were no pain, there could be no diagnosis and cure. He writes, "One can see a biological finality in it: the role of an alarm signal manifesting itself for the preservation of life against the cunning dangers that threaten it in illness."[77] Levinas then turns to the various religious uses of theodicy that "appeal to a meaning that would be peculiar to a metaphysical order and an ethics that are not visible in the immediate lessons of moral consciousness."[78] This is precisely the sort of degrading move that Levinas condemns at the end of the previous section of "Useless Suffering," where he points out that to make an appeal to an invisible God in the face of the suffering of the Other is impossible without "lowering ourselves."[79] And yet this is a move that human beings have consistently made from time immemorial. Levinas points out that prior to its philosophical and theological formalization in Leibniz in the eighteenth century, theodicy was being done, and that it is "as old as a certain reading of the Bible."[80]

Levinas then continues on to discuss the impact of the twentieth-century Jewish Holocaust in the next section of "Useless Suffering," titled "The End of Theodicy." For Levinas, the horrors of Auschwitz effectively bring an end to philosophical defenses of God. This is akin to Nietzsche's notion of the death of God, which is not a literal death of an ontological being that makes epistemic, ontotheological justification impossible, but rather the death of, the uselessness of, the end of, philosophical reasoning in the face of unspeakable horror. What can philosophical reasoning do to explain or justify God after such an atrocity? When Nietzsche proclaims the death of God, he demands a birth of human responsibility, a dawn of a humanity without certain myths that only obscure moral obligation and maintain the status quo. So it is for Levinas. Indeed, Levinas asks a poignant, rhetorical question about Nietzsche: "Did not Nietzsche's saying about the death of God take on, in the extermination camps, the meaning of a quasi-empirical fact?"[81]

Levinas concludes the essay with a discussion of what he calls "The Interhuman Order." This is not a Kantian "kingdom of ends," it is not a Lockean or Hobbesian "state of nature," and it is not a Rawlsian "original position." Instead, it is a moral reality that precedes all hypothetical abstraction and that also precedes every legal and political arrangement between an entity that one would call the state and its citizens. Levinas makes this point when he writes that "The order of politics (post-ethical or pre-ethical) that inaugurates the "social contract" is neither the sufficient condition nor the necessary outcome of ethics."[82] According to Levinas, "In its ethical position, the I is distinct both from the citizen born of the City"[83] and from the Hobbesean notion of the self in the state of nature from which political obligation and legal justification are ultimately derived. The Interhuman Order is, then, not a mere result of political arrangements, but rather prior to them. Prior to the reciprocity of legal "rights" and political obligations, there is an asymmetrical and nonreciprocal moral order where suffering is useless to the Other and useful for me insofar as it quickens my profound moral responsibility to the face of the Other that demands not to be harmed.

Understood phenomenologically, Douglass's life and the lives of slaves were fraught with the uselessness of suffering. Being much more than a mere "refractory synthesis to the Kantian 'I think,'" as Levinas puts it, Douglass was confronted with a world in which his suffering rendered his conceptual and cognitive faculties unable to comprehend what was happening to him and to the other slaves throughout the United States. Thus situated, Douglass finds himself in a place where artistic, first-person narrative will allow him, not to make sense of his situation and the situation of slaves, but rather to express his inner life and the inner lives of the slaves so as to call moral attention to their plight. Fighting through the various theological formations of theodicy that we often resort to by default, as Levinas describes it, Douglass was determined to show, through his humanistic understanding of Christian theology, the uselessness of suffering, and to do so, he used poetry and first person expression that calls us to moral responsibility. This is Douglass's version of a "holy aesthetic," a "poetic said" that disrupts the meaning of ontologized, propositional language with a call to infinite responsibility in the interhuman order. Indeed, after reading Douglass with Levinas on theodicy and suffering, one is left to wonder just how much we degrade ourselves in doing theodicy by appealing to a metaphysical beyond as a means of avoiding the moral demands of the present moment. One can be convinced that we can do better, for how can one even speak of God in the aftermath of not only the Jewish Holocaust but also the trans-Atlantic slave trade and its legacy of Jim Crow, lynching, poverty, and police brutality? Such atrocities demand much more than theoretical musings about God's attributes, as Douglass and Levinas so poignantly remind us.

FROM POETRY TO THE POLITICAL

Douglass and Levinas support a robust, interhuman order of radical moral obligation. Through a suspension of the "theological attitude" that opens the way for a *lebenswelt* of artistic, poetic expression as an act of resistance against oppression, we see an affinity between Douglass and Levinas that may otherwise be overlooked. This chapter has aimed to identify and develop this affinity because overlooking it deprives us of an account of art as a moral resource to resist oppression. Far from the abstractions of analytic theism's reformed epistemology, both Douglass and Levinas want to avoid such abstract theorizations as a matter of morality. Seeking rational explanations for evil is in fact an immoral search for evil's justification. And if one understands evil as rationally justified, then neither Douglass nor Levinas will find such a state of affairs acceptable, as both thinkers are less interested in rational justifications for evil than they are in responsive, moral action to evil. To this point, we have an existential and phenomenological interpretation of Douglass. These two interpretations reveal a Douglass who, in the context of the Incarnational theological framework, is interested in making the word flesh. This is a Douglass that is interested in subjectivity, creativity, and moral responsibility.

In the next chapter, Douglass's moral responsibility takes a social and political turn, as I discuss an aesthetic/political engagement through a reading of Douglass with Kant, in which Douglass's abolition strategy of moral suasion finds itself deeply embedded in a moral anthropology that is at work in Kant's notion of reflective judgment. Douglass's *Narrative* understood as a work of art induces judgments of taste that exhibit disinterestedness, universality, purposiveness, and an appeal to the *sensus communis*, each of which is essential for the philosophical anthropology of moral suasion.

NOTES

1. Job 11:7–9.
2. Matthew 25:40.
3. I John 4:20.
4. For an excellent introduction to the philosophical dimensions of Douglass's work, see *Frederick Douglass: A Critical Reader*, eds. Bill E. Lawson and Frank M. Kirkland (Malden, MA: Blackwell, 1999). Lawson and Kirkland do groundbreaking work in this text, as it is the first collection of essays that view Douglass as a philosopher. As Lawson and Kirkland point out in the introduction, Douglass has a "commitment to argument" that they believe "turns him toward the enterprise of philosophy, because it reflects his ongoing advocacy of intellectual honesty and his willingness to live up to its demands consistently, exposing his reflections to intellectual and political risks and living through existential tensions passionately" (3). The essays in this groundbreaking text in African American philosophy emphasize a broad spectrum of Douglass's thought from within both the analytic and the continental philosophical traditions. Lawson and Kirkland contribute essays that discuss Douglass's philosophical anthropology and its implications for political philosophy, and Lewis R. Gordon contributes a compelling essay on Douglass and existentialism. These essays collectively represent the point of departure for my own philosophical work on Douglass, which is focused on Douglass's philosophical connections to religion and theology in the existentialist and phenomenological philosophical traditions, as well as in some of the more traditional work in the social contract theory of political philosophy.

For discussions of Douglass's religious and theological thought, see my essays, "From Epistemology to Ethics: Theoretical and Practical Reason in Kant and Douglass," which I discussed in the introduction, and "Art, Morality, and the Self: Existentialism in Frederick Douglass and Søren Kierkegaard," in *Existentialist Thought in African-American Literature Before 1940* (Lanham, MD: Lexington Books, 2016), 1–21. These essays are not only my attempts to build upon the groundbreaking work of Lawson and Kirkland by reading Douglass with Kant to turn attention to Douglass's religious and theological thought but also meant to build on the groundbreaking work of Lewis R. Gordon and George Yancy, who read Douglass with Sartre, Fanon, and de Beauvoir, by reading Douglass's engagement with slaveholding Christianity with Kierkegaard, a pre-1940, Christian existentialist philosopher.

Other discussions of Douglass's religious, theological, and political thought include Reginald F. Davis's *Frederick Douglass: A Precursor to Liberation Theology* (Macon, GA: Mercer University Press, 2005), Scott C. Williamson's *The Narrative Life: The Moral and Religious Thought of Frederick Douglass* (Macon, GA: Mercer University Press, 2002), and Waldo Martin's *The Mind of Frederick Douglass* (Chapel Hill: University of North Carolina Press, 1984), especially chapter 7, "The Philosophy and Pursuit of Social Reform." As it relates to these latter texts, my extant work—including this book—is unique in that it is a more explicit philosophical engagement with Douglass and other philosophical figures than the others.

5. Emmanuel Levinas, *Of God Who Comes to Mind*, trans. Bettina Bergo (Stanford, CA: Stanford University Press, 1998), 87.

6. Martin Heidegger, "The Onto-Theo-Logical Constitution of Metaphysics" *Identity and Difference*, trans. Joan Stambaugh (Chicago: University of Chicago Press, 2002), 72.

7. Edmund Husserl, *Ideas for a Pure Phenomenology and Phenomenological Philosophy*, trans. Daniel O. Dahlstrom (Indianapolis, IN: Hackett, 2014), 106–7.

8. Levinas, *Of God Who Comes to Mind*, 87.

9. Pamela Carralero, "A Holy Aesthetic: Recognizing an Art That Is Otherwise Than Art in the Work of Emmanuel Levinas," *Epoché: A Journal of the History of Philosophy* 22, no. 2 (Spring 2018), 512.

10. Ibid., 506.

11. Scott Williamson, *The Narrative Life: The Moral and Religious Thought of Frederick Douglass* (Macon, GA: Mercer University Press, 2002). See especially Williamson's discussion of Waldo Martin, David Blight, and Benjamin Quarles—three Douglass biographers—at pages 141–66.

12. Frederick Douglass, "Too Much Religion, Too Little Humanity," speech delivered on May 9, 1849, in *Frederick Douglass Papers*, vol. 2 (New Haven, CT: Yale University Press, 1982), 189.

13. Here, Douglass, reading the Pauline epistle to Timothy, reclaims Christianity from a neo-Platonic ontological hierarchy that exalts form over matter, logos (word, reason, or language) over sarx (flesh and embodiment) (II Timothy 3:5). Whereas philosophy has logos—word, reason, language in the explanatory, metaphysical sense—as its end, for Christian theology, logos is only the beginning (John 1:1). The end of Christian theology is flesh—a flesh that dwells, that we behold, and that is filled with goodness (John 1:14).

14. Douglass, "Too Much Religion," 180–81.

15. Douglass, in his critique of Christian missionaries, is following the tradition of nineteenth-century Black social and political thought exemplified in the work of David Walker, in his *Appeal, in Four Articles: Together with a Preamble, to the Coloured Citizens of the World, But in Particular and Very Expressly to Those of the United States of America*. There, Walker extensively critiques white Christians for their missionary zeal abroad that fails to address the prevailing suffering and injustice of enslaved Africans within the United States.

16. Sartre's emphasis on responsibility in a war-ravaged Europe echoes Douglass on this point. Sartre wanted humanity to accept full responsibility for the widespread

destruction and carnage in Europe after World War II. See "Existentialism as a Humanism," in *Basic Writings of Existentialism*, ed. Gordon Marino (New York: Modern Library, 2004), 341–68. Lewis Gordon's work has covered the connections between Douglass and twentieth-century existentialism, specifically Sartre and Fanon. See *Existentia Africana: Understanding Africana Existential Thought* (New York: Routledge, 2000) and *Bad Faith and Antiblack Racism* (Amherst, NY: Humanity Books, 1999).

17. See George Yancy, "The Existential Dimensions of Douglass' Autobiographical Narrative: A Beauvoirian Examination," *Philosophy and Social Criticism* 28, no. 3 (2002): 297–320.

18. Frantz Fanon, *Black Skin, White Masks*, trans. Charles Lam Markmann (New York: Grove Press, 1967), 110.

19. Timothy Golden, "From Epistemology to Ethics: Theoretical and Practical Reason in Kant and Douglass," *Journal of Religious Ethics* 40, no. 4 (December 2012): 603–28.

20. Levinas, *Of God Who Comes to Mind*, 87.

21. Frederick Douglass, "Why Is the Negro Lynched?" in *Frederick Douglass: Selected Speeches and Writings*, ed. Philip Foner (Chicago: Lawrence Hill, 1999), 774.

22. Ibid.

23. Ibid.

24. Ibid.

25. Ibid.

26. Ibid.

27. Ibid.

28. Ibid.

29. Ibid., 775.

30. Ibid., 774.

31. Reginald F. Davis addresses this point in his book, *Frederick Douglass: A Precursor to Liberation Theology*. There, he argues that, for Douglass, the point of departure for theological discourse was not abstract theorizing about God's attributes or theodicy, but rather was the actual person and work of Christ among the poor. See Davis, at p. 72. Interestingly, however, despite Douglass's strong criticism of the argument, he also saw great value in it. Indeed, in the same speech in which Douglass criticizes the argument, he says that

> It was a contribution to the cause of liberty. It was largely in favour of the Negro. It was a plain recognition of this manhood, and was calculated to set men to thinking that the Negro might have some other important rights, no less than the religious right to baptism. Thus, with all its faults we are compelled to give the pulpit the credit of furnishing the first important argument in favor of the religious character and manhood rights of the Negro.

See Douglass, "Why Is the Negro Lynched?" in *Frederick Douglass: Selected Speeches and Writings*, ed. Philip S. Foner (Chicago: Lawrence Hill Books, 1975), 775.

32. Douglass, "Too Much Religion, Too Little Humanity," 188.

33. Ibid.

34. Ibid.
35. Ibid., 188–89.
36. Aristotle, *Metaphysics*, 980a.
37. Emmanuel Levinas, *Totality and Infinity*, trans. Alphonso Lingis (Pittsburgh, PA: Duquesne University Press, 1961), 77.
38. Ibid.
39. Ibid., 79.
40. Edmund Husserl, *Ideas for a Pure Phenomenology and Phenomenological Philosophy*, trans. Daniel O. Dahlstrom (Indianapolis, IN: Hackett, 2014), 107.
41. *Epoché: A Journal of the History of Philosophy* 13, no. 1 (2008): 163–83.
42. Carter G. Woodson points out the inherent secularity of philosophical theology when he writes:

> To begin with, theology is of pagan origin. Albert Magnus and Thomas Aquinas worked out the first system of it by applying to religious discussion the logic of Aristotle, a pagan philosopher, who believed neither in the creation of the world nor the immortality of the soul. At best it was degenerate learning, based upon the theory that knowledge is gained by the mind working upon itself rather than upon matter or through sense perception. The world was, therefore, confused with the discussion of absurdities as it is today by those of prominent churchmen. By their peculiar "reasoning," too, theologians have sanctioned most of the ills of the ages. They justified the Inquisition, serfdom, and slavery. Theologians of our time defend segregation and the annihilation of one race by the other. They have drifted away from righteousness into an effort to make wrong seem to be right. (*The Mis-Education of the Negro* [New York: Tribeca Books, 1933], 43)

Here, Woodson elaborates on the consequences of what Heidegger called "ontotheology." This is not to say that Woodson was reading Heidegger, but rather to say that although this quote from Woodson predates Heidegger's essay on the ontotheological constitution of metaphysics, the point that he makes about Aristotle is similar to the point that Heidegger makes about the broader Western philosophical preoccupation with the grounding of being: its "god" is not the God of the Bible; instead, it is an idol of human rationality. The affinity between Woodson and Heidegger here is that what Woodson refers to as Aristotle's "paganism" is a causative factor in producing a god before whom Heidegger says we cannot "dance or sing." As Heidegger puts it, it is the "perdurance" of thought that demands an end to infinite regress resulting in a god of philosophical explanation; a god of anteriority, as I discussed in the introduction. Reading these two thinkers chronologically, one may say that Woodson describes the pagan practice of ontotheology in its racist manifestations—I do this at greater length in another forthcoming book, *Reason's Dilemma: Subjectivity, Transcendence, and the Problem of Ontotheology* (Palgrave Macmillan, under contract)—and Heidegger elaborates on the basis of this sort of Greek philosophical influence on Christian theology.

Another point must be made about Woodson's reading of Aquinas. Jean-Luc Marion challenges the popular notion—one that Woodson seems to embrace—that Aquinas uncritically appropriated Aristotle resulting in the popular use of Greek philosophy in Christian theology. In chapter eight of *God Without Being*, titled "Thomas Aquinas and Ontotheology," Marion argues that Aquinas's distinction between natural and revealed theology excludes God from the realm of being—that is, of the ontotheological—and that it is not until after Aquinas that Christian theology makes the Greek ontotheological move. See Jean-Luc Marion, *God Without Being*, trans. Thomas A. Carlson (Chicago: University of Chicago Press, 2012), 199–236. This point does not negate Woodson's insights, but rather locates the ontotheological starting point after Aquinas in the history of philosophy. Woodson's assertions about Aristotle, his incompatibility with Christian theology, his appropriation by Christian theologians, and the devastating effects of this appropriation on African Americans at the hands of a Greek (pagan) infused Christian theology—even if they came after Aquinas—remain unaffected.

43. William R. Jones, *Is God a White Racist?* (Boston, MA: Beacon Press, 1998), xxiv.

44. Frederick Douglass, *Narrative of the Life of Frederick Douglass, an American Slave*, with preface by William Lloyd Garrison (Boston: Anti-Slavery Office, 1849). Retrieved from https://www.loc.gov/item/82225385/47.

45. Ibid.

46. Ibid., 48.

47. Ibid., 49.

48. Douglass begins discussing Rowena Hamilton at page 49.

49. Ibid., 48.

50. Ibid., 64–65.

51. Donald Gibson, in his essay, "Christianity and Individualism: (Re-)Creation and Reality in Frederick Douglass's Representation of Self," *African-American Review* 26, no. 4 (Winter 1992): 591–603, further argues that the problem of evil is worked out in Douglass's fight with Covey. He writes that Douglass's "ambivalence" with respect to the nature and or existence of God is resolved in Douglass's fight with Covey: "It is of significance that this expression of ambivalence occurs in the Narrative prior to Douglass's fight with Covey, 'the nigger breaker,' for it is my contention that such ambivalence was resolved with the outcome of that confrontation, a moment that also witnessed the birth, in the consciousness of the former (as he sees himself at the time) slave, of an extraordinarily intense and ardent individualism." Although Douglass may have resolved the theological ambivalence of God, Gibson points out that Douglass did so practically—that is, through the fight with Covey—and not through any sort of intellectual problem solving, which is precisely my point here: Douglass, in this narrative, does not seek theoretical and intellectual solutions to the problem of evil. Instead, he sought his resolution through moral action, through a radical affirmation of existential responsibility.

52. Frederick Douglass, "The Anti-Slavery Movement," speech delivered on March 19, 1855, in *The Frederick Douglass Papers*, 47–48.

53. Emmanuel Levinas, *Otherwise Than Being*, trans. Alphonso Lingis (Pittsburgh, PA: Duquesne University Press, 2009), 170.

54. The relationship between art and the ethical in Levinas is complex. See Pamela Carralero, "A Holy Aesthetic: Recognizing an Art That Is Otherwise Than Art in the Work of Emmanuel Levinas," *Epoché: A Journal of the History of Philosophy* 22, no. 2 (Spring 2018): 505–22; Henry McDonald, "Aesthetics as First Ethics: Levinas

and the Altherity of Literary Discourse," *diatrics* 38 (Winter 2008): 15–41; Philipp Theisohn, "Reading the Beyond: Levinas—Literature, Holiness, and Politics," *Naharaim* 1 (2008): 61–80; Jill Robbins, *Altered Reading: Levinas and Literature* (Chicago: University of Chicago Press, 1999); Robert Hughes, *Ethics, Aesthetic, and the Beyond of Language* (New York: State University of New York Press, 2010); Leslie Hill, "'Distrust of Poetry': Levinas, Blanchot, Celan," *MLN* 120 (December 2005): 987; Fabio Ciaramelli, "The Infinite Call to Interpretation: Remarks on Levinas and Art," trans. Ashraf Noor, *Nhaharaim* 6 (November 2012): 357; Gerald Burns, "Should Poetry Be Ethical or Otherwise?" *SubStance* 38 (2009): 72–91; Seán Hand, "Shadowing Ethics: Levinas's View of Art and Aesthetics," in *Facing the Other: The Ethics of Emmanuel Levinas*, ed Seán Hand (Richmond: Curzon Press, 1996), 63–90; Tanja Staehler, "Images and Shadows: Levinas and the Ambiguity of the Aesthetic," *Estetika* 47 (November 2010): 123–43; Edith Wyschogrod, "The Art in Ethics: Aesthetics, Objectivity, and Alterity in the Philosophy of Emmanuel Levinas," in *Ethics as First Philosophy: The Significance of Emmanuel Levinas for Philosophy, Literature, and Religion*, ed. A. Peperzak (New York: Routledge, 1995): 137–48; Francesca Yardenit Albertini, "The Language of the Meeting with the Other and the Phenomenology of Eros: Traces of Aesthetic Thinking in the Philosophy of Emmanuel Levinas," in *Levinas in Jerusalem: Phenomenology, Ethics, Politics, Aesthetics*, ed. Joelle Hansel (New York: Springer, 2009: 157–70); and Silvia Benso, "Aesthethics: Levinas, Plato, and Art," *Epoche* 13, no. 1 (Fall 2008): 163–83.

55. Emmanuel Levinas, "Reality and Its Shadow," in *The Levinas Reader*, ed. Seán Hand (Cambridge, MA: Basil Blackwell, 1989), 129–43.

56. Levinas, *Otherwise Than Being*, 169.

57. Ibid.

58. Ibid.

59. Ibid.

60. Ibid., 5.

61. Ibid.

62. Ibid., 6.

63. Carralero, "A Holy Aesthetic," 511.

64. Ibid.

65. Levinas, *Otherwise Than Being*, 171.

66. Ibid., 169–70.

67. Ibid.

68. Levinas, *Of God Who Comes to Mind*, 87.

69. Ibid.

70. Ibid.

71. Emmanuel Levinas, "Useless Suffering," in *Entre Nous: Thinking of the Other*, trans. Michael Smith and Barbara Harshav (New York: Columbia University Press, 1998), 91.

72. Ibid.

73. Ibid.

74. When Levinas refers to suffering as something more than simply a refractory to the synthesis of the Kantian "I think," it is a reference to the frustration of empirical

cognition which would find itself facing an object of experience in the sensory manifold for which it could not make a conceptual account. So on the Kantian account of knowledge, one could not make a synthetic a priori judgment about such an object, and thus could not claim any knowledge of it. For Kant, this sets the stage for his notion of reflective judgment in the *Critique of Judgment*, where he argues that there is a free play of the imagination and the understanding when there is an intuition without a corresponding concept. The faculty of judgment thus allows for such a concept as the beautiful, in turn enabling reflective judgment to have a degree of artistic creativity that empirical cognition does not permit. I discuss this concept in greater detail in chapter 4, when I turn to Douglass's use of narrative art and poetry as a form of Kantian reflective judgment.

75. Levinas, "Useless Suffering," 94.
76. Ibid.
77. Ibid., 95.
78. Ibid., 95–96.
79. Ibid., 94.
80. Ibid., 96.
81. Ibid., 97.
82. Ibid., 100–101.
83. Ibid., 101.

Chapter Four

A Demand for Universality

Narrative, Art, and the Politics of Moral Suasion

"In the beginning, God created the heavens and the earth. Now the earth was formless and empty. Darkness was on the surface of the deep. God's Spirit was hovering over the surface of the waters. God said, 'Let there be light,' and there was light."

—*Holy Bible*[1]

AESTHETICS AND THE POLITICAL

The previous two chapters are my attempt to develop an existential and phenomenological interpretation of Douglass in the context of an Incarnational theological paradigm. It is from within this Christian theological framework that I have been arguing that Douglass makes the word flesh, in contrast to the reformed epistemology of analytic theism, which, with rationality as its end, employs high levels of abstraction and generality that makes the flesh of Jesus—that is, his historical, social, political, and cultural context—an abstract word. As I argued in the first chapter, analytic theism follows the path of Rawlsian political theory and white Christian theology, which both employ philosophical abstraction to the detriment of urgent moral and political concerns of interest to Black people. So my argument thus far echoes Tertullian's rhetorical dictum "What has Athens to do with Jerusalem?" Indeed, I submit that Athens—the way of philosophical abstraction—has colonized Jerusalem—the site of the Judeo-Christian tradition—insofar as rationality has become, at least for the reformed epistemology of analytic theism, the litmus test of philosophical and theological legitimacy, its anti-foundationalism notwithstanding. And, as I have tried to show thus far, this is a grave mistake that my existential and phenomenological interpretation of Douglass aims to correct. This Christian theological interpretation of Douglass is important because Douglass's own social and political engagements with Christianity occurred in a variety of abolition, post-abolition, reconstruction, and post-reconstruction debates that presupposed certain Christian moral and theological teachings as part of a rational, public discourse. So since Douglass publicly spoke from *within* Christianity *against* Christianity, a Christian theological framework for an interpretation of Douglass is apropos. My interpretation of Douglass has also aimed to show the importance of reading Douglass with white philosophical figures whose work both has a resonance with Douglass's work and is work that Douglass may interrogate at the level of praxis. Thus far, then, I have presented an existential and phenomenological interpretation of Douglass that, unlike the reformed epistemology of analytic theism, makes the word flesh through an attentiveness to urgent moral and political concerns of Black people, and also through the appropriation of white existential and phenomenological theory in praxis.

In this chapter, I continue these efforts with Kant, a different dialogue partner in philosophical aesthetics. My aim is to develop two Kantian interpretations of Douglass. First, I interpret Douglass with Kant in order to show a general resonance between Douglass's and Kant's views on art. I argue that Douglass's understandings of knowledge, morality, and art reflect similar understandings of Kant in his critical philosophy.[2] And second, I want to show that Douglass makes certain Kantian anthropological and aesthetic assumptions that work together in Douglass's politics, specifically in his account of moral suasion as an abolition strategy. As to my first point of interpretation, I draw a connection between Kant and Douglass as it relates to the faculty of judgment and its mediation between the understanding and reason as Kant discusses it in the *Critique of Judgment*. In support of this first interpretation of Douglass with Kant, I first read Kant's epistemology, his moral philosophy, and the *Critique of Judgment* with his essay "On the Miscarriage of All Philosophical Trials in Theodicy," and also with some of Douglass's views on art, and his literary works. In support of my second interpretation of Douglass with Kant, I argue that Douglass's *Narrative* is part of an overall abolition strategy that Frank M. Kirkland has referred to as a "communicative practice of justification." I want to expand upon the work of Kirkland and Bill E. Lawson, as I have done in one of my previously published essays, where I attempted to build upon Kirkland's and Lawson's work on the Kantian features of Douglass's social and political thought by interpreting Douglass with reference to Kant's philosophical theology and rational psychology. In that essay, I argued, *inter alia*, that Douglass makes certain Kantian epistemic assumptions in a moral critique of an argument in favor of baptizing slaves.[3]

In this chapter, however, I want to show the Kantian aesthetic features that are present in Douglass's use of narrative for political purposes and thus continue to build on the work of Kirkland and Lawson.

The chapter proceeds as follows. Before making the arguments that are the substance of the chapter, some discussion is needed to address Kant's racist anthropology and its compatibility with Douglass, whom Kant would very likely have considered subhuman due to his race. This preliminary discussion is one that I have presented in several of my other published works.[4] I present this discussion again here as a prelude to the rest of chapter not only to anticipate objections to my interpretation of Douglass and Kant but also to offer a philosophical hermeneutic that I believe responsibly engages the interpretive problems of race and racism that inevitably arise when Black philosophers are read in conjunction with white philosophers like Kant who are known to hold anti-Black racist beliefs.[5]

After this preliminary discussion, in section three of the chapter, I argue in support of my first Kantian interpretation of Douglass. In this section of the chapter, I discuss Kant's account of the various cognitive faculties: the faculty of the understanding (used to cognize objects of experience in nature), the faculty of reason—practical reason (used under the presupposition of transcendental freedom), and the faculty of judgment, which Kant argues mediates between the understanding and reason. As it relates to practical reason, I discuss Kant's essay "On the Miscarriage of All Philosophical Trials in Theodicy" to show how practical reason demands an honest epistemic silence of Job and eschews the dishonest epistemic hubris of Job's three friends. It is here where Douglass's *Narrative* becomes a work of art, allowing for an expression of Douglass's feelings of pleasure and displeasure that his faculty of judgment leads him to express as art. Judgment is thus neither a mere synthetic a priori cognition of empirical objects nor a mere rational concept without an object, but rather an object with no concept to describe it. In this way, Douglass's work is artistic, for it avoids the rigorous demands of the understanding necessary for synthetic a priori knowledge, on one hand, and reason's flights of fancy that purport to expand reason's reach beyond the world of objects, on the other hand, all while demonstrating the free play of Douglass's imagination and understanding in reflective judgment in such a way that Douglass's use of narrative as art manifests a spirit (*Geist*) that produces a work of artistic genius.

In section four of the chapter, I make my second argument for a Kantian interpretation of Douglass. I want to expand my prior work on the Kantian features of Douglass's philosophical theology to include new work on the Kantian features of Douglass's aesthetics that I believe form, in part at least, the basis for Douglass's abolitionist politics. Here, I draw from Kirkland's account of Douglass as a Kantian-styled, Enlightenment philosopher in his groundbreaking essay "Enslavement, Moral Suasion, and Struggles for Recognition: Frederick Douglass's Answer to the Question—'What Is Enlightenment?'" and Bill E. Lawson's Kantian political anthropology of Douglass in his essay, "Douglass among the Romantics."[6] As I have argued before, in the same vein as Kirkland and Lawson, I do not argue that Douglass is a Kantian, or that he was reading Kant. Instead, I am arguing that there is an aesthetic dimension to Douglass's political work as an abolitionist reflecting what I believe are some deep affinities with Kant's account of judgments of taste. My claim is that Douglass's use of moral suasion, in either of its forms,[7] is grounded in certain Kantian assumptions about human creative capacities and cognitive faculties that relate not only to the creation of the work of art but also to its public perception, a perception that led Douglass to believe that other persons would be motivated, as part of a *sensus communis*, to moral and political action based upon reading his narrative.

I conclude the chapter in section five. There, I reflect on the arguments made in this chapter and look ahead to the final chapter, in which I return to Levinas to develop another dimension of my phenomenological interpretation of Douglass.

PHILOSOPHICAL HERMENEUTICS AND THE JURISDICTION OF HISTORY: A PRELUDE ON KANT AND RACE

Philosophical research has brought much attention Kant's racism over the last thirty years or so. This research has run the gamut of positions, theories, and debates not only about the role of Kant in developing the modern concept of race but also about the extent to which Kant's racist ideas impact his overall critical project and to what extent it may be useful or even advisable to utilize Kantian philosophical frameworks at all in philosophical interpretation, especially when one is reading Kant with Black philosophers.[8] I am not interested in entering these debates, advocating one of these positions over another, or espousing some grand theory purporting to end the debate about the extent to which Kant's critical system is incurably racist, or whether his racist views are merely the product of the time in which he lived. Indeed, engaging in these sorts of debates is worthy of a book on its own. It is enough for my purposes here, however, that significant scholarship in both philosophy (Robert Bernasconi) and Christian theology (J. Kameron Carter) has thoroughly and quite credibly pointed out that Kant plays a significant—indeed a formative—role in the modern construction of race and its influence in both science and Christianity.[9] So it is undeniable that Kant's corpus is, in some sense at least, responsible for the construction and maintenance of a racial taxonomy that lies at the core of the Western imperial, colonial project of justifying white supremacy. Again, there have been extensive arguments about the effects of this on Kant's critical philosophy, but my aim here is not to enter these debates. Instead, I propose an interpretive approach to Kant that facilitates my interpretation of Douglass with Kant by recognizing Kant's racism in such a way that the proverbial "baby" of Kant's insights about knowledge, art, and theology are rescued from the filthy "bathwater" of his racist ideas. Now the objection immediately arises that separating Kant's philosophical views from his racist ideas is precisely what cannot be done. But, as I will argue below, this approach to understanding Kant's racism and its impact on the interpretation of his texts denies the jurisdiction of history that I argued for in chapter 1—not the jurisdiction of the history of the text, but rather the jurisdiction of the history of the interpreter. And to make this argument, I turn to the philosophical hermeneutics of Hans Georg Gadamer in his *magnum opus*, *Truth and Method*.

An interpretation of any philosophical text—indeed, according to Gadamer, any text whatsoever—ought not rely too heavily upon a sort of Enlightenment empiricism, or what I will call a "textual positivism," which is an empiricist hermeneutic that draws conclusions about the meaning of a text based upon notions of "original intent," or "authorial objectives." As applied to Kant, one should not employ textual positivism to assess the viability of Kant's corpus based upon the presence of—or the operation of, for that matter—racist ideas within it. "Textual positivism," as I contemplate the use of that term here, is consistent with the overly narrow modern conception of truth as correspondence, which finds racist ideas—both present and operative—in Kant's texts and thus takes such findings to be conclusive with respect to the use of Kant in subsequent philosophical generations in a way that forecloses the possibility of meaningful advances in philosophical research. The problem with such an approach is that interestingly, at least as it applies to Black philosophy (which is critical of the Enlightenment), it unwittingly pays homage to a central feature of the overall Enlightenment project: it results in the separation of text from self, which, much like the separation of subject from object, is consistent with an epistemic paradigm resulting in a conception of truth as "correspondence" that is far too impoverished to accommodate the dynamic relationship between the author of a text and its interpreter. Gadamer refers to this Enlightenment-oriented shortcoming as "prejudice against prejudice." In other words, there are judgments that interpreters make prior to their engagements with the text which are grounded not in the text, but rather in the myriad social, political, economic, and religious experiences of the interpreter. Enlightenment rationality purports to access the meaning of a text without any attentiveness whatsoever to these sorts of pre-hermeneutical judgments, and claims to access a text's "original meaning," an endeavor which is itself prejudicial. Phenomenologically understood, Gadamer wants to access a pre-theoretical understanding of interpretation by bracketing theoretical notions of the text because for him, what is most important is not to access the text's "original meaning," but rather to access the *lebenswelt* of the interpreter and the resulting *lebenswelt* of the hermeneutical production of the interpreted text. For it is this bracketing that opens up access to the *lebenswelt* of human subjectivity; a world full of experiences that one inevitably brings to the text. It is these experiences that are Gadamer's notion of "effective history," which, I believe, counters the shortcomings of textual positivism and results in an understanding of Kant's texts, racist though they may be, that is conducive to the preservation and progress of knowledge rather than what Gadamer calls the "deformation" of knowledge. In chapter 1, I argued that my concept of the jurisdiction of history counters abstraction in Christian theology through an attentiveness to the historical conditions of the Gospels. Here, reading the jurisdiction of history with Gadamer, one applies it not to historical conditions, but rather to texts. Gadamer writes that "When a naïve faith in scientific method denies the existence of effective history there can be an actual deformation of knowledge. . . . But on the whole the power of history does not depend on its being recognized. This is the power of history over finite human consciousness, namely that it prevails even where faith in method leads one to deny one's own historicity."[10] Hence the title of Gadamer's *magnum opus*, *Truth and Method*: one cannot access the former because the latter has not been properly formulated. Gadamer aims to correct the method to access the "truth," but not truth in the positivistic sense of empirical verification—which seems to be the way of textual positivism—but rather in the more holistic sense of the truth as "understanding."

Gadamer says of his principle of "history of effect" that "Historical consciousness must become conscious that in the apparent immediacy with which it approaches a work of art or a traditionary text, there is also another kind of inquiry in play, albeit unrecognized and unregulated."[11] This other "kind of inquiry in play" is what Gadamer call our "hermeneutical situation" in which "we are always already affected by history," which determines in advance both what seems to us worth inquiring about and what will appear as an object of investigation, and we more or less forget half of what is really there."[12] Indeed, for Gadamer, "we miss the whole truth of the phenomenon—when we take its immediate appearance as the whole truth."[13] Thus, when approaching a text, one must maintain an awareness of how one's history is at work in the hermeneutic endeavor. Suspending our naïve understanding of the text in what Gadamer calls its "immediate appearance" is essential to see "the whole truth of the phenomenon."[14] Keeping this in mind, Gadamer argues that "When a naïve faith in scientific method denies the existence of effective history, there can be an actual deformation of knowledge."[15]

This is the mistake of textual positivism: it ignores effective history and deforms knowledge, creating barriers to philosophical dialogue rather than building bridges over philosophical problems to move the dialogue forward. Another important point to be made here is that significant work on Kant and Black philosophy has already been done, and suggesting that reading Kant with Black philosophers is ill advised because of Kant's racism would do a disservice to this scholarship.[16] Indeed, the previous work on Kant and Black philosophy—some of it on Kant and Douglass that I engage in this chapter—represents Gadamer's notion of "history of effect" already at work in the hermeneutics of those who have produced this scholarship. And my interpretation of Kant and Douglass shows the "history of effect" at work in this chapter.

So, applying this framework to Douglass and Kant, I argue that it would be a deformation of knowledge to avoid interpreting Douglass with Kant because of Kant's racism, its presence in, and indeed even its performative functions in his critical system.[17] Doing so denies the Kant interpreter the opportunity to glean something from Kant's texts—racist though they may be—that can be appropriated and transformed in the interest of philosophical research and the advancement of knowledge. Indeed, an attentiveness to my own mixed-race identity, which I have described in my essay titled "German Chocolate: Why Philosophy Is So Personal," because of my African American father and my German mother, has resulted in this very book being a reflection of the complexities of my own racial and religious identity.[18] I argued in that essay that text and self have merged such that I read Kant—my "German" side—and Douglass—my "Chocolate" side—as two philosophers with similar interests and philosophical projects instead of as oppressor (Kant) and oppressed (Douglass). Again, this is not to deny that race and racism may have roles in Kant's critical philosophy that are central and even performative—propositions that are themselves debatable.[19] But despite this, I, as an interpreter, ought to be granted the opportunity to interpret Kant and Douglass, or any other two thinkers, for that matter, based upon the workings of my effective history—that is, based upon my phenomenological *lebenswelt* of experiences that enable me to see things in the text that no one else can see, thus producing an interpretation that advances philosophical knowledge.[20]

A word of caution is due here, however. I am not advocating a sort of reckless, Protagorean relativism in philosophical hermeneutics, and Gadamer is not advocating such a position, either. This is not a radical claim that texts can mean whatsoever one wishes them to mean, or that one can openly disregard textual evidence that contradicts one's account of the text. Such interpretations are untenable. And again, I make no such claims here. Instead, I am making the much more modest claim that despite the presence and perhaps even the performative function of race in Kant's critical philosophy, it would be a "deformation of knowledge" in the Gadamerian sense to allow Kant's racism to prevent my interpretation of Kant that reads him with Douglass rather than against him as it would also be a "deformation of knowledge" to prevent my use of Douglass by reading him with Kant rather than against him. So rather than reading Kant and Douglass against one another, my own sense of history informs my hermeneutic endeavor, resulting in an appropriation and transformation of Kant such that he can be read with Douglass and vice versa. This hermeneutic approach advances rather than deforms knowledge. So what I deny is not that race and racism are present or even performative in the Kantian corpus, but rather that their presence and their performative function ought not preclude a reading of Douglass with Kant or vice versa that would prevent the furtherance of philosophical conversation with dialogue partners that, at first glance—the glance of the naïveté of the hermeneutical "natural attitude"—appear to be incompatible. With my bracketing of such a naïve approach to the text, the advance of knowledge is assured through a phenomenological access to my effective history grounded in my *lebenswelt*, which merges with both Douglass's and Kant's texts in a manner that furthers rather than halts philosophical dialogue. It is to this philosophical dialogue—to this conversation between Kant and Douglass—that I now turn.

KANT, DOUGLASS, AND ART

My first interpretation of Douglass with Kant is based upon what I believe to be a strong resonance between the conclusions that Kant reaches in his epistemology, his moral philosophy, and his account of aesthetics, and Douglass's views on art in two of his speeches, and some of his works of art (his *Narrative of the Life of Frederick Douglass, An American Slave* and his novella, *The Heroic Slave*). As Kirkland and Lawson have both argued, Douglass, though not a Kantian in explicit terms, makes some of his arguments employing certain Enlightenment-inspired anthropological presuppositions such as rationality, dignity, and autonomy. So I begin my comparison of Kant and Douglass with Kant. First, I discuss the broad contours of Kant's critical philosophy—what Kant terms "The Canon of Pure Reason." This discussion will analyze the broad conclusions of each of Kant's three Critiques, according to the three basic questions that Kant claims constitute the entirety of reason's speculative and practical interests. These questions are "What can I know?" "What ought I do?" and "What may I hope?" Each of these questions corresponds to different parts of Kant's critical philosophy. The first two questions relate to Kant's epistemology, and his ethics. And the third question is connected to his ethics, his theology, and his aesthetics. Against this backdrop of Kant, the stage is set for an analysis of Douglass's work and its comparison to the broader conclusions of Kant's critical philosophy, especially his views on aesthetics in relation to his views on science and morality.

Kant and the Canon of Pure Reason

Three basic questions are at the core of Kant's critical philosophy, and for Kant, at the core of speculative and practical reason itself: (1) What can I know? (2) What ought I to do? and (3) What may I hope? These three questions provide the framework for what Kant calls the "canon" of pure reason: the totality of all a priori principles of the correct use of our epistemic faculties.[21] Kant's answers to these three questions demonstrate the role of the various cognitive faculties (the understanding, reason, and judgment); their corresponding governing a priori principles of lawfulness, final purpose, and purposiveness over the "mental powers" of cognition, desire, and the feeling of pleasure or displeasure; and, finally, their respective applications to nature, freedom, and art. By raising these three questions and providing answers to them, Kant is attempting to live up to the inscription in the temple of the Delphic oracle to "know thyself." This imperative inspired Socrates to know himself by recognizing his fundamental lack of knowledge relative to the politicians, the poets and the artisans.[22] And Kant's critical philosophy aims to do something similar: to critique the rational capacities of human beings so that we can fully appreciate and respect the limits of knowledge, and thereby better understand our place in the world. This is why the critical philosophy is "Copernican" in nature: it aims to reinstate human beings to the center of epistemic, moral, and aesthetic life, despite the Copernican decentering of humanity from the physical world according to the laws of nature. So these three questions and their answers demonstrate that Kant's critical philosophy is profoundly both Socratic and Copernican: we "know" ourselves better because we not only understand our epistemic abilities but also learn to resituate ourselves at the center of a moral world after the natural world has displaced us. Kant's answers to each of these three questions is discussed below.

What Can I Know?

The answer to the first question, "What can I know?" according to Kant, is that our knowledge is restricted to the limitations of our cognitive faculty that Kant calls the "understanding." The understanding brings objects of experience under the categories of pure reason, enabling us to form synthetic a priori statements about them, and this is, for Kant, what alone counts as knowledge. In attempting to refute David Hume's skepticism, Kant makes transcendental arguments to show that there is a component of our cognition that is necessary and universal, and not merely contingent, as Hume argued.

Hence there is Kant's account of causation in the "Analogies of Experience" in the "Transcendental Analytic" of the *Critique of Pure Reason*, where Kant argues that causation is not a property of objects, but rather a cognitive category of the knowing subject. And Kant makes a similar argument against his rationalist target, Gottfried Leibniz. For instead of theoretical reason making knowledge claims about speculative metaphysics, the subjective structure of human cognition circumscribes knowledge to objects of experience that appear within the spatiotemporal framework of the understanding. Kant thus labels the first question about what we can know "speculative," as it restricts speculative, metaphysical thinking about God, freedom, and the soul to the limitations of the understanding. So as to the first question, Kant gives an account of scientific, natural laws and how the understanding guarantees the truth of our knowledge by overcoming skepticism through the employment of an a priori cognitive structure, on one hand, while restricting the domain of our knowledge to objects of experience, on the other hand. This is what Kant calls the "land of truth," or nature: we can only "know" that which conforms to the conceptual framework of human cognition.

It is important to remember that for Kant, our epistemic limitations do not result in a repudiation of that which cannot be known, such that one can say with Hume that if we do not see it empirically, it therefore does not exist. No. Such a claim is as dogmatic for Kant as Leibniz's claims about speculative metaphysics. Hence Kant's point about the dogma of empiricism, cast in terms of the difference between Epicurus and Plato:

> But when empiricism itself as frequently happens, becomes dogmatic in its attitude towards ideas, and confidently denies whatever lies beyond the sphere of its intuitive knowledge, it betrays the same lack of modesty; and this is all the more reprehensible owing to the irreparable injury which is thereby caused to the practical interests of reason. The contrast between the teaching of Epicurus and that of Plato is of this nature. Each of the two types of philosophy says more than it knows. Epicurus encourages and furthers knowledge, though to the prejudice of the practical; Plato supplies excellent practical principles, but permits reason to indulge in ideal explanations of natural appearances, in regard to which a speculative knowledge is alone possible to us—to the neglect of physical investigation.[23]

Epicurus and Plato roughly correspond to Kant's targets of Hume on the side of empiricism and Leibniz on the side of rationalism. As Kant puts it, "Each of the two types of philosophy says more than it knows." So instead of claiming knowledge of that which is beyond the a priori structure of our conceptual scheme, Kant's aim is not to dogmatically claim—as Hume does—that such a realm does not exist, but rather that we cannot know it. This is why Kant distinguishes between limits (*Schranke*) and bounds (*Grenze*). Limits restrict knowledge within certain parameters. In contrast, bounds assume something beyond us. Kant defines the distinction in this way: "Bounds (in extended beings) always presuppose a space existing outside a certain definite place and inclosing it; limits do not require this, but are mere negations which affect a quantity so far as it is not absolutely complete."[24] Kant points out that mathematics and the natural sciences are limited. Kant writes, "In mathematics and natural science human reason admits of limits but not of bounds, viz., that something indeed lies outside it, at which it can never arrive, but not that it will at any point find completion in its internal progress."[25] For Kant, the "enlarging of insights in mathematics and the possibility of new discoveries are infinite; and the same is the case with the discovery of new properties of nature, of new forces and laws, by continued experience and its rational unification."[26] But Kant cautions that "limits cannot fail to be seen here; for mathematics refers to appearances only, and what cannot be an object of sensuous intuition (such as the concepts of metaphysics and of morals) lies entirely without its sphere. It can never lead to them, but neither does it require them."[27] So it is that for Kant, while mathematics and the natural sciences are unlimited in their disciplinary applications, there are limits (*Schranke*) facing both disciplines as they are restricted to objects of experience that are mere appearances and not things in themselves. In contrast to mathematics and natural science, there is speculative metaphysics, which, according to Kant,

> leads us toward bounds [*Grenze*] in the dialectical attempts of pure reason (not undertaken arbitrarily or wantonly, but stimulated thereto by the nature of reason itself). And the transcendental ideas, as they do not admit of evasion and yet are never capable of realization, serve to point out to us actually not only the bounds of the use of pure reason, but also the way to determine them.[28]

Speculative metaphysics is as rational as mathematics and the natural sciences in its origin, but in its operation, unlike mathematics and the natural sciences, it does not yield knowledge. Instead, speculative metaphysics reminds us that there is something beyond us that is unknowable. Thus, Kant's point that metaphysical speculation shows us "not only the bounds of the use of pure reason, but also the way to determine them." So Kant limits empirical knowledge by way of affirming its narrow scope to objects as appearances of a possible experience, and articulates bounds for metaphysical speculation by negating knowledge of what is beyond our rational, cognitive abilities; bounds that affirm room for something beyond us, while denying that we can have any synthetic a priori knowledge of it. Hence Kant's famous dictum that his aim was to "deny reason, in order to make room for faith." The answer to the question "What can I know?" tells us not that mathematical and scientific truths are the only truths that there are, but rather that our cognitive faculty of the understanding restricts our knowledge to just those truths, while our rational inclination to metaphysical speculation reminds us that there is much more beyond mathematics and natural science that we simply cannot know. The next question ("What ought I to do?") allows for morality what epistemology disallows altogether, which is to say that, for Kant, practical reason's interest in freedom is distinct from theoretical reason's interest in knowledge. So practical reason must see itself—morally speaking, not ontologically—as if (*als ob*) it can exceed the bounds (*Grenze*) of the sensible world in a way that theoretical reason cannot. This is discussed in more detail in the next subsection.

What Ought I to Do?

The second question in Kant's canon of pure reason is a practical question and is beyond the scope of the *Critique of Pure Reason* because its interest is moral, not transcendental. That is, the question of what one ought to do is a moral question that does not, through the use of transcendental argument, purport to refute skepticism by demonstrating the a priori components of human cognition. Instead, this question concerns an interest of reason in its practical rather than its theoretical employment. Theoretical reason's interest is in nature, where the a priori categories of the understanding subsume the particular under the universal to make synthetic a priori judgments that yield knowledge. Each judgment contains one concept and one intuition, the subjective form of which is space and time. For example, if I was to say, "There is my cat, Felix," this is a synthetic a priori statement that counts as knowledge because the universal concept ("cat") subsumes the particular intuition ("Felix") within a space, "There" at a certain time, "is." These are the sorts of things that we can know, including, as previously discussed, mathematics and the natural sciences. Again, this is Kant's "land of truth," and it is the operation of the understanding working in the interest of theoretical reason, which aims to produce a rational account of nature that allows for mathematical and scientific progress.

But practical reason has a different aim. The answer to the question "What ought I to do?" is an answer that concerns practical reason's interest in freedom. Among the most basic concerns of Kant's critical philosophy is how one can be moral in the midst of natural laws that dictate the operations of the natural world. How does the notion of what one "ought" to do even make any sense, considering the overwhelming presence of mechanistic, inexorable, natural laws? Kant, in his resolution of the third antinomy of causal necessity and freedom in the *Critique of Pure Reason* points out that the basis for practical, moral freedom is transcendental freedom, which is the necessary presupposition of freedom that is required for the assignment of praise and blame. Kant argues from his malicious lie example that there may be myriad reasons for someone's motive in telling a malicious lie. One may be motivated, Kant argues, by "defective education, bad company . . . the viciousness of a natural disposition insensitive to shame, in levity and thoughtlessness,"[29] and so forth. But, according to Kant, we do not allow any of these factors to absolve the person who told the lie from responsibility for telling the lie. Instead, for Kant, we hold a person accountable for a malicious lie that he or she has told precisely because we base our blame "on a law of reason whereby we regard reason as a cause that irrespective of all the above-mentioned empirical conditions could have determined, and ought to have determined, the agent to act otherwise."[30] Kant's point here is that despite the presence of empirical conditions which, in the natural world according to the understanding would dictate outcomes a priori, human beings have a spontaneous causality at work that exempts them from the weight and pull of natural causality in matters of morality. So it is that one may say a hungry animal that scavenges food by taking it from another animal is operating according to the laws of natural causality: the animal's hunger is the cause of taking the food from another animal. The scavenging animal lives based on nature's law of cause and effect. But for Kant, human beings are different from animals. If a hungry human being undertakes a similar course of action to a scavenging animal, taking food from another human being, we refer to that human being as a criminal who has committed theft and as one who is also morally contemptible for that theft. So it is that human beings have a spontaneous causality that functions independent of natural causes. Again, how can this be? In his resolution the third antinomy, Kant argues that causality and necessity are consistent with one another because they each belong to different human standpoints. Causality belongs to the standpoint of humans as empirical beings. But freedom belongs to the standpoint of humans as intelligible beings. Kant explains:

> Man is one of the appearances of the sensible world, and . . . one of the natural causes the causality of which must stand under empirical laws. Like all other things in nature, he must have an empirical character. This character we come to know through the powers and faculties which he reveals in his actions. In lifeless, or merely animal, nature we find no ground for thinking that any faculty is conditioned otherwise than in a merely sensible manner. Man, however, . . . knows himself also through pure apperception; and this, indeed, in acts and inner determinations which he cannot regard as impressions of the senses. He is thus . . . on the one hand phenomenon, and on the other hand . . . a purely intelligible object. We entitle these faculties understanding and reason. . . . That our reason has causality, or that we at least represent it to ourselves as having causality, is evident from the imperative which in all matters of conduct we impose as rules upon our active powers. "*Ought*" expresses a kind of necessity and . . .

connection with grounds . . . found nowhere else in the whole of nature. The understanding can know . . . only what is, what has been, or what will be. We cannot say that . . . nature ought to be other than what in all these time-relations it actually is. When we have the course of nature alone in view, "*ought*" has no meaning whatsoever. It is just as absurd to ask what ought to happen in the natural world as to ask what properties a circle ought to have. All that we are justified in asking is: what happens in nature? What are the properties of the circle?[31]

Kant resolves the antinomy of causal necessity and freedom by concluding that in one sense—that of the sensible world—human beings are subject to the laws of causal necessity, but that in another sense—that of the intelligible world—human beings have a causality of their own which acts independent of natural laws. Kant points out that moral language, the "ought," points us toward a sort of disruption of the natural world insofar as it suggests a spontaneous causality independent of natural laws, for we cannot say that anything in nature "ought" to be either this or that way, but rather only that nature "is" thus and so. So as beings who are subject to the laws of nature, we have the cognitive faculty of the understanding. But as beings who are moral, we are independent of causal laws and have the faculty of reason. The understanding operates under the laws of nature to provide us with a stable knowledge of the natural world, and reason operates under the law of freedom—the categorical imperative—to provide human beings with autonomy from nature and a sense of dignity as moral beings, who unlike beings in the animal world, are not instinct-driven, but rather who are rational beings, capable of acting only in accord with principles that they will to be universal laws. This is the categorical imperative, and it demands absolute duty to the moral law, which, in order for an action to have moral worth, must be the determining ground of the will, which Kant also refers to as the power of the soul that he calls desire.[32] If feeling or inclination determine one's will, then one is living by a hypothetical imperative that nature governs—that is, one's will to produce a certain outcome consistent with one's desires. But Kant, the consummate deontologist, argues against this sort of morality and in favor of one's desires being subordinate to one's duty to the moral law.

With this in mind, a certain picture of Kant's moral subject emerges. Kant's moral subject is situated between its duty to the moral law, on one hand, and its feeling and inclination, on the other hand. Both clamor for the moral attention of the moral subject's will. All actions based on the moral subject's feeling and inclination are based on the law of cause and effect, showing the moral subject to be not autonomous, but rather heteronomous in that the law of cause and effect from nature determines the moral subject's actions. In contrast, all moral actions based on the moral subject's duty to the moral law have no regard for consequences, and are thus independent of the natural law of cause and effect, showing the moral subject to be an autonomous being that is capable of acting independent of nature. It is in this portrait of Kant's moral subject that the cognitive faculties of understanding and reason, along with their a priori principles, are clarified. For whereas the constitutive a priori principle of lawfulness for the power of theoretical cognition is in the faculty of the understanding and is applied to nature, the constitutive a priori principle of final purpose for the power of desire (the will) is in the faculty of reason and applies to freedom. The a priori principle of lawfulness needed for theoretical cognition is a reference to the regularity and predictability of nature, with its law-like qualities that determine our capacity for synthetic a priori knowledge.[33] The a priori principle of final purpose is a reference to the will as a "higher power of desire" that rises above inclination and feeling as it "carries with it pure intellectual liking for its object," which is the moral law.[34] It is in this way that human beings are simultaneously both subject to and independent from the laws of nature.

Kant's concept of reason as it applies to morality is critical in explaining the nature of the will and moral action, but Kant also divides the faculty of reason in two, arguing that there is theoretical reason and practical reason. Generally speaking, reason is that cognitive faculty that is driven toward an absolute totality of the unconditioned when the unconditioned is given. It is not bound to the limitations of sensible experience, and naturally reaches beyond the sensible world, falling into epistemic failure as it relates to rational psychology and its attempt to attain knowledge about the immortality of the soul (the paralogisms of pure reason), rational cosmology and its attempt to attain knowledge of the world (the antinomies of pure reason), and rational theology and its attempt to attain knowledge of God (the transcendental ideas). Reason thus naturally leads to a condition of epistemic failure in which its attempt at realizing a totality is frustrated. This is reason in its theoretical sphere of employment.

Reason also has a practical sphere of employment. Practical reason has primacy over theoretical reason in Kant's critical philosophical system. In the *Critique of Practical Reason*, Kant builds upon his conclusion of transcendental freedom in the *Critique of Pure Reason* by making the point that practical reason must do what theoretical reason cannot do: see human beings as a causality independent of nature in an intelligible world of freedom rather than a sensible world of nature. Kant's claim that practical reason has primacy over theoretical reason means that practical reason has a certain interest in morality that demands its extension beyond the sensible world to allow for human beings to see themselves as intelligible beings possessed of a causality that is independent of nature. And for Kant, this must be, for the moral law, and not inclination or feeling, has to be the sole determining ground of the will. Kant thus writes in the *Critique of Practical Reason*:

> The concept of freedom alone allows us to find the unconditioned and intelligible for the conditioned and sensible without going outside ourselves. For, it is our reason itself which by means of the supreme and unconditional practical law cognizes itself and the being that is conscious of this law (our own person) as belonging to the pure world of understanding and even determines the way in which, as such, it can be active. In this way it can be understood why in the entire faculty of reason *only the practical* can provide us with the means for going beyond the sensible world and provide cognitions of a supersensible order and connection, which, however, just because of this can be extended only so far as is directly necessary for pure practical purposes.[35]

Kant is not making any ontological claims about freedom here. Indeed, Kant himself acknowledges that making such claims would contradict the conclusions that he has reached about the dialectical structure of cosmological speculation in the *Critique of Pure Reason*. Instead, Kant argues that practical reason has an interest in morality such that human beings must see themselves as causalities that are independent of nature, and that are inhabitants of an intelligible, as well as a sensible world. If, for example, one could not see oneself outside of the sensible realm, then time would determine our actions rather than freedom. Again, Kant's words are instructive:

> The concept of causality as *natural necessity*, as distinguished from the concept of causality as *freedom*, concerns only the existence of things insofar as it is *determinable in time* and hence as appearances, as opposed to their causality as things in themselves. Now if one takes the determinations of the existence of things in time for determination of things in themselves (which is the most usual way of representing them), then the necessity in the causal relation can in no way be united with freedom; instead they are opposed to each other as contradictory. For, from the first it follows that every event, and consequently every action that takes place at a point of time, is necessary under the condition of what was in the preceding time. Now, since time past is no longer within my control, every action that I perform must be necessary by determining grounds that are not within my control, that is, I am never free at the point of time in which I act.[36]

Time can determine the nature of objects of experience as appearances, but it cannot determine human nature as things in themselves. If time was determinative in this fashion, then, according to Kant, one could never be morally free, as previous temporal conditions would, according to the law of cause and effect, determine present outcomes. Practical reason must thus able to see the human being as a member of an intelligible world as if (*als ob*) the human being is free as a thing in itself. This is a move that theoretical reason cannot make.

Through Kant's epistemology and his moral philosophy, we are presented with a picture of a human being as a subjectivity that is complex and multifaceted. On one hand, human beings are subject to the laws of nature, while, on the other hand, human beings are independent of nature. On the former account of theoretical reason, human beings are objects that move in space just as other objects move in space, but on the latter account, human beings are subjects who freely make moral decisions, as they are endowed with an autonomy from nature and inclination, and a dignity of their personhood that prevents them from acting based on instincts and inclination as cause is to effect. The next subsection explores what human beings can hope for considering these limitations of the understanding and reason.

What May I Hope?

The third question in Kant's canon of pure reason is "What may I hope?" Kant rephrases this question: "If I do what I ought to do, what may I then hope?"[37] This question is a hybrid in that it is both practical and theoretical. Kant explains that the practical side of the question is connected to hoping, which is directed at happiness, and that the theoretical side of the question is connected to knowing, which is directed at truth. The practical side of the third question is a "clue" to answering the theoretical side of the third question, and ultimately answering the speculative question of what we can know.[38] Kant explains:

> For all *hoping* is directed to happiness, and stands in the same relation to the practical and the law of morality as *knowing and the law of nature* to the theoretical knowledge of things. The former arrives finally at the conclusion that something is (which determines the ultimate possible end) *because something ought to happen*; the latter, that something is (which operates as the supreme cause) *because something happens*.[39]

For Kant, the notion that the practical side of the third question is a clue to answering the theoretical side of the third question is seen in an analogy between hope and happiness in the sphere of practical reason and scientific, natural laws and knowledge in theoretical reason. Hope is to happiness what natural laws are to knowledge: hope is directed at happiness, which is what ought to happen, while natural laws are directed at knowledge because of what actually does happen. The practical side of the question "What may I hope?" is a clue because one must hope for a happiness that ought to happen, but that one cannot know will happen. This clue, in turn, tells us that all that we can "know" is what actually does happen based upon natural, scientific laws. And so the practical side of the question "What may I hope?" answers both the theoretical side of the question and the speculative question. I must hope because I cannot know.

Hoping, though directed at happiness, is subject to the practical law of morality (what Kant calls the "categorical imperative"), even as knowing is subject to the law of nature and to the strictures of theoretical reason (the understanding). When one hopes, one longs for happiness, even as when one knows, one attains truth. Kant's analysis here is important because he gestures toward what will become, one year after the publication of the second edition of the *Critique of Pure Reason*, his argument for a moral, rational belief in God in the *Critique of Practical Reason*. So it is that this third question is theological in nature because it addresses practical reason's interest hope and happiness, which, Kant will argue in the *Critique of Practical Reason*, only a belief in God can satisfy. But what are we to make of Kant's assertion that practical reason has an interest in hope and happiness? What is this assertion's connection to practical reason's reliance on transcendental freedom? And how does it connect to Kant's argument for a moral belief in God, thus making the question "If I do what I ought to do, then what may I hope?" a theological question? To address these questions, it is important to recount Kant's argument for a moral and belief in God. For in doing so, the contrast between nature and freedom in Kant becomes clearer as it relates to my argument about Douglass and Kant on art and theology.

Practical reason has an interest in hope and happiness precisely because transcendental freedom ensures an autonomy from the causality of nature in favor of a spontaneous causality of freedom that enables Kant's moral subject to freely determine the will according to its duty to the moral law. This means that one's actions can be moral through the power of free choice without regard to feeling or inclination. But this has its disadvantages, as one must do what is right without regard for the consequences of one's actions, which may often be unfavorable. Duty does not lead to happiness. And herein lies the problem: duty does not lead to happiness, and yet practical reason has both hope and happiness as its principal interests. In the *Critique of Practical Reason*, Kant writes that the moral law "must also lead to the possibility of the second element of the highest good, namely happiness proportioned to that morality, and must do so as disinterestedly as before, solely from impartial reason."[40] The morality that Kant references in this statement is the morality of one who consistently makes the moral law the "supreme determining ground of the will."[41] If one does this, then one will surely be a moral being who is worthy of happiness. But happiness will always be elusive to one who is faithful to the moral law, because the fulfillment of duty will often bring unpleasant consequences that will likely make Kant's moral agent rather unhappy, especially since Kant defines happiness as "the state of a rational being in the world in the whole of whose existence everything goes according to his wish and will, and rests, therefore, on the harmony of nature with his whole end as well as with the essential determining ground of his will."[42] Happiness thus implies a condition in which one would be able to produce moral desert in direct proportion to one's commitment to the moral law. But, for Kant, this state of affairs is unattainable because "the acting rational being in the world is, however, not also the cause of the world and of nature itself," so "there is not the least ground in the moral law for a necessary connection between the morality and the proportionate happiness of a being belonging to the world as part of it and hence dependent upon it, who for that reason cannot by his will be a cause of this nature and, as far as his happiness is concerned, cannot by his own powers make it harmonize thoroughly with his practical principles."[43] So the rational moral agent, as a finite being cannot bring about the happiness necessary to make the highest good attainable, for while one can be moral, one is unable to perfectly proportion moral desert to happiness. This, then, for Kant demands a belief in "the existence of a cause of all nature, distinct from nature" to cause happiness in proportion to morality. With this belief, the attainment of the highest good is now possible because no moral agent can bring about the necessary element of happiness in proportion to morality. This can only be hoped for, however, because Kant's account of moral agency demands duty, which again, will often likely result in disappointment rather than happiness.

This discussion of Kant's three questions gives us the following answers. What I can know is limited to the world of sensibility, what I ought to do is freely commit myself to the moral law for the sake of duty and duty alone, and what I may hope for is that my moral commitments to duty and to the moral law will one day result in my happiness, implying that I may believe in a God who will apportion moral desert in direct proportion to my moral efforts. Kant's answers to these three questions leave us, however, with some questions. What happens while I am waiting for my happiness and I remain disappointed because of my commitment to duty? Am I only bound to see myself as an abstract, moral subject without any feeling whatsoever? What does the denial of feeling in morality imply for other facets of one's personhood that may incline toward creativity? I address these questions in the next subsection where I discuss the third part of Kant's critical trilogy, *The Critique of Judgment*—specifically, his account of aesthetic judgment. In this next subsection, I will also discuss Kant's essay "On the Miscarriage of All Philosophical Trials in Theodicy," connecting it to Kant's moral theory and his theory of artistic creativity.

Kant's *Critique of Judgment*

Thus far, we have seen that Kant's epistemology and his moral philosophy include his account of two cognitive faculties. In the *Critique of Pure Reason*, Kant argues for the existence of a priori categories that operate in the faculty of the understanding, and that, as applied to nature, yield synthetic a priori knowledge. Our knowledge based upon the understanding is limited, however, as one can only know objects of a possible experience that present themselves in space and time, which are the a priori forms of subjective intuition. The understanding subsumes the particularity of objects under the universality of concepts, and what we can know is in one sense negated through the concept of limitation (*Schranke*), and enlarged through the concept of bounds (*Grenze*), in which something is presupposed beyond the limits of the understanding. Although reason, in its theoretical employment, inevitably extends itself beyond the bounds of experience, its demand for a totality that will produce knowledge in rational psychology (the soul), rational cosmology (freedom), and rational theology (God) remains unfulfilled. Reason's mental power of cognition is restrained in that its only application is to nature through natural laws. In contrast, the *Critique of Practical Reason* allows for practical reason to see the human being as independent of natural causality such that practical reason concludes that one must live "as if" (*als ob*) one is free, despite the epistemic failure at its attempt to prove itself to be free, as in the antinomies of the *Critique of Pure Reason*. Practical reason also allows for an argument that it is moral to believe in God as a being who is able to bring about the highest good (the union of happiness and morality), by a perfect apportionment of happiness to morality—something that human beings are unable to do. This belief makes the highest good attainable, and thus a belief in God is rational according to the demands of practical reason. Neither the belief that one is free nor the belief in God are ontological claims; that is, they are not claims about freedom and God as objects of experience with real existences, but rather are claims made about the practical rationality of the beliefs themselves. What we can hope is, for Kant, determined in part by what we can know and by what we ought to do: since our knowledge is limited, our moral lives are the site of responsibility and accountability, the quality of which is determined by our faithfulness to the moral law, which must determine our will. As there are no guarantees that my morality will ever bring about happiness, what I may hope for is a day when the God that I have believed in through my practical reason will properly apportion moral desert such that I will then have happiness commensurate with my virtuous moral conduct.

Kant is often caricatured as a harsh, duty-based philosopher because of his denial of feeling in moral deliberation, his emphasis on duty, and the portrait of his moral subject as an abstract self who is situated between inclination and feeling, on one hand, and the moral law, on the other hand. He is styled as a moral taskmaster, who, in his Pietist, Lutheran tradition, emphasizes abstract duty to the exclusion of common sense, real life situations. Similar caricatures of his work in epistemology and metaphysics have cast Kant as an atheist philosopher, or as a skeptic, whose work, despite his protestations of being viewed in this way, is a danger to Christianity and to religious beliefs in general. After all, Kant is known as "the Great Destroyer" for his critique of the traditional arguments for God's existence. But the problem with such interpretations and caricatures of Kant is that they are fundamentally inattentive to other parts of his corpus that problematize them. For example, if one only reads the "Transcendental Aesthetic" and the "Transcendental Analytic" of the *Critique of Pure Reason*, one might think that Kant is simply trying to vindicate the claims of Newtonian physics, with no interest in (or perhaps even a hostility toward) religion. But reading the *Critique of Pure Reason* in its entirety, one sees that Kant has a certain regard for the arguments for the immortality of the soul, freedom, and God's existence. For Kant, the faculty of reason crafts these arguments intentionally rather than haphazardly. So Kant is not asserting that the claims of rational psychology, rational cosmology, and rational theology are merely the product of a garbled, disorganized, and irrational mind. Instead, such claims emanate from the very nature of reason itself insofar as it seeks the unconditioned whenever the conditioned is given. Thus it is that all of the arguments for God's existence, for example, are endowed with rational integrity, but they are subject to the boundary of sensory experience. And it is with this restriction of reason that Kant sets the stage for his account of morality by using the epistemic failure of psychological, cosmological, and theological speculation as a pivot to a subjective life of moral responsibility and authentic religious practice.

To avoid these mischaracterizations of Kant's critical philosophy, it is important to understand the role of the third installment in Kant's critical trilogy, the *Critique of Judgment*. The *Critique of Judgment* is concerned with an analysis of the power of judgment generally, and, specifically, it is concerned with aesthetic and teleological judgments. For our purposes, aesthetic judgments are my focus. Kant does two things in the *Critique of Judgment* that are important for our consideration of Douglass as it relates to aesthetic judgments: first, he provides for an expanded role of the imagination in perception, and second, he makes a space for feelings of pleasure and displeasure that connect with the imagination's more expansive role. I argue that it is the expanded role of the imagination in our perceptual experience and its connection to feeling—something off limits in both Kant's moral philosophy and his epistemology—that transforms both Kant's notion of the self as an epistemic placeholder that is the transcendental unity of apperception from the *Critique of Pure Reason* and the duty-driven self of the *Critique of Practical Reason* into a self in the *Critique of Judgment* that is able to feel and to be creative in the face of situations that escape both the grasp of conceptual subsumption of the particular under the universal and the duty-driven morality that leaves one hoping for happiness commensurate with virtue because of a disregard of feeling and inclination out of a sense of commitment to the moral law. I begin with a broad discussion of the place of the *Critique of Judgment* in Kant's critical philosophy.

Kant describes the *Critique of Judgment* as mediating between the *Critique of Pure Reason* and the *Critique of Practical Reason*. Kant understands the *Critique of Judgment* as bridging the gap between the understanding, which is the cognitive faculty that facilitates empirical knowledge, and reason, which is the cognitive faculty that is the basis for morality. Kant argues that judgment is the cognitive faculty that makes room for possibility in a way that the understanding and reason do not, for the understanding leaves the entire substrate of nature "wholly undetermined," and reason, through the categorical imperative, determines the entire substrate of nature as if one is free. While the understanding determines nothing as it relates to our moral nature, and reason determines our moral nature through transcendental freedom, the faculty of judgment allows for one to, through the unrestrained power of the imagination, find concepts for the intuitions presented to us in experience. This results in neither an undetermined nor a determined substrate through the understanding or reason, but in a substrate that is *determinable*. The understanding is the basis for knowledge because empirically speaking, for each concept there is a corresponding intuition that is subsumed. Reason cannot be the basis for knowledge because, unlike the understanding, there are concepts but there are no corresponding intuitions. So reason does not yield knowledge because although there are ideas of the soul, freedom, and God, there are not spatiotemporal intuitions of these ideas, and therefore the concepts of reason are empty. This is, of course, the first half of Kant's famous dictum that "thoughts without concepts are empty, intuitions without concepts are blind."[44] As it relates to the faculty of the understanding, this statement is true, for again, reason has psychological, cosmological, and theological concepts that are themselves empty because of the lack of spatiotemporal objects, and intuitions without concepts would, in Kant's words, be blind; that is, objects would present themselves to us in experience and could not be known, effectively "blinding" us from all manner of empirical cognition. Kant's dictum holds true for the faculty of the understanding. The faculty of judgment, however, presents a scenario in which there are intuitions without any corresponding concepts; there is a particular without a universal. The cognitive faculty of judgment addresses this problem, not as reason would do, with a mere "random groping" of concepts searching for intuitions, but rather with a search for concepts under which the observable particular may be subsumed. And it is this searching for concepts that Kant refers to as "reflective judgment," in which the imagination and the understanding are at "free play" with one another.

The role of imagination in Kant's epistemology is radically different from its role in Kant's aesthetics. In both his epistemology and his aesthetics, the imagination mediates between sensibility and the understanding. In the *Critique of Pure Reason*, the imagination schematizes intuitions to present them to the understanding consistent with their subjective temporal form. Some explanation of the schematism will be helpful in both understanding the role of imagination in Kant's epistemology and contrasting it with his aesthetics.

After Kant makes his argument for the transcendental deduction of the categories in the *Critique of Pure Reason*, he admits that while he has shown that the categories of pure reason apply to objects of experience, there is a problem of heterogeneity. That is, the categories of pure reason and intuitions are too different from one another for the conclusions of the transcendental deduction of the categories to work. The categories are a priori and intuitions are sensible, so in this sense they are too different from one another in order to enable the understanding to perform its work of subsumption, and thus yield synthetic a priori knowledge. There must be something that allows for homogeneity, something that Kant calls "a third thing," which has a commonality with both a priori concepts and sensuous intuitions in order for the former to apply to the latter. Kant describes the problem:

> In all subsumptions of an object under a concept the representations of the object must be homogenous with the concept; in other words, the concept must contain something which is represented in the object that is to be subsumed under it. . . . But pure concepts of the understanding being quite heterogeneous from empirical intuitions, and indeed from all sensible intuitions, can never be met with in any intuition. For no one will say that a category, such as that of causality, can be intuited through sense and is itself contained in appearance. How, then, is the subsumption of intuitions under pure concepts, the application of a category to appearances, possible?[45]

Kant claims to have solved this problem of heterogeneity through arguing that there must be "some third thing, which is homogeneous on one hand with the category, and on the other hand with the appearance, and which thus makes the application of the former to the latter possible."[46] Kant will call this "third thing" a "transcendental schema."[47] And this "third thing" is the transcendental determination of time, for, according to Kant, time is not only an a priori subjective form of intuition but also contained in every empirical representation of the sensory manifold.[48] Kant labels "the formal and pure condition of the sensibility to which the employment of the concept of understanding is restricted" the "schema of the concept."[49] And the understanding's procedure in the schema Kant calls "the schematism of pure understanding."[50] It is this formal and pure condition of sensibility—the schema itself—that is "always a product of the imagination."[51] But the schema of an object must be distinguished from the image of the object because "the synthesis of imagination aims at no special intuition, but only at unity in the determination of sensibility."[52] Kant gives the example of five points being put next to one another (.....). This, he argues, is an image of the number five. But the schema of the number five, or of any other number, for that matter, is "the representation of a method whereby a multiplicity . . . may be represented in an image in conformity with a certain concept," rather "than the image itself."[53] Kant explains this distinction between the image of an object and its schema as follows: "The concept 'dog' signifies a rule according to which my imagination can delineate the figure of a four-footed animal in a general manner, without limitation to any single determinate figure such as experience, or any possible image that I can represent in concreto, actually presents."[54] Images themselves are thus made possible through the reproductive, imitative work of the a priori imagination, which mediates between a priori concepts and sensible intuitions, allowing the categories to apply to intuitions that present themselves in the sensory manifold as determinations of appearances in time. So in the *Critique of Pure Reason*, the imagination plays a foundational role in Kant's epistemology in that its mediation between sensibility and the understanding allows the understanding to subsume intuitions under concepts and yield synthetic a priori knowledge. The role of imagination in Kant's epistemology is consistent with Kant's notion of the self that he presents in the *Critique of Pure Reason*. This self is the transcendental unity of apperception, which is an intermediate conception of the self falling between Hume's account of the self as a mere passive bundle of perceptions and the Cartesian notion of an immortal self that can outlive the death of the body. Kant needs this conception of the self because, as he points out, "The 'I think' must accompany all of my perceptions." Kant will argue that all of our perceptions must abide somewhere and that the self is the place where they abide. But this self is merely transcendental in nature; that is, it is a transcendental presupposition, a necessary condition for the possibility of experience. This account of the self is, then, a sort of epistemic placeholder that gives a home to the cognitive activity of synthetic a priori knowledge.

The nature of the faculty of judgment, is, however, different from the understanding, and thus the imagination plays a different role in aesthetic, reflective judgments in the *Critique of Judgment* than it does in the synthetic a priori judgments of the *Critique of Pure Reason*. Whereas the understanding yields knowledge through the application of concepts to intuitions, reflective judgments have intuitions that present themselves without concepts. On the former account, the imagination functions according to the strictures and rigor of the understanding's application to the laws of nature such as cause and effect. But on the latter account, since the intuitions present themselves without any concepts to subsume them, the imagination, instead of mediating between sensibility and the understanding to yield knowledge, is actually at what Kant calls "free play" in which it assumes a role that is productive, original, and creative as opposed to being merely reproductive and imitative. And unlike the imagination's functioning according to the a priori principle of lawfulness and its application to nature in the *Critique of Pure Reason*, in the *Critique of Judgment*, the imagination not only assumes a role of creativity, productivity, and originality but also is connected to feelings of pleasure or displeasure in the subject, where it operates under the a priori principle of purposiveness; that is, the imagination's role in the *Critique of Judgment* is to find purposiveness where experience presents no purposiveness at all in the absence of concepts that will subsume the intuitions given in experience.

Two things have now happened that are very significant for both the role of the imagination and the nature of the self in Kant's critical philosophy. First, the imagination's role in reflective judgment sets the stage for artistic expression because of its productive, creative capacity to produce something original. And second, the self has ceased to be a mere epistemic placeholder that houses the perceptions that compose empirical cognition. Instead, the self is now a being that has feelings of pleasure and displeasure, and, because the imagination is free from the strictures of the understanding, the understanding can connect with those feelings to produce works of art that have *Geist*, or spirit, and may even be considered so original as to be called works of artistic genius. Kant thus gives us the picture of a self that is both feeling and creative. This feeling and creativity is important when one faces intuitions that have no concepts—that is, when one faces situations that induce either pleasure or displeasure that escape the rigor and lawfulness of epistemic predication, and is free to use the power of one's imagination to produce something creative and original that will help one grapple with the feelings of pleasure or displeasure in the form of works of art. We saw this at work in chapter 2, where I discussed the role of art in Kafka's novel, *The Trial*. Recall that Titorelli, the painter, was confronted with the absurdity of an oppressive bureaucracy and in the midst of that oppression and absurdity, his imagination, at free play with his understanding, enabled him to paint portraits of the judges of the court as *he saw them*. One can hear a faint echo of Kant in the work of Friedrich Nietzsche, who argues that a healthy culture is one in which the Dionysian realm of tragedy is not ignored at the expense of Socratic rationalism. Nietzsche, despite many differences from Kant, does emphasize the importance of feeling in both its role in the production of art and its role in the human self.

Kant's *Critique of Judgment* helps to explain, perhaps, how one manages the feelings of pleasure or displeasure while longing for the realization of the highest good: works of art help us to constructively display our feelings of pleasure or displeasure in the face of the myriad frustrations, disappointments, and moments of joy and happiness that face us throughout life. In the *Critique of Judgment*, one thus sees the culmination of the Kantian self as a being invested with cognitive power that is used to understand nature; as a being invested with dignity because of a freedom from natural causes that governs the desire of one's will; and as a being with feeling that produces works of art while in search of an evasive sense of purpose—a purposiveness found in artistic production that emanates from feeling. A good illustration of art produced in this way is found not only in Kafka and in Nietzsche but also in the Bible, a text that concerned Douglass throughout his life as a public intellectual. Indeed, in the Bible, we see that nothing is created until the spirit moves (Genesis 1:2). Similarly, in art, nothing is created until one's *Geist*, or spirit, has moved. And what is so compelling about the biblical account of creation is that the spirit moves under conditions that are empty, chaotic, and terrifying, for before we are told that the spirit moved, we are told that the Earth "was without form, and void," and that "darkness was upon the face of the deep."[55] To be without form is to be chaotic, to be void implies an emptiness, and darkness implies fear. It is under these conditions that creation occurs when God speaks light into the darkness in Genesis 1:3. Similarly, when one is confronted with such feelings of displeasure in the face of chaos, emptiness, and fear in their lives based upon an intuition that presents itself and that one cannot explain, one's imagination is at free play with the understanding and is able to, like the creation account in the Bible, create something to bring purpose to that which does not appear to be purposive whatsoever. The chaos of life, its feelings of emptiness, and its terrifying circumstances thus lay the foundation for creative interventions that are animated with the power of the human *Geist*, a spirit that moves to create meaning and order from such hostile conditions. We see such hostile conditions in the lives of slaves like Douglass, and of biblical characters like Job. In both Douglass's and Job's situations, their intense feelings of displeasure allow for a movement of their *Geist* in such a way as to produce poetic language. And this is often the case with poetry. Kierkegaard points out, through his pseudonym, Victor Eremita, in *Either/Or* that poetry emerges from dreadful existential conditions:

> What is a poet? An unhappy person who conceals profound anguish in his heart but whose lips are so formed that as sighs and cries pass over them they sound like beautiful music. . . . And people crowd around the poet and say to him, "Sing again soon"—in other words, may new sufferings torture your soul, and may your lips continue to be formed as before, because your screams would only alarm us, but the music is charming.[56]

Kierkegaard, through his pseudonym, is making the point that the finest poetic language results from the worst life conditions. It seems that for the poet, the more intense the pain—or the joy—the more beautiful the poetry. To put this in Kantian terms, the more intense the feelings of pleasure or displeasure, the more the imagination abides by its productivity and originality, yielding a work of fine art. As I will discuss below, the hostile conditions of life beset Job, and they most certainly beset Douglass, and both of them produced works of art in the midst of their pain: Job in some of the most poetic passages in the Bible, and Douglass in the form of his *Narrative*. Significantly, Kant's account of Job occurs in the context of the problem of theodicy that I took up in the previous chapter. That Kant discussed Job in the context of a failure of theodicy says something about art and its relationship to rational explanation—namely, that the creativity of the former humanizes us while the abstractions of the latter are dehumanizing insofar as they neglect the power and temerity of the human spirit in the face of suffering and evil. So it is that neither Job nor Douglass was interested in theodicies or free will defenses, as the reformed epistemology of analytic theism would be. Instead, rational reconciliations of God's divine attributes is far less important than the courageous and creative expressions of the human spirit. This is why Kant condemns the discourse of Job's three friends, and lauds Job for his epistemic humility. I first discuss Job, and then I turn to Douglass.

In his essay "On the Miscarriage of All Philosophical Trials in Theodicy," Kant examines the biblical character, Job, and his response to his plight. Job is a biblical character who was morally upright and wealthy. Through a series of sudden and tragic events, Job loses his wealth and his physical health. His three friends, Eliphaz, Zophar, and Bildad, hear of his plight and go to visit him. What ensues is an exchange between Job and his friends that addresses the philosophical problem of evil and suffering. Kant, in writing about this dialogue between Job and his three friends, points out that while neither Job nor his friends actually know anything about his plight, and thus provide us no real insight into the reason for his suffering, Job's friends exhibit a hubris, while Job exhibits a spirit of courage and honesty:

> Job speaks as he thinks, and with the courage with which he, as well as every human being in his position, can well afford; his friends, on the contrary, speak

> as if they were being secretly listened to by the mighty one, over whose cause they are passing judgment, and as if gaining his favor through their judgment were closer to their heart than the truth. Their malice in pretending to assert things into which they yet must admit they have no insight, and in simulating a conviction which they in fact do not have, contrasts with Job's frankness—so far removed from false flattery as to border almost on impudence—much to his advantage. . . . If we now consider the theoretical position maintained by each side, that of Job's friends might convey more of an appearance of greater speculative reason and pious humility; before any court of dogmatic theologians, before a synod, an inquisition, a venerable congregation, or any higher consistory in our times . . . Job would likely have suffered a sad fate. Hence only sincerity of heart and not distinction of insight; honesty in openly admitting one's doubts; repugnance to pretending conviction where one feels none, especially before God (where this trick is pointless enough)—these are the attributes which, in the person of Job, have decided the preeminence of the honest man over the religious flatterer in the divine verdict.[57]

Here, Kant condemns Job's three friends in terms of his critical philosophy. When Kant writes that Job's friends employ "speculative reason and pious humility," he makes the point that Job's three friends are essentially employing the faculty of understanding to Job's situation and thus are extending the reach of theoretical reason beyond the bounds of the sensory manifold of intuition. Job, their friend, in his pitiful condition, becomes an object to be subsumed under the concept of God's righteous judgment. Hence Eliphaz's claim that Job must have done something wrong because "who, being innocent, has suffered?" This misapplication of theoretical reason leads to a moral degradation in Job's three friends because they now see themselves as defending God against any charges of injustice, and in doing so, have manufactured a façade of self-righteousness. Without any regard for Job whatsoever, his three friends cling to an ontotheological mode of reasoning, applying notions of cause and effect to Job's situation as though they know the will of God directly. This sort of commitment to the interests of theoretical reason over and above a genuine concern for Job is akin to what happens in the reformed epistemology of analytic theism: abstraction leads to a neglect of those who suffer because rational consistency not only is more important than one's suffering but also justifies it.

Job's three friends would have done well to acknowledge the significance of their silence upon seeing their friend. For when they saw Job, their well-to-do friend, destitute and covered in sores and ashes, they fell silent with him for seven days and seven nights.[58] No one said anything. This silence represents the failure of the understanding to subsume Job's situation under a concept that could help them "know" exactly what was wrong with Job. To be sure, Job presented himself to them as an object of experience, but they had no concept to describe what they saw, they were literally speechless in the face of such devastation to their friend. And instead of allowing their power of judgment to connect with their feelings of displeasure at the sight of seeing their friend in such a predicament and to allow their imagination to speak creative words of comfort to him, when they reopened their mouths and began to speak, they did so while still allowing the understanding to proceed according to the dictates of theoretical reason rather than reflective judgment and, as such, missed an opportunity to move from the logical, propositional use of language to its more poetic, artistic use. Job, by contrast, broke his silence with a poetic lament that resonates with Kant's insights about poetry as fine art from the *Critique of Judgment*. There, Kant describes poetic imagery as a manifestation of the imagination's free play with the understanding:

> A poet ventures to give sensible expression to rational ideas of invisible beings, the realm of the blessed, the realm of hell, eternity, creation and so on. Or again he takes things that are indeed exemplified in experience, such as death, envy and all the other vices, as well as love, fame, and so on: but then, by means of an imagination that emulates the example of reason in reaching [for] a maximum, he ventures to give these sensible expression in a way that goes beyond the limits of experience, namely, with a completeness for which no example can be found in nature. And it is actually in the art of poetry that the power [i.e., faculty] of aesthetic ideas can manifest itself to full extent. Considered by itself, however this power is actually only a talent (of the imagination).[59]

After the seven-day silence ends, Job's discourse transitions from the propositional to the poetic. To put it in Kantian terms, Job's productive and original aesthetic imagination, at free play with the understanding has connected with his intense feelings of displeasure. Job's power of reflective judgment attempts to find a purposiveness in his tragic situation—and it must, for there are no concepts to correspond to the intuition that is the devastation of his life—and he does so through the power of artistic expression in the elegy that is chapter three of the book of Job, where he curses the day of his birth, asking darkness to "claim" it; asking the day of his birth to "hope" for light but find none; giving "eyelids" to the morning; and giving his mother's womb "doors" to be shut. Of course, physical darkness does not make "claims," days do not "hope," morning has no "eyelids," and a mother's womb has no literal "door." But as Kant points out, the poet, through the power of imagination connected to feeling in reflective judgment and searching for purposiveness in the face of an intuition without concepts, creates a work of art by giving "sensible expression in a way that goes beyond the limits of experience, namely with a completeness for which no example can be found in nature." And this is precisely what Job does in the third chapter of the biblical book that bears his name: the power of his poetic imagination, at free play with his understanding, connects to his intense feelings of displeasure in search of a purposiveness of his situation and a concept for the visible intuitions of his ravaged life, and he produces a work of art in the form of poetic expression by attributing things to objects of experience that take the reader beyond the limits of experience.

In contrast to Job, his friends never make the move to the poetic. Instead, they remain in the propositional mode of discourse, in which their imagination is restricted to a mediation between sensibility and the understanding. So when they break their silence, they are not connected to feeling at all, but instead are looking for ways to subsume Job under the concept of "wrongdoer" because of the intuition that presents itself to them as a phenomenon that must be comprehended instead of a friend that must be comforted. It is ultimately their commitment to theodicy (that is, their commitment to a rational explanation for evil—akin to the commitment to theodicy and free will defense that one sees in the reformed epistemology of analytic theism) that prevents a genuine connection to feeling and leaves them with a series of dogmatic explanations for Job's plight that are nothing more than the sorts of pretensions to transcendent insight that Kant argues are not the domain of theoretical reason. Instead of being selves of feeling and compassion, Job's three friends approach his plight as selves and as persons who are devoid of feeling; who are ultimately epistemic placeholders in the form of the transcendental unity of apperception, behaving as though they have knowledge that they do not have. This also makes them morally contemptible because of their dishonesty in the face of their friend's tragedy that causes them to present themselves as having a divine knowledge and insight that they, epistemologically speaking, simply do not have.

In chapter 3, I discussed how, unlike the reformed epistemology of analytic theism Levinas and Douglass resisted theodicy through Douglass's emphasis on the poetic expression of the saying, as opposed to the ontology of the said. And here, we see an intersection of Levinas, Douglass, and Kant on theodicy, as Kant also references artistic and poetic expression (the poetic "saying") as a means of stemming the tide of ontotheological thinking that seeks rational grounds (the politically—ontologized "said") at the expense of moral concerns. Based upon chapter 3 and what I have argued thus far in this chapter, both Douglass and Kant reject theodicy because of epistemic failure, and it is precisely this epistemic failure that opens a creative, imaginative aperture, allowing Douglass to express artistically what neither the understanding will allow him to express empirically nor what practical reason prevents him from expressing morally. I now return to Douglass to make this argument.

Douglass, Personhood, and Art

Thus far throughout this chapter, we have seen Kant's conception of the human develop from his assessment of our cognitive faculties (*Critique of Pure Reason*) and our moral capacity to see ourselves as free beings (*Critique of Practical Reason*). Kant's critical trilogy culminates with an account of how human beings are also beings that feel and that have creative capacities which show themselves in works of art stemming from the power of imagination and its connection to feeling in a search for purposiveness in the face of intuitions for which there are no concepts (*Critique of Judgment*). We took Job as an example of this from Kant's essay on theodicy, connecting it with the previous chapter on Douglass's rejection of theodicy as a suspension of the "theological attitude," and his deep connection to Levinas's ethical demands of the poetic "saying" as opposed to the ontologized nature of the said. I now turn to Douglass to show, as others have argued, the Kantian resonance in Douglass's thought.[60]

To make this connection between Douglass and Kant, I turn to Douglass's works. First, I examine Douglass's conception of the person from the appendix to his 1855 autobiographical narrative, *My Bondage and My Freedom*, which is his December 1, 1850, speech titled "The Nature of Slavery." There, Douglass gives what I believe is a Kantian philosophical anthropology. I discuss how Douglass's arguments in this speech bring us closer to the moral reasons that Kant provides for rational psychology in the paralogisms of pure reason, the resolution of the third antinomy of rational cosmology in the *Critique of Pure Reason*, and to the nature of rational theology, also in the *Critique of Pure Reason*. Douglass's conception of human personhood, when read with Kant, shows a strong presence of Kantian themes in Douglass's thought. Douglass's account of the human person continues in the second text that I examine, which is his novella, *The Heroic Slave*. It is in this section where I will build upon the groundbreaking work of Bill E. Lawson, who has argued that moral suasion has certain Kantian moral and anthropological features that Douglass used to his advantage.[61] Among these is a rational appeal to slave owners about the wrongness of slavery because of its inconsistency with the dignity and autonomy of rational beings. It is here that I argue that Douglass can be understood to be making this appeal along the lines of not only Kant's moral philosophy but also his aesthetics. Third, I discuss Douglass's narrative strategy from his *Narrative*, and his 1861 speech, "Pictures and Progress," arguing that his literary technique is a type of poetic expression that is neither propositional knowledge—as it would be if it were operating according to what Kant would call the "understanding"—nor moral silence—as would be the case if it were operating in contrast to the self-righteousness of Job's three friends. I submit that this is why Douglass is able to express himself through narrative and poetry with aesthetic feeling according to the power of judgment, when both empirical cognition and practical reason demand his stoic silence, as it did for Job in Kant's essay on theodicy. Instead, Douglass's narrative methodology is one that reveals his spirit (*Geist*) or feeling, allowing him a mode of expression that lies between the rigorous certainty of predication needed for the attainment of synthetic a priori knowledge, on one hand, and the uncertainty of epistemic failure combined with stoic moral duty, on the other. Through a careful examination of these texts and speeches, I try to show not only that Douglass's views on human personhood and art are similar to Kant's but also—and more important—that the epistemic preoccupations of analytic theism, a style of philosophical theology that is geared to humanity's rational faculty, but that does nothing to address the urgent moral and aesthetic demands of human personhood, is fundamentally inadequate to address moral and political concerns as compared with my aesthetic interpretation of Douglass.

"The Nature of Slavery"

Douglass's speech titled "The Nature of Slavery" has as its thesis that the real nature of slavery is to eliminate the qualities that distinguish persons (Black slaves) from property (ordinary chattel). The real nature of slavery is not measured simply by its devastating physical effects on slaves, but rather by those characteristics of slavery which eliminate the intellectual and emotional life of the slave. Douglass argues essentially that slavery is a turning of nature against itself, because for Douglass, the true nature of human beings is to be free, not enslaved. Douglass makes this point when he writes that in order for slavery to persist "Nature must cease to be nature; men must become monsters; humanity must be transformed; Christianity must be exterminated; all ideas of justice and the laws of eternal goodness must be utterly blotted out from the human soul."[62] So it is that for Douglass, the real experiment would not be emancipation, but rather slavery, which he argues is utterly failing. In support of the humanity of the slave, Douglass argues that the legal system deprives slaves of their personhood because "The slave is a human being, divested of all rights—reduced to the level of a brute—a mere 'chattel' in the eye of the law—placed beyond the circle of human brotherhood."[63] Douglass, then, like Kant, understands the fundamental nature of human beings to be a nature that is free and unencumbered by the heteronomous will of another person. Indeed, it is accurate, I think, to claim that both Douglass and Kant situate human personhood in a natural world in which human beings are free beings.

There are many other uniquely human traits of the slave other than freedom which must be overlooked, ignored, or eliminated in order for slavery to thrive as it was thriving in Douglass's day. Indeed, the true character of slavery does not become apparent until one looks beyond the physical oppression to the emotional and psychological toll of slavery, which says much more about its treacherous and vile nature. Douglass makes his argument in this way:

> The physical cruelties [of slavery] are indeed sufficiently harassing and revolting; but they are as a few grains of sand on the sea shore, or a few drops of water in the great ocean, compared with the stupendous wrongs which it inflicts upon the mental, moral, and religious nature of its hapless victims. It is only when we contemplate the slave as a moral and intellectual being, that we can adequately comprehend the unparalleled enormity of slavery, and the intense criminality of the slaveholder. I have said that the slave was a man. "What a piece of work is man! How noble in reason! How infinite in faculties! In form and moving how express and admirable! In action how like an angel! In apprehension how like a God! The beauty of the world! The paragon of animals!"[64]

Here, Douglass speaks of slaves as human beings in several ways that are rather Kantian. First, he points out that slaves have natures that are "mental, moral, and religious." Second, the slaves are described as "moral and intellectual beings." Third, slaves are human in that they are admirable pieces "of work," who are "noble in reason" and "infinite in faculties." This language displays a strong resonance with Kant's account of human beings as rational beings of dignity and nobility who are both intellectual and moral and who have a variety of faculties, including the understanding that governs their cognitive power according to the a priori principle of lawfulness that applies to nature; their faculty of judgment, which reflectively governs their feelings of pleasure and displeasure according to the a priori principle of purposiveness that applies to art; and their faculty of reason, which governs the power of their will manifested as desire according to the a priori principle of final purpose that applies to freedom. Douglass and Kant thus have similar understandings of the human person.[65]

Douglass continues his discussion with a description of the slave in terms that continue to be strikingly Kantian in nature. He writes:

> The slave is a man, "the image of God," but "a little lower than the angels;" possessing a soul, eternal and indestructible; capable of endless happiness, or immeasurable woe; a creature of hopes and fears, of affections and passions, of joys and sorrows, and he is endowed with those mysterious powers by which man soars above the things of time and sense, and grasps, with undying tenacity, the elevating and sublimely glorious idea of a God. It is such a being that is smitten and blasted. The first work of slavery is to destroy all sense of high moral and religious responsibility. It reduces man to a mere machine. It cuts him off from his Maker, it hides from him the laws of God, and leaves him to grope his

way from time to eternity in the dark, under the arbitrary and despotic control of a frail, depraved, and sinful fellow-man. As the serpent-charmer of India is compelled to extract the deadly teeth of his venomous prey before he is able to handle him with impunity, so the slaveholder must strike down the conscience of the slave before he can obtain the entire mastery over his victim.[66]

This passage again indicates several Kantian themes. Kant, in the *Critique of Pure Reason*, argues that despite the failure of rational psychology to yield synthetic a priori knowledge, it still has the positive benefit of restricting our knowledge in such a way that it helps us to pivot from reason in its speculative, theoretical employment to the use of practical reason, in which the notion of an immortal soul is much more useful morally than it is ontologically. After arguing extensively against the claims of the rational psychologist in the paralogisms of pure reason, Kant sums up his assessment of rational psychology by concluding that rational psychology, despite its failure to produce knowledge "keeps us, on the one hand, from throwing ourselves into the arms of a soulless materialism, or, on the other hand, from losing ourselves in a spiritualism which must be quite unfounded so long as we remain in this present life."[67] Aside from mediating between materialism and spiritualism, Kant argues that the epistemic failure of rational psychology is theoretical "reason's hint to divert our self-knowledge from fruitless and extravagant speculation to fruitful practical employment."[68] Douglass brings us closer to Kant's moral reasoning about rational psychology in two ways. First, Douglass commits himself to the rejection of a "soulless materialism" when he proclaims that the slave possesses "a soul, eternal and indestructible."[69] This is not to say that Douglass is committed to a Cartesian-styled rational psychology—I have argued elsewhere that he is not[70]—but rather that Douglass is aware, as is Kant, of the moral importance of seeing people as more than simply flesh and bone. And second, a careful study of Douglass's criticism of Reverend Godwin's argument for Negro baptism shows that Douglass, like Kant, understood morality to be more important than metaphysics. Reverend Godwin was an eighteenth-century pastor who argued that slaves could be baptized because, although their master owned their bodies, their souls belonged to God. Douglass at first acknowledges this argument as beneficial for recognizing slaves had souls and thus humanizing them. But he then criticizes the argument for its "metaphysical" nature, concluding that it was much like the argument in which "the white man got the turkey and the Indian got the crow."[71] Douglass points out the shortcoming of the argument when he writes that "When the Negro looked for his body, that belonged to his earthly master; when he looked around for his soul, that had been appropriated by his heavenly Master; and when he looked around for something that really belonged to himself, he found nothing but his shadow, and that vanished into the air, when he might most want it."⁷² Godwin's argument was premised upon a Cartesian psychological dualism that Kant argues can be harmful to morality when it is left unchecked. As Kant points out, it is the limitations on rational psychology that are reason's "hint" for us to turn our attention away from metaphysical speculation and toward moral action. Douglass, I submit, says something similar about Godwin's argument. Douglass concludes of Godwin's argument that "He only saw part of the truth. He saw that the Negro had a right to be baptized, but he could not all at once see that he had a primary and paramount right to himself."⁷³ Douglass, then, like Kant, would likely argue for pivoting away from an overly theoretical, Cartesian psychological dualism toward a more practically oriented argument for an immortal soul as one finds in Kant's *Critique of Practical Reason*. Douglass is, I think, far more interested in an *unendliche gehend* (endless progress) toward morality than he is in a fixed, speculative metaphysical account of the soul that is morally lacking because of its quest for epistemic certainty. Here we see another connection between the theoretical abstractions of analytic theism and their failure to address moral concerns, for even as reason is the principal concern in their form of philosophical theology and urgent moral and political concerns are overlooked, so did Godwin overlook the pressing moral and political concern of American chattel slavery because of his principal interest in a rational, Cartesian-styled account of the soul that actually helped Christian theology to justify American chattel slavery.

Douglass also points to "those mysterious powers by which man soars above the things of time and sense, and grasps, with undying tenacity, the elevating and sublimely glorious idea of a God."⁷⁴ This reads much like the following passage from Kant's *Critique of Pure Reason*, where Kant discusses reason in its quest for the unconditioned being of God whenever anything conditioned is given:

> If we admit something as existing, no matter what this something may be, we must also admit that there is something which exists necessarily. For the contingent exists only under the condition of some other contingent existence as its cause, and from this again we must infer yet another cause, until we are brought to a cause which is not contingent, and which is therefore unconditionally necessary. This is the argument upon which reason bases its advance to the primordial being.⁷⁵

Douglass articulates the procedure that Kant identifies for reason's quest for the unconditioned whenever the conditioned is given: we soar "above the things of time and sense" and grasp "with undying tenacity, the elevating and sublimely glorious idea of a God." This language suggests that Kant and

Douglass are referencing a similar rational procedure by which rational theology argues for the existence of God.

Douglass's speech also resonates with Kant's aesthetics, for he points out that the feeling of the slave leads to the production of works of art in the form of singing and dancing. This connects with the above-quoted passage from Douglass where he writes that the slave is "a creature of hopes and fears, of affections and passions, of joys and sorrows." Douglass is making the point that slaves are capable of experiencing feelings of pleasure and displeasure in the face of unbearable intuitions for which there are no corresponding concepts. Under such conditions, the slave's imagination is at free play with the understanding and, through its connection to the feelings of pleasure or displeasure, creates works of art under the a priori principle of purposiveness, giving purposiveness to their status as creative beings in the face of that which escapes epistemic articulation and conceptual subsumption. So it is that Douglass writes that any song, dance, or merriment from the slaves proves nothing except "that though slavery is armed with a thousand stings, it is not able entirely to kill the elastic spirit of the bondman. That spirit will rise and walk abroad, despite whips and chains."[76] The *Geist* of the slave—the slave's spirit—remains capable of artistic production because of the faculty of reflective judgment that produces a universally communicable judgment as purposive in the face of an experience that has no apparent purpose or is absurd.

So, in Douglass's speech "The Nature of Slavery," we see deep affinities between Douglass and Kant. These affinities are in the areas of philosophical anthropology, ethics, psychology, epistemology, rational theology, and aesthetics. Across these philosophical subfields, the commonality is that both Douglass and Kant have a rich conception of the human person as an intellectual being, a free moral being, and a feeling, creative, imaginative, and artistic being.

The Heroic Slave

In addition to his speeches, his abolitionist, and his post-abolition writings, Douglass penned a novella, *The Heroic Slave*. In this work of fiction that was based upon an actual slave mutiny aboard the US brigantine *Creole* in November 1841, Douglass tells the story of Madison Washington, a slave who longs to be free. Douglass had as his objective in writing *The Heroic Slave*, according to Bill E. Lawson, "to write as if the institution of slavery cannot or did not wholly shape blacks."[77] Lawson's essay on Douglass argues that the reason there are Kantian overtones in *The Heroic Slave* is because Douglass was in a position where, politically and morally, he had to reject John Locke's empiricism. If Locke is right about "nothing being in the mind that is not first in the senses," and if human beings are actually a "tabula rasa" at birth, waiting for their experiences to "write" upon them, then all that Douglass could ever have been was a slave.[78] So, for Lawson, Douglass needs a way to avoid empiricism's determinism. To put this in de Beauvoirian terms—as George Yancy has[79]—Douglass needed to show that he was not merely a socially and politically determined essence that preceded his existence, but rather that he had an existence that preceded his essence; that he could, as a dignified, autonomous, rational being, have some say as to who he was and who he was destined to become. Lawson, interpreting Douglass and Kant, interprets Douglass with transcendentalist themes, but he still does so in a manner that invests Douglass with the freedom he needs to choose a way of life for himself:

> I want to argue that Douglass's use of "manhood" places him squarely in the Romantic tradition with a deep connection to the Transcendentalists. The Transcendentalists, it should be remembered, reject the empiricism of Locke for the idealism of Kant. Their use of Kant puts their understanding of what it means to be human in a very different light from that of the empiricist . . . [Kant] thought that those philosophers who adhered to either the rationalism of Descartes or the empiricism of Locke had reasoned wrongly about human knowledge acquisition.[80]

Lawson goes on to point out that Kant's epistemology defends the view that human beings are active with respect to their acquisition of knowledge, and that this sort of cognitive contribution to experience gives human beings a certain conception of the self that is rational, free, and dignified. This is important, because this is exactly the way that Madison Washington, the protagonist of *The Heroic Slave*, is portrayed not only, as Lawson points out, as a being that is both human and free, in a Kantian sense in terms of his form, but also in terms of other Kantian characteristics such as intellect, morality, and reflection and creativity, which resonate strongly with Kant's aesthetics. Douglass describes Madison Washington as one who "had the head to conceive, and the hand to execute."[81] Washington was a *man* of both thought and action. In Kantian terms, one would say that Washington was both an intellectual and a moral being capable of theoretical and practical reasoning. So one can argue that Washington has the cognitive faculties of the understanding and reason.

In addition to having the cognitive faculties of understanding and reason, Washington has the faculty of judgment that mediates between the understanding and reason that completes him as a human being in the Kantian sense. Washington can subsume objects under concepts through the employment of his understanding as an intellectual being under the a priori principle of lawfulness as applied to nature; not only can Washington make the moral law the determining ground of his will, rather than feeling or inclination through the use of his practical reason as a moral being under the a priori principle of final purpose as applied to freedom, but Washington can also reflect on intuitions that present themselves to him in consciousness, and, though there be no corresponding concepts for those intuitions, he can, reflectively, through the free play between his imagination and understanding, connect himself to feelings of pleasure and displeasure under the a priori principle of purposiveness and produce a work of art in the form of poetry. Consider the following passage from the opening of *The Heroic Slave*, a soliloquy, where Washington is lamenting his condition as a slave:

> What, then, is life to me? It is aimless and worthless, and worse than worthless. Those birds, perched on you swinging boughs, in friendly conclave, sounding forth their merry notes in seeming worship of the rising sun, though liable to the sportsman's fowling-piece, are still my superiors. They live free, though they may die slaves. They fly where they list by day, and retire in freedom at night. But what is freedom to me, or I to it? I am a slave,—born a slave, an abject slave,—even before I made part of this breathing world, the scourge was plaited for my back; the fetters were forged for my limbs. How mean a thing am I. That accursed and crawling snake, that miserable reptile, that has just glided into its slimy home, is freer and better off than I. He escaped my blow, and is safe. But here am I, a man,—yes, a man!—with thoughts and wishes with powers and faculties as far as an angel's flight above that hated reptile,—yet he is my superior, and scorns to own me as his master, or to stop to take my blows. When he saw my uplifted arm, he darted beyond my reach, and turned to give me battle. I dare not do as much as that.[82]

Before discussing the Kantian aesthetic dimensions of this passage, I want to make a point about its Kantian moral dimensions in light of Lawson's work that has yet to be made. Notice that Washington says that "even before I made part of this breathing world, the scourge was plaited for my back; the fetters were forged for my limbs." Kant wants to address the question of how one can be considered morally free in a world of Newtonian, deterministic, natural laws. Washington here asks a similar question, but the laws that constrain his freedom are not the laws of nature, but rather the laws of chattel slavery. That is, Washington is reflecting on the question of how it will be possible for him to be free considering that, as Lawson points out, on a Lockean empiricist view, all Washington—or Douglass—could ever be was a slave. But even as Kant claims that we see ourselves as beings who are independent of natural laws—dignified, autonomous, rational beings—Washington, later in the soliloquy, determines that despite the shackles and fetters of American chattel slavery, he will choose to be free. He says, "I will stand it no longer.

What others have done, I will do. These trusty legs, or these sinewy arms shall place me among the free."[83] Washington, despite the social, political, and legal system of American chattel slavery—the analog to the natural laws of Newtonian physics—was determined to see himself as a free, rational, dignified being. Douglass, then, through Washington's character in the story, shows another strong resonance with Kant's moral philosophy as it relates to the very foundations of Kant's notion of transcendental freedom: even as Kant argues for a notion of transcendental freedom in the midst of inexorable, mechanistic, natural laws, Douglass embraces a view of Black humanity that demands to see itself as free, despite the mechanistic—indeed, practically Manichean—weight of social and political laws that purport to determine Black people as slaves.

Now to address the aesthetic dimensions of this passage from *The Heroic Slave*, the following points are significant. First, Washington is in reflection. That is, he finds himself "answering each heavy blow of a cruel master with doleful wails and piteous cries" and is "galled with irons." Washington is thus having spatiotemporal experiences, emanating from the sensory manifold, and for which there are no concepts. So he is in a mode of reflective judgment. Neither his understanding nor his practical reason are of any use to him. The understanding is of no use to him because his conception of himself as a free being is plainly at odds with his iron fetters and mournful tears. Subsumption of himself as free in the context of chattel slavery reduces his natural condition to a complete absurdity; and since the understanding operates under the a priori principle of lawfulness and applies to nature, it is this disruption of the natural order that makes Washington's employment of the cognitive faculty of the understanding useless. So, beyond the crude, positivistic concept of "slave," which, again, is contrary to Washington's nature as a free being and thus absurd, he has no concepts to claim knowledge of what is happening to him. Objects of experience—his iron fetters and his mournful tears—present themselves to him, but due to the lack of concepts, provide no synthetic a priori knowledge beyond his condition as a slave, which is unnatural and absurd. Washington's practical reason is of no use to him because his feelings of displeasure have overwhelmed him, and he does not make his feelings the determining ground of the power of desire rooted in his will. Instead, his feelings are the basis for the production of a work of art, insofar as his imagination is at free play with his understanding and is looking for purposiveness in a world where there is none. It is in this context that Washington turns to poetic reflections on nature and treats the birds and a snake as though they have human capacities for transcendental freedom, contrasting them with himself. This is consistent with Kant's claim in the *Critique of Judgment* that "A poet . . . takes [things] that are indeed exemplified in experience . . . by means of an imagination that emulates the example of reason in reaching [for] a maximum, he ventures to give . . . sensible expression in a way that goes beyond the limits of experience, namely, with a completeness for which no example can be found in nature."[84] Birds and snakes fly and crawl instinctively, but Washington's feelings of displeasure over his plight as a slave have connected themselves to his imagination, which has, in turn, freed of the constraints of empirical cognition, produced a poetic, artistic reflection on nature. In some sense, as I will discuss more in the next section on the Kantian dimensions of Douglass's use of narrative, Douglass views Washington, I believe, as a portrait of himself, or certainly of the self that he wants to project to those who read his work.

Lawson's philosophical work on Douglass produces a Kantian interpretation of Douglass that is social and political in nature. What I have tried to do here is to build upon Lawson's work by showing how Douglass's aesthetics resonate with Kant's. Like Lawson, I am not making any strong claims about Douglass having read Kant or being a Kantian. But I do think that we can better understand Douglass's use of art through a Kantian interpretation of his work, for as Lawson points out, Kant "is particularly helpful in understanding Douglass."[85]

Narrative

Another place where one can see Kantian aesthetic features in Douglass's works is in Douglass's use of narrative. Here, it is important to revisit the problem that I am calling the problem of anteriority. I briefly discuss this problem in the introduction and I discuss it in more detail in chapter 2 as it relates to Kierkegaard and Douglass. The problem of anteriority is the problem of epistemic failure in the face of philosophical demands for knowledge as viewed in the context of Moses's demand for God to reveal Himself to him. God tells Moses that his front cannot be seen, and instead of seeing God's front, Moses sees God's backside. God's specific statement to Moses is that "Thou canst not see my face: for there shall no man see me and live."[86] I would argue that this notion of being unable to see God's face and live can be interpreted more broadly than a literal depravation of life. Living, life, and "live," as the Bible uses that term here can also refer to the sense of spirit, imagination, and creativity that our epistemic limitations afford us. After all, if human beings were able to see God's face, there would be no need for poetic expression. It is in this way that human beings, though limited in speculative metaphysical knowledge, are thus morally and aesthetically well disposed. As for our moral disposition, Kant addresses what he calls "the wise adaptation of the human being's cognitive faculties to his practical vocation" in the *Critique of Practical Reason*. In section nine of book two, Kant argues that our epistemic limitations should be viewed as advantageous to us rather than as a detriment. Kant begins his argument by recalling the conclusions of the *Critique of Pure Reason* as it relates to theoretical reason's capacity for transcendent insight in speculative metaphysics, pointing out that it seems that humanity has been deprived of something beneficial. Kant writes, "Nature then seems here to have provided for us only in a stepmotherly fashion with the faculty needed for our end."[87] Kant then questions what the resulting condition would be if theoretical reason afforded such speculative metaphysical insight. He argues that "Unless our whole nature were at the same time changed, the inclinations, which always have the first word, would first demand their satisfaction and, combined with reasonable reflection, their greatest possible and most lasting satisfaction under the name of happiness."[88] Kant then contrasts the clamor of the inclinations with the demands of the moral law: "the moral law would afterward speak, in order to keep them within their proper limits and even to subject them all to a higher end which has no regard to inclination."[89] Here one can see the portrait of Kant's moral agency at work: the will is situated between feeling and inclination, which demand happiness, and the moral law, which demands duty. Epistemic failure thus allows for a tension between feeling and the moral law, on Kant's view. But, Kant argues, this tension would vanish if epistemic failure was replaced with epistemic fulfillment. Kant writes:

> But instead of the conflict that the moral disposition now has to carry on with the inclinations, in which, though after some defeats, moral strength of soul is to be gradually acquired, God and eternity with their awful majesty would stand unceasingly before our eyes. . . . Transgression of the law would, no doubt, be avoided: what is commanded would be done; but because the disposition from which actions ought to be done cannot be instilled by any command, and because the spur to activity in this case would be promptly at hand and external, reason would have no need to work itself up so as to gather strength to resist the inclinations by a lively representation of the dignity of the law: hence most actions conforming to the law would be done from fear, only a few from hope, and none at all from duty, and the moral worth of actions, on which alone in the eyes of supreme wisdom the worth of the person and even that of the world depends, would not exist at all. As long as human nature remains as it is, human conduct would thus be changed into mere mechanism in which, as in a puppet show, everything would gesticulate well but there would be no life in the figures. . . . Thus what the study of nature and of the human being teaches us sufficiently elsewhere may well be true here also: that the inscrutable wisdom by which we exist is not less worthy of veneration in what it has denied us than in what it has granted us.[90]

Kant's point here is profound. As we are currently situated, our epistemic limitations demand attention to the subjective self, and we must, through the conflict between the moral law, on one hand, and our feeling and inclination, on the other hand, along with our will in between, strive for the moral law to be the determining ground of our will, and the more that we strive because of this tension, the more we build moral character. This is what Kant means when he uses the phrase "moral strength of soul" in the above passage. Our moral fiber is developed through theoretical reason's epistemic failure, and turning from objectivity in knowledge to subjectivity in morality. But if our transcendent knowledge gave us exactly what theoretical reason demands—if we were given the ability, in Moses's terms, to see God's face, his front, his anterior—then we would see God; that is, God's "awful majesty would stand unceasingly before our eyes," as Kant puts it. Under these conditions, our conformity to the law would be out of fear of punishment, hope for happiness, and without any regard at all for duty. And so it is that for Kant, we would perform according to the law based upon external, heteronomous influence instead of the internal, autonomous will and the self-legislated, rational moral law. There would never be any genuine moral development. As Kant puts it, everything would, as in a puppet show, move well, but there would be no "life" in the figures. This is precisely why no one can see God and "live": the realization of an epistemic totality would have the consequence of depriving human beings of the opportunity to develop moral character.

And the problem of anteriority is not just a moral problem; it is also an aesthetic problem, for if theoretical reason can grasp—that is, if it can rationally explain the existence of God—then creative, imaginative, artistic expression would be unnecessary. The difference between God's front and God's back is the difference between an intellect which demands a philosophical explanation of God, and the emotions, which can only offer gratitude and thanksgiving to God. The demand to see God's front is the logic of propositions, and the reality of seeing God's back is the creativity of poetry. In Kantian terms, God's face is the understanding and practical reason, which both demand compliance with a priori principles that do not allow for feeling or for creative expression. God's backside, however, is where one sees how an intuition without a concept—as Moses did—allows the imagination and understanding to be at free play with one another, and how the imagination connects to the intense feelings of pleasure or displeasure, allowing something artistic to be created. There is, then, a linguistic shift from philosophical explanation to poetic expression as it relates to the demands of rational theology and its resultant epistemic failure. The problem of anteriority is important here because I am interested in how Douglass's narrative operates aesthetically as a testimony that mediates between the rigors of the conceptual predication of the understanding, on one hand, which would demand Douglass's silence, and the stoic-like endurance for one's commitment to the moral law, on the other hand, that would likewise demand Douglass's silence. Neither the understanding nor practical reason's governance of his will allow him to speak with feeling. But narrative, as a work of art, functions reflectively as Douglass's imagination is at free play with his understanding and is connected to his feelings of pleasure and displeasure, thus enabling him to create and tell a story that both the understanding and practical reason forbid him to tell. Consider that Douglass not only tells his story but also effectively creates a persona for each of his three narratives. This is why, according to Henry Louis Gates, Douglass's biographies all have a similar structure: Douglass created personas for his autobiographical narratives because of his concern for how he would be perceived in future generations. Gates points out that,

> above all, Douglass was demonstrably concerned with the representation in written language of his public self, a self Douglass created, manipulated, and transformed, if ever so slightly, through the three fictive selves he posited in his three autobiographies. . . . When I choose to call these selves fictive ones, I do not mean to suggest any sense of falsity or ill intent; rather, I mean by fictive the act of crafting or making by design, in this instance a process that unfolds in language, through the very discourse that Douglass employs to narrate his autobiographies.[91]

My point here is that what allowed Douglass to create those personas in the first place is the testimonial nature of narrative itself; for in Kantian terms, when one tells a story, neither the understanding nor practical reason allow the storyteller to employ feeling and imagination. As Gates points out, this literary creation is "a process that unfolds in language, through the very discourse that Douglass employs to narrate his autobiographies." This process is indeed one that unfolds in language and in the discourse that Douglass uses as his narrative. This discourse, I argue, is artistic and poetic rather than epistemic and propositional; that is, Douglass's faculty of judgment works reflectively, allowing him to deploy language in its poetic rather than propositional mode. Douglass can use a language that contains as much of a poetic description of his emotional condition as it does a propositional language that describes the brute facts surrounding his enslavement. It is here that one may speak of the difference between the facts and the truth. The understanding limits the storyteller to the historical facts of what happened. But Douglass, who, as I will discuss in the next section of this chapter, as a matter of political strategy, wanted his readership to be moved to end slavery, could not merely recite the facts of his enslavement. No. If Douglass wanted his narratives to have the right political effect, the emotional and psychological truths of his enslavement had to bolster the fact of his enslavement. It is the combination of facts and emotion that comprise the full truth of Douglass's story, making his autobiographical narratives works of art. One may recall Douglass's criticism of the Garrisonians, who wanted Douglass to simply stick to the "facts" of his enslavement and leave the "philosophy" to them. Douglass, however, couldn't bear this sort of limitation, not only because he wanted to make philosophical arguments against slavery—which he did rather well—but also to demonstrate his feeling and sentiment in a creative manner that would be much more effective than simply factual recitation of what happened to him. We also see this distinction between facts and the truth in Douglass's speech "Pictures and Progress." There, he writes:

> The dead fact is nothing without the living impression. Niagara is not fitly described when it is said to be a river of this or that volume falling over a ledge of rocks two hundred feet, nor is thunder when simply called a jarring noise. This is truth, but truth disrobed of its sublimity and glory. A kind of frozen truth, destitute of motion itself—it is incapable of producing emotion in others.[92]

Douglass's speech here articulates the difference between the truth as "a kind of frozen truth"; that is truth without feeling, or, put another way, the scientific "facts" about Niagara Falls and the *truth* of Niagara Falls, which is the truth that includes both the "sublimity and glory" that can only be captured through an artistic description of Niagara Falls. Such an artistic depiction of Niagara Falls will, unlike its scientific counterpart, produce emotion in its audience. The production of emotion is important for Douglass because, as I will argue in the final section of this chapter, he understood that his narrative methodology was an integral part of a much larger political strategy of abolition in the form of moral suasion.

JUDGMENTS OF TASTE AND THE POLITICS OF MORAL SUASION

Douglass not only created works of art that resonate with Kant's aesthetics but also used the works of art that he created as part of a broader political strategy of moral suasion that furthered the cause of abolition. And he did so through an appeal to what he saw as universal and necessary features of human experience, culminating in an appeal to a universal community of rational persons that he hoped would, after reading his *Narrative*, be motivated to abolish American chattel slavery. I argue in this section of the chapter that Douglass's *Narrative* is intended to provoke a certain response among its readership through the use of moral suasion that enables the readership to make reflective judgments of taste that are consistent with Kant's four moments of aesthetic judgment from the *Critique of Judgment*.

The notion of judgment is a basic component of human experience throughout Kant's entire critical philosophy. In our perceptual experience, we make epistemic judgments about objects based upon a priori categories of empirical cognition. In our moral experience, we make ethical judgments about moral action based upon the universally binding, self-legislated moral law that is the categorical imperative. And our aesthetic experience is no exception, for as I have been arguing throughout this chapter, we make reflective judgments—Kant also calls them judgments of taste—because unlike the judgments of theoretical reason, which determine nothing beyond the bounds of empirical cognition, and the moral judgments of our ethical life, which determine humans as free beings based upon the notion of transcendental freedom, aesthetic judgments make our experience determinable based on the free play between the imagination and the understanding.

In Kant's terms, these judgments of taste that Douglass's *Narrative* is intended to provoke are disinterested in quality insofar as Douglass's *Narrative* is not beautiful because it is pleasurable, but rather that it is pleasurable because it is beautiful; second they are universal in quantity in that the claim of beauty is made as if (*als ob*) the *Narrative* is made with an objective property of beauty; third, they are purposive in relation, compelling the readership to view the *Narrative* as the product of a rational will; and finally, such judgments of taste have the modality of necessity as an appeal to a rational *sensus communis* of autonomous persons who, after reading Douglass's *Narrative*, are expected to feel morally and politically bound to abolish slavery and pursue a consistent and humane course of political action toward slaves, who must now be treated as rational ends-in-themselves, rather than merely as means to the end of white economic, social, and political interests.

Douglass's *Narrative* and the Moment of Quality

The first of Kant's four moments of aesthetic judgment is the moment of quality. The quality of judgments of taste is that they are fundamentally disinterested in the object that one claims is beautiful. By interest, Kant means "what we call the liking we connect with the presentation of an object's existence. Hence such a liking always refers at once to our power of desire, either as the basis that determines it, or at any rate, as necessarily connected with that determining basis."[93] So to say that a judgment of taste is disinterested is to say that any claim to beauty with respect to an object will not be based upon anything about the object or one's desire for the object, but rather will be a reference to how "the subject feels himself, [namely] how he is affected by the presentation." If we make claims about the object, we make a logical judgment. But with judgments of taste, we are referencing the feelings of pleasure and displeasure engendered in the subject. So a judgment of taste makes a claim of beauty based upon subjective feeling rather than something in the object itself connected to the subject's desire. In the end, disinterest characterizes the first moment of aesthetic judgment such that we take pleasure in something because we judge it to be beautiful, rather than judge something beautiful because we find it pleasurable.

Douglass's *Narrative* is "beautiful" in a Kantian sense insofar as one makes a reflective judgment of taste about it that is disinterested. That is, one does not claim that the *Narrative* is beautiful because it pleasurable; instead, one finds the *Narrative* pleasurable because it is judged to be beautiful. As a reflective judgment, judgments of taste about Douglass's *Narrative* from its readership are made based upon the subjective feelings of pleasure and displeasure that lead them to, in their search for a concept, call the *Narrative* beautiful. For example, in William Lloyd Garrison's preface to Douglass's *Narrative*, he claims that "He who can peruse it without a tearful eye, a heaving breast, an afflicted spirit . . . must have a flinty heart, and be qualified to act the part of a trafficker."[94] Garrison's use of such emotive language conveys the strong message that as he read Douglass's *Narrative*, it caused him to have "a tearful eye, a heaving breast," and "an afflicted spirit." His endorsement of the *Narrative* brings with it his own feelings of pleasure and displeasure rather than any claim about the *Narrative* itself as an object of experience. So it is that the *Narrative* is beautiful not because Garrison found the *Narrative* desirable as an object, as something to merely possess, but instead because he has judged it to be beautiful based upon the feelings of pleasure and displeasure—displeasure over Douglass's condition, pleasure over the motivation to abolition—that the *Narrative* has aroused within him. Garrison's judgment of taste is disinterested, as was the aim for the rest of Douglass's readership: arouse feelings of displeasure that will lead to a judgment, based on those feelings, that the reader finds Douglass's *Narrative* "beautiful," in this Kantian sense.

Douglass's *Narrative* and the Moments of Quantity and Modality

The second moment of judgments of taste, quantity, is connected to the first moment of quality. If a judgment of taste has nothing at all to do with the object but is instead based on the subject's feelings of pleasure—again, in this case, Garrison's feelings of pleasure due to an increased motivation to abolition—then it stands to reason that one cannot help "requiring a similar liking from everyone because he cannot discover, underlying this liking, any private conditions, on which only he might be dependent, so that he must regard it as based on what he can presuppose in everyone else as well."[95] One cannot discover any such private conditions, because, according to the first moment of quality as being disinterested, there is no desire for anything in the object itself, but rather only an expression of feeling with reference to the subject. So, one "will talk about the beautiful as if beauty were a characteristic of the object and the judgment were logical."[96] Although judgments of taste are not logical, empirical judgments, we treat them as such because "all interest is kept out of" such judgments.[97]

Douglass's abolition strategy was one that demanded an appeal to universality in order for it to be effective. It would be pointless for Douglass to publish his *Narrative* unless he believed that it would evoke such emotion and sentiment that he could make a moral appeal to all people. If American chattel slavery was universally wrong—and Douglass argued vociferously that it was—then any appeal for its abolition must also have a universal appeal. And, for Douglass, this universal appeal for abolition was made based, in part at least, upon the anthropological presupposition that all human beings have feeling, reason, and are free to act upon the things that move them emotionally and appeal to their rationality. This is what Frank M. Kirkland referred to as Douglass's engagement in a "communicative practice of justification." Kirkland writes of Douglass that he "freely makes public use of his reason; he experiences freedom of thought and speech in the public sphere where the autonomous voluntary association and reasoned communication of free and equal individuals occur."[98] And this was Douglass's strategy for abolition that he pursued with the publication of his *Narrative*: the readership would comprehend the magnitude of slavery's devastating moral and emotional toll on the slaves and on their masters, and, because of that comprehension, the readership would demand an immediate end to American chattel slavery. In other words, if one reader was moved to consider the *Narrative* "beautiful" as a means to abolition, that reader brought with that judgment the expectation that other readers would see the *Narrative* in the same way. This strategy resonates strongly with the Kantian moment of aesthetic judgment as to quantity in Garrison's endorsement of Douglass's *Narrative* in its preface:

> This Narrative contains many affecting incidents, many passages of great eloquence and power; but I think the most thrilling one of them all is the description Douglass gives of his feelings, as he stood soliloquizing respecting his fate, and the chances of his one day being a freeman, on the banks of the Chesapeake Bay—viewing the receding vessels as they flew with their white wings before the breeze, and apostrophizing them as animated by the living spirit of freedom. Who can read that passage, and be insensible to its pathos and sublimity? Compressed into it is a whole Alexandrian library of thought, feeling, and sentiment—all that can, all that need be urged in the form of expostulation, entreaty, rebuke, against that crime of crimes—making man the property of his fellow man! O, how accursed is that system, which entombs the godlike mind of man, defaces the divine image, reduces those who by creation were crowned with glory and honor to a level with four-footed beasts, and exalts the dealer in

human flesh above all that is called God! Why should its existence be prolonged one hour? Is it not evil, only evil, and that continually? What does its presence imply but the absence of all fear of God, all regard for man, on the part of the people of the United States? Heaven speed its eternal overthrow![99]

Garrison asks a rhetorical question implying that everyone who reads Douglass's poetic account of freedom would be moved by "its pathos and sublimity." This is Kant's second moment of aesthetic judgment—quantity—at work, for Garrison demonstrates a strong expectation that the same passage that moved him will move all others who read it. Indeed, this may be considered a reflective judgment at the meta level because it is a reflective judgment on a reflective judgment of Douglass himself, as he poetically, through the power of his imagination at free play with his understanding, assigns human characteristics like moral freedom to nature. This is, of course, consistent with Kant's account of what poets do.[100] Not only does Garrison convey an expectation of universal agreement with his assessment of this passage in Douglass's *Narrative*, but he also moves straight through to the desired outcome, which is the immediate abolition of American chattel slavery, arguing that slavery should not be "prolonged one hour," that it is "evil, only evil," and that divine power should "speed its eternal overthrow." It is in this sense that the quantity of universality and the modality of necessity as it relates to Kant's account of aesthetic judgment may be read together, for the demand for universality regarding claims of taste not only claims that others will agree with me but also presupposes that I will be able to meaningfully communicate my ideas to a community of rational persons who have a common sense—that is, a sense of connectedness to the community in virtue of certain shared cognitive features and functions (understanding, judgment, and reason). Douglass's narrative strategy is thus seen in this passage from Garrison's preface, and this political strategy resonates strongly with Kant's aesthetics: Garrison makes a reflective judgment of quality that is disinterested in that it is based upon his subjective feelings of pleasure and displeasure through the reading of Douglass's *Narrative*, and he expects others to be similarly moved to end American Chattel slavery as he is. Garrison's expectation is, in turn, based upon one of the key assumptions of his and Douglass's strategy of moral suasion—namely, that all human beings share certain characteristics, and when these characteristics are appealed to in the right fashion, humanity can reach a place of universal agreement about the moral wrongness of American Chattel slavery and abolish it. This was the political strategy of moral suasion as Douglass and Garrison employed it. Interpreting Douglass in this way, I believe, demonstrates that Douglass, through a Kantian-styled aesthetic framework, pursues social and political freedom. Douglass uses art in the service of politics to pursue justice.

Reading Douglass's *Narrative*, then, induces a reflective judgment that is disinterested in its quality, in that there is no interest in or desire for the *Narrative* as an object, that is universal in its quantity, in that the absence of desire carries with it an expectation that others will also judge the *Narrative* beautiful, and that is necessary in its modality insofar as it predicates communication with others upon certain Kantian assumptions as it relates to shared cognitive operations. Douglass himself certainly wished people to have this sort of universal opinion of his *Narrative* because of what he thought was the universal wrongness of American chattel slavery. And in order to do that, Douglass must have believed that he could communicate the wrongness of American chattel slavery to other similarly disposed rational persons, making his reflective judgment necessary in its modality.

Douglass's *Narrative* and the Moment of Relation

Objects that people consider to be beautiful often appear to have no purpose whatsoever. This is more the case with natural objects such as sunsets, mountain peaks, or sea sides. Kant's third moment of aesthetic judgment is straightforward when considering natural objects such as these because, Kant argues, we see sunsets, mountain peaks, and sea sides *als ob* (as if) they are the product of a rational will. It is in this sense that we can see natural objects as having *Zweckmäßigkeit ohne Zweck* (purposiveness without a purpose). But even human artistic productions can appear to us as having no purpose, despite that they were made for a purpose. Artists have reasons and motivations for their work. But the artist's motivation or purpose for the work is irrelevant with respect to judgments of taste, which originate in the subjective feelings of pleasure or displeasure in the subject, and have nothing at all to do with the object. The judgment that Douglass's *Narrative* is a beautiful literary work, for example, has nothing at all to do with Douglass's motivations in creating the work, but rather in the subjective feeling of the readership. And while it may be true that Douglass intends to produce that subjective feeling in his audience, a judgment of taste will not be based on Douglass's motivations. Instead, the judgment will be based on the subjective feelings themselves, which are not only disinterested but also communicable through the moments of quantity (universality) and modality (necessity) to an audience that is assumed to be similarly moved because those in that audience are—just as Douglass is—emotional, rational, and free.

So one who judges Douglass's *Narrative* as beautiful because of its purpose, makes a judgment that is interested insofar as it attributes the concept of beauty to the object itself. Again, this is not what Garrison is doing with his endorsement of Douglass's *Narrative* in the preface. But one who judges

Douglass's *Narrative* as beautiful because of their feelings of pleasure or displeasure which are communicable through discursive practices that assume an anthropological universality in the form of a *sensus communis*, are moving toward political action. This is what Garrison did, and what both he and Douglass hoped that his entire readership would also do. What Kant's third moment of aesthetic judgment adds to the experience of Douglass's readership is that despite the vast cultural, social, and political gaps between whites and Blacks during chattel slavery that would have caused many whites to see Douglass as subhuman, those same whites must now presuppose that the *Narrative* itself is the product of a rational will. White readers must view the *Narrative als ob* (as if) it had a purpose, which forces them to recognize Douglass's personhood, and thus the personhood of every other slave.

FROM THE POLITICAL TO THE SOCIAL: A RETURN TO LEVINAS

This chapter has argued for two Kantian interpretations of Douglass. First, I have argued that there is a general resonance between Kant's critical philosophy and Douglass's conceptions of the human being, morality, knowledge, and art. In support of this interpretation, I have tried to show that Douglass's *Narrative* functions as a type of art that enables him to speak poetically from his experience rather than epistemically from his cognition. To put it in Kantian terms, Douglass's *Narrative*, his novella *The Heroic Slave*, and his view of art in his 1861 speech "Pictures and Progress" are the result of neither the understanding nor practical reason, but rather of his faculty of judgment that operates reflectively.

My second interpretation of Douglass explored the relationship between Douglass's art and his politics—specifically, his use of moral suasion. I have argued that reading Douglass's *Narrative* allows for one to make claims of taste about intuitions that lack concepts, and that exhibit disinterestedness, universality, purposiveness, and necessity as part of Douglass's political strategy of abolition through moral suasion. Douglass demonstrates reflective judgment; he occupies a creative space where he can speak according to the free play between his imagination and his understanding rather than remain silent due to the demands of epistemic certainty, on one hand, and the stoic silence of practical reason, on the other. As Kant points out in the *Critique of Judgment*, the understanding functions—as he argued in the *Critique of Pure Reason*—to unite concepts with intuitions, but because of the bounds of theoretical reason, the substrate is left undetermined, and practical reason functions—as he argued in the *Critique of Practical Reason*—to postulate certain religious beliefs and beliefs about freedom as rationally acceptable but ontologically uncertain, as in the arguments for transcendental freedom, which determine the substrate with the view that one must live *als ob* (as if) one is free. In contrast to the understanding and practical reason, Kant argues that aesthetic judgments make the substrate *determinable*, rather than undetermined because of the *Grenze* (bounds) of theoretical reason, or determined because of the presupposition of transcendental freedom, allowing for a "free play" between the understanding and the imagination. And Douglass indeed determines his judgments of taste using this notion of "free play" artistically so as to appeal to the shared cognitive features and functions of all human beings, who form the *sensus communis* that demands that all rational beings not only assent to his claims of taste but also recognize the plight of slaves in the system of American chattel slavery. The moral and the aesthetic are bound together in both Douglass and Kant. And the moral, the aesthetic, and the political are bound together in Douglass.

Thus far, I have attempted to develop a philosophical and Christian theological interpretation of Douglass that makes the word flesh, as compared with the reformed epistemology of analytic theism, which makes the flesh a word. To make my case, I have interpreted Douglass with four dialogue partners: Kierkegaard and Kafka represent my attempt at an existential interpretation of Douglass, Levinas is my attempt to interpret Douglass phenomenologically, and by reading Douglass with Kant's critical philosophy, especially his aesthetics, I have tried to show the relationship between art and the political in Douglass, interpreting him as an aesthetic-political thinker. Throughout this interpretive study of Douglass, my claim has been that as compared with the reformed epistemology of analytic theism, my existential, phenomenological, aesthetic, and political interpretation of Douglass is more consistent with the moral imperatives of Christianity as seen in the context of an Incarnational theological paradigm.

In the next and final chapter of this interpretation of Douglass I continue to argue in support of my claim through a return to Levinas to present a social interpretation of Douglass. I interpret Douglass's well-known and formative experience fighting Covey, the "slave-breaker," as a microcosm of the social totality in which all slaves found themselves. It is in the midst of this totality that Douglass forges his personhood, and displays a resistance that problematizes the epistemic impulse behind the institution of American chattel slavery. The resistance that Douglass showed becomes normative, not in the literal, physical sense of a fight, but rather in terms of a metaphorical, ongoing struggle to be free that American Black people ought to embrace with a Derrick Bell–inspired sort of courage. In Levinas's terms, Douglass represents infinity that resists totality.

NOTES

1. Genesis 1:1–3.

2. I also include Kant's philosophical theology here, which is essentially the conclusions of his epistemology in the *Critique of Pure Reason*, along with his essay "Religion within the Limits of Reason Alone" and his essay on Job, "On the Miscarriage of All Philosophical Trials in Theodicy."

3. See Timothy J. Golden, "From Epistemology to Ethics: Theoretical and Practical Reason in Kant and Douglass," *Journal of Religious Ethics* 40, no. 4 (2012): 603–28.

4. A similar discussion on the interpretation of Kant with Douglass can be found in chapter 4 of my forthcoming book, *Reason's Dilemma: Subjectivity, Transcendence, and the Problem of Ontotheology* (New York: Palgrave Macmillan, under contract), and in my essay, "From Epistemology to Ethics: Theoretical and Practical Reason in Kant and Douglass," 623–26.

5. See Frank M. Kirkland, "Enslavement, Moral Suasion, and Struggles for Recognition: Frederick Douglass's Answer to the Question—'What Is Enlightenment?'" in *Frederick Douglass: A Critical Reader*, eds. Frank M. Kirkland and Bill E. Lawson (Malden, MA: Blackwell, 1999), 243–310. In this essay, Kirkland acknowledges the racism of David Hume. See page 258.

6. See Kirkland's essay in *Frederick Douglass: A Critical Reader* (Malden, MA: Blackwell, 1999), 243–310, and Lawson's essay, "Douglass among the Romantics," in *The Cambridge Companion to Frederick Douglass*, ed. Maurice Lee (Cambridge: Cambridge University Press, 2009), 118–31.

7. Frank Kirkland argues that there are two forms of moral suasion in Douglass's work. First, there is a version of moral suasion "that rests on moral sentimentalism and whose advancement of reasons is rhetorically saturated," and second there is a version of moral suasion "that hinges on natural law and whose advancement of reasons is discursively amplified." See Kirkland, "Enslavement, Moral Suasion, and Struggles," 264–65.

8. See Robert Bernasconi's essays, "Who Invented the Concept of Race? Kant's Role in the Enlightenment Construction of Race," in *Race*, ed. Robert Bernasconi (Malden, MA: Blackwell, 2001), 11–36; "Will the Real Kant Please Stand Up: The Challenge of Enlightenment Racism to the Study of the History of Philosophy," *Radical Philosophy* 117, no. 1 (2003): 13–22; and "Kant's Third Thoughts on Race," in *Reading Kant's Geography*, eds. Stuart Elden and Eduardo Mendieta (Albany: State University of New York Press, 2011), 291–318. See also Tommy J. Curry's essay, "Shut Your Mouth When You're Talking to Me: Silencing the Idealist School of Critical Race Theory," *Georgetown Journal of Law and Modern Critical Race Perspectives* 3, no. 1 (2012): 1–38.

9. See J. Kameron Carter, *Race: A Theological Account* (London: Oxford University Press, 2008), for a discussion of Kant's contribution to race in Christian theology; for Kant's contributions to the concept of race in philosophy, see the citations to Robert Bernasconi's work in the previous note.

10. Hans Georg Gadamer, *Truth and Method*, trans. Joel Weisenheimer and Donald G. Marshall (London: Continuum, 2004), 300.

11. Ibid., 299–300.
12. Ibid., 300.
13. Ibid.
14. Ibid.
15. Ibid.
16. For example, see Kirkland's "Enslavement, Moral Suasion and Struggles" and Lewis R. Gordon's "Douglass as an Existentialist," both in *Frederick Douglass: A Critical Reader*, and Bill E. Lawson's "Douglass among the Romantics," in *The Cambridge Companion to Frederick Douglass*. See also Ronald T. Judy, "Kant and Knowledge of Disappearing Expression," in *A Companion to African-American Philosophy*, eds. Tommy L. Lott and John P. Pittman (Malden, MA: Blackwell, 2006), 110–24.
17. Emmanuel Eze and Eduardo Mendieta both argue that Kant's racism is not merely present in his corpus but also plays an integral, performative role in his conceptions of humanity, race, and gender. See Emmanuel Eze, "The Color of Reason," in *Post-Colonial African Philosophy: A Critical Reader*, ed. Emmanuel Chukwudi Eze (Cambridge, MA: Blackwell, 1997), 103–40, and Eduardo Mendieta, "Geography Is to History as Woman Is to Man: Kant on Sex, Race, and Geography," in *Reading Kant's Geography*, eds. Stuart Elden and Eduardo Mendieta (Albany: State University of New York Press, 2011), 345–68.
18. See my essay "German Chocolate: Why Philosophy Is So Personal," in *Philosophy and the Mixed Race Experience*, ed. Tina Fernandes Botts (Lanham, MD: Lexington Books, 2016), 231–66.
19. Again, I have no interest in entering this debate here. But for a discussion of my critique of Eze's position, see my essay, "From Epistemology to Ethics," 623–26. See also Thomas E. Hill and Bernard Boxill, "Kant on Race," *Race and Racism*, ed. Bernard Boxill (London: Oxford University Press, 2001), 448–71.
20. Consider Charles Mills's 2018 essay "Black Radical Kantianism," in which Mills argued for an emancipatory politics within a Kantian ethical framework. Charles W. Mills, "Black Radical Kantianism," *Res Philosophica* 95, no. 1 (January 2018): 1–33.
21. Immanuel Kant, *Critique of Pure Reason*, trans. Norman Kemp Smith (New York: St. Martin's Press, 1965), A796/B825–A797/B826. This text will hereafter be referred to in the notes as CPR.
22. Plato, *Apology*, 21a–23d.
23. Kant, CPR, A471/B499, A472/B500.
24. Kant, *Prolegomena to Any Future Metaphysics That Will Be Able to Come Forward as Science*, trans. James W. Ellington (Indianapolis, IN: Hackett, 2001), 86.
25. Ibid., 87.
26. Ibid.
27. Ibid.
28. Ibid.
29. Kant, CPR, A554/B582.
30. Ibid., A555/B583.
31. Kant, CPR, A546/B574–A547/B575.

32. Immanuel Kant, *Critique of Judgment*, trans. Werner S. Pluhar (Indianapolis, IN: Hackett, 1987), 37–38. This text is hereafter referred to as CJ.

33. CJ, 37.

34. Ibid.

35. Immanuel Kant, "Critique of Practical Reason," in *Practical Philosophy*, trans. Mary Gregor (Cambridge: Cambridge University Press, 2006), 224. This text is hereafter referred to as CPrR.

36. Kant, CPrR, 215–16.

37. Kant, CPR, A808/B833.

38. Ibid., A804/B832–A806/B834.

39. Ibid.

40. Kant, CPrR, 240.

41. Ibid.

42. Ibid.

43. Ibid.

44. Kant, CPR, A51/B75.

45. Kant, CPR, A137/B176–B177/A138.

46. Ibid.

47. Ibid.

48. Ibid., A139/B178.

49. Ibid., A140/B179.

50. Ibid.

51. Ibid.

52. Ibid.

53. Ibid.

54. Ibid., A141/B180.

55. *Holy Bible*, Genesis 1:2 (King James Version).

56. Kierkegaard, *Either/Or*, volume I, trans. Howard V. Hong (Princeton, NJ: Princeton University Press, 1987), 19.

57. Kant, "On the Miscarriage of All Philosophical Trials in Theodicy," in *Religion and Rational Theology*, ed. and trans. Allen Wood and George Di Giovanni (Cambridge: Cambridge University Press, 1996), 32–33.

58. *Holy Bible*, Job 2:11–13 (King James Version).

59. Kant, CJ, 183.

60. See Kirkland, "Enslavement, Moral Suasion, and Struggles," and Lawson, "Douglass among the Romantics."

61. Lawson, "Douglass among the Romantics."

62. Frederick Douglass, "The Nature of Slavery," in *Douglass: Autobiographies* (New York: Library of America, 1996), 423–24.

63. Ibid., 419.

64. Ibid., 420.

65. Insofar as this statement represents my interpretation of Douglass and Kant that is guided by my own hermeneutic prejudices—prejudices that, according to Gadamer, are inevitable—I would refer those who would object to this statement in the text to my discussion earlier in this chapter in my prelude on Kant and race.

66. Ibid., 420–21.
67. Kant, CPR, B421.
68. Ibid.
69. Douglass, "The Nature of Slavery," 420.
70. See my essay, "From Epistemology to Ethics."
71. Frederick Douglass, "Why Is the Negro Lynched?" in *Frederick Douglass: Selected Speeches and Writings*, ed. Philip S. Foner (Chicago: Lawrence Hill, 1999), 775.
72. Ibid.
73. Ibid.
74. Ibid.
75. Kant, CPR, A584/B612.
76. Douglass, "The Nature of Slavery," 422.
77. Lawson, "Douglass among the Romantics," 126.
78. Ibid., 127.
79. See George Yancy, "The Existential Dimensions of Frederick Douglass's Autobiographical Narrative: A Beauvoirian Examination," *Philosophy and Social Criticism* 28, no. 3 (2002): 297–320.
80. Lawson, "Douglass among the Romantics," 124–25.
81. Frederick Douglass, "The Heroic Slave," in *Frederick Douglass: Selected Speeches and Writings*, ed. Philip S. Foner (Chicago: Lawrence Hill Press, 1996), 222.
82. Ibid., 221.
83. Ibid.
84. Kant, CJ, 183.
85. Lawson, "Douglass among the Romantics," 118.
86. *Holy Bible*, Exodus 33:20 (King James Version).
87. Kant, CPrR, 257.
88. Ibid., 257–58.
89. Ibid., 258.
90. Ibid.
91. Henry Louis Gates Jr., *Figures in Black: Words, Signs, and the "Racial" Self* (London: Oxford University Press, 1987), 103.
92. Douglass, "Pictures and Progress," 462.
93. Kant, CJ, 45.
94. William Lloyd Garrison, "Preface," in Frederick Douglass, *Narrative of the Life of Frederick Douglass, an American Slave* (Boston: Anti-Slavery Office, 1849). Retrieved from https://www.loc.gov/item/82225385/.
95. Kant, CJ, 54.
96. Ibid.
97. Ibid.
98. Kirkland, "Enslavement, Moral Suasion, and Struggles," 252.
99. Garrison, "Preface," viii.
100. Kant, CJ, 183.

Chapter Five

An Ethical Metaphysics of the Flesh

Narrative, Theology, and Justice

"But the unclean spirit, when he is gone out of the man, passes through waterless places, seeking rest, and doesn't find it. Then he says, 'I will return into my house from which I came out,' and when he has come back, he finds it empty, swept, and put in order. Then he goes, and takes with himself seven other spirits more evil than he is, and they enter in and dwell there. The last state of that man becomes worse than the first. Even so will it be also to this evil generation."

—*Holy Bible*[1]

DOUGLASS AND LEVINAS ON SOCIAL LIFE AS THE ETHICAL

American chattel slavery had both social and political dimensions. This is what Douglass means when he speaks on "the legal and social relation of master and slave."[2] Of this legal and social relation, he says, "A master is one—to speak in the vocabulary of the southern states—who claims and exercises a right of property in the person of a fellow-man. This he does with the force of law and the sanction of the southern religion."[3] In the previous two chapters, I have addressed the relationship of Douglass's *Narrative* both as an art form and as an aesthetic act of political resistance. In chapter 3, reading Douglass with Levinas, I attempted to show how Douglass's *Narrative* and his poetic sensibilities operate phenomenologically to suspend what I termed the "theological attitude" in favor of an aesthetic turn away from theodicy and the problem of evil and toward a poetic "saying" that resists the abstractions of philosophical and theological reflection inherent in theodicy and in free will defenses. And in chapter 4, reading Douglass with Kant, I argued that a Kantian aesthetic played an integral role in the politics of moral suasion, enabling Douglass to portray himself as a rational, moral being. As such a being, I concluded that Douglass was capable of self-expression in the form of a universal appeal to the readership of his *Narrative* based upon the presupposition of shared cognitive features to help bring about the demise of American chattel slavery. In both of these aesthetic/political interpretations of Douglass, the word is made flesh through robust political engagement with oppression in a manner consistent with the Incarnational theological paradigm that I outlined in chapter 1. As compared with the reformed epistemology of analytic theism, which purports to be a Christian approach to the philosophy of religion, I have been arguing that my existential, phenomenological, and aesthetic interpretation of Douglass is the better of the two approaches because in shunning the hyper-rational in favor of the subjective, the political, and the aesthetic, Douglass is best able to address moral, social, and political exigencies that confront the oppressed, particularly Black people. The reformed epistemology of analytic theism cannot address these exigencies precisely because in its attempt to prove that a belief in God is rational, it exalts reason over history—a concept that I have introduced called "the jurisdiction of history"—and it aims to philosophically see God's anterior rather than, because of a recognition of epistemic failure and a respect for epistemic limitations, being content to see God's posterior poetically—a concept that I have introduced called the "problem of anteriority."

This chapter shifts from a political to a social interpretation of Douglass. According to Douglass, whereas the "force of the law" justified the political dimension of American chattel slavery, it was the "sanction of the southern religion" that justified the social dimension of American chattel slavery.[4] To articulate this social interpretation of Douglass, I now return to Levinas and try to show that Douglass experiences what Levinas himself experienced when the Nazis captured him in 1940: a social and political seizure with an ample—and deeply problematic—amount of philosophical and theological support. With Levinas, I argue that philosophy and theology are complicit in oppression insofar as they help to develop and maintain what Levinas calls a "totality," or a logically grounded social order that truncates human personhood in the interest of epistemic and metaphysical domination and control. In order to develop this social interpretation of Douglass, I analyze his fight with Covey, the "slave-breaker," reading it against the backdrop of Levinas's concepts of ethical metaphysics, totality, infinity and subjectivity, and what he calls the "vassalage" of religion to reason.[5] It is with this last point that I situate the reformed epistemology of analytic theism as being in a subordinate position to the primacy of philosophical inquiry, which, I argue, is what makes the reformed epistemology of analytic theism ignore the social, moral, and the political due to reason's weighty interests in epistemic justification and metaphysical explanation. This discussion is important, because for Douglass, what justifies the social dimension of American chattel slavery is the "sanction of southern religion."[6] And for Douglass, this religion is a corrupt brand of Christianity, as exemplified in the life of Covey, the "Christian" "nigger breaker," who, like the reformed epistemology of analytic theism, separates his theological beliefs from moral, social, and political concerns.

My social interpretation of Douglass develops in two phases. First, following this introduction to the chapter, in the next section, I provide a broad background discussion of Levinas's notion of an "ethical metaphysics." Within that section, there are, in turn, three subsections that are discussions of various concepts in Levinas that are important for my social interpretation of Douglass. The first of these subsections is a discussion of Levinas's concept of "totality," the second, a discussion of Levinas's concepts of "infinity" and subjectivity, and the third discusses Levinas's criticism of abstraction in rational theology. I examine these concepts in Levinas as background for my social interpretation of Douglass throughout the rest of the chapter, which is based on Douglass's fight with Covey as Douglass discusses it in his *Narrative*. Reading Douglass with Levinas through Douglass's fight with Covey both supports my thesis about the shortcomings of the reformed epistemology of analytic theism and advances a meta-philosophical interpretation of American chattel slavery with strong explanatory force. That is, I submit that Douglass's fight with Covey, when read with Levinas, raises serious questions about the advisability and morality of establishing a social life with epistemic and metaphysical foundations that exclude ethical considerations. What my interpretation of Douglass's fight with Covey demonstrates is that, in the end, such an exclusion of ethical considerations in the founding of social institutions leads to oppression, which, in turn, demands a perpetual struggle for such institutions to be ethical and justice oriented, resulting in a struggle on a much broader scale that is narrowly represented in the fight between Douglass and Covey.

With this background in place, the second phase of my interpretation of Douglass is an analysis of the social metaphysics and social epistemology that is the "totality" in which Douglass finds himself in his *Narrative*. Indeed, Douglass's fight with Covey—which I introduce in this section of the chapter—is an encounter of two persons within Douglass's *Narrative* that represent Levinas's notions of totality (Covey) and infinity (Douglass). The subsections in this section of the chapter correspond to the subsections on Levinas: there is one on Douglass's world of American chattel slavery as representing Levinas's notion of totality, another on Douglass and Levinas's notions of infinity and subjectivity, and finally a section on how the fight between Douglass and Covey represents a struggle to maintain a unity between theological beliefs and morality. In the first subsection of the chapter on Douglass and totality, I draw from philosopher Cynthia Nielsen's work. Specifically, I am interested in her analysis of Douglass's fight with Covey, where she discusses the notion of the panopticon, which is a metaphysical and epistemological means of maintaining social control. When Covey assaults Douglass, he is acting within an oppressive epistemological framework where Douglass is already "known" as a slave. Within this epistemological framework, Douglass, on Levinas's account, becomes the mere *noema* of a *noesis*, preserving only the minimal amount of transcendence that is necessary to epistemically maintain Douglass as an "object" "to" and "for" Covey. Thus transformed into an intentional object, Covey achieves a simultaneous intelligibility and unintelligibility: on one hand, Covey can render Douglass intelligible to himself, but, on the other hand, Douglass is made to play a role of a slave, in which Douglass is made unintelligible to himself.

In the next subsection on Douglass, infinity, and subjectivity, I argue that when Douglass resists Covey, Covey's subjectivity is, as Levinas argues in *Otherwise than Being*, "thrown back onto itself" in a sort of "anarchic passivity." Anarchic in that Covey is no longer an autonomous, self-regulating subject operating according to the laws of his own instrumental rationality and freedom. Covey is made passive in the sense that now instead of acting on Douglass, he himself is acted upon by the infinity of Douglass as the Other. Douglass's narrative methodology, when read with Levinas in this way, thus makes the Word flesh: it transforms the overly theoretical reflections of "infinity" as a concept into the existentially/phenomenologically lived experience of Douglass.

And finally, I contrast the theology of Covey with that of Douglass in an attempt to demonstrate that Douglass advocates a theology of the flesh that is consistent with the biblical imperative to tend to the "least of these" (Matthew 25:40, 45), whereas Covey champions belief to the exclusion of authentic moral and religious (Christian) practice; a sort of religion that, in its epistemic and metaphysical commitments, more resembles the neglect of moral and religious practice in the reformed epistemology of analytic theism than it does the authentic religion demanded in the Bible (James 1:26–7). I then conclude.

Before I begin, I make two clarifications as it relates to Levinas. First, it is, I think, important to give some preliminary remarks on two of Levinas's concepts: "totality" and "infinity." Although I will discuss these concepts later in the chapter as part of Levinas's broader project of an ethical metaphysics, I introduce them briefly here to provide some initial familiarity that will help to clarify my discussion of them later in the chapter. And second, I want to provide some background on Levinas's motivations for his philosophical project of an ethical metaphysics, as I think that a brief elucidation of the impetus for his philosophical work will be useful for understanding why I believe Levinas to be a compatible dialogue partner for Douglass, and thus further clarify my social interpretation of Douglass through his fight with Covey.

PRELIMINARY REMARKS ON "TOTALITY" AND "INFINITY"

A concept that is central to Levinas's philosophical work is what he terms "totality." Totality is the tendency of philosophy, conceived of as a project of epistemic and metaphysical justification, to subject all of being to the conditions of rational intelligibility. With its strong epistemic and metaphysical predilections, totality attempts to make all things both knowable and rational according to the dictates of the *logos*, or reason. But when philosophy has its way, according to Levinas, it makes all of being conform to its rational demands at a great human social cost. And that cost is the identity of people, who often present themselves before philosophical reason as that which cannot be made rational and intelligible, which is to say that people have identities that transcend the limits of philosophical knowledge. The problem for Levinas is that despite this transcendence, persons are still made to conform to the conditions of rational intelligibility and the ego's demands such that they so conform, have their identities truncated, and become social and political amputees in the interest of epistemic and metaphysical justification. We often see this manifested in the vast array of stereotypes that are distortions of who people really are. Indeed, people must be so distorted if reason is to have its way because the concept of totality does not tolerate transcendence. Anything that is alien to reason, any alterity or strangeness, especially as it relates to persons, is unacceptable because of reason and its desire for knowledge. Totality thus results in a sort of social violence in which persons are left distorted and ersatz versions of themselves because philosophical reasoning demands intelligibility. Totality is connected to the very nature of philosophy, which is the acquisition of epistemic and metaphysical truth that can be rationally articulated and defended.

Infinity is a concept that philosophy is prone to discuss abstractly, but for Levinas, who invests infinity with theological language, there is no interest in the abstractions of conceptual analysis. Levinas interprets infinity differently than in classical philosophical theology. It is through the development of Levinas's notion of *l'Autre* (the Other) that infinity is personified in the face, which becomes a metaphor for the vulnerability of marginalized and oppressed people. It is the face of the widow, the orphan and the stranger—that is, the Other is the face of the oppressed. And it is this face that places moral demands on Levinas's moral subject, holding it hostage, subjecting it to insomnia, decentering it, and putting its autonomy, freedom, and its rationality in crisis. For Levinas, infinity is God Himself in the face of the Other. The concepts of totality and infinity work together in Levinas to form a dynamic of oppression (totality) and resistance to that oppression (infinity). Whereas totality attempts to make that which is transcendent immanent to the ego, infinity resists totality and preserves transcendence in such a way as to facilitate an asymmetrical relation between the ego and the Other in which the ego is led into a wakeful vigilance—what Levinas refers to as "insomnia"—for the moral well-being of the infinity that the Other represents. So totality and infinity are involved in a struggle with one another. And it is in Douglass's fight with Covey that Levinas's concepts of totality and infinity come into sharper focus through Douglass's use of narrative. Levinas's concepts become Douglass's reality. Moreover, as I briefly discuss below in the next section, before totality and infinity were concepts for Levinas they were also his reality.

DOUGLASS AND LEVINAS

It has been said of Levinas that the chief interest motivating his notions of "totality," "the Other," and "infinity" was his survival in a German prison camp "under difficult and humiliating circumstances, while his family, with the exception of his wife and daughter, perished."[7] The violence of World War II and the Nazi-directed, systematic extermination of Jewish people was, according to Levinas, performed with the complicity of a certain philosophical and theological thinking that displaces alterity and installs the interests of metaphysics and epistemology as masters that dominate the strangeness, perplexity, and uniqueness of that which is foreign to a free, rational self. It is for this reason that Levinas wants to, through his notion of ethical metaphysics or ethics as first philosophy, get behind the rational, free self of moral theory in an attempt to place moral obligation at the foundations of social life rather than epistemology and metaphysics. Indeed, Levinas would argue that once the free, rational, philosophical self is displaced and replaced with the primacy of an ethical obligation to the Other, the world becomes far more just. This, then, is Levinas's project: the ego that sees its moral obligation to the Other prior to anything else and acts upon it. On this view, instead of deriving moral principles from reason, epistemic and metaphysical principles are derived from morality. If this had been the case, then perhaps there would have been no Holocaust and Levinas and his family would not have endured such oppression. I believe Levinas to be right about this. And I also believe that his experiences in the German prison camp liken his experience to Douglass's experience living through American chattel slavery. Indeed, as I have pointed out in chapter 3, while the worst atrocity of the twentieth century was the Jewish Holocaust, the preceding three centuries were stained with the scourge of chattel slavery, both before and after the founding of America, and which eventually fractured America in the form of the Civil War. Levinas was a survivor of oppression, as was Douglass. Moreover, they both advocated for resistance to oppression, seeking a much-improved social order based not on the advancement of philosophical knowledge, but rather on principles of justice in concrete human relationships. For these reasons, I believe that Douglass and Levinas are quality dialogue partners that will provide my social interpretation of Douglass with strong explanatory force.

LEVINAS AND ETHICAL METAPHYSICS

To have a fuller appreciation for Levinas's notion of ethics as first philosophy, it is important to be familiar with certain epistemic and metaphysical tendencies that Levinas believes are at the foundation of Western philosophy. So before discussing Levinas's concepts of totality, infinity, subjectivity, the Other, transcendence, and immanence, some discussion of Aristotle is necessary, because the tendency of Western philosophy that Levinas finds so troubling is present both in Aristotle and prior to him, as Aristotle recounts the history of pre-Socratic philosophy in his treatise, *Metaphysics*.

The first sentence of Aristotle's *Metaphysics* is compelling. There, he writes "All human beings, by nature, desire to know."[8] The term that Aristotle uses to describe "desire to know" is the Greek word *oregontai* (ὀρέγονται), and it implies a stretching forward, a hand reaching out in the distance to grasp something to bring it closer for inspection so that it can be comprehended and understood. For Aristotle, the driving force of human beings is epistemic. That is, we seek to know the first causes and principles of all things. Aristotle writes:

> [W]e do not regard any of the senses as wisdom; yet surely these give the most authoritative knowledge of particulars. But they do not tell us the "why" of anything—e.g., why fire is hot; they only say that it is hot. . . . We have said in the *Ethics* what the difference is between art and science and the other kindred faculties: but the point of our present discussion is this, that all men suppose what is called wisdom to deal with the first causes and the principles of things. . . . Since we are seeking this knowledge, we must inquire of what kind are the causes and the principles, the knowledge of which is wisdom.[9]

Although Aristotle appreciates the role of the senses in the acquisition of knowledge, the type of knowledge that the senses provide for us is inferior to another type of knowledge—namely, that of causes. So we may avoid touching hot objects on the stovetop, for example, which is a good sort of practical knowledge to have, but merely knowing that the frying pan is hot is knowledge that qualitatively differs from the knowledge of why the object is hot. Aristotle is interested in the knowledge of "the first causes and the principles of things" because he believes that wisdom is found in "why" things are as they are rather than just that things are a certain way. So, for Aristotle, the highest wisdom will be a knowledge of the first principles and causes of things. This will result in a knowledge of being, or what is, and this, in turn, is known as metaphysics or ontology, which has become, for many, synonymous with the very project of Western philosophy itself: philosophy is understood as the love of wisdom (*sophia*), understood as intellectual understanding and comprehension that provides a rational account of all that is, or of being in general.

But Levinas claims that Aristotle's desire to explain the first causes of things originates much earlier in Greek philosophical thinking. He points to the Milesian philosophers—widely considered to be the first philosophers in the history of Western philosophy—as the originators of this epistemic and metaphysical desire to know. Levinas writes that the "pre-Socratic philosophers" formulated "their wisdom by declaring that all is this or that all is that."[10] I return to this discussion of pre-Socratic philosophy below, but I allude to it here to point out just how deeply Levinas believes this problem is philosophically rooted. In contrast to Aristotle, Levinas believes that our first principles ought to be ethical rather than epistemic or metaphysical. That is, Levinas argues that the first thing that one encounters in the world is not an object to be known, but is instead the face of another person who demands that I do her no harm. So whereas Aristotle's "desire to know" produces the imagery of a confident, self-assured hand stretching forth in the distance to grasp an object and bring it closer for inspection so that it can be known, Levinas's understanding of ethics as first philosophy brings to mind a fundamentally different sort of imagery: a hand is stretching forth, to be sure, but it is a hand connected to a person who, having abandoned the primal quest for knowledge, is preoccupied with her moral obligation to the face of the other person and thus stretches for a hand to help rather than to know the first causes and principles of things. And this hand, unlike the steady, confident hand of Aristotle that reaches forth to grasp and to comprehend, is a hand that, overwhelmed with the magnitude of the moral obligation in the face of the Other, is in crisis as it confronts a moral obligation of overwhelming magnitude. In Levinas, then, moral obligation precedes both metaphysics and epistemology. Hence the phrases "ethics as first philosophy" and "ethical metaphysics." For Levinas, the epistemic and metaphysical preoccupations of Western philosophy have made it complicit constructing frameworks of oppression, where the alterity and strangeness of the Other is disregarded in favor of a manner of social and political organization that fixes reality into a unified whole that, while convenient for the self, is detrimental to the Other. Divesting that which is unknown to the self of its alterity and strangeness solely for the interests of reason is a sort of epistemic and metaphysical violence that determines anything foreign according to the conditions of intelligibility of a philosophical (rational) self. Rather than something—or someone—being allowed to present themselves as they are (*kath-auto*), the *logos* of the free, rational self determines what all things shall be. We thus construct a social, epistemic, and metaphysical framework of oppression that, through a variety of socially constructed meanings, truncates the true identity of others by sacrificing their alterity on the altar of philosophical explanation.[11] The following discussion on Levinas is intended to discuss some of the details as to how Levinas supports his view with his notions of totality, infinity, subjectivity, the face, the Other, transcendence, and immanence. There may be some repetition, but it is necessary to provide the proper context and details of the parts of Levinas's philosophical oeuvre that compose my social interpretation of Douglass.

Totality

Levinas's notion of totality has two traits that are important for my social interpretation of Douglass. First, Levinas situates totality at the beginning of Western philosophy. For Levinas, there is something problematic about the very nature of philosophical inquiry, as he views philosophy as an attempt to establish a unified whole (a totality) from the freedom of the *logos*. This is, in part, similar to the previous discussion on Aristotle. But here, I want to give a more detailed discussion of the pre-Socratics and their connection to Aristotle's quest for knowledge. So it is more of a continuation of this discussion rather than a repetition of it. And second, the rational demand for a unified whole is not confined to the realm of an intellectual puzzle or a sort of abstract thought experiment. Instead, the demand for a totality develops into a sort of rationality that has, for Levinas, at least, an oppressive social dimension that expands beyond the rational thought of individual persons to the social and political organization of unified whole, of a society, of a homogenized group of abstract "persons" whose alterity and uniqueness are subject to truncation by the ruminations and abstractions of a free and rational self. I begin with a discussion of how Levinas situates totality in the history of philosophy.

The concept of totality is at the core of Levinas's attempt to develop an "ethical metaphysics." Drawing from Aristotle, Levinas, in his essay, "Totality and Totalization," points out that the concept of totality "is treated among the fundamental terms of thought in Book Alpha of the *Metaphysics*."[12] What Levinas means by this is that Aristotle, like his pre-Socratic predecessors, is interested in the first causes and principles of things. So, in Book Alpha of *Metaphysics*, totality "is treated among the fundamental terms of thought," because Aristotle discusses the pre-Socratics in terms of his own assessment of whether their views successfully answer the question of why things are as they are as they are, since metaphysics is itself, according to Aristotle, the science of the first causes and principles of things. For example, after writing brief summaries of the Milesian philosophers and Anaxagoras and Empodocles, Aristotle criticizes their work as follows: "From these facts one might think that the only cause is the so-called material cause.... However true it may be that all generation and destruction proceed from some one or more elements, why does this happen and what is the cause?"[13] Aristotle is making the argument here that only part of the story has been told, for although the Milesian ontologies of earth, air, fire, and water may explain natural phenomena as we perceive them, such ontologies do not explain the origin—that is, the cause—of earth, air, fire, and water. In order to provide that explanation, Aristotle argues that the much more comprehensive science of first principles and causes will be necessary, for only then can the totality of what is be properly explained and justified according to the *logos*, which is the aim of the philosophical endeavor. This is why, according to Levinas, totality is at the core of the Western philosophical project: it represents reason's attempt to render all of being philosophically explainable as metaphysical first causes.

The second characteristic of totality in Levinas that is important for my social interpretation of Douglass is that totality expands beyond metaphysical and epistemic reflection and establishes a world beyond itself. In "Totality and Totalization," Levinas writes that "The true function of totalizing does not consist in looking at being, but in determining it by organizing it."[14] Consistent with the aim of philosophical explanation is totality's desire for determination and organization. It is this determination and organization of being that is the origin of history as totalization: "Whence the idea of the temporal or historical dimension of totality; history being not just any element to totalize, but totalization itself."[15] For Levinas, history marches forth—perhaps in an Hegelian-like manner—such that there is with history a negation of errors within a given historical era "by the action of reasonable men, that is, guided by the universal, transforming nature into culture or isolating reason from the immediate of the datum."[16] That is, totalization as history is so all encompassing that truth itself is an amalgam of truth and error, that "reasonable"—philosophically inclined, rational persons—absorb in the interest of progressing toward a unified expression of thought. Of this, Levinas writes:

> There is, here, progression toward the whole, the movement of history itself, or the dialectic movement of thought. Both superannuated truth and its negation are "determinant" for the "new" truth that "does not fall ready-made from heaven," but results from that historical determination. Error is kept in its being gone beyond. It is not outside of truth, which is total when no negation is any longer possible, or when no new determination is necessary. Totalization is the history of humanity *qua* realization of rational universality in mores and institutions, in which thought (the subject) is no longer out of step with that which is thought (substance), in which nothing remains other for reason, i.e., in which being is freedom.[17]

It is the last sentence of this passage that is the most telling. For in it, Levinas makes the point that totality is the very unfolding of history itself in which a rational subjectivity comprehends all substance—all of being—such that "nothing remains other for reason." In this sense, "being is freedom" because there is nothing whatsoever that is foreign to the self. This puts the self in the position that "allows one to grasp at once the whole and its parts, seen in the light of the whole."[18] Levinas returns to Aristotle to continue his description of the end result of totality as the unfolding of history amounting to "the whole being, as in Aristotle, the finality of the parts itself. Total presence of being to itself, or self-consciousness, the whole as the end of history is not empty; it is the reality in its concretization and most complete determination."[19] Levinas concludes his description with a historical reference, claiming that history portrays "A lucid and free humanity, of which the nineteenth century believed itself to be the glorious dawn."[20] As I will discuss below, a tragic irony in the nineteenth century was that, on one hand, as Levinas put it, there was a "the glorious dawn" of rational and scientific progress. On the other hand, the nineteenth century was, as Douglass put it, an era of "man-stealing," in which the march of reason's instrumental and technological progress, when juxtaposed against the awful realities of American chattel slavery, represents the great moral failure of the previous two centuries. And I would argue that a similar tragic irony existed in the twentieth century, for as I pointed out in chapter 3, Levinas, like Douglass, inhabited a world in which there was great technological and scientific progress, no doubt attributable to the march of reason through history, but in this same world, there was the genocidal treatment of the Jewish people.[21] So, in both instances, we inhabit worlds that are rich in rational, philosophical knowledge, on one hand, but that, on the other hand, are morally impoverished. Perhaps such ironies exist because "Totalization is the history of humanity *qua* realization of rational universality in mores and institutions."[22] So again, we see first that totality is deeply entrenched within the history of philosophy; that is, for Levinas, totality is inscribed into the very foundations of philosophy, which is conceived of as metaphysics or ontology. And second, this entrenchment is so firm, that Levinas views history itself as the phenomenon of totalization, in which there is nothing outside of the self; the self, the ego, is the site of all truth, which is conceived of as the obsolete being absorbed into the present, and moving, with the assurance that comes from the freedom of immanence, toward a rational end. With this freedom comes the establishment of rational institutions. And when rationality becomes institutionalized, it prepares the way for totality to assume its social dimension, which Levinas discusses in *Totality and Infinity*.

Levinas understands totality, in his essay, *Totality and Infinity*, to be a concept that is connected to war, which is, in turn, the dimension of being that predominates Western philosophy. In the preface to *Totality and Infinity*, Levinas defines war as reason, which manifests itself in politics. He writes, "The art of foreseeing war and of winning it by every means—politics—is henceforth enjoined as the very exercise of reason. Politics is opposed to morality, as philosophy to naïveté."[23] Philosophical thinking is an exercise of reason that leads to politics (war), which, for Levinas, "renders morality derisory."[24] Philosophy thus leads to war, and war to a diminution of morality. Philosophy leads to war because of the concept of totality: "The visage of being that shows itself in war is fixed in the concept of totality, which dominates Western philosophy,"[25] and morality becomes insignificant because of the dominance of philosophy. Philosophy as totality—that is, as a tendency to compose a metaphysical and epistemological whole—understands being itself as war, as conflict, as violence that is harmful to people. Levinas points out that "We do not need obscure fragments of Heraclitus to prove that being reveals itself as war to philosophical thought, that war does not only affect it as the most patent fact, but as the very patency, or the truth, of the real."[26] Heraclitus, of course, is known for his metaphysics of tension, where the compresence of opposites causes conflict among the four elements, leading to flux, which Heraclitus understands to be the fundamental characteristic of all that is. Levinas draws from this to show that the Heraclitean compresence of opposites becomes a metaphor for the conflict of being that is war and that comes from the philosophical use of reason that totalizes all that is. For Levinas, the notion of a "harsh reality" is a redundancy, and it creates "an objective order from which there is no escape."[27] In this objective order—a social order—"Individuals are reduced to being bearers of forces that command them unbeknown to themselves. The meaning of individuals (invisible outside of this totality) is derived from the totality."[28] Philosophical reason understands reality as conflict and constructs a totality in which people cease to be people, but instead become instruments of the rationality that founds their society. People in this society are controlled by a reasoning unbeknownst to them, and this constitutes a sort of violence, which is much broader than just physical violence. Levinas explains that "violence does not consist so much in injuring and annihilating persons as in interrupting their continuity, making them play roles in which they no longer recognize themselves, making them betray not only commitments but their own substance, making them carry out actions that will destroy every possibility for action."[29] With all things thus known, and people thus subject to violence within the totality, the stage is set for Levinas's conception of freedom, of which he offers a strong critique.

When Levinas criticizes the notion of freedom, it is not a critique of political freedom as such, but rather a critique of a certain sort of freedom of a self—a subjectivity—that is "free" to totalize within a certain economy of enjoyment that does violence to the Other. Levinas writes that "Freedom does not resemble the capricious spontaneity of free will; its ultimate meaning lies in this permanence in the same, which is reason. Cognition is the deployment of this identity; it is freedom."[30] Levinas is not being critical of the notion that a person would be free in the sense of being free from restraint. He is instead being critical of a freedom that comes from a certain use of reason that is epistemically and metaphysically driven to create a totalized whole that manifests itself as war and does violence to people in the name of the very philosophical reasoning that is at the foundation of such a social order. So, for example, Levinas would not be critical of Douglass for wanting to be free, but rather he would be highly critical of Covey and of the system that Covey represents, which is founded on the sort of philosophical reasoning that generates the totality that was American chattel slavery. It is Covey who, through a perverse sort of Kantian-styled empirical cognition, brings the particular who is Douglass under the universal concepts of "slave," and "nigger," in order to "grasp," "comprehend," and "seize" him. This is the sort of freedom that Levinas finds problematic: a freedom in which a self may, according to the dictates of an oppressive epistemic and metaphysical order, "know" that which is presented to him, even if the knowing truncates the true identity of Douglass, who is much more than a slave. It is this sort of immanence in which Douglass always already presents himself to Covey within the confines of Covey's socially conditioned intelligibility that limits Douglass to the role of slave. This is the "cognition" that deploys a Socratic-type of identity from Plato's *Meno*. Levinas explains:

> Western philosophy has most often been an ontology: a reduction of the other to the same by interposition of a middle and neutral term that ensures the comprehension of being. This primacy of the same was Socrates's teaching: to receive nothing of the other but what is in me, as though from all eternity I was in possession of what comes to me from the outside—to receive nothing, or to be free.[31]

Levinas is making his point about the nature of totality in terms of a Socratic immanence. In this passage, he makes an allusion to Plato's dialogue, *Meno*, in which the learner's paradox is resolved with reference to Plato's theory of the Forms and the kinship of the soul with the Forms prior to one's birth. This was discussed at length in chapter 2 with respect to Kierkegaard, but a brief recitation is warranted again here. The learner's paradox begins with question of how the truth can be learned. The problem is raised with the disjunction that either one knows the truth or one does not know the truth. If one knows the truth, then one cannot learn what one already knows, and if one does not know the truth, then one will not recognize it when one finds it. Socrates resolves this puzzle with the claim that the soul was in kinship with the Forms prior to birth, and so all that needs to happen is for one to be asked the right questions to jar one's memory so that one can recognize the truth when one sees it. This is the doctrine of recollection: the soul is already familiar with the Forms and will recollect the truth when the soul finds it. This is consistent with Levinas's claim that the truth is already "in" the self, "as though from all eternity" the self "was in possession of what comes to me from the outside." This is the sort of immanence that puts the self in a state of freedom, in which all things that purport to be transcendent to the self can be understood as being completely absorbed within the totality. Again, the reference to Covey is appropriate here, for it is Covey who truncates Douglass's transcendence, making him immanent to him—and for him—as Douglass is already contained within the totalizing grasp of the rational, war-like, oppressive, epistemic, and metaphysical framework that was American chattel slavery.

Subjectivity and Infinity

Subjectivity, the self, the ego, is, in the context of the totality that I have been describing, rational, free, centered, and undisturbed. Always at home with itself in an economy of enjoyment, the subject of totality deploys rationality to reinforce the epistemic and metaphysical totality that it has created. This is the subjectivity that Levinas describes in *Totality and Infinity*. But there is another conception of subjectivity in Levinas, which he describes in his important text, *Otherwise than Being*. This subjectivity is not free, and does not inhabit an economy of enjoyment, but instead is a subject that finds itself in a crisis responding to the Other as an infinity that overflows it with its demand not to be harmed. The heteronomous moral obligation to the Other effectively decenters the self, leaving it destitute and helpless before the Other's moral demands. What I want to do in this subsection is discuss Levinas's description of this subjectivity, contrasting it to the subjectivity of *Totality and Infinity* and connect it to the concept of infinity, as it is this contrast and connection that lays the foundation for my interpretation of the fight between Douglass and Covey.

Levinas points out with his concept of totality that epistemology and metaphysics drive the tendencies of the subject in Western philosophy. In its incessant quest for first principles and causes, the subject's twin aims of securing a grand theory of all that is and securing grounds for knowledge of all that presents itself to it, the self thus has a tendency to secure itself before it secures its moral obligation to the Other. This is why Levinas finds traditional moral theory (deontology, consequentialism, and virtue ethics) so problematic: such moral theories are derived from rational principles, and as such do not represent any moral advance, but rather subordinate morality to the interests of reason. Instead of securing the moral subject on such rational footing, Levinas wants to get behind this free, secure, rational, moral subject and show that instead of deriving moral principles autonomously from reason, that moral principles are instead derived heteronomously from the face of the other person who makes the moral demand to do no harm. Situating morality in this way effectively decenters the rational moral subject and puts it in a position of "anarchic passivity."[32] What Levinas means by this phrase is that his moral subject is unable to derive moral principles from self-legislated moral laws as one does in deontology; from a rational calculation of the greatest good for the greatest number, as one does in utilitarianism; or from the location of a rational mean between two extremes, as one does in virtue ethics. In all three of these instances, there are rational principles that govern moral choices. In contrast to this secured, free, rational, moral subject, Levinas's moral subject is held hostage to the infinite moral demands of the Other. So there is "anarchy" in the sense that there are no rational laws from which one derives moral obligation. Instead, moral obligation comes from outside the subject, from the infinity of the Other, which ruptures totality. Unlike a Kantian ethics, in which moral obligation results from auto-affection, giving itself the moral law, for Levinas, the moral obligation is utterly heteronomous, as the self gets its moral obligation from the Other. Levinasian subjectivity is put into a state of anarchic passivity, because the auto-affection associated with the moral law and an active subjectivity that calculates and deliberates prior to moral action is nonexistent in the face of the Other. There is, then, no "law" unto the self. So there is anarchy. And there is likewise no time for activity of the self in moral deliberation as there is with either the utilitarian or the deontological moral agent. So Levinasian subjectivity is passive. Levinas describes this condition of anarchic passivity as being held hostage. He writes:

> Diachrony is the refusal of conjunction, the nontotalizable, and, in this sense, infinite. But in the responsibility for the Other . . . for another freedom, the negativity of this anarchy, of this refusal of the present, of appearing, or the

immemorial, commands me and ordains me to the Other . . . to the first one on the scene, and makes me approach him, makes me his neighbor. It thus diverges from nothingness as well as from being. It provokes this responsibility against my will, that is, by substituting me for the Other . . . as a hostage. All my inwardness is invested in the form of a despite-me-for another. Against my will for-another, that is signification par excellence and the sense of oneself . . . of the self . . . that accusative that derives from no nominative; it is the very fact of finding oneself while losing oneself.[33]

Levinas is emphasizing the radically different nature of a centered, rational, free subject with the subjectivity that is in crisis in the face of the Other's heteronomous moral obligation. He begins with what one may argue is an allusion to his notion of the saying, with his reference in the first sentence of this passage to "diachrony," or the slippage and changes in language over time that seemingly resists the fixed ontology of the said. Diachrony "refuses conjunction," is "nontotalizable," and is "infinite." This implies that the fluidity of language indicates that which opposes the fixed meaning that totality wants to attribute to it and thus resists totality altogether. And it is within this flux that the nature of subjectivity changes as well, for the subjectivity of totality becomes substitutable insofar as the Other has taken the ego "as a hostage," for the Other "makes me approach him, makes me his neighbor," provoking an infinite moral responsibility "against my will." There is thus a certain reversal of the self for the Other. But this is not a reversal of reciprocity. That is, it is not simply a mere change of positioning such that the Other will now do to the self what the self has done to the Other. Instead, the Other opens a dimension of height that is utterly asymmetrical in which the self confronts the divinity of the face. Moreover, it seems that Levinas resonates with the Christian tradition in the last line of this passage, for to find "oneself while losing oneself," echoes the admonition of Jesus that "He that findeth his life shall lose it: and he that loseth his life for my sake, shall find it."[34]

In contrast to the subjectivity that experiences the anarchic passivity of an ethics as first philosophy, Levinas argues that both Spinoza and Hegel attempt to ground the self in a larger whole to secure it against the unknowability of the Other by constructing a higher rational order where all things are knowable according to reason. In *Totality and Infinity*, Levinas writes of this approach to subjectivity that "The I can indeed, to justify itself, enter upon a different course: it can endeavor to apprehend itself within a totality. This seems to us to be the justification of freedom aspired after by the philosophy that, from Spinoza to Hegel, identifies will and reason."[35] This approach is, to some degree, grounded in the epistemic desire that Aristotle points out in the first sentence of the *Metaphysics*, discussed earlier, which is that "All human beings by nature, desire to know." Western philosophy thus secures the self by stabilizing it within a larger unified whole, and the self's first task is to acquire knowledge; to grasp; to seize; to reduce alterity to conditions of intelligibility. In *Otherwise than Being*, Levinas writes of this approach to subjectivity that "We have been accustomed to reason in the name of the freedom of the ego—as though I had witnessed the creation of the world, and as though I could only have been in charge of a world that would have issued out of my free will. These are presumptions of philosophers, presumptions of idealists! Or evasions of irresponsible ones. That is what Scripture reproaches Job for. He would have known how to explain his miseries if they could have devolved from his faults! But he never wished evil!"[36] Levinas's reference to Job here is significant in that God rebuked Job for reasoning as if he understood the world—indeed, as if he created it. So it is that when God spoke to Job out of the whirlwind, interrogating Job as to the extent of his knowledge, Job fell silent. This interaction between God and Job says something about the self-assured ego of rational subjectivity for Levinas: that, despite its assurances, it knows very little and ought to be humbled.

And Levinas's Job reference is significant for another reason, which is that it makes a significant point about the inverse relationship between the ego and its attendant epistemic hubris, as opposed to the humility of a self that relinquishes a quest for knowledge at the expense of moral concerns. This point is best elucidated from an interpretation of the book of Job as a whole. One might reasonably view Job as a type of Christ; an innocent man who suffers. Moreover, one might likewise view the book of Job as a microcosm of the entire Bible; it begins in paradise, there is a fall, and at the end of the story, there is restoration. But the restoration comes at the expense of epistemological and metaphysical preoccupations; for whereas Job was restored when he relinquished his quest for knowledge, acknowledging his epistemic limitations after God spoke to him,[37] Adam and Eve fell when they ate of the fruit of the tree of knowledge of good and evil. Thus it is that to seek knowledge is to fall and to relinquish the quest for knowledge is to be restored. I have written of this elsewhere where I argued that the fall of Adam and Eve according to the Judeo-Christian narrative results from the deception that good and evil are merely objects of knowledge.[38] Good and evil are to be lived subjectively, rather than known objectively; and when we fail to see this, we become "addicted" to knowledge; that is, we seek knowledge at the expense of ethics, at the expense of our moral obligation to the Other. This is Levinas's principal objection to the orientation of Western philosophy: an orientation in favor of a self-sufficient ego that is prepared for epistemic and metaphysical exploration and domination without regard for the alterity of the other.

The picture of subjectivity is, then, for Levinas, quite different than what one sees throughout most of Western philosophy: it is a portrait of a self that is in crisis, and that is absolutely responsible first and foremost, not for its acquisition of knowledge or its ontological theory, but rather for the face of the Other. For Levinas, the self begins in an economy of enjoyment that is disrupted at the sight of the Other, and from that moment of disruption forward, the self is held hostage to the Other, and experiences what Levinas calls an "insomnia" for the Other, a vigilance and a wakefulness; a disturbance that creates a restlessness in the self such that the self must satisfy the demands of the other.[39]

Levinas on Theological Abstraction

The concept of God in Levinas is unorthodox. Rather than locating God in a metaphysical beyond, for Levinas, God is found in the face of the other person. It is this relocation of God that facilitates the primacy of the ethical relation in concrete human interaction as opposed to an epistemic relation to a belief in a supreme being that is transcendent to the sensible world. Levinas makes this point when he writes "the concept of God possessed by the believers of positive religions [is] ill disengaged from the bonds of participation," and such religious believers are those "who accept being immersed in a myth unbeknown to themselves."[40] Hence, Levinas refers to his concept of infinity as "the metaphysical relation," the "dawn of a humanity without myths" in which there is an atheism that "conditions a veritable relationship with a true God καθ' αὐτό."[41] Levinas's use of the Greek term *kath-auto* is significant because it is translated as a thing that gives itself. This means that the concept of God is, for Levinas, not something that must conform to the epistemic and metaphysical demands of intelligibility associated with the *logos*—as is the case, for example, with the reformed epistemology of analytic theism—but is instead something that appears to the self which the self cannot contain or philosophize. This something is beyond the comprehension of the ego and so instead of the ego controlling the terms God's appearance, it is infinity that appears on its own terms. This infinity is God appearing in the face of the other person, who imposes itself on the ego, making a moral demand to do it no harm. So the very notion of the transcendence of God, conceived of as a being that is beyond this world, is, for Levinas, morally unacceptable insofar as such a conception of God obscures and neglects concrete ethical relationships between human beings. Levinas thus rejects traditional notions of transcendence in favor of a "transcendence in immanence," as in one's transcendent moral obligation to others existing in the immanent world of concrete social relationships in which the transcendence is not a transcendence of God as a Supreme Being, but rather as the face of the other person that gives itself to the ego in such a way as to impose an infinite moral obligation upon the ego. This is why Levinas writes in *Totality and Infinity* that "To posit the transcendent as stranger and poor one is to prohibit the metaphysical relation with God from being accomplished in the ignorance of men and things. The dimension of the divine opens forth from the human face. A relation with the transcendent free from all captivation by the Transcendent is a social relation."[42]

There can be no theology at all for Levinas apart from human social relationships. Levinas emphasizes this point in *Totality and Infinity*, which was made earlier in chapter 1 with parts of this quote from Levinas, but it bears repeating here:

> Metaphysics is enacted in ethical relations. Without the signification they draw from ethics theological concepts remain empty and formal frameworks. The role Kant attributed to sensible experience in the domain of the understanding belongs in metaphysics to interhuman relations. It is from moral relationships that every metaphysical affirmation takes on a "spiritual" meaning, is purified of everything with which an imagination captive of things and victim of participation charges our concepts. When I maintain an ethical relation I refuse to recognize the role I would play in a drama of which I would not be the author or whose outcome another would know before me. . . . Everything that cannot be reduced to an interhuman relation represents not the superior form but the forever primitive form of religion.[43]

Levinas here claims that grand theological narratives prevent rather than facilitate ethical relationships between human beings. It is a "primitive form of religion" to play a role "in a drama of which I would not be the author or whose outcome another would know before me." Here, Levinas is referencing the various theological narratives of different religions and denominations, which tend to have predetermined outcomes in which each person in the "in group" plays a role in bringing about an end to the drama that fits the viewpoint of the religion that weaves the narrative. Levinas is rejecting this sort of religious and theological orientation in favor of a concrete ethical relationship between human beings that causes one to reach beyond the narrow confines of sectarian dogma. Indeed, as I argued in chapter 1, the ethical relationship is so fundamental in Levinas that, as he points out, in a Kantian sense, it supplies the sensory material for theological concepts. Kant makes the point that concepts without intuitions are empty. Biblically speaking, however, one would simply say that "faith without works is dead."[44] Hence the sweeping language of the final sentence of the above passage with its use of the word "everything": theology apart from concrete ethical relations is a morally inferior religion that paves the way for the religious hypocrisy of clinging to beliefs at the expense of authentic moral practice. And it is this sort of "primitive form of religion," this hypocrisy that results from the separation of theology from moral praxis, that is, as I will argue in the next section, the religion of Covey that Douglass so vigorously and vociferously resists.

DOUGLASS AND SOCIAL REFORM AS RESISTANCE

Douglass lived a life of staunch resistance to oppression. His *Narrative* reveals a journey of a person from slavery to freedom that not only chronicles his awareness of his condition but also reveals a relentless desire to resist slavery and be free from his oppression. We see this desire early on in his *Narrative* when he becomes literate and begins to read: "The more I read, the more I was led to abhor and detest my enslavers. I could regard them in no other light than a band of successful robbers, who had left their homes and gone to Africa, and stolen us from our homes, and in a strange land reduced us to slavery."[45] He continues on describing how he longed to be free from slavery: "The silver trump of freedom had roused my soul to eternal wakefulness. Freedom now appeared, to disappear no more forever."[46] Douglass managed to channel this intense desire to be free into a life spent pursuing freedom both from slavery and from its legacy, and this meant that his life would become a life of resistance; it meant that he would have to resist slavery through an escape from it and then through becoming a staunch opponent of slavery from outside of the institution. And this would not be easy. To the contrary, it would demand much from him and, as he would soon learn, the collective efforts of those—Black and white—in the abolition movement. Both during the struggle for abolition and after, Douglass would find himself trying his best to inspire his fellow freedom fighters with the importance of agitation and its role in progress and social reform. From his earlier statements such as "If there is no struggle, there is no progress"[47] to his much later claim that the Christian Gospel is not good news unless it is actually true,[48] Douglass consistently defended the need for social struggle.

Indeed, it is the point of this interpretive study of Douglass and the philosophy of religion to compare Douglass's relentless social, political, and moral engagement with what I have been arguing is the colossal failure of the reformed epistemology of analytic theism to similarly engage such important issues, especially in light of its purported interest in Christianity. Douglass too, of course, is heavily engaged with the Christian theological tradition because, as Waldo E. Martin Jr. has pointed out, "The fervid moral spirit born of evangelical Protestantism constituted a vital element of nineteenth-century social reform. Mere secular reform would not suffice. . . . The ideal social reformer was a peerless Christian and moral giant."[49] So since both Douglass and the reformed epistemology of analytic theism have strong Christian influences, the framework for this study is Incarnational; that is, if the nature of the Christian Gospel is that there is good news because the Word of God became flesh, then any sort of philosophical or theological thought that made the flesh a word would be problematic. And this is what I have argued throughout, and what I continue to argue here: that the reformed epistemology of analytic theism, through its philosophical and theological abstractions, makes the social life of Jesus theologically and philosophically irrelevant. In support of this argument, I have pointed out how Douglass eschews abstraction in favor of an authentic subjectivity, a deep and abiding moral sensibility in his rejection of theodicy, and an aesthetically informed politics. It is, I think, fair to say that there is substantial evidence suggesting that Douglass's life was indeed a life of social resistance to oppression.

Douglass's ultimate act of resistance, however, is his well-known fight with his overseer, Covey. This fight with Covey was formative for Douglass, as it is the point in his life when he considered himself to have ceased to be chattel and had become a person. That this experience was transformative for Douglass is found in his description of it in his *Narrative*, when, before the description of the fight, he writes, "I have already intimated that my condition was much worse, during the first six months of my stay at Mr. Covey's, than in the last six. The circumstances leading to the change in Mr. Covey's course toward me form an epoch in my humble history. You have seen how a man was made a slave; you shall see how a slave was made a man."[50] And Douglass's commentary after the fight with Covey likewise indicates the fight's importance to his life:

> This battle with Mr. Covey was the turning-point in my career as a slave. It rekindled the few expiring embers of freedom, and revived within me a sense of my own manhood. It recalled the departed self-confidence, and inspired me again with a determination to be free. The gratification afforded by the triumph was a full compensation for whatever else might follow, even death itself. He only can understand the deep satisfaction which I experienced, who has himself repelled by force the bloody arm of slavery. I felt as I never felt before. It was a glorious resurrection, from the tomb of slavery, to the heaven of freedom. My long-crushed spirit rose, cowardice departed, bold defiance took its place; and I now resolved that, however long I might remain a slave in form, the day had passed forever when I could be a slave in fact. I did not hesitate to let it be known of me, that the white man who expected to succeed in whipping, must also succeed in killing me. From this time I was never again what might be called fairly whipped, though I remained a slave four years afterwards. I had several fights, but was never whipped.[51]

When Douglass writes that "He only can understand the deep satisfaction which I experienced, who has himself repelled by force the bloody arm of slavery," he does, I think, lay the foundation for the normativity of social resistance to oppression. For Douglass to experience "deep satisfaction" on the micro level, what will be the experience on a broader scale if other slaves, and those who are interested in and support their freedom, likewise resist and repel "by force the bloody arm of slavery"? Douglass, I think, believes that his experience becomes normative, creating, as I discussed in chapter 4, a universal appeal to the moral side of humanity, demanding not only condemnation and active resistance to American chattel slavery but also its abolition.

What I want to do here is detail the background of the fight with Covey and then, in each of the three sections below, discuss different aspects of the fight that I believe, when read with certain concepts in Levinas, yield an interpretation of this watershed event in the life of Douglass that, on a micro level, helps us to better appreciate the importance of Douglass's much broader program of social resistance.

Douglass's fight with Covey is chronicled in chapter ten of his *Narrative*. As Douglass describes the circumstances preceding the fight with Covey, he fell sick while performing the chore of fanning wheat. Since the task was multi-person and interdependent, when Douglass fainted from his illness, the entire process halted. When Covey heard that the fan stopped turning, he immediately came to see what happened, and when the other slaves told him that Douglass had fainted, he asked where Douglass was and, upon finding him and asking him what was wrong, assaulted Douglass by kicking him multiple times and then hitting him in the head with a piece of wood. This blow to Douglass's head caused him to bleed profusely, and, when Douglass began to recover from this wound, as his strength returned to him, he determined to tell his master what happened; in order to do that, Douglass had to walk seven miles. After setting out on this seven-mile walk, Covey, knowing that Douglass was leaving, demanded that he return, but Douglass ignored him. When Douglass arrived at his master's house, he pleaded to be sent elsewhere, away from Covey's supervision, but to no avail. Douglass's master told him that he could stay the night but had to leave early in the morning the next day, which was Saturday. Douglass left as instructed, and on his way back, Covey spotted him walking and came after him with a whip, but Douglass was able to hide in the height of the corn. Douglass spent all day on Saturday in the woods, and Saturday night he ran into a fellow slave named Sandy Jenkins. Sandy gave Douglass a root and told him to carry it on his right side; as long as he did so, he would never be whipped again. Sandy claimed it had worked for him. On Sunday, Douglass arrived back to Covey's, only to find that Covey spoke to him "very kindly" and "passed on towards the church."[52] Douglass was prepared to discredit the root that Sandy Jenkins gave to him the night before, but after such an unusually welcoming reception from Covey, Douglass admits that Covey's reception of him made him "begin to think that the was something in the root which Sandy had given"[53] him. And if it was not Sunday—Covey's day of religious observance—Douglass would have accepted Sandy's endorsement of the root as "something more than" he "at first had taken it to be."[54]

But on Monday morning, everything changed. While Douglass was tending to the horses as he had been instructed to do, "Covey entered the stable with a long rope"[55] and, catching Douglass by the legs, attempted to bind him. This is when Douglass, for the first time, resisted Covey and declared himself to be a person rather than chattel. Douglass writes of this moment:

> As soon as I found out what he was up to, I gave a sudden spring, and as I did so, he holding to my legs, I was brought sprawling on the stable floor. Mr. Covey seemed now to think he had me, and could do what he pleased; but at this moment—from whence came the spirit I don't know—I resolved to fight; and, suiting my action to the resolution, I seized Covey hard by the throat; and as I did so, I rose. He held on to me, and I to him. My resistance was so entirely unexpected, that Covey seemed taken all aback. He trembled like a leaf.[56]

According to Douglass, he and Covey "were at it for nearly two hours."[57] And it is in these two hours that sixteen years of slavery is defeated, for Douglass writes that he was sixteen years old when he resisted Covey. This two-hour struggle would end, but Douglass's struggle against slavery and its legacy would not. From age sixteen until he died, there would be a life of resistance that was for the benefit of not only himself but also every other slave, and in some sense, for the benefit of all humanity. There are more details to the fight and its overall context within Douglass's *Narrative*, but I am reserving the discussion of such details for what follows, which is an analysis of certain aspects of the fight that resonate with Levinas's notions of totality, infinity and subjectivity, and the abstractions of rational theology, each to be discussed in separate subsections.

Douglass and Totality

The philosophical implications of Douglass's fight with Covey are significant. As Levinas points out, the metaphysical and epistemological impulse of philosophy drives reason to bring all things within a larger whole so that such things can be "grasped," "known," "understood," and "comprehended" according to the rational order that philosophy has installed. But the problem is that conceiving of reality in this way is harmful because among the things that are "grasped" and "understood" are human beings. And human beings have particularities and a uniqueness that transcends the grasping of reason. So a problem arises when that which is transcendent is purported to be made immanent to philosophical reason: it is truncated, cut off, short-circuited, and made into something that it is not. Philosophy, then, with its totalizing tendencies, brings with it an epistemic and metaphysical violence that causes people to, in Levinas's words, "play roles in which they no longer recognize themselves."⁵⁸ As discussed earlier in the chapter, Levinas points out how philosophy founds institutions that facilitate the interests of reason by executing reason's directives in social and political life.

That Douglass lived in such a philosophical and social order is, I think, undeniable. As I argued in chapter 2 with reference to the work of American legal scholar Ariela J. Gross, states—political subdivisions—developed an entire system of laws to govern the institution of American chattel slavery. The state thus presided and litigated—according to the dictates of reason, no less—the business of trading human flesh. In chapter 2, I drew from Gross's work to demonstrate that the paradoxical formation of Black subjectivity not only originates in the antebellum slavery courts of the American south but also reaches far beyond those courts of law to connect with the emergence of Black subjectivity in the twenty-first century in the form of quotidian interactions of police officers and African American citizens such as Byron Ragland, for example. Here, however, Gross's work is important for another reason, which is that when viewing the antebellum courts through Levinas, all of the components of a totality are present: there is the philosophical formation of a social and political institution that does violence to human beings that is grounded in a certain metaphysical and epistemological understanding of the world. The philosophical theology of the day justified slavery in the abstract,⁵⁹ and the legal and social institutions of the day justified slavery in concrete factual situations.

Consider Douglass's statement in his 1850 speech, "The Nature of Slavery," in which he argues that masters rule over slaves "with the force of the law." Of the law of slavery and its enforcement, Douglass writes, "The law gives the master absolute power over the slave. He may work him, flog him, hire him out, sell him, and, in certain contingencies, *kill* him, with perfect impunity."⁶⁰ Now generally, it is the case that there is almost always some coercive element of law. The law forces us to do things that we otherwise would not do. Indeed, Jacques Derrida discusses this phenomenon in his essay "Force of Law" when he points out that "there is no law without enforceability and no applicability or enforceability of the law without force, whether this force be direct or indirect, physical or symbolic . . . brutal or subtly discursive."⁶¹ Derrida's argument may be reconstructed here in the form of a hypothetical syllogism: (1) If there is a law, then it is enforceable. (2) If the law is enforceable, then force may be used in its execution. Therefore, if there are laws, then force will be used in their execution. Again, Derrida's claim is that this is true of any law whatsoever, but I submit that the force needed to execute or enforce the laws of American chattel slavery was especially disturbing because of the dehumanizing nature of that institution. Indeed, to properly characterize the nature of the sort of "force" that the law of American chattel slavery demands, some etymology of the word "enforcement" is in order.

As I pointed out in chapter 2 regarding Byron Ragland and Wesley Michel, "enforcement" is derived from the French word of identical spelling that implies not only a strengthening and a fortification but also "rape." This puts the nature of American chattel slavery into sharper focus. For now, the nonconsensual nature of American chattel slavery's legal and social structure is understood for what it is: a raping of sorts in which enslaved African Americans are "owned" against their will, with all of the attendant indignities and dehumanizing practices that rape implies. American chattel slavery, the legal and social system in which Douglass abides, is indeed a totality as Levinas contemplates the meaning of that term. In this sort of oppressive epistemic and metaphysical framework, there was no room for anything to exist outside of it. Indeed for a slave to resist was aberrant behavior to be met with a violent reorientation to the system from which they were resisting. Such resistant behavior on part of a slave may even be considered to be, in a perverse sort of way, "irrational," as though American chattel slavery was the normal, natural condition of human beings. But in a sense, slavery was "rational" and "natural" insofar as it was endemic to the contorted view of nature that the proponents of American chattel slavery defended. Under their "reasoning," Douglass would argue—and did argue—that wrong was made right and right was made wrong. Douglass was undoubtedly a denizen of this philosophically, theologically, politically, socially, and legally justified totality. There was no escape from this totality without severe and enduring consequences. And although American chattel slavery's legalities constituted a system of positive law, their enforcement—that is, their use to, etymologically speaking, "rape" slaves—was indeed a totality, it was a far cry from justice.

To better appreciate the nature of the totality of chattel slavery as it is represented in Douglass's fight with Covey, it is important to emphasize some of Covey's personal characteristics as Douglass describes them. Douglass's description of Covey gives Covey an air of omnipresence and omniscience. According to Douglass, Covey's "comings were like a thief in the night. He appeared to us as a being ever at hand. He was under every tree, behind every stump, in every bush, and at every window on the plantation."[62] As a result of his seeming omnipresence, Covey's "work went on in his absence almost as well as in his presence; and he had the faculty of making us feel that he was ever with us."[63] This description accurately depicts, I think, Levinas's notion of totality: an all-encompassing epistemic and metaphysical framework in which the conceptual violence of slavery dictates Douglass's every move. Indeed, not only is the framework all encompassing, but so is the surveillance. The surveillance is the totality in action; it is the execution of the concept, "slave"; it is a praxis that brings application to the oppression that begins as a violent concept. So when Levinas points out that "The neutralization of the other who becomes a theme or an object—appearing, that is, taking its place in the light—is precisely his reduction to the same," such language contemplates the all-encompassing gaze of Covey, which reduces Douglass (and the rest of his slaves) "to the same"—that is, to the same concept of "slaves" that exist for him, rather than as human beings who have their own interests, histories, and uniqueness independent of him. This is why Levinas continues on to point out that "To know ontologically is to surprise in an existent confronted by that which it is not this existent, this stranger, that by which it is somehow betrayed, surrenders, is given in the horizon in which it loses itself and appears, lays itself open to grasp, becomes a concept."[64] Levinas makes several important points in this brief passage regarding philosophy's culpability in the construction of totality, which is at work in the relationship between Douglass and Covey. First, philosophy is indicted at the beginning of the passage as complicit in the metaphysical and epistemic project of "knowing," by connecting it to the "surprise" of an "existent" who is "confronted by that which it is not this existent," meaning that one of the functions of a philosophically constructed totality is to, in surprising fashion, transform someone from who they are into someone who they are not. This sort of transformation is so shocking that it renders the person so helpless, so "open to grasp," as to become "a concept." This sort of language brings to mind philosopher George Yancy's extensive and compelling phenomenological account of racial embodiment as a sort of confiscation in which the white gaze distorts an existent, returns it to the existent in distorted fashion, and transforms the Black body from a person into a concept such as "criminal," "hyper-sexual," and so forth. For Yancy, the white gaze is responsible for the construction of a white-supremacist epistemic and metaphysical field in which Black bodies that are persons cease to be persons and instead they become concepts of the white racist imaginary. Something similar is happening to Douglass here because of Covey's gaze: Douglass and the other slaves are violently transformed from persons into concepts. This is, I submit, Levinas's notion of totality at work. Moreover, philosopher Cynthia Nielsen has pointed out the connection between Covey's surveillance tactics and Michel Foucault's notion of panoptic surveillance which I think also demonstrates the social totality of American chattel slavery that Douglass confronted. In her discussion of the Panopticon as found in the work of Jeremy Bentham, she points out that the architectural structure of Panopticon created, as with Covey, "an ever-present gaze."[65] This became an effective means of control of prisoners, who, Nielsen writes, "internalized the gaze." Nielsen continues, "Once the gaze was internalized, the actual presence of the warden observing the prisoner was rendered unnecessary. The docile body was thus formed, having come into existence by way of active and passive disciplinary practices and spatial-shapings (e.g., the architectural design of the prison itself)."⁶⁶ Douglass thus writes, "Mr. Covey succeeded in breaking me. I was broken in body, soul, and spirit. My natural elasticity was crushed, my intellect languished, the disposition to read departed, the cheerful spark that lingered about my eye died; the dark night of slavery closed in upon me; and behold a man transformed into a brute!"⁶⁷

So it is that after enough surveillance and surprise, Douglass and the rest of the slaves internalize Covey's panoptic gaze, and they work, believing that at all times that they are being watched and can be seized upon and subject to physical violence at any moment. But preceding the physical violence is the conceptual violence of transforming persons into things. Douglass has just shown us how totality makes him a slave in the eyes of Covey. In the next subsection, I will argue that it is Levinas's notion of infinity that makes Douglass a person in Covey's eyes.

Douglass, Infinity, and Subjectivity

If we take Douglass's claim that "You have seen how a man was made a slave; you shall see how a slave was made a man"⁶⁸ seriously, then one can, I think, argue that Levinas's concept of infinity undoes what totality attempts to do. That is, totality makes Douglass—a person—into a slave, and infinity makes Douglass—a slave—into a person. With this contrast in mind, I now turn to a discussion of Douglass in his fight with Covey as infinity that resists totality. Covey's epistemic and metaphysical assurances of Douglass as a "slave" crumble beneath the weight of Douglass's assertion of his personhood, and, in the midst of the fight between Douglass and Covey, not only does Douglass effect a physical reversal of fortune, but he also effects a metaphysical and epistemic transformation that throws Covey into a crisis, making him unable to see Douglass as a slave. And here is where Levinas's notion of infinity transforms the self-assured, free, subjectivity of Covey into an anarchic, passive subjectivity in crisis. To appreciate this transformation, it is, I think, important to set forth Douglass's account of the fight, which he describes as follows:

> Mr. Covey entered the stable with a long rope; and just as I was half out of the loft, he caught hold of my legs, and was about tying me. As soon as I found what he was up to, I gave a sudden spring, and as I did so, he holding to my legs, I was brought sprawling on the stable floor. Mr. Covey seemed now to think he had me, and could do what he pleased; but at this moment—from whence came the spirit I don't know—I resolved to fight; and, suiting my action to the resolution, I seized Covey hard by the throat; and as I did so, I rose. He held on to me, and I to him. My resistance was so entirely unexpected, that Covey seemed taken all aback. He trembled like a leaf. This gave me assurance, and I held him uneasy,

causing the blood to run where I touched him with the ends of my fingers. . . . He asked me if I meant to persist in my resistance. I told him I did, come what might; that he had used me like a brute for six months, and that I was determined to be used so no longer. With that, he strove to drag me to a stick that was lying just out of the stable door. He meant to knock me down. But just as he was leaning over to get the stick, I seized him with both hands by his collar and brought him by a sudden snatch to the ground . . . we were at it for nearly two hours.[69]

Douglass's account of his fight with Covey in this passage exemplifies Levinas's notion of infinity and, with it, a transformed subjectivity. As discussed in the previous section of the chapter, for Levinas, infinity is the one thing that totality is unable to bring within its grasp. Drawing from Descartes's third meditation, in which Descartes argues that the idea of God is so overwhelming to him that it was impossible that it originated from him, Levinas argues that infinity overwhelms the consciousness of the free self, and holds it hostage. This is precisely what happens at the micro level in Douglass's fight with Covey, and it has far-reaching implications at the macro level. Rather than Covey seizing, grasping, and overwhelming Douglass with physical force, it is Douglass who "seized Covey hard by the throat" and "seized" Covey "with both hands by his collar and brought him by a sudden snatch to the ground." Douglass's resistance, like Covey's oppression, comes with a seizure and a grasping, but this is not a reciprocity or a symmetry. In contrast, Douglass becomes greater than Covey's oppression in that it fundamentally changes the nature of their relationship, in that, from that moment onward, Douglass points out that "I was never again what might be called fairly whipped," despite remaining a slave for four more years. Douglass thus personifies an infinity that overwhelms the subjectivity of Covey's totalizing epistemic and metaphysical gaze, transforming Covey from a self-assured, free subjectivity into a subjectivity that is now at the mercy of Douglass, who holds Covey "hostage," and whose effect on Covey is infinite insofar as he will never whip Douglass again. Covey's subjectivity is also problematized in that his freedom is now thrust into a state of what Levinas calls "anarchic passivity." Again, Levinas uses the language of anarchy to describe the lawless condition in which a subjectivity finds itself facing the infinity of the Other. What makes this condition lawless is that the rigorous, law-like certainty of a Kantian-styled epistemic cognition and predication that would purport to bring Douglass, a sensible intuition, under the concept of "slave" is now completely obliterated because of Douglass's resistance. So instead of actively functioning to think Douglass as an object of his consciousness (that is, as the *noema* of a *noesis*), Covey is thrown into a lawless—anarchic—condition in which he ceases to be active, and instead must now be passive as it relates to his understanding of Douglass. Douglass is no longer there "for" Covey but is now a subjectivity that is there "for" Douglass. And this is Levinas's conception of subjectivity: the ego (Covey) at the mercy of the infinite Other (Douglass). But again, this reversal is neither symmetrical nor reciprocal, for Covey's oppression was temporary, but Douglass's resistance was permanent. So Douglass's fight with Covey, in this transformation of subjectivity thus creates a dimension of what Levinas would call "height," in which

> The Other (*l'Autre*) thus presents itself as a human Other (*Autrui*); it shows a face and opens the dimension of height, that is to say, it infinitely overflows the bounds of knowledge. Positively, this means that the Other puts in question the freedom which attempts to invest it; the Other lays him- or herself bare to the total negation of murder but forbids it through the original language of his defenseless eyes.[70]

The application of this passage to Douglass and Covey is compelling. Douglass presents himself to Covey during the fight as a human being who "infinitely overflows the bounds" of Covey's "knowledge." Covey's certainty of Douglass as a slave is overwhelmed in Douglass's assertion of his personhood. Douglass has thus put Covey's freedom into question by laying himself "bare to the total negation of murder." That is, Douglass risked his life in resistance, but, in another sense, he forbade the taking of his life through the "original language" of his "defenseless eyes" or through his vulnerability. In making himself vulnerable to Covey the way that he did, Douglass effectively stripped himself of every defense under slave law. He was thus utterly "defenseless" in his vulnerability. In this way, Douglass's infinity effects not a simple reciprocal reversal of physical fortune, but rather a complete transformation of subjectivity in which Douglass's infinity disrupts Covey's freedom, overwhelming his "knowledge" of him as a slave with a "height" that, while taking a great risk and making himself completely vulnerable, demands that Covey do him no harm. Douglass's "infinity" is also significant in another sense. It is, I believe, not only a reference to the never-ending nature of the moral obligation that Douglass imposed on Covey during the fight but also a reference to Douglass's ongoing, infinite moral obligation to resist oppression. Through his resistance to Covey, Douglass learned that his moral obligation to resist oppression was far greater than himself insofar as it would require that he be a moral defender of freedom from oppression for many others throughout the rest of his life as a public intellectual, as in, for example, his support for the anti-lynching campaign of Ida B. Wells.[71]

As I have argued throughout, Douglass's use of narrative is strategic in its aim to communicate normativity in terms of the wrongness of slavery. And in chronicling the fight with Covey, Douglass's use of narrative is a way of communicating normativity in terms of the resistance to slavery. What Douglass does on the micro level, he expects to be done beyond the pages of his *Narrative*. Otherwise, there is little value in recounting the story of the fight, for unless other slaves and those who support abolition see the humanity of the slaves as a real possibility as seen in Douglass's resistance to slavery, it is unlikely that Douglass's *Narrative* would be able to communicate the compelling moral need for abolition.

Covey's Theology as the Flesh Made Word

Considering Covey's strong religious piety, the fight between Covey and Douglass, as set forth in Douglass's narrative form, has, I think, profound theological implications. As I argued in the previous subsection of this chapter, Douglass's use of narrative enables what occurs on the micro level to be understood in broader terms, as with Douglass's resistance to Covey, which Douglass himself wanted to be a message to others that resistance to slavery was normative. Here, I argue that the fight between Covey and Douglass represents a larger theological struggle: the struggle between an epistemically and metaphysically driven religious experience that separates social life from one's theology, on one hand, and a religion that views theology as inextricably connected to the flesh of human experience, on the other hand. Covey and the reformed epistemology of analytic theism represents the former, and Douglass and the theology of a responsible, politically and morally engaged Christianity represents the latter.

At the core of the differences between the reformed epistemology of analytic theism (Covey's approach to Christianity) and my existential, phenomenological, aesthetic/political, and social interpretation of Douglass is the relationship between theology and justice. It is important at the outset to make some clarifications. When I identify Covey's approach to religion with the reformed epistemology of analytic theism, I am not making any strong claims about Covey actually doing conceptual analysis and interrogating epistemic foundationalism. Instead, to identify Covey's approach to religion with the reformed epistemology of analytic theism as I am doing is to make the much weaker, yet still morally significant claim that Covey's radical separation of his theology from his moral life is akin to the reformed epistemology of analytic theism's use of philosophical abstraction to ignore more pressing moral, social, and political concerns of justice. Covey's separation of religion from morality is the result of inverting the Christian soteriological paradigm, for when one makes the flesh of Jesus into a word, one disregards the jurisdiction history and creates a religion for oneself in which there is no moral accountability. At the foundation of the relationship between theology and justice is, then, a still deeper connection to the relationship between reason and history: to separate one's theology from justice is to allow one's reason to exert authority over history rather than allowing history to assert its authority—its jurisdiction, as I have argued in chapter 1—over reason. When reason wins the day, the moral imperatives of justice are ignored, and theological abstractions, whether they be theoretical in the case of the reformed epistemology of analytic theism, or whether they be practical in the case of Covey, inevitably occlude much more compelling moral, social, and political considerations. So it is that Covey can exhibit strong personal piety while owning slaves; he can beat a human being within inches of his or her life on Monday through Saturday, but on Sunday he can "respect the Sabbath." And in a similar manner, the reformed epistemology of analytic theism can, on one hand, purport to, through its rigorous philosophical articulations of theodicy and free will defenses, claim to be doing God a great service, while, on the other hand, ignoring so many of the moral, social, and political issues that its own Judeo-Christian tradition demands be addressed. So, again, the identification of Covey with the reformed epistemology of analytic theism is not a claim that Covey engaged in a conceptual analysis of God and His attributes. It is instead a claim that Covey is able to separate his theology from justice, as does the reformed epistemology of analytic theism. With this clarification in mind, I now turn to my argument.

The separation of theology from justice is the exaltation of reason over history that makes for the flesh to be made a word. Philosophical abstractions—like those of the reformed epistemology of analytic theism—will, through a vast array of epistemic and metaphysical nuance, construct a notion of God that, although consistent with the rigors of philosophical analysis, is utterly bereft of any social, moral, or political concerns. We see this religious hypocrisy at work in the life of Covey, whose brand of false religion makes the word flesh. Again, Covey is not an analytic theist in the strong sense, but that is not my point. Instead, my point is that Covey lives a life that is consistent with the results of the reformed epistemology of analytic theism: theology is separated from justice such that Covey can call himself a Christian and have absolutely no regard for the suffering that he inflicts upon other human beings in his own life.

Douglass describes Covey as an intensely religious man whose piety was strong. So it stands to reason that the piety with which he lived would yield a life of moral virtue. But it was not so, for Douglass says that despite Covey's intense piety, that his "*forte* consisted in his power to deceive. His life was devoted to planning and perpetrating the grossest deceptions. Everything he possessed in the shape of learning or religion, he made conform to his disposition to deceive."[72] The contrast with Levinas's concept of God and the ethical relation is strong on this point. Consider that Covey makes religion "conform to his disposition to deceive." In other words, Covey's belief in God was not a God who gives Himself *kath-auto*, in the face of the other person who demands that I conform my behavior to its presence in my life. Instead, Covey's "god" must conform "to his disposition" of deception. Covey's separation of theology from morality and justice has thus resulted in an idol of his white, racist, slaveholding imaginary such that his "god" is adaptable to his ends and purposes rather than Covey being amenable and adaptable to God's ends and purposes as dictated within the context of a concrete ethical relationship. Perhaps this explains Covey's fervor and enthusiasm, as Douglass points out that Covey would "make a short prayer in the morning, and a long prayer at night; and, strange as it may seem, few men would at times appear more devotional than he."[73] Covey was so passionate because his religion enabled his immorality to the point of him deceiving himself into believing, in Douglass's words, "that he was a sincere worshipper of the most high God" even as he was facilitating adultery for the sake of expanding his collection of slaves.[74] It thus seems that Covey's most effective form of deception was his self-deception resulting from his separation of theology from justice.

When Douglass fought Covey, he resisted totality, transformed subjectivity as the face of infinity, and revolted against a system of false religion that separated theology from justice; that made the flesh of Jesus an abstract word through its disregard of the jurisdiction of history. Douglass's use of narrative enables us to see this struggle in normative terms such that when Douglass's audience—which includes us in the twenty-first century—reads his *Narrative*, his audience is thoroughly inspired to resist as Douglass himself resisted. And even as Douglass was not the same when he resisted, but rather was forever changed and felt obligated to resist for the rest of his life, I believe that Douglass expects that his audience—indeed even his twenty-first-century audience would be likewise inspired to a lifetime of such resistance.

THE INFINITY OF SOCIAL RESISTANCE

Douglass's life was a life of resistance to an oppressive social order. In this chapter, I have read Douglass with Levinas to develop a social interpretation of Douglass that can be explained in terms of the dynamic between totality and infinity as embodied in the fight between Douglass and Covey. It is this fight that transforms Covey's and Douglass's respective subjectivities, forever changing their relationship and freeing Douglass from slavery. Although the fight with Covey did not free Douglass in the legal sense, it did free Douglass as a practical matter; for Douglass lives his life from the moment of the fight onward "as if" he is free. Significantly, then, Douglass did not find actual freedom in his resistance, but was nonetheless free from slavery. Through Douglass's use of narrative, the description of his fight with Covey is the basis for a normative demand to resist injustice in the face of religious hypocrisy.

But beyond the arguments of this chapter, there are, I think, some additional questions and observations. For example, what is the moral import of Douglass's self-motivated practical manumission from slavery? That is, Douglass recognized that his resistance to American chattel slavery extended beyond his fight with Covey to a moral obligation of social resistance to oppression that endured a lifetime. What does this mean for twenty-first-century readers of his *Narrative*? I submit that Douglass's recognition of resistance demands a similar commitment to the perpetuity of moral resistance in the face of oppression from today's society. The social conditions that confronted Douglass are certainly not identical in today's world, but there are, indeed, no shortage of social injustices in contemporary life that demand our moral commitment to resist them. To enumerate them and discuss them here would be tantamount to another book-length study, so I will restrict my commentary to raising the question of whether today's world is up to the challenge on an individual level as Douglass was up to the challenge during his life. Are people prepared to assume the moral responsibility to resist oppression as Douglass did, not just "in the moment" in their individual lives but also for the rest of their lives, for infinity? And although the problems with Christianity today are not identical to Douglass's day, it is, I think, fair to say that certain strains of Christianity—what Cornel West has called "Constantinian Christianity"[75]—are as integral in maintaining systemic forms of oppression today as they were in Douglass's time, and, regrettably, what is called the "conceptual analysis" of the philosophy of religion, through its incessant abstractions, enables such injustices through the separation of theology from justice today just as it did for Covey. This book represents my attempt, in the spirit of Douglass, to offer a competing interpretation of Christian philosophy to the reformed epistemology of analytic theism to show what philosophy of religion ought to be. I hope that presenting this alternative can perhaps be a corrective to this state of affairs, for as long as philosophical theology ignores justice and morality at the level of praxis; as long as the jurisdiction of history is disregarded; as long as rational demands exalt ontotheological conceptions of "god," seeking to see God's anterior; as long as poetic orientations to Christianity that respect epistemic limitations and are content to see God's "backside" are dismissed as philosophically insignificant, the problem of anteriority will continue to frustrate moral progress.

Again, my interpretation of Douglass presented throughout this study is intended to at least grapple with these problems, and at most to correct them. I likely will not achieve the latter, but if I achieve the former, I will be successful. For even as Levinas articulated the concept of infinity, and even as Douglass lived the concept of infinity, to grapple with these questions rather than to provide definitive answers to them is the preferred result, for conceding either that there are no easy solutions or that the racial problems at the core of Christian philosophical thinking are permanent demands a level of moral resistance that is likewise permanent—that is, a resistance to injustice that is infinite in nature. If I can at least move philosophy and its relationship to Christian theology in this direction, I will have been successful. Whether I am successful will be left up to you, the reader.

NOTES

1. Matthew 12:43–45 (World English Version).
2. Frederick Douglass, "The Nature of Slavery," in *Douglass: Autobiographies* (New York: Library of America, 1996), 419.
3. Ibid.
4. Ibid.
5. Emmanuel Levinas, "God and Philosophy," in *Basic Philosophical Writings*, eds. Adrian T. Peperzak, Simon Critchley, and Robert Bernasconi (Bloomington: Indiana University Press, 1996), 129.
6. Ibid.
7. Hilary Putnam, "Levinas and Judaism," in *The Cambridge Companion to Emmanuel Levinas*, ed. Simon Critchley and Robert Bernasconi (Cambridge: Cambridge University Press, 2002), 33.
8. Aristotle, *Metaphysics*, 980a22.
9. Ibid., 981b10–982a5.
10. Emmanuel Levinas, "Totality and Totalization," in *Alterity and Transcendence*, trans. Michael B. Smith (New York: Columbia University Press, 1999), 50.
11. See especially my discussion of the philosophical background of the deadly encounter between Trayvon Martin and George Zimmerman in my essay "Two Forms of Transcendence: Justice and the Problem of Knowledge," in *Pursuing Trayvon Martin: Historical Contexts and Contemporary Manifestations of Racial Dynamics*, eds. George Yancy and Janine Jones (Lanham, MD: Lexington Books, 2012), 73–84.
12. Levinas, "Totality and Totalization," 39.
13. Aristotle, *Metaphysics*, 984a, 17–20.
14. Levinas, "Totality and Totalization," 47.
15. Ibid.
16. Ibid.
17. Ibid., 47–48.
18. Ibid., 48.
19. Ibid.
20. Ibid.
21. Indeed, some scholars have argued that the term "genocide" can be anachronistically applied to characterize the treatment of Indigenous Americans, whose plight American chattel slavery often overshadows. For example, see Benjamin Madley,

An American Genocide: The United States and the California Indian Catastrophe, 1846–1873 (New Haven, CT: Yale University Press, 2016). Moreover, it seems that the proliferation of technology leads to a crisis of conscience, for in the nineteenth century, in the midst of emerging industrialized society and mass culture, there is American chattel slavery and, in the twentieth century, what Edmund Husserl called the "mathematization" of nature led to a "crisis of the European sciences," for the same technological advances that purported to move civilization forward were leading to the proliferation of nuclear weaponry and were doing nothing to curb the advance of national socialism in Hitler's Germany.

22. Levinas, "Totality and Totalization," 48.

23. Emmanuel Levinas, *Totality and Infinity: An Essay on Exteriority*, trans. Alphonso Lingis (Pittsburgh, PA: Duquesne University Press, 1969), 21.

24. Ibid.

25. Ibid.

26. Ibid.

27. Ibid.

28. Ibid., 22.

29. Ibid., 21.

30. Ibid., 43.

31. Ibid.

32. See generally Emmanuel Levinas, *Otherwise than Being or Beyond Essence*, trans. Alphonso Lingis (Pittsburgh, PA: Duquesne University Press, 1998).

33. Levinas, "Essence and Disinterestedness," in *Basic Philosophical Writings*, 118.

34. *Holy Bible*, Matthew 10:39 (King James Version). Jesus repeats this admonition in Matthew 16:25, perhaps indicating some importance of the moral principle at stake here, which is that in the Judeo-Christian tradition, moral obligations to others precede the demand of the self for epistemic and metaphysical truth. Merold Westphal cites this Bible passage with reference to the relationship between subjectivity and transcendence in Kierkegaard, making the point that there is an inverse relationship between transcendence and the self such that "the greater the intensity of transcendence, the greater the intensity of subjectivity; or, more specifically, subjectivity is a matter of degree, and it increases with the degree of self-transcendence evoked by the transcendence to which it is relative. This hypothesis, of course, is not neutral; for it suggests that the self increases as its autonomy decreases and decreases as it becomes more nearly absolute." See Merold Westphal, "Inverted Intentionality: Being Addressed," in *Levinas and Kierkegaard in Dialogue* (Bloomington: Indiana University Press, 2008), 140.

35. Levinas, *Totality and Infinity*, 87.

36. Levinas, *Otherwise Than Being*, 122.

37. See *Holy Bible*, Job 42:10.

38. See my essay "Epistemic Addiction: Reading 'Sonny's Blues' with Levinas, Kierkegaard, and Nietzsche," *Journal of Speculative Philosophy* 26, no. 3 (2012).

39. Levinas, "God and Philosophy," in *Basic Philosophical Writings*, 132.

40. Levinas, *Totality and Infinity*, 77.

41. Ibid.

42. Ibid., 78.
43. Ibid., 79.
44. *Holy Bible*, James 2:26 (King James Version).
45. Douglass, *Narrative*, 40.
46. Ibid., 41.
47. Frederick Douglass, "The Significance of Emancipation in the West Indies," in *The Frederick Douglass Papers*, vol. 3, ed. John W. Blassingame (New Haven, CT: Yale University Press, 1985), 204.
48. Frederick Douglass, "'It Moves,' or the Philosophy of Reform," in *The Speeches of Frederick Douglass*, eds. John McKivigan, Julie Husband, and Heather L. Kaufman (New Haven, CT: Yale University Press, 2018), 394.
49. Waldo E. Martin Jr., *The Mind of Frederick Douglass* (Chapel Hill: University of North Carolina Press, 1986), 168.
50. Douglass, *Narrative*, 65–66.
51. Ibid., 72–73.
52. Ibid., 70.
53. Ibid.
54. Ibid., 70–71.
55. Ibid., 71.
56. Ibid.
57. Ibid., 72.
58. Levinas, *Totality and Infinity*, 21.
59. Myriad philosophical and theological arguments were advanced in support of American chattel slavery. See Mark A. Noll, *The Civil War as a Theological Crisis* (Chapel Hill: University of North Carolina Press, 2006).
60. Douglass, "The Nature of Slavery," in *Douglass: Autobiographies*, 419.
61. Jacques Derrida, "Force of Law," in *Acts of Religion*, ed. and trans. Gil Anidjar (New York: Routledge, 2002), 233.
62. Douglass, *Narrative*, 61.
63. Ibid., 60.
64. Levinas, *Totality and Infinity*, 43–44.
65. Cynthia Nielsen, *Foucault, Douglass, Fanon, and Scotus in Dialogue: On Social Construction and Freedom* (New York: Palgrave Macmillan, 2013), 47.
66. Ibid., 48.
67. Douglass, *Narrative*, 63.
68. Ibid., 66.
69. Ibid., 71–72.
70. Levinas, "Transcendence and Height," in *Basic Philosophical Writings*, eds. Adrian T. Peperzak, Simon Critchley, and Robert Bernasconi (Bloomington: Indiana University Press, 1996), 12.
71. Douglass expressed his support for Ida B. Wells in a letter written to her in 1892. This communication is chronicled in *Southern Horrors and Other Writings: The Anti-Lynching Campaign of Ida B. Wells, 1892–1900*, ed. Jacqueline Jones Royster (Boston, MA: Bedford/St. Martin's, 1997), 51.
72. Douglass, *Narrative*, 61.

73. Ibid.

74. Douglass describes how Covey channeled his religious enthusiasm into producing more slaves by purchasing a slave woman and forcing her to maintain a sexual relationship with a male slave who was married. Ibid., 62–63.

75. Cornel West, *Democracy Matters: Winning the Fight against Imperialism* (New York: Penguin Press, 2004). See especially chapter 5, titled "The Crisis of Christian Identity in America."

Epilogue

Toward a Philosophical Theology of History: Narrative and Resurrection

"It happened, as they were burying a man, that behold, they spied a band of men; and they cast the man into the tomb of Elisha: and as soon as the man touched the bones of Elisha, he revived, and stood up on his feet."

—*Holy Bible*[1]

ABSTRACTION, CONSCIOUSNESS, AND TIME AS HISTORY

Among the most obscure miracles recorded in the Bible is the story of a dead man who was resurrected when he was thrown into the sepulcher of Elisha and his corpse "touched" Elisha's bones. Elisha was a prophet in Israel who was said to have had twice the amount of divinely imparted supernatural power as Elijah, his prophetic predecessor. Only one verse is devoted to this miraculous event, and one may even miss it but for a close reading of the biblical text. This text is my point of departure for the conclusion of this book because I interpret it as saying much not only about the ground covered up to this point but also about how this ground is connected to the trajectory of some of my future philosophical research. What I want to do in the few remaining pages is interpret this biblical account of a resurrection in Kantian terms, emphasizing the relationship between consciousness and time understood as history. I then want to use this Kantian framework to augment the importance of "the jurisdiction of history," which is a concept that I discussed in chapter 1 and that serves not only as the principle undergirding Douglass's uses of narrative but also as an organizing concept for some of my future research. This consciousness-based, Kantian temporal framework eschews abstraction in favor of historical and temporal considerations; it is thus consistent with the Incarnational theological interpretation of the word made flesh that I have tried to develop up to this point. The Kantian notion of time as history represents another way of doing what I do with the Incarnational theological paradigm throughout this book: it critiques abstraction for its fundamental moral shortcomings.

Why a Kantian-styled, temporal framework? Because it is instructive for appreciating the importance of history and its relationship to the problem of abstraction as depicted in the account of the resurrection from the biblical story I have been discussing here; it helps one appreciate the philosophical significance of the miracle for what it tells us about abstraction's destructive influence on human beings. The dead man in this obscure miracle recorded in the Book of Second Kings experienced a physical death that, symbolically, implies something much more significant: it represents his disconnection from consciousness, from history, from a past—that is, from time itself. Being disconnected from time understood as history in this manner implies a death in senses that are other than physical (e.g., the social, political, moral, cultural, and spiritual). And this is what abstraction does: it severs the connection between consciousness and time such that one is separated from one's history, from one's past, and experiences a social, political, moral, cultural, and spiritual death. According to Kant, the severance of time from consciousness would make empirical cognition impossible, for we are beings who are situated—indeed, saturated—in time, which, through its notions of coexistence and succession, determines our inner sense of objects, making our perception of those objects possible. I submit that in a similar manner, the man's death in the resurrection story represents such a severance of consciousness from time and from history. A brief exposition of Kant's conception of time will be useful to explain how this is so.

To be sure, Kant's metaphysical exposition of time in the "Transcendental Aesthetic" of the *Critique of Pure Reason* is not about the resurrection of the dead. Indeed, Kant's scientific sensibilities would likely lead him to reject a literal interpretation of any notion that a dead person can be resurrected by merely coming into contact with another dead person's bones. Such matters were simply not his concern in his metaphysical exposition of time. Instead, he was concerned with the conditions of possibility for the empirical cognition of objects, with the universal and necessary features of human experience that make our perceptions possible in the first place and that, once discovered, would prescribe limits on human knowledge that would effectively foreclose any theoretical, synthetic, a priori knowledge of miracles whatsoever. But here, I want to think Kant's account of time otherwise by arguing that the empirical cognition of objects and their relationship to time—to our "inner" sense, as Kant calls it—along with the temporal notions of coexistence and succession, say something to us about not only empirical cognition but also history, our connection to it, and what happens when philosophical abstraction severs that historical connection. Even as one would be unable to experience empirical cognition without the condition of time that determines our inner sense of objects as either coexistent or successive, one is unable to experience life itself without the condition of history that determines not only our consciousness of objects but also our self-consciousness.

So, for Kant, time is not merely an objective means of measurement for how fast objects move in space; rather, it is subjective in nature, belonging to human consciousness. In his important chapter on the schematism in the *Critique of Pure Reason*, which immediately follows the transcendental deduction of the categories, Kant points out the "heterogeneity" between the concepts of the understanding and empirical intuitions. There must be some link between the two, some "third thing" that bears the features of both objectivity and subjectivity so that concepts can have an empirical application. This "third thing" is time, which, on one hand, is akin to the categories in its universality and its necessity and which, on the other hand, is akin to "appearance, in that time is contained in every empirical representation of the manifold."[2] Kant concludes that "an application of the category to appearances becomes possible by means of the transcendental determination of time, which, as the schema of the concepts of understanding, mediates the subsumption of the appearances under the category."[3] Human consciousness is, then, for Kant, immersed in time, which makes our experience of objects possible. To separate ourselves from time is, for Kant, to make empirical cognition, our very means of navigating the world, impossible, for time is a universal condition of possibility for any experience of objects. Without time understood as history, as a past, one's very identity is as imperceptible as the empirical cognition of objects without time. Kant's placement of time within consciousness asserts that time, that the past, that history, is an indispensable component of empirical cognition. And I am arguing here that it is also an indispensable component of cultural, personal, social, national, moral, spiritual, and political identity. To separate our consciousness, ourselves, from time is to die.

In contrast, to be connected with history is to live, which is precisely what happens when the dead man is thrown into the sepulcher of Elisha: he comes into contact with Elisha's bones, with a historical figure from the past, with time, with history, and it is precisely this reconnection with history that resurrects him. Throughout this book, I have argued that the abstractions of the philosophy of religion as represented in analytic theism have, despite the anti-foundationalism of their reformed epistemology, severed the connection between the Christian consciousness and history, resulting in an ersatz brand of Christianity that has the "form of godliness" but lacks any real moral power.[4] Hence there is the difference between the abstract reflections of Platonic recollection and the radical conversion experience of Christianity that Johannes Climacus discusses in Kierkegaard's *Philosophical Fragments*. The former was the way of Covey's religion of slaveholding Christianity, while the latter was the true conversion experience that Douglass demanded of slaveholding Christians. It took a re-engagement with history to restore the true spirit of life to the dead man in the biblical account of resurrection. Indeed, it was because of his reconnection with Elisha's bones—with the bones of a person who had twice the spirit of Elijah—that his own spirit, his consciousness, his connection to his temporality, to his past, to his history, was restored, and he was thus "resurrected." It is in the moral and spiritual interests of Christianity that I have tried to develop the concept of the "jurisdiction of history." Through this concept, I make the Kantian move of situating human consciousness in an inescapable network of historical—that is, temporal—considerations that will preserve its connection to time and prevent the pernicious encroachments of philosophical abstraction, which, in the philosophy of religion, assume the form of an incessant, ontotheological, conceptual analysis of God's attributes and remove from Christianity the authentic spirit that Douglass's use of narrative preserves through its deep connections to time as history.

As I have mentioned earlier, I believe that the problem of abstraction in the philosophy of religion is represented in Tertullian's age-old question "What hath Athens to do with Jerusalem?" Tertullian did not contemplate the theological problem of philosophical abstraction that Black Americans would face in the modern and postmodern West, but such problems, as I have discussed throughout this book, persist nonetheless, especially in political philosophy and Christian theology. I have attempted to show throughout how philosophical thinking (Athens) has intruded upon—indeed, colonized—Christian theology (Jerusalem). I have argued that abstraction in the form of analytic theism is morally problematic for Christianity in a way that Douglass's use of narrative is not. In Incarnational theological terms, I have argued that whereas abstraction leads to analytic theism's transformation of the historically and culturally situated, incarnate *logos* into the abstract *logos* of conceptual analysis, Douglass's use of narrative is more consistent with the Christian Incarnational paradigm of the word made flesh. I developed this interpretation starting from the problem of abstraction in the philosophy of religion that is akin to the same problem in political philosophy, as presented in the work of Charles Mills in *The Racial Contract*, and in Christian theology, as presented in the work of James Cone in *The Cross and the Lynching Tree*: abstraction results in a neglect of historical and moral considerations that demand Christianity's moral attention and political engagement. Then, reading Douglass with Kierkegaard, Kafka, Levinas, and Kant, I have attempted to develop an existential and phenomenological interpretation of Douglass's use of narrative intended as a moral, social, and political corrective to the abstractions of analytic theism's reformed epistemology.

I now want to connect this book to some of my forthcoming research in both jurisprudence and Black male studies; two philosophical subfields in which abstraction is, in my view, as problematic as it is in the philosophy of religion. This research will, on one hand, affirm the poetic use of narrative and testimony as it relates to jurisprudence but will, on the other hand, demonstrate some fundamental shortcomings of narrative and testimony within a Christian theological context as it relates to Black male studies insofar as an over-reliance on narrative and testimony can produce epistemic domination by ignoring both empirical data and certain aspects of history that frustrate the prevailing norms of theorization, norms that are often unwittingly beholden to racist ideology. In jurisprudence, narrative maintains the deep connection between consciousness and time understood as history, but in gender studies, an inauthentic form of narrative—one that aims to maintain a certain status quo—severs the connection between consciousness and time understood as history. The former use of narrative maintains a spirit of resistance to abstraction's oppressive conceptualization of equality as sameness in the work of Derrick Bell. But the latter use of narrative abandons time as history in the interest of maintaining an epistemic framework of oppression relative to Black men. I detail some of this forthcoming work below.

ABSTRACTION AND NARRATIVE IN JURISPRUDENCE

Abstraction in American jurisprudence is prominent in the conceptual, ahistorical analysis of the Equal Protection Clause of the Fourteenth Amendment to the United States Constitution; it arises from the United States Supreme Court's commitment to a color-blind, Rawlsian, political liberalism of the sort that Mills critiques in *The Racial Contract* and in a commitment to a formalist theory of adjudication that theorizes law as an a priori, transcendent reality. I take up this problem of abstraction and narrative's use to curb its influence in American law in my essay titled "Liberalism, Christendom, and Narrative: Paradox and Indirect Communication in Derrick Bell and Søren Kierkegaard."[5] In this essay, I argue that the abstractions of a color-blind, political liberalism have stripped the Fourteenth Amendment of its historical moorings. In doing so, consciousness is, in a Kantian sense, severed from time as history, resulting in a jurisprudence that, as Derrick Bell has argued, simply allowed racial injustice to adapt in ways that maintain white domination, for color-blindness in jurisprudence leads to the ultimate severance from the historical realities surrounding the ratification of the Fourteenth Amendment during American Reconstruction that were specifically designed to aid newly freed slaves in securing the political and civil rights of American citizenship. With the color-blind consciousness thus severed from time understood as history, the Supreme Court can simply treat "equal protection" of the law as an identical sameness that fails to account for historical realities. And the results are decisions of the Supreme Court that interpret the Fourteenth Amendment—an amendment that, again, was ratified for the benefit of newly freed slaves—in ways that, in bizarre fashion, work as nullifying remedial measures designed for Black Americans as unconstitutional, in the interest of vindicating claims of racial discrimination against whites.

In this way, color-blind liberalism leads to a sort of delusion of racial progress and integrationist hope in America's political discourse that resembles the delusions of the Danish State Church in Kierkegaard's Denmark with respect to the authenticity of their Christianity. I argue that this similarity leads Bell to deploy narrative as a form of indirect communication in order to remove the delusions of liberalism as Kierkegaard used indirect communication remove the delusion of Danish Christians that Christianity was easily lived as a matter of abstract, philosophical knowledge. Bell, I argue, like Kierkegaard, turns to the use of narrative to engender a sort of double reflection: (1) the reader will see themselves in the narrative, and (2) the reader will subjectively appropriate the lessons learned in the interest of a perpetual moral resistance against racism. Both Bell and Kierkegaard use narrative strategies as forms of indirect communication (Bell through the revisionist, yet historical, nature of his creative nonfiction and Kierkegaard through pseudonymous appeals to the history of the Christian faith as present in certain biblical motifs) to reconnect a cultural consciousness to time as history so as to "resurrect" the culturally, morally, and politically dead consciousness with a spirit of enthusiasm and authenticity. For Kierkegaard, this takes the form of an inward, unscientific, and passionate relation to the Christian faith. And for Bell, this takes the form of a relentless resistance to anti-Black racism, despite its permanence. Narrative thus restores the connection between consciousness and time as history in both of these thinkers that leads to a social, political, spiritual, and cultural "resurrection." To couch it in terms of our epigraph, the "bones" of history, present in the creative articulation of historical events (Bell) and reflection on biblical motifs (Kierkegaard), resurrect a dead social consciousness, whether it be within Christendom or without.

ABSTRACTION AND NARRATIVE IN GENDER STUDIES

As in jurisprudence, abstraction works in gender studies to develop and maintain an epistemic framework of oppression. Rather than demonstrating a vigilant attentiveness to the historical dimensions of race and racism, some aspects of contemporary gender theory rely upon the abstract concepts of "men" and "women" apart from their historical foundations in ways that fail to account for racial and ethnic complexities that complicate the mere "man-ness" and "woman-ness" of abstract concepts. A notable exception to this situation is that intersectional feminism enables Black women and other women of color to claim the duality of their racial and gender identity to account for how they simultaneously experience both race-based and gender-based oppression. Having thus theorized their identity, Black women have successfully seized control—and rightly so—of their dual identities in a manner that suits their interest. I am not passing adverse judgment on this sort of theorizing as such, for it is in the best interests of Black women to control their group identity. Indeed, as Charles Johnson has keenly observed, "black women have succeeded in culturally 'defining' themselves in their own terms and not those of the racial (or gender [sic]) Other."[6] Intersectionality is a theory that serves Black women well.

But this theorization comes at a cost. For example, it has recently been argued that intersectional feminism is based upon accounts of Black men that deploy oppressive tropes and mythologies regarding Black male sexuality as inherently predatory and violent. These mythopoetic constructions of Black men impede the visibility of Black male vulnerability and victimization insofar as the concept of "men" marks all men, including Black men, as violent and predatory when the historical and empirical record contradicts these characterizations.[7] Hence Tommy J. Curry's trailblazing work in Black male studies, which, through Curry's concept of the Man-Not, aims to contrast the historical and empirical realities of Black male life with the shifting sands of gender theory, which, Curry argues, is too often grounded in an academically popular but oppressive anti-Black misandry.

Curry's recent work has emphasized intersectionality's reliance on anti-Black, misandric criminological and sociological theories from the twentieth century.[8] In his essay titled "Decolonizing the Intersection: Black Male Studies as a Critique of Intersectionality's Indebtedness to Subculture of Violence Theory," Curry argues that Kimberlé Crenshaw's iteration of intersectional feminism is based upon subculture violence theory that comes from racist criminological and sociological characterizations of Black men. Curry also points out the problematic theory of bell hooks, who, in his view, quite wrongly (and in the absence of any empirical support) assumes that Black men dominate and oppress Black women in some sort of attempt to be like white men. Curry argues that the proliferation of such theories harmfully reifies a mythopoetic Black male pathology that not only contradicts empirical data about egalitarian attitudes of Black men toward Black women and the presence of loving Black fathers who care for their children but also prevents the visibility of the vulnerability and victimization of Black boys and men, especially as seen the work of Stacey Patton, who argues that Black mothers are often abusive to Black boys,[9] and Thomas Foster, who points out that Black men were victims of sexual oppression during chattel slavery.[10] Moreover, the severance of consciousness from time as history manifests itself in gender studies through a historically uninformed notion of American patriarchy, which fails to account for American patriarchy's origin in white racial solidarity between white women and white men,[11] rather than as a concept involving gender, as in contemporary gender theory. A consciousness connected to time as history will not simply deploy the term "patriarchy" in some general sense apart from its racial origins to the detriment of Black men. But a consciousness committed to abstraction will—and does—do just that. There is, then, a proliferation of theory due to abstraction in gender studies. Such theorizing becomes a form of epistemic domination over Black men insofar as their vulnerability and victimization are chronically unseen while their personhood is incessantly pathologized. There is always something "wrong" with a Black man in virtue of their manhood. And when this pathologizing is made theological, Black men—especially Black Christian men—find themselves facing an anti-Black misandry recast as "the Word of God."

I critique this problem in my forthcoming essay titled "On a Hill Far Away: The Problem of Black Male Death in Black Christianity." In this essay, I draw from the work of womanist theologian Delores S. Williams and religion scholar Ronald Neal to argue that Christian soteriology posits the death of Black men as essential for the salvation of the Black community. I then turn to a discussion of *kyriarchy*, a term coined by Elizabeth Schüssler Fiorenza, who purports to make the reach of intersectionality more expansive as a theological concept that she believes can better account for the complexities of identity that exist throughout the myriad hierarchies of social life. I critique Fiorenza's notion of *kyriarchy* because it draws heavily—and uncritically—from Crenshaw's intersectional feminism, which, as I point out earlier in the essay drawing from Curry's work, is ultimately indebted to twentieth-century racist criminological and sociological theories about Black men. Anti-Black misandry is thus theologized, and the abstraction of "man" then receives the ultimate homiletic and exegetical imprimatur: it is preached from pulpits and becomes the "Word of God," leaving Black Christian men in ecclesial spaces unable to find the spiritual nurture and rest that a religious community ought to provide.

My next monograph, which I have titled *Now I See: Epistemic Addiction, Black Male Death, and the Resurrection as Eschatology*, expands my discussion of Black male vulnerability to a much broader, more extensive critique of the Black ecclesia. My aim in this monograph is to further develop the concept of "epistemic addiction" as a problem of abstraction by connecting it to the principle of sufficient reason, which I will argue Gottfried Leibniz did not invent but rather discovered. I argue that at the core of the seemingly incessant pathologizing of Black men is the principle of sufficient reason's philosophical drive for explanation, a philosophical drive that truncates Black male identity in the interest of theoretical reflection—hence the problem of epistemic addiction and its connection to Black male death.

In this work, I want to recover a Christian species of Black nationalism in the nineteenth-century Black abolitionist thought of people such as Reverend Lewis Woodson, Maria Stewart, and David Walker. Interpreting these thinkers with William H. Ferris's notion of the "Negro-Saxon," I work toward developing a philosophical theology of history that has an eschatology for Black men that is one of purpose and hope rather than the social death attendant to abstraction in the form of epistemic addiction. Such purpose and hope will ultimately be tantamount to a figurative resurrection from an abstraction-induced death.

NEW BEGINNINGS

As odd as it may seem to end this book with the phrase "new beginnings," those words aptly describe this project. My reflections on Douglass within these pages represent a beginning of further philosophical work in phenomenology and existential philosophy, jurisprudence, Black male studies, African American philosophy, critical race theory, and the philosophy of religion, work that interrogates abstraction as a source of epistemic domination and that emphasizes the power of narrative to both resist such domination as art and politics and facilitate it when, despite its status as narrative, it becomes "*a* narrative" that severs consciousness from time as history and, being thus made ahistorical, condemns the oppression of some while facilitating oppression toward others, who are often Black men. I look forward to continuing this work and to further philosophical work on Douglass, in addition to the future work that I have referenced here. I look forward to more "new beginnings."

NOTES

1. *Holy Bible*, II Kings 13:21 (World English Version).
2. Immanuel Kant, *Critique of Pure Reason*, trans. Norman Kemp Smith (New York: St. Martin's Press, 1965), A138/B177–A139/B178.
3. Ibid., A139/B178.
4. *Holy Bible*, II Timothy 3:5.

5. This essay is a chapter in my edited book titled *Racism and Resistance: Essays on Derrick Bell's Racial Realism* (Albany: State University of New York Press, 2021).

6. Charles Johnson, "A Phenomenology of the Black Body," *Michigan Quarterly Review* 32, no. 4 (1993): 599–613.

7. Tommy J. Curry, "Decolonizing the Intersection: Black Male Studies as a Critique of Intersectionality's Indebtedness to Subculture of Violence Theory," in *Critical Psychology Praxis: Psychosocial Non-Alignment to Modernity/Coloniality*, ed. Robert Beshara (New York: Routledge, 2021).

8. Ibid.

9. Stacey Patton, *Spare the Kids: Why Whupping Children Won't Save Black America* (Boston, MA: Beacon Press, 2017).

10. Thomas Foster, *Rethinking Rufus: Sexual Violations of Enslaved Men* (Athens: University of Georgia Press, 2019).

11. See Louise Michele Newman, *White Women's Rights: The Racial Origins of Feminism in the United States* (New York: Oxford University Press, 1999).

Bibliography

Albertini, Francesca Yardenit. "The Language of the Meeting with the Other and the Phenomenology of *Eros*: Traces of Aesthetic Thinking in the Philosophy of Emmanuel Levinas," in *Levinas in Jerusalem: Phenomenology, Ethics, Politics, Aesthetics*, ed. Joelle Hansel (New York: Springer, 2009), 157–70.

Alston, William P. *Perceiving God: The Epistemology of Religious Experience* (Ithaca, NY: Cornell University Press, 1991).

Aristotle. *Metaphysics*.

———. *Politics*.

Bell, Daniel M., Jr. *Liberation Theology After the End of History: The Refusal to Cease Suffering* (London: Routledge, 2001).

Bell, Derrick. *And We Are Not Saved: The Elusive Quest for Racial Justice* (New York: Basic Books, 1987).

Benso, Silvia. "Aesth-ethics: Levinas, Plato, and Art," *Epoché: A Journal of the History of Philosophy* 13, no. 1 (2008): 163–83.

Bernasconi, Robert. "Kant's Third Thoughts on Race," in *Reading Kant's Geography*, eds. Stuart Elden and Eduardo Mendieta (Albany: State University of New York Press, 2011), 291–318.

———. "Who Invented the Concept of Race? Kant's Role in the Enlightenment Construction of Race," in *Race*, ed. Robert Bernasconi (Malden, MA: Blackwell, 2001), 11–36.

———. "Will the Real Kant Please Stand Up: The Challenge of Enlightenment Racism to the Study of the History of Philosophy," *Radical Philosophy*, 117, no. 1 (2003): 13–22.

Broadie, Sarah. "Rational Theology," in *The Cambridge Companion to Early Greek Philosophy*, ed. A. A. Long (New York: Cambridge University Press, 1999), 205–24.

Burns, Gerald. "Should Poetry be Ethical or Otherwise?" *SubStance* 38 (2009): 72–91.

Carralero, Pamela. "A Holy Aesthetic: Recognizing an Art That Is Otherwise Than Art in the Work of Emmanuel Levinas," *Epoché: A Journal of the History of Philosophy* 22, no. 2 (Spring 2018): 505–22.

Carter, J. Kameron. *Race: A Theological Account* (Oxford: Oxford University Press, 2008).

Ciaramelli, Fabio. "The Infinite Call to Interpretation: Remarks on Levinas and Art," trans. Ashraf Noor, *Nhaharaim* 6 (November 2012): 357.

Cone, James H. *A Black Theology of Liberation* (Maryknoll, NY: Orbis Books, 1970).

———. *The Cross and the Lynching Tree* (Maryknoll, NY: Orbis Books, 2011).

———. *God of the Oppressed* (Maryknoll, NY: Orbis Books, 1997).

Curry, Tommy J. "Shut Your Mouth When You're Talking to Me: Silencing the Idealist School of Critical Race Theory," *Georgetown Journal of Law and Modern Critical Race Perspectives* 3, no. 1 (2012): 1–38.

Davis, Reginald F. *Frederick Douglass: A Precursor to Liberation Theology* (Macon, GA: Mercer University Press, 2005).

Derrida, Jacques. "Force of Law," in *Acts of Religion*, ed. and trans. Gil Anidjar (New York: Routledge, 2002), 228–98.

Douglass, Frederick. "The Anti-Slavery Movement," speech delivered on March 19, 1855, in *The Frederick Douglass Papers*, vol. 3, ed. John W. Blassingame (New Haven, CT: Yale University Press, 1985), 47–48.

———. "The Heroic Slave," in *Frederick Douglass: Selected Speeches and Writings*, ed. Philip S. Foner (Chicago, IL: Lawrence Hill Press, 1996), 219–47.

———. "'It Moves,' or the Philosophy of Reform," in *The Speeches of Frederick Douglass*, eds. John McKivigan, Julie Husband, and Heather L. Kaufman (New Haven, CT: Yale University Press, 2018), 374–400.

———. *Narrative of the Life of Frederick Douglass, an American Slave*, with preface by William Lloyd Garrison (Boston: Anti-Slavery Office, 1849). Retrieved from https://www.loc.gov/item/82225385/.

———. "The Nature of Slavery," in *Douglass: Autobiographies* (New York: Library of America, 1996), 419–24.

———. "Pictures and Progress," speech delivered on December 3, 1861, in *The Frederick Douglass Papers*, vol. 3, ed. John W. Blassingame (New Haven, CT: Yale University Press, 1985), 462.

———. "The Significance of Emancipation in the West Indies," in *The Frederick Douglass Papers*, vol. 3, ed. John W. Blassingame (New Haven, CT: Yale University Press, 1985), 183–208.

———. "Too Much Religion, Too Little Humanity," speech delivered on May 9, 1849, in *Frederick Douglass Papers*, vol. 2 (New Haven, CT: Yale University Press, 1982), 174–93.

———. "Why Is the Negro Lynched?" in *Frederick Douglass: Selected Speeches and Writings*, ed. Philip Foner (Chicago: Lawrence Hill, 1999), 750–76.

Du Bois, W. E. B. *Black Reconstruction in America* (New York: Oxford University Press, 2007).

Eze, Emmanuel. "The Color of Reason," in *Post-Colonial African Philosophy: A Critical Reader*, ed. Emmanuel Chukwudi Eze (Cambridge, MA: Blackwell, 1997), 103–40.

Fanon, Frantz. *Black Skin, White Masks*, trans. Charles Lam Markmann (New York: Grove Press, 1967).

Feuerbach, Ludwig. *The Essence of Christianity*, trans. George Eliot (Amherst, NY: Prometheus Books, 1989).

Gadamer, Hans Georg. *Truth and Method*, trans. Joel Weisenheimer and Donald G. Marshall (London: Continuum, 2004).

Garrison, William Lloyd. "Preface," "The Narrative of the Life of Frederick Douglass," in *Douglass: Autobiographies* (New York: Library of America, 1996).

Gates, Henry Louis, Jr. *Figures in Black: Words, Signs, and the "Racial" Self* (London: Oxford University Press, 1987).

Gibson, Donald. "Christianity and Individualism: (Re-)Creation and Reality in Frederick Douglass's Representation of Self," *African-American Review* 26, no. 4 (Winter 1992): 591–603.

Gordon, Lewis R. *Existensia Africana: Understanding Africana Existential Thought* (New York: Routledge, 2000).

Green, Ronald M. "Enough Is Enough! 'Fear and Trembling' Is Not about Ethics," *Journal of Religious Ethics* 21, no. 2 (1993): 191–209.

Gross, Ariela J. *Double Character: Slavery and Mastery in the Antebellum Southern Courtroom* (Athens: University of Georgia Press, 2006).

Hand, Seán. "Shadowing Ethics: Levinas's View of Art and Aesthetics," in *Facing the Other: The Ethics of Emmanuel Levinas*, ed. Seán Hand (Richmond: Curzon Press, 1996), 63–90.

Hartman, Saidiya. *Scenes of Subjection: Terror, Slavery, and Self-Making in Nineteenth Century America* (Oxford: Oxford University Press, 1997).

Hedges, Paul. "Radical Orthodoxy and the Closed Western Theological Mind: The Poverty of Radical Orthodoxy in Intercultural and Interreligious Perspective," in *The Poverty of Radical Orthodoxy*, eds. Lisa Isherwood and Marko Zlomislic (Eugene, OR: Wipf and Stock, 2012), 119–43.

Hegel, Georg Wilhelm Friedrich. "The Science of Logic," in *Hegel's Logic*, trans. William Wallace (London: Oxford University Press, 1975), 3.

Heidegger, Martin. "The Onto-Theo-Logical Constitution of Metaphysics," in *Identity and Difference*, trans. Joan Stambaugh (Chicago: University of Chicago Press, 2002), 42–74.

Hill, Leslie. "Distrust of Poetry: Levinas, Blanchot, Celan," *MLN* 120 (December 2005): 987.

Hill, Thomas E., and Bernard Boxill. "Kant on Race," in *Race and Racism*, ed. Bernard Boxill (London: Oxford University Press, 2001), 448–71.

Holy Bible. World English Version.

Hughes, Robert. *Ethics, Aesthetic, and the Beyond of Language* (New York: State University of New York Press, 2010).

Husserl, Edmund. *Ideas for a Pure Phenomenology and Phenomenological Philosophy*, trans. Daniel O. Dahlstrom (Indianapolis, IN: Hackett, 2014).

Isherwood, Lisa, and Marko Zlomislic. *The Poverty of Radical Orthodoxy* (Eugene, OR: Wipf and Stock, 2012).

Johnson, Charles. "A Phenomenology of the Black Body," *Michigan Quarterly Review* 32, no. 4 (1993): 599–613.

Jones, William R. *Is God a White Racist? A Preamble to Black Theology* (Boston, MA: Beacon Press, 1998).

Judy, Ronald T. "Kant and Knowledge of Disappearing Expression," in *A Companion to African-American Philosophy*, eds. Tommy L. Lott and John P. Pittman (Malden, MA: Blackwell, 2006), 110–24.

Kafka, Franz. *The Trial*, trans. Breon Mitchell (New York: Shocken Books, 1998).

Kant, Immanuel. *Critique of Judgment*, trans. Werner S. Pluhar (Indianapolis, IN: Hackett, 1987).

———. "Critique of Practical Reason," in *Practical Philosophy*, trans. and ed. Mary J. Gregor (Cambridge: Cambridge University Press, 1996), 257.

———. *Critique of Pure Reason*, trans. Norman Kemp Smith (New York: St. Martin's Press, 1965).

———. "On the Miscarriage of all Philosophical Trials in Theodicy," in *Religion and Rational Theology*, trans. George di Giovanni (Cambridge: Cambridge University Press, 1996), 24–37.

———. *Prolegomena to Any Future Metaphysics That Will Be Able to Come Forward as Science*, trans. James W. Ellington (Indianapolis, IN: Hackett, 2001).

Kierkegaard, Søren. *Concluding Unscientific Postscript to Philosophical Fragments*, trans. Howard V. and Edna H. Hong (Princeton, NJ: Princeton University Press, 1992).

———. *Either/Or*, volume I, trans. Howard V. Hong (Princeton, NJ: Princeton University Press, 1987).

———. *Philosophical Fragments*, ed. and trans. Howard V. and Edna H. Hong (Princeton, NJ: Princeton University Press, 1985).

———. *The Point of View for My Work as an Author*, trans. Howard V. and Edna H. Hong (Princeton, NJ: Princeton University Press, 1998).

———. *The Sickness Unto Death: A Christian Psychological Exposition for Upbuilding and Awakening*, ed. and trans. Howard V. and Edna H. Hong (Princeton, NJ: Princeton University Press, 1980).

Kirkland, Frank M. "Enslavement, Moral Suasion, and Struggles for Recognition: Frederick Douglass's Answer to the Question—'What Is Enlightenment?'" in *Frederick Douglass: A Critical Reader*, eds. Frank M. Kirkland and Bill E. Lawson (Malden, MA: Blackwell, 1999), 243–310.

Lawson, Bill E. "Douglass among the Romantics," in *The Cambridge Companion to Frederick Douglass*, ed. Maurice Lee (Cambridge: Cambridge University Press, 2009), 118–31.

———. "Introduction," in *Frederick Douglass: A Critical Reader*, eds. Bill E. Lawson and Frank M. Kirkland (Malden, MA: Blackwell, 1999).

Levinas, Emmanuel. "Essence and Disinterestedness," in *Basic Philosophical Writings*, eds. Adrian T. Peperzak, Simon Critchley, and Robert Bernasconi (Bloomington: Indiana University Press, 1996), 109–28.

———. "God and Philosophy," in *Basic Philosophical Writings*, eds. Adrian T. Peperzak, Simon Critchley, and Robert Bernasconi (Bloomington: Indiana University Press, 1996), 129–48.

———. *Of God Who Comes to Mind*, trans. Bettina Bergo (Stanford, CA: Stanford University Press, 1998).

———. *Otherwise Than Being*, trans. Alphonso Lingis (Pittsburgh, PA: Duquesne University Press, 2009).

———. *Otherwise Than Being or Beyond Essence*, trans. Alphonso Lingis (Pittsburgh, PA: Duquesne University Press, 1998).

———. "Reality and Its Shadow," in *The Levinas Reader*, ed. Seán Hand (Cambridge, MA: Basil Blackwell, 1989), 129–43.

———. *Totality and Infinity: An Essay on Exteriority*, trans. Alphonso Lingis (Pittsburgh, PA: Duquesne University Press, 1969).

———. "Totality and Totalization," in *Alterity and Transcendence*, trans. Michael B. Smith (New York: Columbia University Press, 1999), 39–51.

———. "Transcendence and Height," in *Basic Philosophical Writings*, eds. Adrian T. Peperzak, Simon Critchley, and Robert Bernasconi (Bloomington: Indiana University Press, 1996), 11–31.

———. "Useless Suffering," in *Entre Nous: Thinking of the Other*, trans. Michael Smith and Barbara Harshav (New York: Columbia University Press, 1998), 91–101.

Madley, Benjamin. *An American Genocide: The United States and the California Indian Catasrophe, 1846–1873* (New Haven, CT: Yale University Press, 2016).

Marion, Jean-Luc. *God Without Being*, trans. Thomas A. Carlson (Chicago: University of Chicago Press, 2012).

Marsden, George. "The Collapse of American Evangelical Academia," in *Faith and Rationality: Reason and Belief in God*, eds. Alvin Plantinga and Nicholas Wolterstorff (Notre Dame, IN: Notre Dame University Press, 1983), 219–64.

Martensen, Hans Lassen. "Rationalism, Supernaturalism, and the *principium exclusi medii*," in *Mynster's "Rationalism, Supernaturalism" and the Debate about Mediation*, ed. and trans. Jon Stewart (Copenhagen: Museum Tusculanum, 2009), 127–44.

Martin, Waldo. *The Mind of Frederick Douglass* (Chapel Hill: University of North Carolina Press, 1984).

McDonald, Henry. "Aesthetics as First Ethics: Levinas and the Alterity of Literary Discourse," *diatrics* 38 (Winter 2008): 15–41.

Mendieta, Eduardo. "Geography Is to History as Woman Is to Man: Kant on Sex, Race, and Geography," in *Reading Kant's Geography*, eds. Stuart Elden and Eduardo Mendieta (Albany: State University of New York Press, 2011), 345–68.

Mills, Charles W. "Black Radical Kantianism," *Res Philosophica* 95, no. 1 (January 2018): 1–33.

———. *The Racial Contract* (Ithaca, NY: Cornell University Press, 1997).

———. "Rawls on Race/Race in Rawls," *Southern Journal of Philosophy* 47, no. S1 (2009): 161–84.

Myers, Ched. *Binding the Strong Man: A Political Reading of Mark's Story of Jesus* (Maryknoll, NY: Orbis Books, 2008).

Newman, Louise Michele. *White Women's Rights: The Racial Origins of Feminism in the United States* (New York: Oxford University Press, 1999).

Nielsen, Cynthia. *Foucault, Douglass, Fanon, and Scotus in Dialogue: On Social Construction and Freedom* (New York: Palgrave Macmillan, 2013).

Nietzsche, Friedrich. *Twilight of the Idols*, trans. Duncan Large (London: Oxford University Press, 1998).

Noll, Mark A. *The Civil War as a Theological Crisis* (Chapel Hill: University of North Carolina Press, 2006).

Pinn, Anthony. *Why Lord? Suffering and Evil in Black Theology* (New York: Continuum, 1995).

Plantinga, Alvin. "A Defense of Religious Exclusivism," in *Philosophy of Religion: An Anthology*, eds. Michael Rea and Louis Pojman (Stamford, CT: Cengage Learning, 2015), 645–59.

———. *God, Freedom, and Evil* (New York: Harper and Row, 2002).

———. "The Reformed Objection to Natural Theology," *Proceedings of the American Catholic Philosophical Association* 54 (1980): 49–62.

Plato. *Apology*.

———. *Republic*.

Putnam, Hilary. "Levinas and Judaism," in *The Cambridge Companion to Emmanuel Levinas*, ed. Simon Critchley and Robert Bernasconi (Cambridge: Cambridge University Press, 2002).

Rawls, John. *A Theory of Justice* (Cambridge, MA: Harvard University Press, 1971).

Robbins, Jill. *Altered Reading: Levinas and Literature* (Chicago: University of Chicago Press, 1999).

Rosenberg, Rae. "The Whiteness of Gay Urban Belonging: Criminalizing LGBT Youth of Color in Queer Spaces of Care," *Urban Geography* 38, no. 1 (2016): 137–48.

Royster, Jacqueline Jones. *Southern Horrors and Other Writings: The Anti-Lynching Campaign of Ida B. Wells, 1892–1900* (Boston, MA: Bedford/St. Martin's, 1997).

Smith, James K. A. *Introducing Radical Orthodoxy: Mapping a Post-Secular Theology* (Grand Rapids, MI: Baker Academic Publishing, 2004).

———. *Speech and Theology: Language and the Logic of Incarnation* (London: Routledge, 2002).

Smith, James K. A., and Shane R. Cudney. "Postmodern Freedom and the Growth of Fundamentalism: Was the Grand Inquisitor Right?" *Studies in Religion/Religieuses* 25 (1996): 35–49.

Sartre, Jean Paul. "Existentialism as a Humanism," in *Basic Writings of Existentialism*, ed. Gordon Marino (New York: Modern Library, 2004), 341–68.

Staehler, Tanja. "Images and Shadows: Levinas and the Ambiguity of the Aesthetic," *Estetika* 47 (November 2010): 123–43.

Stauffer, John. "Frederick Douglass and the Aesthetics of Freedom," *Raritan* 25, no. 1 (2005): 114–36.

Stewart, Jon, ed. *Mynster's "Rationalism, Supernaturalism" and the Debate about Mediation* (Copenhagen: Museum Tusculanum, 2009).

Theisohn, Philipp. "Reading the Beyond: Levinas—Literature, Holiness, and Politics," *Naharaim* I (2008): 61–80.

Tritten, Tyler. "The Contingency of God," *Heythrop Journal* 59, Issue 3 (2018): 448–55.

Walker, David. *Appeal, in Four Articles: Together with a Preamble, to the Coloured Citizens of the World, But in Particular and Very Expressly to Those of the United States of America* (Baltimore, MD: Black Classic Press, 1993).

Ward, Jane. "White Normativity: The Cultural Dimensions of Whiteness in a Racially Diverse LGBT Organization," *Sociological Perspectives* 51, no. 3 (2008): 563–86.

Welz, Claudia. "Kierkegaard and Phenomenology," in *The Oxford Handbook of Kierkegaard*, ed. John Lippitt and George Pattison (London: Oxford University Press, 2013), 440–63.

West, Cornel. *Democracy Matters: Winning the Fight against Imperialism* (New York: Penguin Press, 2004).

Westphal, Merold. "Inverted Intentionality: Being Addressed," in *Levinas and Kierkegaard in Dialogue* (Bloomington: Indiana University Press, 2008), 138–51.

———. "Teleological Suspensions," in *Levinas and Kierkegaard in Dialogue* (Indianapolis: Indiana University Press, 2008), 45–57.

Williamson, Scott C. *The Narrative Life: The Moral and Religious Thought of Frederick Douglass* (Macon, GA: Mercer University Press, 2002).

Wolterstorff, Nicholas. "Can a Belief in God Be Rational," in *Faith and Rationality: Reason and Belief in God*, eds. Alvin Plantinga and Nicholas Wolterstorff (Notre Dame, IN: Notre Dame University Press, 1983), 136.

———. "Introduction," in *Faith and Rationality: Reason and Belief in God*, eds. Alvin Plantinga and Nicholas Wolterstorff (Notre Dame, IN: Notre Dame University Press, 1983), 3.

Woodson, Carter G. *The Mis-Education of the Negro* (New York: Tribeca Books, 1933).

Wyschogrod, Edith. "The Art in Ethics: Aesthetics, Objectivity, and Alterity in the Philosophy of Emmanuel Levinas," in *Ethics as First Philosophy: The Significance of Emmanuel Levinas for Philosophy, Literature, and Religion*, ed. A. Peperzak (New York: Routledge, 1995), 137–48.

Yancy, George. "The Existential Dimensions of Douglass' Autobiographical Narrative: A Beauvoirian Examination," *Philosophy and Social Criticism* 28, no. 3 (2002): 297–320.

Index

abolition, 17, 73, 74, 101, 103, 176–78, 208, 216; movements for, 68, 114, 206; and moral suasion, 71; strategies, xiii, 132, 174, 180
abolitionists, 83, 91, 114, 134, 166
absolute difference, 56–57
abstract indeterminacy, 59
abstraction, 7, 35, 44, 58, 99, 111, 121, 131, 157, 195; Alston, 24; in American jurisprudence, 229; and analytic theism, xiii, 28, 31, 33, 36, 52, 60, 158, 228; Bell, 229; and Black men, 232; and Christianity, 10, 22, 30; Cone, 30; and contractarianism, 19; critiques of, 19, 226; Douglass, 38, 76, 106, 207, 225; and embodiment, 18–19; and epistemic addiction, 232–33; and epistemic domination, 233; and epistemology, 18, 28; and Fourteenth Amendment, 229; and gender studies, 230–33; and Greek philosophy, 60; Hegel, 59–60, 63; and history, 24, 37, 136, 225, 229; in jurisprudence, 229–30; and justice, 36–37; Kierkegaard, 59–60, 76; Levinas, 189, 209; logical, 51–52; and materiality, 21; Mills, 28, 36; and morality, 228; and philosophy of religion, 219, 227–29; and political philosophy, 10, 28–30, 33; and rationality, 34; and reformed epistemology, 33, 122, 229; and resurrection account, 226, 227–28; and theology, 10, 19, 22–24, 28, 30–32, 189; theoretical, 34, 36, 165; and thought experiments, 7; and white thought, 19–20, 37–38
accountability, 35, 150, 216
actus reus, 82
Adams, Marylin McCord, xiv
aesth-ethics, 110–15
aesthetic judgment, 174–75
aesthetics, xii–xiii; and the political, 131–34; as political resistance, 187; and social theory, 18
African Americans, 30, 77, 97, 137; and historical remembrance, 80; and legal systems, 79, 84, 210; lynching, 32; Niebuhr on, 48n43; and philosophy, 41–42, 233; and racial violence, 79; and racism, 80; slavery, 211; and theology, 32–33
Africans, xiii, 32, 72, 116
Afrocentrism, 30
agency, 87; slaves and, 43, 83
"Alpha and Omega," 21

243

Index

Alston, William P., x, 19–20, 24, 25–26, 27, 46n20; and M-beliefs, 26
alterity, 11, 14, 191–92, 195; and intelligibility, 203; and transcendence, 115
America: and African Americans, 181; antebellum, 66, 78; citizenship, 230; Civil War, 193; Constitution, 48n47; founders, 48n43; history, 4; jurisprudence, 229; legal systems, 53, 79, 81–82, 84, 91, 229; and manifest destiny, 116; oppression, 36–37; patriarchy, 232; politics, 230; and racism, 80; Reconstruction, 229; slavery, xiii, 5–6, 31–32, 41, 54, 71, 84, 87, 98–99, 109, 113, 165, 168–69, 174, 177–79, 181, 187–89, 192–93, 197, 199–200, 208, 210–12, 219
American Civil War, 193
analytic theism, 11–12, 26, 27–28, 35, 47n40, 73–74, 85, 98, 100, 116, 157–58, 190; and abstraction, xiii, 10, 18, 24, 28, 31, 33, 36, 52, 60, 122, 165, 207, 216–17, 227–29; and Black thought, 33, 188; and Christian belief, x, 10, 28, 37, 44, 52–53, 62, 206, 219; and Covey, 189, 216–17; critique of, 3, 5, 52, 206; and Douglass, 11, 18–20, 37, 76, 78, 112, 131–32, 162, 181, 188; and evil, 99, 118, 160; and *logos*, 24, 204; and morality, x, 12, 52, 189, 217; and ontotheology, xiv, 8–9, 99; and parity argument, 4; and phenomenology, 3, 12, 216; and philosophy of religion, 19, 30; and rationality, 7, 24, 27, 31, 51, 53, 111; and Scholasticism, 6; and subjectivity, 62; and suffering, 118; and theodicy, 160; and theology, 38, 52, 111, 131, 188
anarchic passivity, 14, 190, 201–2, 214
Anaxagoras, 196
Angst, 43
anteriority, 7–9, 71–75, 89, 101, 110–11, 116, 170, 172, 188, 219

anti-Black racism, 81
antinomies, 142–45, 150, 161
apperception, 143, 151, 154, 160
Aquinas, Thomas, ix, 3, 126n42
Areopagus, ix
Aristotelian logic, 54–57, 59, 61, 70
Aristotle, ix, 2–3, 54–56, 126n42, 193–97; Hegel on, 54–55; Levinas on, 194–97; *Metaphysics*, 23, 31–32, 40, 106, 193, 196, 202; *Poetics*, 32; *Politics*, 31–32; principle of identity, 56; on slavery, 32
art, xiii, 11, 37, 45, 115, 139, 168, 233; and Bible, 156–57, 160; Douglass, 8, 38, 87, 89, 123, 132–33, 138, 162–63, 170, 173–74, 178, 180–81; Douglass's *Narrative* as, 13, 180; Gadamer, 136; and *Heroic Slave*, 169; Kafka, 88, 155; Kant, 132, 135, 156, 157, 159, 174; Kierkegaard, 68; as moral resource, 122; and moral suasion, 134; Nietzsche, 156; and oppressive regimes, 88; production of, 156, 166; as reflection, 170; vs. science, 193; and slavery, 89, 166; and theology, 148; and understanding, 155
art forms, 9, 13, 52, 100, 110, 115, 187
artistic expression, 38, 89, 155, 159, 172
artistic genius, 133, 155
atheism, xiv, 100, 107, 204
Athens, ix, 3, 131, 228
attributes of God, 109, 110–11, 118, 122, 158, 217, 228
Auld, Captain Thomas, 64–65
Auschwitz, 121
Aut/aut (Either/Or), 59
autobiographical narratives, as works of art, 75, 98, 100, 112, 161, 173
autonomy, 44, 85, 98, 138, 144, 147, 148, 161, 192
Autrui, 215

Baldwin, James, 20, 81; "Sonny's Blues," x–xii

baptism, 64, 67; of slaves, xii, 102–4, 125n31, 132, 164–65
Barth, Karl, 19
beauty, 163, 175–76, 177, 179
Beauvoir, Simone de, 43, 102, 167
beliefs, 2, 25–27, 66, 109; Alston, 26; and Christianity, 4, 27–28, 51, 70; Climacus, 64; doctrinal, 62, 65, 70; Douglass, 52, 105; Enlightenment, 25; foundationalism, 25, 27; Kant, 133, 148–59, 150, 181; Kierkegaard, 70, 75; Levinas, 204–5; Plantinga, 26–27; and rationality, 2, 25–27, 53, 148; and slavery, 51, 84, 98; Wittgenstein, 46n20; Wolterstorff, 25
Bell, Daniel, 5
Bell, Derrick, 48n47, 181, 229–30
Benso, Silvia, 110
Bentham, Jeremy, 212
Bernasconi, Robert, 134
Bible, 190; and Aristotle, 32; and Covey, 66; creation account, 75, 156; and Levinas, 121; resurrection account, 225, 226, 227–28; Job, 156–57, 159, 203; Moses, 72, 170; and slavery, 102–3
Bible Society, 102
Bildad, 157
Black abolitionism, 5, 166, 206, 233
Black Americans, 36, 206, 228, 230
Black bodies, 78, 79, 81, 84, 212
Black male studies, 229, 231, 233
Black men: and Christianity, 232; Curry, 231; and feminism, 231; and gender studies, 232; identity, 233; misandry toward, 231–32; oppression of, 229, 231–33
Black people, 131–32; Douglass, 32, 188; identity, 37; and legal systems, 81; and philosophy, 6; and racism, 80–81, 84; and slavery, 77, 82–83, 87, 162, 169, 180; and theology, 6, 48n48; and white thought, 7
Black philosophy, xiii, 5–6, 13, 19, 33, 39, 43, 134, 135, 137

Black subjectivity, 78, 80–82, 91, 210
Black theology, xiii, 5–6, 13, 19–20, 30–31, 33
Black women, 231
Book of Acts, ix
Bryant, William Cullen, 114

canon, 37–38, 41, 44–45, 139
Carralero, Pamela, 117
Cartesian thought, 72, 104, 154, 164–65
Castille, Philando, 77
causality, 142–46, 148, 150, 153
causa sui, 2
causation, 2, 140
Christianity, xiv, 66–67, 229; and abstraction, 10, 228; Auld, 64–65, 67; Baldwin, xii; beliefs, 19, 24, 27, 35–36, 51–52, 60, 62–63, 70; Climacus, 4, 11, 62–64, 71, 228; community, 11, 53–54, 62, 64–65, 71; Cone, 7, 30; Constantinian, 219; Covey, 65–67, 189–90, 205, 216–19; and culture, xii, 54, 64, 71; denominations, 9; and doctrine, 70, 105; Douglass, 10, 17–18, 20, 44, 53, 60, 101–2, 104, 132, 181, 189, 206, 216, 219, 228; and Enlightenment, 3–4; Hegel, 59, 61–62; and history, 35, 53, 227; and Incarnationalism, 18, 22, 37, 44, 62, 228; Kant, 134, 151; Kierkegaard, 54, 62, 68–71, 230; Levinas, 202; and morality, x, 227–28; Mynster, 59; philosophical approach to, 61–62; and philosophy, ix, 3, 10–11, 19, 23, 37, 44, 52–53, 58, 61–63, 70, 101, 219–20; and racism, 5, 32, 52; and slavery, xiii, 4–6, 10–12, 31–33, 51–52, 71, 91, 98, 101, 103, 162, 228; soteriology, xii, 232; and theology, ix–x, xiii, 3–5, 7, 10, 17–19, 21–24, 28, 30–31, 33, 35–37, 41, 54, 58, 60–61, 122, 131, 134, 136, 165, 188, 220, 228; and white supremacy, 6, 31, 32, 35, 38

church, as institution, 6, 30, 64, 66, 101–3
Civil Rights Bill, 103
Climacus, Johannes (Søren Kierkegaard), 4, 11, 23, 47n37, 60–64, 66–67, 70–72, 75, 93n30, 228
cognition, 69, 139, 141, 146, 150, 180, 199; and experience, 167; finite, 55; human, 140, 142; rational, 120; theoretical, 145
cognitive faculties, 121, 133–34, 139, 141, 144–45, 150, 152, 161, 167, 169–70
coherence theory, 4, 114–15, 116
colonialism, 28, 30, 35, 135
color-blindness, 229
complacency, moral, 35, 54, 106
complicity, 35, 38, 188, 192, 194, 212
concentration camps, 98
conceptual analysis, 37–38, 44, 118, 191, 216–17, 219, 228
Cone, James H., 5, 7, 10, 19–20, 28, 30–31, 32–33, 35, 37, 48n43, 48n48, 228
consciousness, 12, 55, 73, 227–28, 230, 232; absolute, 109; cultural, 230; Douglass, 13, 168, 214; finite, 136; Husserl, 109; Kant, 226–27, 229; Kierkegaard, 54; Levinas, 119–20, 214; moral, 120; of objects, 227; and time, 225–26, 229–30
consequentialism, 201
Constantinian Christianity, 219
Constitution (American), 48n47, 103
contract, social, 29, 121
contractarianism, 19, 28
conversion, 60–62, 64–65; genuine, 12, 62, 76, 91; religious, 64, 66
Copernican philosophy, 139
corpus juris, 82, 83
correspondence theory, 4, 135
corruption, 31, 35, 41, 91; moral, 65; religious, 67
Covey, Edward, 199, 200; and Christianity, 65–67, 189–90, 205, 216–19; fight with Douglass, 14, 73–74, 112, 127n51, 181, 188–91, 192, 201, 207–9, 211–12, 213–16, 218–19; vs. Freeland, 65–66; and slavery, 65, 199, 212–13, 215, 217–18, 223n74, 228; and subjectivity, 14, 190, 214
creation (divine), 4, 20–21, 75, 156, 159, 177, 203
creativity, 11, 39, 73, 75, 88, 91, 100, 122, 155, 157, 167, 170; artistic, 18, 76, 149; of poetry, 172
critical philosophy (Kant), 14, 132, 135, 137–39, 142, 151–52, 155, 158, 175, 180–81
Cruz, Ramon, 79
Cukor, Christopher, 80–81
Cullen, Countee, 20
Curry, Tommy J., 231–32

Danish State Church, 11, 54, 60, 68, 91, 230
Danish theology, 53, 55, 58, 60–61, 230
datum, 12–13, 119, 196
Davis, Reginald F., 105, 125n31
death, 23, 159, 207, 232; of God, xii, 121; physical, 35, 154, 226; of religion, 7; spiritual, 73, 226
deity, as philosophical concept, 2, 40, 99
deontology, 117, 201
Derrida, Jacques, 210
Descartes, René, 25, 107–8, 167, 214
determinism, 34, 167
dignity, Kantian concept of, 44, 138, 144, 147, 156, 161, 163
dikē, 111
discourse, 27, 83, 98, 157, 160, 173; ontologized, 116; poetic, 101; political, 230; pro-slavery, 118; public policy, x; rational, 89, 115; subversive, 115; theological, 6
diversity, Hegelian concept of, 56–57
divine attributes, 107, 157
divine image, 177
divine knowledge, 160

divine power, 178
divine providence, 101
divinity, 23, 58–59, 106, 108–10, 118, 202, 205
doctrine, 1, 61; of Christianity, xi, 17, 62–63, 71, 105; of Hegelian theology, 70; of Incarnation, 58; objective, 51; of recollection, 200
Douglass, Frederick: and abolitionism, 17, 44, 68, 73, 74, 90–91, 103–4, 123, 132–34, 166, 173, 177, 180, 206; and abstraction, 105–6, 207; and the absurd, 76–91; aesthetic interpretation of, 9–10, 17–18, 28, 37, 44, 162, 181, 188, 216; and Aristotle, 32; and artistic expression, xiii, 10, 88–89, 110–18, 132, 138, 156, 160, 161–74; and Auld, 64–65; and baptism of slaves, xii, 102–4, 125n31, 132, 164–65; and Christianity, x, xii, 10–12, 17–18, 20, 44, 51, 53, 60, 62, 66–67, 71, 74–75, 100–105, 110, 122, 131–32, 181, 189–90, 206, 219, 228; and Covey, 14, 65, 73–74, 111–12, 127n51, 181, 188–91, 192, 199, 201, 205, 207–9, 211–12, 213–16, 217–19, 223n74; death of grandmother, 112–14; and Godwin, xii, 102–4, 164–65; and existentialism, xiv, 11, 76, 87, 91, 181; and Garrison, 104, 177–80; and Hegel, 60; *Heroic Slave*, 166–70; and Husserl, 54, 92, 99; and identity, xii, 85–86, 190, 199, 212–13, 215; and Incarnationalism, 18, 122, 131; and infinity, 190, 209, 213–15, 218–19; and Job, 156–57, 161; and Kafka, 12, 53–54, 76, 76–91; and Kant, xii–xiii, 13–14, 20, 37–38, 40–44, 123, 132–35, 137–38, 148, 151, 157, 160–67, 170, 173–76, 178–81, 188, 214; and Kierkegaard, xiii–xiv, 11, 53–76, 90–91, 170; and Levinas, 12–14, 54, 92, 97–109, 116, 122, 181, 187–205, 218; and moral suasion, 123, 174–80; and Mr. Gore, 86–87; and phenomenology, 9–10, 99, 101–15, 134, 181; and philosophy, 19, 37–38, 44, 72–74, 76, 101, 118, 174, 181; and poetry, 113–14, 118; and problem of evil, 100, 110–14, 122; and slavery, xii–xiii, 14, 38, 43–44, 51–52, 54, 64, 74–77, 84–87, 90, 94n44, 97–98, 101–4, 112, 114, 116, 156, 161–68, 173–74, 177–81, 187–89, 206, 208, 210–12, 215–16, 218–19; and subjectivity, 214–15, 218; and theodicy, 112, 114, 119, 160; and totality, 212, 218; and use of narrative, x, 11–14, 18, 33, 40, 45, 52, 68, 72–73, 75–76, 99–100, 106, 110, 115, 118, 120, 122, 133, 161–62, 172–74, 176, 178–80, 187, 189–90, 216, 218, 228; and Weeden, 67; and white thinkers, 37–39, 41–45
doxa, xiii
doxastic practices, 25–26, 46n20
Du Bois, W. E. B., 20; *Black Reconstruction in America*, 48n47

ego, 14, 117, 119–20, 192, 198, 200, 202–4, 215
Eleatic doctrine, 62
Elijah, 225, 228
Elisha, 225, 227–28
Ellison, Ralph, 19, 35
emancipation, 64, 162
Emancipation Proclamation, 10, 72
embodiment, 18–24, 212
empirical cognition, x
Empodocles, 196
Enlightenment, xiv, 2–4, 18, 25, 101, 133–35, 138
Epicureans, ix
Epicurus, 140
epistemic addiction, x–xii
epistemic domination, xi
epistemic intelligibility, xi
epistemic interests, critique of, xii

epistemology, xii–xiv, 2, 18, 22, 40, 107, 109, 138, 151, 153, 166, 194; and abstract discussions, 24; and analytic theism, x, 47n40; and Christian belief, x; Enlightenment, 4; and justifications for religious beliefs, xii; and metaphysics, 192, 201; moral critique of, x; religious, 24; social, 189; verificationist, 26

Eremita, Victor, 59, 156

ethical metaphysics, xiv, 11, 107, 110, 187–220

ethical relations, 22, 52, 115, 204–5, 217

ethics, xiii, 22, 30, 48n48, 100, 106–7, 109, 110, 120–21, 138, 166, 192, 194, 202–3, 205

Eurocentrism, 43

Eve, 203

evidentialism, 24–25

evil, 1, 12–13, 65, 71, 99–100, 110–14, 118, 127n51, 157, 160, 178, 187, 203; rational justifications for, 52–53, 122

existentialism, xiv, 11–12, 17–18, 38–39, 43, 76, 91, 233

existential subjectivity, 11, 28, 51, 53, 59–62, 65, 67, 70, 73–76, 86–91; and art, 11; and communication, 68; importance of, 54, 85

Exodus, 8

faculties, 143, 145, 150–52, 158–59, 166, 168, 171, 211; of judgment, 13, 132–33, 152, 154, 163, 167, 180; perceptual, 69; of reason, 75, 133, 144–46, 162, 163

faith, 3, 23, 61–63, 67, 70–71, 136, 141; absence of, 62; abstract, 104–5

Fanon, Frantz, 102

fear, 43, 156, 163, 166, 171; of God, 178; of punishment, 172; and social control, 78

Fifteenth Amendment, 103

final purpose, principle of, 139, 145, 163, 168

finitude, 14, 23, 55

flesh made word, xiii, 10, 17–45, 52, 62, 65, 68, 76, 111, 131, 181, 187–220, 226, 228

Foster, Thomas, 232

Foucault, Michel, 212

foundationalism, 4, 25–27, 131, 227

Founding Fathers, 48n43

Fourteenth Amendment, 229–30

free choice, 148

freedom, 86, 89, 98, 152, 162–63, 168, 177–78, 181, 190, 192, 197–98, 200, 215; existential, 12, 88; Kant on, 139–40, 142–46, 148, 150–51, 156; Levinas on, 199, 202–3; moral, 142, 178; natural, 29; political, 34, 36, 72, 178, 199

Freeland, William, 65–66

free will defense, 1, 31, 52–53, 114, 157, 160, 188, 217

free will theodicy, 1, 52

Fricker, Miranda, xiii

Gadamer, Hans Georg, xiv, 39, 135–38; *Truth and Method*, 135–36

Garner, Eric, 77

Garnet, Henry Highland, 5

Garrison, William Lloyd, 74, 104–5, 176–80

Gates, Henry Louis, 173

Geist, 13, 133, 155–56, 162, 166

gender studies, 229, 230–33

Genesis, 156

Gibson, Donald, 114, 127n51

God: all-powerful, 120; and analytic theism, 3; belief in, 1, 24, 27, 51–52, 73, 74, 148, 150, 188; epistemic justification for, 98; and eternity, 171; existence of, 7, 26, 166, 172; and humanity, 58, 70; idea of, 107–8, 214; Incarnation of, 61; infinite, 108; invisible, 121; involvement in history, 31; and Job, 203; in

Levinas, 204; mystery of, 59, 97; omnipotent, 112; omnipresent, 111; ontological account of, 8, 72; theoretical consideration of, x; transcendence of, 73, 99–100, 109, 204; understanding of, 8–9
"god of philosophy," ix, 3, 32, 107
Godwin, Morgan, xii, 103–4, 165
Golden Rule, 22
Good Samaritan, 105–6
Gordon, Lewis R., xiii–xiv, 43, 102
Gospel, 5, 20, 24, 28, 73, 206
Grenze, 140–41, 142, 150, 181
Gross, Ariela J., 12, 78, 82, 210

happiness, 147–50, 152, 156, 163, 171, 172
Hebrews, 20, 23, 31
Hegel, Georg Wilhelm Friedrich, 53, 54–60, 61, 202; and Aristotle, 59; and Kierkegaard, 63; logic, 55, 58–59, 70, 71; and mediation of divinity, 59, 62, 70–71; theology, 54, 61–62, 70–71
Heidegger, Martin, ix, 2–3, 8, 32, 40, 99, 107, 126n42
Heraclitus, 198
hermeneutics, xiv, 39, 133, 134–38
Hesiod, x
history, importance of, 226
Hobbes, Thomas, 28, 121
Holocaust, 87, 98, 99, 106, 109, 121–22, 193; and Levinas, 192
holy aesthetic, 100–101, 122
Homer, x, 21
hooks, bell, 231
Hopkins, Rigby, 67
human nature, 21, 23, 146, 171
Hume, David, 25, 139–40, 154
Husserl, Edmund, 3, 11–12, 20, 39, 44, 97, 99–100, 107; on God's transcendence, 109; and Levinas, 38, 54, 92; methodology, 12, 119
hypocrisy, 67, 116; religious, 51, 64, 205, 217, 219

identity, 34–35, 84, 191; Aristotle, 56; Douglass, 86, 91, 118, 199; gender, 37, 231; group, 231; Hegel, 55–56; importance of, 91; Kafka, 85; national, 30; political, 227; principle of, 54–57, 59; and race, 37, 82, 231–32; religious, 39, 137; of slaves, 12, 82; social, 82
imagination, 73, 151–57, 168–70, 172–73, 175, 178, 180–81; aesthetic, 159; poetic, 160; power of, 159–60, 161; role of, 153–54
imago Dei, ix
imago hominis, ix, 31
immanence, 21, 61, 70, 72, 91, 108, 116, 119, 193, 195, 198–200, 209; of God, 99; in language, 115; transcendence in, 204
imperialism, 30, 35
Incarnation/Incarnationalism, 10, 11, 18–19, 21–22, 23, 24, 28, 51, 54, 58–59, 61, 62, 65, 67, 70, 76, 91, 122, 131, 181, 188, 206, 226, 228
Incarnational theology, 11, 18, 20–21, 37, 53, 58, 62, 70, 91
indirect communication, 12, 68–69, 89–90, 229–30
infinite regress, 3, 40
infinity, xi, 40, 99; Douglass, 190, 213–15, 218–19; Levinas, 14, 106–7, 117, 181, 189–93, 195, 200–201, 204–5, 209, 213–14, 219; and subjectivity, 188–89, 209
injustice, 7, 28–30, 35–37, 101, 111, 220; and God, 2, 112, 158; racial, 4, 229; social, 219
intellect, xv–xvi, 2, 74–75, 167, 172, 213
intelligibility, 115, 116–17, 195, 203–4; conditioned, 199; human, 72, 107; metaphysical, xi
intersectional feminism, 231
intersectionality, 231–32
intuition, 22, 25, 156, 168, 205; empirical, 153, 227; Husserl,

97; Kant, 142, 152–55, 158–61, 172, 180; sensible, 153–54, 214; sensuous, 141, 153; spatiotemporal, 152
inwardness, 64–65, 67, 70–71, 74, 88, 202

Jeremiah, 23
Jerusalem, 3, 105, 131, 228
Jesus Christ, ix–x, 10, 18, 20, 22–24, 31, 36, 60–61, 103, 104–5, 203; death, 32; life, 35; parabolic language, 53
Jewish people, 192, 197
Jewish religion, 70
Jewish thinkers, 39
Jim Crow, 4, 6, 30, 98, 122
Job, 13, 133, 156–60, 161–62, 203
John the Baptist, 104, 105
Jones, William R., 5, 111
Judeo-Christian tradition, 3, 20–21, 23, 35, 40, 100, 106, 113, 131, 217
judgment, 13, 33, 58, 132–33, 139, 142, 152, 154, 158–59, 162–63, 167; aesthetic, 149, 151, 174–75, 177–78, 180, 181; empirical, 177; ethical, 48n43, 175; logical, 175; moral, 175; pre-hermeneutical, 135; reflective, 178–79; of taste, 123, 134, 174–77, 179–80, 181; teleological, 151; theoretical, 12, 175
jurisdiction, 17, 33–34, 58, 77, 217; of history, 10, 24, 28, 31, 34–37, 39, 52, 134–38, 188, 218–19, 228; human, 35; legal, 33
jurisprudence, 229–30, 233
justice, 18–19, 24, 34, 37, 53, 66, 102, 106, 108, 111, 115, 162, 178, 187, 189, 193, 211, 216–19; and morality, 219; perfect, 36; social, 30

Kafka, Franz, 11–12, 20, 38–39, 44–45, 53–54, 76–78, 84–87, 91, 155–56, 181, 228

Kant, Immanuel, x, xii–xiii, 2, 11, 13–14, 20, 22, 37–44, 85, 129n74, 132–35, 137–81, 188, 205, 228; account of Job, 157; aesthetics, 138–39, 153, 166–67, 174, 178; "Analogies of Experience," 140; conception of time, 226; concept of reason, 145; on consciousness, 226; *Critique of Judgment*, xii, 13, 132, 149, 150–60, 161, 169, 174, 180; *Critique of Practical Reason*, 9, 145, 148, 150, 152, 161, 165, 170, 180; *Critique of Pure Reason*, 13, 140, 142, 145–46, 148, 150, 151–52, 153–55, 161, 164–65, 171, 180, 226–27; and Douglass, 44, 132–33, 148, 161, 170, 180; epistemology, 132, 138, 147, 150, 153–54, 167; ethics, 201; interpretations of, 14, 137–38, 151; and Kierkegaard, xiii, 41; on mathematics, 85; notion of time, 226; "On the Miscarriage of All Philosophical Trials in Theodicy," 13, 132, 133, 149, 157; philosophical anthropology, 161; philosophical theology, 132; pure reason, 142, 147; racism, xiv, 41, 133–35, 137–38; on theodicy, 15n4, 160, 161; *The Trial*, 12, 53–54, 76–78, 84–91, 155
kath-auto, xi, 204
Kierkegaard, Søren, xi–xiv, 20, 38–39, 41, 43, 44, 62–64, 67–71, 74, 76, 85, 89–91, 156–57, 170, 181, 200, 229; and Christianity, 64; *Concluding Unscientific Postscript to Philosophical Fragments*, 11, 70; and Denmark, 68, 71, 230; and Hegel, 54–60; on indirect communication, 68; and Baldwin, xi; and Kafka, 11, 38, 45, 181; and Kant, xiii, 41; on knowledge, 69; *Philosophical Fragments*, 11, 53, 60, 62, 64, 66, 70, 72, 228; and pseudonymity, 93n30; *Repetition*, xi. See also Climacus, Johannes

Kirkland, Frank M., xii, 132–34, 138, 177, 182n7
knowledge, x–xi, 22, 39, 55–57, 61, 106, 132, 135–42, 150, 155, 160, 164, 180, 191, 193–95, 201, 203, 215; acquisition of, 167, 193, 204; empirical, 141, 152; of God, 108, 145; historical, 69; human, 72, 140, 226; intuitive, 140; objective, 46n20, 68–69, 71, 85; practical, 194; propositional, 13, 161; and rationality, 25; speculative, 140, 170; theoretical, 9, 147; transcendent, 172
kyriarchy, 232

"land of truth" (Kant), x, 85, 140, 142
language, 20–21, 100, 111, 114–17, 159, 163, 165, 202, 205, 212, 214; poetic, 156; propositional, 110, 122, 173; theological, 14, 65, 191; written, 173
l'Autre (Levinas), xi, 106, 191, 215
lawfulness, principle of, 139, 145, 155, 163, 169
law of cause and effect, 144, 146
Lawson, Bill E., xii–xiii, 132, 134, 166, 168, 170
learner's paradox, 60–61, 200
Lebenswelt, 4, 107, 110, 119, 122, 136–38
legal systems, 53–54, 77–79, 83–84, 91, 162, 169
Leibniz, Gottfried, 24, 121, 140, 233
Levinas, Emmanuel, xii, 11, 20, 39, 44, 101, 110, 161, 180, 193–206, 205, 215; and abstraction, 189, 204–5; on art, 115; and atheism, 100, 107; and Baldwin, xi; conception of freedom, 199; and Douglass, 13–14, 54, 92, 97–109, 115, 118, 121–22, 181, 187–93, 208, 210, 218, 228; and ethical metaphysics, 193–95; and ethics, 107, 115, 121, 190; and first principles, 106; and God, 108, 116, 120, 204–5, 217; and Holocaust, 106, 121; and Husserl, 12, 38; and infinity, 14, 107, 190–93, 200–204, 213–14, 219; and Job, 203; and Kant, 22; and language, 116–17; and Nietzsche, 121; and Other, 14; *Otherwise than Being*, xi; and phenomenology, 8, 12, 38, 119, 134, 181; on poetry, 114; and social contract, 121; and subjectivity, 200–204; and suffering, 12, 118–20, 122, 128n74; and theodicy, 119–20, 122, 160; and theology, 27, 116, 204–5; and totality, 14, 189, 191–93, 195–200, 209–12; *Totality and Infinity*, xi, 106, 108, 198, 200, 202, 204–5; "Useless Suffering," 12, 100, 118–21; on violence, 79
liberalism, 229–30
liberation theology, xiii; and critique of radical orthodoxy, 6; critiques of, 5; Latin American, 5
liberty, 33–34, 36, 41
Locke, John, 25, 28–29, 121, 166–67
logic, 172; Hegel, 53, 54–56, 58; speculative, 55–56, 58, 63
logos, ix–x, 3, 9–10, 20–22, 24, 28, 31, 51, 72, 74, 106–7, 111, 113, 116–17, 191, 195–96, 204, 228
Longfellow, Henry Wadsworth, 114
lynching, 4, 6–7, 32, 98, 122; campaigns against, 215

Mackie, John L., 1–2, 111
manifest destiny, 116
Marion, Jean-Luc, 8, 126n42
Martensen, Hans Lassen, 58–59, 70
mathematics, 141–42
M-beliefs, 26
metaphysics, x, 70, 104, 141, 151, 164, 196, 198, 201, 205; and epistemology, 2, 22, 107, 109, 192, 194; ontotheological dimension of, 2; social, 189; speculative, 140–41, 171
Michel, Wesley, 80–82, 84
Milbank, John, 5–6
Miletus, Thales of, 21, 106, 194, 196

Mills, Charles W., 6–7, 10, 19, 28–30, 31, 34, 36; *The Racial Contract*, 7, 29–30, 228, 229
misandry, 231–32
moral action, 18, 52, 105, 107, 120, 122, 144–45, 165, 175, 201
moral agency, 83–84, 148–49, 201
moral imperatives, 181, 217
morality, xii–xiii, 4, 22, 28, 37–39, 43, 45, 76, 122, 132, 139, 142–52, 164–65, 167, 172, 180, 189–90, 192, 198, 216, 219; and Christianity, x; and justice, 218; subordinate to reason, 201
moral law, in Kant, 144–45, 148–49, 150–52, 168, 171–72, 201
moral life, 4, 9, 216
moral obligation, 35, 105–6, 108, 120–21, 192, 194, 200–202, 203; infinite, xi–xii, 204, 215; Kant, 201; radical, 122; of social resistance, 219
moral praxis, 44, 205
moral reform, 68, 74
moral responsibility, xi–xii, xiv, 3, 11, 31, 85–87, 101–2, 109, 113, 117, 121–23, 219; infinite, 99, 202; radical, 107; and religious practice, 151
moral suasion, xiii, 13, 71, 123, 132, 134, 161, 174, 178, 180, 188
moral subject, 144–45, 149, 151, 191, 201
moral theory, 38, 44, 149, 192
Mosaic Law, 105
Moses, 8–9, 72–73, 111, 116, 170, 172
music, xiii, 2–3, 89, 157
Myers, Ched, 35
Mynster, Bishop Jakob Peter, 58, 59
mythos, x

narrative methodology, in Douglass, 5, 13–14, 18, 33, 40, 100, 106, 162, 174, 190
Narrative of the Life of Frederick Douglass, an American Slave, 11, 13, 52–54, 64–65, 67, 73–74, 75, 76–78, 84–85, 88, 91, 123, 132–33, 138, 157, 161, 170, 174–76, 178–80, 187–89, 206–9, 216, 218–19
National Socialism, 116
Native Americans, 30
natural laws, 140, 142, 144, 147, 150, 168–69; scientific, 87
natural sciences, 55, 85, 141–42
natural world, 32, 139, 142–44, 162
Nazis, 87, 188
neglect of praxis, xii
Newtonian physics, 151, 168–69
Niebuhr, Reinhold, 7, 19–20, 32, 48n43
Nielsen, Cynthia, 190, 212
Nietzsche, Friedrich, xi, 121, 155–56; and Baldwin, xii; *The Birth of Tragedy*, xii; and death of God, xii;
noema of a *noesis*, 14, 119, 190, 214
noncontradiction, principle of, 54–56, 59

objectivity, 11, 51, 85, 88, 227; and morality, 172; and subjectivity, 172
objects of experience, 139–41, 146, 150, 153, 158, 160, 169, 176
omnipotence, 111
omnipresence, 211
omniscience, 110–12, 211
ontology, xii, 102, 116–18, 160, 194, 196, 198–99; and epistemology, xii, 47n40; fixed, 202; of God, 7–8
ontotheology, ix, 5–8, 31, 32, 40–41, 111, 116, 228; critiques of, xiii–xiv, 5; dangers of, 41; defense of, xiv; and phenomenology, 8
oppression, 9, 30, 35, 37, 48n47, 81, 88, 98–99, 117, 155, 188–89, 192–93, 195, 206–7, 211, 233; epistemic framework of, xiii, 229–30; gender-based, 231; and legal systems, 77; physical, 163; political, 28–29, 87, 98, 116; resistance to, 122, 215, 219; sexual, 232

paganism, 63–64, 70, 71
panopticon, 190, 212
parity argument, 4, 26
Paul (Apostle), ix
personhood, 62, 82, 109, 147, 149, 161–62, 180–81, 188, 213, 215, 232
phenomenology, x, xiv, 3, 7–8, 10–11, 97, 101, 111, 137, 233; aesthetic, 8; and Black suffering, 52, 91–92, 118; Douglass, 12, 17–19, 28, 37–39, 44, 91, 100, 112, 181, 188, 216; Husserl, 109; Levinas, 12, 99–100, 119; and religious experience, 8
philosophers, xv, 19, 26, 98, 167, 203; ancient Greek, 21; atheist, 151; pre-Socratic, 194; white, 13, 20, 37–39, 41–43, 133
philosophical abstraction, 10, 23, 29, 34, 39, 44, 106, 131, 188, 216–17, 228
philosophical argumentation, 9, 72–74, 76
philosophical hermeneutics, 39, 133, 134–38, 137
philosophical knowledge, 40, 57, 59, 89, 137, 191, 193, 197, 230
philosophical reasoning, 23, 102, 121, 191, 198–99, 209
philosophical theology, 23, 32, 73, 107, 118, 162, 165, 210, 219, 225; Christian, x; classical, 191; of history, 233; Wolterstorff, 24
philosophy, ix, 2–3, 10, 18, 21, 27, 75, 118; academic, 40–41; Aristotle, 194; Douglass, 174, 212; Hegel, 55–56, 57–59; Kant, 134, 140; Kierkegaard, 62; Levinas, 106, 108, 188, 191, 195, 197–98, 209; moral, 132, 138, 147, 150–51, 161, 169; pre-Socratic, 106, 193–94; of religion, 6–8, 12, 14, 19, 28, 30, 33, 35, 37, 108, 188, 206, 219, 227–29, 233; Spinoza, 202; white, 37–38
piety, 35–36, 64, 102, 216–17
Plantinga, Alvin, x, 1–2, 4, 20, 24, 26–27, 53, 111

Plato, ix, 94n44, 140; dialogues, 60, 200; *Meno*, 60–61, 199–200; recollection, 11, 60–61, 66, 70, 72, 228; *Republic*, 76
pleasure, 78; and displeasure, 133, 139, 151, 155–57, 163, 166, 168, 172–73, 175–76, 178–80
poetic expression, 10, 13, 160, 161, 170, 172; as act of resistance, 122
poetry, 9, 97, 99–100, 106, 112, 172; Douglass, 110, 113–15, 118–19, 122, 162, 168; Kant, 159; Kierkegaard, 156–57; Levinas, 114–15
political philosophy, 10, 19, 35; and abstraction, 31, 33; Mills, 7, 10, 19, 28, 30–31, 37, 228; Rawls, 7
political theory, 19, 29–31, 35, 131; social, 45
politics, 17, 37–38, 106, 115, 121, 178, 180, 198, 233; and moral suasion, 13, 174, 188
practical reason, 13, 133, 139, 142, 145–48, 150, 160, 162, 164, 168–69, 172–73, 180–81
praxis, xii–xiii, 20, 38–39, 44–45, 132, 211, 219
pre-Socratics, 195–96
pseudonyms, use of, 11, 68, 71
pure reason, 22, 139, 141, 147, 153, 161, 164
purposiveness, 123, 139, 155–56, 159–60, 161, 163, 166, 168–69, 179–80

race, 6, 14, 32, 38; Kant, 134, 137; modern construction of, 134; and racism, 13, 30, 133, 137–38, 231
racial oppression, 5–7, 33, 35
racial taxonomy, 134
racism, 6, 13, 30, 80–81, 229–30, 231; and Christianity, 38; Kant, 37–38, 41, 133–34, 136–38
radical orthodoxy, 5–6
Ragland, Byron, 78–79, 81–82, 84
rational cosmology, 145, 150–51, 161
rationalism, 140, 167

rationality, 3–4, 23–25, 27–28, 31, 40, 51, 74–75, 79, 116, 131, 138, 177, 192, 195, 198; objective, 88; ontological, 74
rational psychology, 13, 132, 145, 150–51, 161, 164–65
rational theology, 27, 38, 115, 119, 145, 150–51, 161, 166, 172, 189, 209
Rawls, John, 7, 19, 28–29, 30, 34, 36, 121, 131, 229
reason, x, xii, 1–3, 21, 24, 34–35, 37, 40, 44, 110–11, 147, 159, 171, 178, 188, 191, 195–96, 216; Douglass, 133, 163, 165, 177; Hegel, 59; Heidegger, 75; Kant, 13, 75, 132–33, 138–46, 150–52, 164–65, 167, 170; Leibniz, 233; Levinas, 28, 197–99, 201–3, 209–10; Plato, 140; Schelling, 8
reformed epistemology, of analytic theism, x, 2–4, 7, 10–12, 18–20, 24–28, 30–33, 35, 37, 44, 51–52, 60, 62, 73–76, 78, 85, 98, 111, 122, 131–32, 157–58, 160, 181, 188–90, 204, 206–7, 216–17, 219, 227, 229
Reid, Thomas, 4, 25–26
religion, xiii, 2–4, 6, 8, 23, 27, 32, 34, 37, 51–52, 55, 63, 66, 71, 73, 100; ancient Greek, 21; Covey, 216–18; Douglass, 101–2, 110, 112, 189–90, 206, 216; Levinas, 205
religious belief, x, xii–xiii, 1–2, 4, 26–28, 67, 109, 151, 181
religious experience, xiii, 8, 26, 62, 65, 91, 135, 216
religious practice, 51, 67, 151, 190
resistance, 48n47, 60, 81, 101, 122, 181, 192–93, 206–7, 209, 215–16, 218–20, 229; moral, 219–20, 230; political, 187
resurrection, ix, 225, 226, 227–28
Rousseau, Jean-Jacques, 28–29

Sartre, Jean-Paul, 82, 102, 124n16
sarx, 21, 23, 111

Schelling, Friedrich, 8
Scholasticism, 6
Schüssler Fiorenza, Elizabeth, 232
science, 3–4, 25, 55, 64, 70, 134, 139, 193
self, xii–xiv, 14, 67–68, 87, 98, 103, 108, 120; Douglass, 170; Hobbes, 121; Hume, 154; Kant, 151–52, 154–55, 167; Kierkegaard, 41; Levinas, 106, 115, 119, 195, 197–204
slaveholders, 48n43, 66–67, 75, 103, 163–64
slaveholding Christianity, xii, 51, 103
slavery, 4, 10, 12, 17, 19, 30–32, 41, 48n47, 52–53, 60, 66, 68, 75–77, 81, 83–86, 90, 98, 100–104, 112, 114, 118, 161, 162–63, 166, 168–69, 173–75, 177–78, 180, 193, 206–11, 213, 215–16, 218–19, 232; abolishing, 104; as American institution, xiii, 32, 181, 188–89, 210; cause for, 75; courts, 84, 210; defense of, 83; dehumanizing character of, 89; descriptions of slaves, 82; plight of, 100, 181; psychological toll of, 163
slaves: baptizing, xii, 102–4, 125n31, 132, 164–65; escaped, 18, 38–39, 76; former, 72, 118; freed, 17, 72, 90, 230; women, 113
slave songs, xiii, 88–89
slave trade, 72, 103, 122
Socrates, 60–61, 139, 199–200
soul: human, 162; immortal, 164–65; moral strength of, 171–72
Spinoza, Baruch, 202
St. Augustine, ix, 118
state of nature, 7, 28–29, 31, 121
Stauffer, John, 32
Stewart, Jon, 56
Stewart, Maria, 5, 233
Stoics, ix
storytelling, 51–52, 75; artistic, 72; narrative, 106
subjectivity, xi, xiii, 3, 8, 11–12, 18, 28, 37–39, 41, 45, 46n20, 51, 68, 73, 77,

91, 122, 147, 172, 188–90, 193, 195, 199, 209, 213–16, 227; active, 201; free, 214; Levinas, 200–204; passive, 213; transformed, 214, 218
subsumption, 153, 169, 227; conceptual, 152, 166
suffering, 11–13, 18, 33, 71, 97, 99–101, 110, 112–15, 118–22, 157–58, 217
supernaturalism, 59
Supreme Court, 72, 230

temporality, 35, 80, 228
Tertullian, 3, 131, 228
testimony, 73–75, 82, 84, 110–11, 172, 229; narrative, 9; poetic, x
textual positivism, 135–37
theodicy, 12–13, 15n4, 31, 52–53, 125n31, 132–33, 149, 157, 160, 161–62, 187–88, 207, 217; critique of, 99, 118–19; overcoming, 97–123
theological imagination, 32–33
theological positivism, 4, 15n6
theology: academic, 19; moral, 19–20, 32; natural, 27; postmodern, 5; speculative, 7; white, 30–32, 35
theology of liberation, Black, 30
Tillich, Paul, 19, 78
Titorelli, 88, 89, 155
totality, xiii, 14, 40, 106, 145, 181, 188, 196–200; Douglass, 189–90, 209–13, 218; Levinas, 189–93, 195, 195–202, 209, 214
transcendence, 21, 70, 91, 108–9, 115–16, 190, 192–93, 195, 204

transcendental freedom, 133, 142, 145, 148, 152, 169, 175, 181
Transcendentalists, 167
Tritten, Tyler, 7–8

violence, 7, 78, 107, 192, 198–99, 210; physical, 79, 199, 213; racial, xiii, 4, 79, 118

Walker, David, xiii, 5, 233
Weeden, Daniel, 67
Wells, Ida B., 215, 222n71
West, Cornel, 219
Western philosophy, 3, 21–22, 98, 106, 115, 193–95, 198–99, 201–3
Westphal, Merold, 221n34
white domination, 80–81, 229
white gaze, 78–79, 82, 84, 212
whiteness, 81
white people, 29–30, 37–38, 43, 73, 80, 83–84, 103, 180, 230
white supremacy, 6, 28, 32, 38, 135
Whittier, John Greenleaf, 112–13, 114
Wittgenstein, Ludwig, 46n20
Wolterstorff, Nicholas, x, 20, 24–25, 27
Woodson, Carter G., 126n42
word: and flesh, xiii, 11, 13–14, 18, 24, 44, 53, 122, 131–32, 181, 187–220; of God, xiii, 22–23, 36, 44, 206, 232
World War II, 98, 192

Xenophanes, 73

Yancy, George, xiii–xv, 43, 78, 81, 102, 167, 212

About the Author

Timothy J. Golden is professor of philosophy at Walla Walla University in College Place, Washington. He is the author of *Reason's Dilemma: Subjectivity, Transcendence, and the Problem of Ontotheology* (2022) and the editor of *Racism and Resistance: Essays on Derrick Bell's Racial Realism* (2021).

www.ingramcontent.com/pod-product-compliance
Lightning Source LLC
Chambersburg PA
CBHW020113010526
44115CB00008B/813